POPULISM IN THE SOUTH REVISITED

Edited by James M. Beeby

Populism in the South Revisited
NEW INTERPRETATIONS AND NEW DEPARTURES

University Press of Mississippi / *Jackson*

www.upress.state.ms.us

The University Press of Mississippi is a member of the Association of American University Presses.

Copyright © 2012 by University Press of Mississippi
All rights reserved
Manufactured in the United States of America

First printing 2012

∞

Library of Congress Cataloging-in-Publication Data

Populism in the South revisited : new interpretations and new departures / edited by James M. Beeby.
    p. cm.
  Includes index.
  ISBN 978-1-61703-225-7 (cloth : alk. paper) — ISBN 978-1-61703-233-2 (ebook) 1. Populism—Southern States—History—19th century. 2. Southern States—Politics and government—1865–1950. 3. Working class—Political activity—Southern States—History—19th century. 4. Southern States—Race relations—Political aspects—History—19th century. 5. Political culture—Southern States—History—19th century. I. Beeby, James M., 1969–
  JK2372.P67 2012
  320.56'62097509034—dc23   2011024031

British Library Cataloging-in-Publication Data available

CONTENTS

vii .... Acknowledgments

ix .... Introduction: Populism in the American South
—JAMES M. BEEBY

3 .... "The Race Cry Doesn't Scare Us"... Or Does It?:
Populism and Race in Grant Parish, Louisiana
—JOEL SIPRESS

36 .... "Workingmen's Democracy" in the Deep South:
The Knights of Labor in Georgia Politics, 1884–1892
—MATTHEW HILD

56 .... "Of Whom Shall the Third Party Be Composed?": Urban
Laborers and the Origins of the People's Party in Dallas, Texas
—ALICIA E. RODRIQUEZ

82 .... Agrarian Rebel, Industrial Workers: Tom Watson and the
Prospects of a Farmer-Labor Alliance
—MICHAEL PIERCE

101 ...... "Hard Times Is the Cry": Debt in Populist Thought in
North Carolina
—DAVID SILKENAT

128 ...... Reconceptualizing Black Populism in the New South
—OMAR H. ALI

145 ...... Creating a New South: The Political Culture of Deep
South Populism
—LEWIE REECE

177...... "[T]he Angels from Heaven Had Come Down and Wiped Their Names off the Registration Books": The Demise of Grassroots Populism in North Carolina
—JAMES M. BEEBY

199...... Agrarian Producerism after Populism: Socialism and Garveyism in the Rural South
—JAROD ROLL

227 ..... List of Contributors

231...... Index

ACKNOWLEDGMENTS

This edited collection started with an idea during a conversation at the Southern Historical Association (probably like so many good ideas). After some thought and following the publication in 2008 of my monograph on the Populist movement in North Carolina, I decided it was time to bring together some of the latest scholarship on Populism in the American South into one edited collection, for the use of scholars and students alike. Little did I know that this project would consume a lot of my time but also, and more important, it would introduce me to some exciting new research and to several excellent historians who are as fascinated with Populism as myself. Now that the project comes to fruition, I think it is only right to thank those who made this collection possible.

Edited collections take a lot of time and work, especially for the editor, but it is a labor of love. The project also goes smoothly if the contributors stick to deadlines and the overall theme of the book. I was very fortunate that each contributor was a joy to work with and thus I would like to thank each of them for their respective essays and for meeting all the deadlines and responding to various questions and editorial suggestions in a timely manner. I believe each essay is stronger because of this close collaboration. So thank you, Omar H. Ali, Matthew Hild, Michael Pierce, Lewie Reece, Alicia E. Rodriquez, Jarod Roll, David Silkenat, and Joel Sipress. I look forward to further collaborations and to keeping up with your research agendas.

I would again like to thank everyone at the University Press of Mississippi who invested a great deal of time and effort into the production of this book. I appreciate the strong support and total professionalism of my editor, Craig Gill, throughout the entire process. Over the past six years, Craig has asked questions, reassured me during each stage of the process, and strongly supported the publication of my monograph and now this edited collection. I would also like to thank the anonymous reader who gave substantive and insightful comments that strengthened this collection beyond measure.

I would like to thank the generous support of my colleagues and friends at Indiana University Southeast. A research release time each semester at

Indiana University Southeast enables me to remain an active researcher and scholar in my field, and I am grateful to both my dean and my colleagues in history for their support in my research. I would like to acknowledge the tireless work of the Indiana University Southeast library staff, the secretaries in the School of Social Sciences, as well my colleagues in history for their good cheer and intellectual stimulation throughout the process. My students at Indiana University Southeast have inspired me to continue researching and bringing the subject matter of Populism alive to students and scholars, and I thank each of them for that inspiration. I have also benefited from the insights and intellectual camaraderie of many others, including Gregg Cantrell, Liette Gidlow, Jonathan Haws, Bob Miller, Donald Nieman, Kelly Ryan, and David Wall, and I would like to thank each of them for listening and discussing intellectual ideas and research questions and for their good grace. And last but not least, thank you to my loving wife, Robin Wallace, for the myriad of ways that she supported me throughout this whole enterprise.

INTRODUCTION
Populism in the American South

—James M. Beeby

Populism in the American South has long fascinated historians and students. The political insurgency of the People's Party and its failed attempt to reorient society and the economy is an important story in the history of the United States. The history of American Populism is well documented but remains a site of historical disagreement and debate. This collection of essays, by a relatively new generation of scholars, attempts to refine that debate and offer new interpretations of the meaning of the Populist revolt. The focus of this collection is Populism in the American South. Although the Populist movement was a national movement with national aims and ambitions, Populism in the South exhibited regional traits and dealt with specific issues and political traditions. Southern Populists had to negotiate the complex world of race, the legacy of Reconstruction, and the almost solid one-party Democratic rule of the region. The scarecrow of race and the activism of African Americans also make the story of the South different from the rest of the nation. Although Populism was a national movement and much of the ideology and political ideas of the People's Party influenced local activists, the way that Populists organized, campaigned, and formed alliances was due to the realities of life in the rural areas or the bustling small towns of the South. How Populism played out on the ground was informed as much by local realities as by lofty political ideals and national platforms. The essays in this book are case studies that analyze local politics in the South (broadly defined), how Populists organized at the grassroots, how Populists viewed and worked with African Americans and Republicans, the complex role of African Americans within the movement itself, and the knotty relationship of the People's Party, urban laborers, and reformed-minded Democrats. Each of the authors in this volume subtly analyzes historical contingency and carefully weighs the effect of Populism in the American South. Case studies are common but these studies add more depth and broaden our understanding on the meaning of southern Populism. This collection brings together some of the latest research and pathbreaking interpretations on Populism in the South, at a time when the nation is witnessing renewed calls for a new third-party movement.

The Populist movement was the largest mass movement for political and economic change in the history of the American South until the civil rights movement of the 1950s and 1960s, and part of a long tradition of dissent in the South. The Populist movement in this book is defined as the Farmers' Alliance and the People's Party, as well as the Agricultural Wheel and Knights of Labor in the 1880s and 1890s. The Populists threatened the political hegemony of the white racist southern Democratic Party during Populism's high point in the mid-1890s and threw the New South into a state of turmoil. The Populist movement in the South began in the 1870s and early 1880s, when the Southern Farmers' Alliance organized farmers across the South to push for a major overhaul of economic policy and the enactment of the subtreasury, and set up cooperative endeavors between farmers to increase the prices of crops and reduce production costs. Throughout the 1880s and 1890s, as the membership of the Farmers' Alliance radicalized but eventually declined in number, the People's Party rose in its place. The Populists organized politically, debated economic and social policy, and campaigned for political office across the South, and in some locations gained power, often in the face of intense intimidation, terrible violence, and widespread electoral fraud. Populists attempted to bring honest and fair elections, an end to machine rule, and fundamental economic change. For example, Populists campaigned for "equal rights to all and special privileges to none," democracy for all, as well as the tenets of the Omaha platform, free silver, and an end to the machine rule of the Democrats (in the South). In short, the Populists hoped to reorient southern society in a more progressive direction. The mid-1890s witnessed the highwater mark of Populism in the South, as the People's Party gained hundreds of local offices, and elected state legislators, U.S. congressmen, and even a U.S. senator. In some areas of the South the Populists gained power on their own, while in other areas they aligned with African Americans and the Republican Party. However, in many areas of the South the Populists could not organize themselves into a coherent movement or gain political office to enact change. The forces of resistance were strong. Ultimately, in all areas of the South, the Populists lost power and by the end of the century, the party withered and died. Many Populists returned to the Democratic Party, while others joined the lily-white Republicans; still others gave up on politics altogether. After 1896, the southern Democrats co-opted many of the economic planks of the Populist platform, though their Progressive-era reforms were far more limited and certainly not the same as those proposed by the People's Party. As C. Vann Woodward, the dean of southern history, noted, the Populists were one of the "forgotten alternatives" in the South, along with Unionists and Republicans, a third party that attempted to transform the lives of the southern farmer and laborer. Although the Populists ultimately failed in most of their programmatic endeavors, their story and legacy is no less important.

The Populists were one, albeit the largest and most significant, of a series of independent political movements in the South after the Civil War. From 1865 until the early 1900s, the South was rocked by a series of independent candidates and third parties, such as the Greenbackers, who battled the entrenched Democrats for control. The conservative Democrats tried to maintain a vice-like grip on power and patronage in the South, but this grip was never total and internal divisions within the Democratic Party (often between so-called reformers and the conservative Bourbon Democrats) opened up fissures in the polity. In addition, organizations such as the Knights of Labor and the Southern Farmers' Alliance represented the aspirations of those in the middle or at the lower rungs of the economic ladder and each sought to restructure southern society toward the needs of the small farmers, laborers, sharecroppers, and the poor. The Southern Farmers' Alliance in particular attempted to improve the conditions of middling to small-scale farmers who experienced a marked decline in crop prices, increased interest rates on debt, and higher prices for seed, transportation, and basic food items during the 1880s. The federal government offered little or no relief to farmers, and southern state governments largely ignored the plight of farmers. By the early 1890s, when it was clear to most laborers and farmers that the conservative Democrats would not bring about substantive change, these nonpartisan organizations made the ultimate political decision and formed an independent third party, the People's Party.[1]

The historical treatment of Populism is vast. Since the 1930s, and the seminal work of John D. Hicks, historians have sought to understand the nature of the Populist insurgency in the United States. Why did the 1880s and 1890s witness such an uprising? Was it just a consequence of a severe economic recession that lasted from the late 1870s and reached its worst levels in the early 1890s? What political and social transformations in the Gilded Age ushered in a culture of dissent that culminated in the Populist movement? How did radicals, small farmers, and laborers see the monumental economic and social changes of the burgeoning industrial economy and what future did they see for producerism? Were Populists forward looking and reformers or were they conservative and nostalgic for a bygone era? Were southern Populists racists? Historians such as C. Vann Woodward, Richard Hofstadter, Norman Pollack, Robert McMath, and Lawrence Goodwyn have offered fascinating interpretative insights into the farmers' insurgency, which culminated in the People's Party, and each historian offered compelling and sophisticated arguments over the nature, impact, and significance of the Populist uprising. As one historian noted, the scholarship on Populism ebbs and flows, and during the 1970s to the late 1980s, the academy produced a particularly strong body of work. This scholarship on Populism began to ebb somewhat in the 1990s, but there were still historians studying the rich stories of the Populist insurgency.[2]

Beginning in the new millennium, a new generation of historians emerged to reevaluate the Populist insurgency. This volume of essays concentrates upon the Populist revolt in the American South from the 1880s until the early twentieth century. Although the Populist insurgency was strong in the Mountain West, Kansas, and elsewhere, southern Populism was different in many ways to the rest of the nation. The political traditions, history, and the centrality of race made the South a unique region. It is true that the People's Party was a national mass movement, with national conventions, nationally known speakers and writers, and widespread communication among leaders at all levels that sought political change at the federal level, yet the nature of the Populist revolt varied according to region. Over the past ten years, the academy has witnessed a flurry of substantive, articulate, and innovative studies of Populism and the notion of dissent in the South. Many of these scholars owe a great deal to the preeminent scholars of southern history, but the new research has moved in different directions and offered fresh interpretations on the nature and significance of the Populist revolt. This volume includes many of these scholars, but it is by no means exhaustive, and this book does not address all the intricate details of the Populist movement in the South. However, what these scholars have in common is that they demonstrate the far-reaching impact of the Populist movement. In short, the Populist movement was as much a political movement as an economic and social movement for change. Although it was a national movement, it manifested itself in different ways in different regions of the nation. There are problems with a sectional framing of Populism, but on the ground, Populism in the South was different from that in the West or in the Midwest. Although the Populists attempted to push for a national movement, it is also clear that throughout the life of the insurgency tensions and differences existed among Populist leaders in Kansas and Texas and among those in North Carolina and Georgia.[3]

An important area of research in Populism in the South is local activism on the ground. Populism relied on local leaders, small-town newspapers, and dedicated activists and precinct captains to get out the vote during elections. Case studies of grassroots Populism in the South are a fertile ground to explicate the nature of the Populist revolt and to understand the strengths and weaknesses of the Populists. The first essay in this volume pays close attention to the local dynamics behind the rise and fall of the Populist Party and the tensions over issues of race and political organization. Joel Sipress analyzes the efforts of Populists in Grant Parish, Louisiana, to work with African Americans to throw out the entrenched Democrats. He argues that in the early 1890s white Populists rejected the white political solidarity and instead called for an interracial coalition of laboring classes to push through economic and political reforms. Sipress argues that historians should analyze Populists' political actions toward African Americans rather than white attitudes. Despite overtures toward the local black leadership in Grant Parish, Sipress notes that a long history of autonomous black political action and tensions over class interests put an end to interracial alliance. The tensions in Grant Parish point out the problems Populists had in organizing a mass movement of whites and blacks, especially after 1892.

The relationship between Populists and organized labor in the South has received a great deal of interest from historians over the past ten years. The second essay in this book, by Matthew Hild, analyzes the Knights of Labor in Georgia and the ways in which the brief organizing of the Knights paved the way for the electoral success of both labor candidates and Populists in some cities and counties in the 1890s. In short, Hild discerns that the Knights of Labor's political legacy was greater than its limited accomplishments in the 1880s. Through a close examination of the Knights of Labor's organizing activities in Columbus, Atlanta, and Augusta, Hild convincingly argues that the Knights helped to create the political culture and leadership for the Populist insurgency in Georgia and even furnished several local leaders. What is clear from a statewide comparative study is that the Populist insurgency had deep roots and committed relationships with organized labor.

The third essay in this book, by Alicia E. Rodriquez, also focuses on organized labor, but this time in Dallas, Texas, and during the Populist revolt of the late 1880s and early 1890s. Southern historians often overlook urban Populism, perhaps in part because the South was predominantly rural. But Rodriquez's detailed study of urban laborers and activists in a New South city shows that Populism had strong support in some southern cities and that urban laborers were crucial in the organization of the People's Party, especially in Texas. Grassroots activism and leaders played a pivotal role in the political insurgency of the 1890s. Local activists, Rodriquez argues, employed labor-organizing strategies to build a vibrant third-party movement in Dallas, and eventually across the state. Rodriquez points out that the collaboration among workers, the Farmers' Alliance, and independents was crucial in building an insurgency. But, Populism in Dallas quickly faded after 1892, Rodriquez argues, because key leaders returned to the Democrats, and election fraud undermined the organizational abilities of the Populists.

The relationship between organized labor and Populism was not without friction, however. The fourth essay in this book, by Michael Pierce, broadens the analysis of southern Populism by focusing on the relationship between Populist leader, Tom Watson, and labor organizing in the Midwest and North. Tom Watson was the key leader of the People's Party in the South (he was the Populist vice presidential candidate in the 1896 election debacle), and much is known about Watson and his economic, political, and racial views. However, Pierce focuses on an often-overlooked part of Watson's Populist leadership. Pierce points out that Watson was very hostile to labor unions and workers in the North and Midwest because he believed the labor leaders and trade unionists wanted to take over the People's Party. Pierce argues that Watson turned his back on the growing Populist insurgency in the Midwest, which ultimately crippled the national insurgency and prevented an alliance of the laboring and farming classes. In some ways, Watson epitomizes the tensions within the Populist movement.

Statewide studies of southern Populism are large in number, in part because each state had its own history, political tradition, and unique set of individuals and leaders who risked their political careers, and even their lives, to take up the gauntlet of reform. In many ways, the statewide approach is perhaps the most common form of study of Populism. However, historians are now focusing on key themes in the Populist insurgency within a state, in order to understand the nature of the Populist revolt. David Silkenat offers a statewide thematic essay focused on North Carolina, the one state where the Populists achieved statewide power, in order to understand how the Populists saw the issue of debt, and how debt influenced Populist attempts to reform the state economy. Silkenat places the Populists' notion of debt in the *long duree* and traces the development of attitudes toward and the rhetoric of debt. Silkenat notes that by the 1880s and 1890s, white farmers saw debt as a form of slavery and oppression. He argues that debt relief was a central tenet of North Carolina Populism, but once the Populists achieved power in the mid-1890s, they were unable to pass much in the way of debt relief, in part because they achieved power in alliance with Republicans, who were less than enthusiastic about wholesale debt reform.[4]

The relationship between Populists and African Americans has long interested historians. Most historians note that the Populists shared the same racist attitudes toward African Americans as Democrats (and indeed, white Republicans). Most of the historical literature to date focuses on the racial attitudes of whites, and some of the literature focuses on the Populists' electoral strategies with blacks, such as political cooperation with African Americans, and efforts to build a new sort of movement. Several historians have noted that white Populists played a role in the disfranchisement policies of the South at the end of the nineteenth century and therefore they were the party not only of white metal (silver) but also the white man. Omar H. Ali's historiographical essay seeks to approach the issue of race and African Americans and the Populist insurgency from another direction. Instead of seeing black Populism as an appendage to the Populist Party, Ali places black Populism in context and as part of a long tradition of independent African American political action after the Civil War. Ali, through a regionwide analysis, argues that black Populism had its own political integrity and used a variety of methods to advance the political and economic interests of the black communities in the South. Ali sees this at work in the Colored Farmers' Alliance, black fraternal organizations, black churches, and finally in black Populism. Black Populists ran independent candidates for office and created cooperative and coalition campaigns when needed. Ali correctly reminds us that black Populism was the largest African American movement in the South prior to the civil rights movement.[5]

Regionwide studies of southern Populism are significant. Perhaps the most famous study of regional Populism is by Bruce Palmer. But to date, most historians focus on either the national level, state level, or a case study. Each southern state produced a distinctive Populist insurgency. This local and statewide approach was a both a strength and a weakness for the Populists, and it was especially problematic for the national movement for reform. Local leaders and activists did not often see eye to eye on state policy, and they spent a great deal of time and energy in political jockeying for office and power. Indeed, when it came to organizing, campaigning, and voting, grassroots activists often ignored the edicts and pressure from the state party leaders. The unique nature of state Populism makes it difficult to offer generalizations about how and why Populism rose and fell, at least politically, in the South. In some states, Populism fizzled out quickly, while in other states, it lasted after the 1896 election. Lewie Reece's synthesis of Populism in the Deep South (essentially Alabama, Georgia, Louisiana, and Mississippi) sheds light on the complexity of local organizing, alliances with African American voters, and how Populists tried to organize for elections throughout the 1890s. Reece places the Populist insurgency into the context of indigenous radical movements that challenged the Democrats for power. He notes that the Populists were part of a broader critique of the New South society. Reece illuminates the myriad ways that the Democrats used intimidation, fraud, and violence, along with disfranchisement, to restrict the Populists in the Deep South and prevent a broad political realignment. Reece offers some useful comparisons of the Populists in the Deep South.

In the penultimate essay in this volume, James M. Beeby examines how the Populists in the eastern section of North Carolina tried to organize white and black voters to resist the resurgence of the Democrats and push back against the disfranchisement campaign of 1900, during the twilight of the Populist Party. Using contested election testimony, which is often the only way to get to the voices of the rank-and-file Populists, Beeby argues that white Populists attempted to register African Americans and get out the black vote, even after the passage of the disfranchisement amendment. Although white Populists held racist views, they did believe in the political rights of all men, black and white, and they risked their lives to see an honest and fair count. The decline of southern Populism and its impact on the economic and political life of the South is far more subtle than the political implosion of the 1896 election.

In the final essay, Jarod Roll explores the career of producerist thought and rhetoric following the demise of the People's Party. Roll describes how white Socialists and then African Americans in the Garvey Movement (through the United Negro Improvement Association) in the South, as well as Oklahoma and Missouri, used producerist rhetoric to challenge the corporate powers and political elites in the early twentieth century. Even though both white and black organizations failed to stop the reorganization of the southern agricultural economy, Roll skillfully elucidates how the legacy and ideas of Populism far outlasted the political organization of the People's Party. Roll clearly indicates that both the Socialists and the

Garveyites used the Populists' organizing tactics, employed Populist rhetoric, and adhered to a producerist ideology to offer a radical alternative to the exploitative nature of corporate farming. Roll's essay stretches the accepted boundaries of the South and the typical historical framework of Populism, but his essay offers a new approach to the long-term legacies of the Populist revolt and its producerist ideology.

It is clear from this volume that race and class issues dominated the Populist insurgency in the South. In many ways, the issues at work within the People's Party and the Populist movement as a whole are the same as the central issues in southern history. Class interests are readily apparent, particularly in places such as Grant Parish, Louisiana, or Dallas, Texas. But, so, too, are race and racism. What is striking is how racism often circumscribed the limits of Populist dissent and prevented unity along class lines, especially but not exclusively in the Deep South. However, it is also clear that African Americans and whites often did come together, however briefly and despite mutual suspicion, to espouse and, in some cases, enact significant economic and political change. It is also clear that African Americans were not merely an appendage of the Farmers' Alliance or the People's Party. The Populists were a product of their time, but the essays of this volume convincingly argue that the Populists sought to reorient southern society in a more progressive way, both politically and economically; in one state, North Carolina, they even succeeded for a few years. In addition, the Populists were forward looking and embraced change; they wanted an active and engaged federal government, a producer economy, and an end to the one-party dominance of the Democrats in the South. Although many Populists were conservative, and many held racist views, they could and did see beyond the "scarecrow" of race. The threat of the Populists to the established order is apparent if one analyzes the reaction of the Democrats. The Democrats used all the tools at their disposal to frighten voters, restrict the franchise, and even kill off their opponents. They succeeded. Thus, by 1900, the People's Party was a shadow of its former self, destroyed by internal bickering and internecine warfare over electoral strategy, a bungled 1896 presidential election, and a resurgent Democratic Party that pulled out all the stops to regain power. The South entered a period of one-party rule, Jim Crow, and disfranchisement that lasted until the civil rights movement of the 1950s and 1960s. Each of these essays informs us that we have much to learn from the Populist insurgency and that the Populists and their allies do not fit into neat interpretive boxes. For a brief period, the Populists offered an alternative vision for the South. Although the scholarship on Populism ebbs and flows, it is exciting to see a period of intellectual engagement and new research on one of the largest and most significant mass movements in southern history.[6]

Notes

1. This book is not an exhaustive history of southern Populism. This introduction does not offer a detailed historiography of Populism or indeed southern Populism. However, for those interested in Populist historiographical publications, see William F. Holmes, "Populism in Search of Context," *Agricultural History* 64 (Fall 1990): 26–58; Worth Robert Muller, "A Centennial Historiography of American Populism," *Kansas History: A Journal of the Central Plains* 16 (Spring 1993): 54–69; and Robert McMath Jr., Peter H. Argersinger, Connie L. Lester, Michael F. Magliari, and Walter Nugent, "*Agricultural History* Roundtable on Populism," *Agricultural History* 83 (Winter 2008): 1–35.

2. The literature on Populism is vast. The following is a list of key texts and is by no means exhaustive. The key early work is John D. Hicks, *The Populist Revolt: A History of the Farmers' Alliance and People's Party* (Minneapolis: University of Minnesota Press, 1931). Other significant works that still set the historiographical debate include C. Vann Woodward, *Origins of the New South* (Baton Rouge: Louisiana State University Press, 1951); C. Vann Woodward, *The Strange Career of Jim Crow* (New York: Oxford University Press, 1955); Richard Hofstadter, *The Age of Reform: From Bryan to FDR* (New York: Random House, 1955); Norman Pollack, *The Populist Response to Industrial America* (Cambridge, MA: Harvard University Press, 1962); Robert McMath, *Populist Vanguard: A History of the Southern Farmers' Alliance* (Chapel Hill: University of North Carolina Press, 1975); Lawrence Goodwyn, *Democratic Promise: The Populist Movement in America* (New York: Oxford University Press, 1976).

Since the 1960s and into the mid-1990s, a large number of statewide biographies of Populists emerged. A few fine examples include Theodore Soloutos, *Farmer Movements in the South, 1865–1933* (Berkeley and Los Angeles: University of California Press, 1960); Walter Nugent, *The Tolerant Populists: Kansas, Populism, and Nativism* (Chicago: University of Chicago Press, 1963); Gene Clanton, *Kansas Populism: Ideas and Men* (Lawrence: University Press of Kansas, 1969); Sheldon Hackney, *Populism to Progressivism in Alabama* (Princeton, NJ: Princeton University Press, 1969); T. Clinch, *Urban Populism and Free Silver in Montana* (Missoula: University of Montana Press, 1970); William Rogers, *The One Gallused Rebellion: Agrarianism in Alabama, 1865–1896* (Baton Rouge: Louisiana State University Press, 1970); Peter Argersinger, *William Peffer and the People's Party* (Lexington: University Press of Kentucky, 1974); J. E. Wright, *The Politics of Populism: Dissent in Colorado* (New Haven, CT: Yale University Press, 1974); Roger L. Hart, *Redeemers, Bourbons, and Populists: Tennessee, 1870–1896* (Baton Rouge: Louisiana State University Press, 1975); Robert Cherny, *Populism, Progressivism and the Transformation of Nebraska Politics* (Lincoln: University of Nebraska Press, 1981); Steven Hahn, *The Roots of Southern Populism: Yeomen Farmers and the Transformation of the Georgia Upcountry, 1850–1890* (New York: Oxford University Press, 1983); Donna Barnes,

Farmers in Rebellion: The Rise and Fall of the Southern Farmers' Alliance and People's Party in Texas (Austin: University of Texas Press, 1984); Barton Shaw, *The Wool Hat Boys: Georgia's Populist Party* (Baton Rouge: Louisiana State University Press, 1984); William I. Hair, *Bourbonism and Agrarian Protest: Louisiana Politics, 1877–1900* (Baton Rouge: Louisiana State University Press, 1985); Lala Carr Steelman, *The North Carolina Farmers' Alliance: A Political History, 1887–1893* (Greenville, NC: Eastern Carolina University Press, 1985); Worth R. Miller, *Oklahoma Populism: A History of the People's Party in Oklahoma Territory* (Norman: University of Oklahoma Press, 1987); Gregg Cantrell, *Kenneth and John B. Rayner and the Limits of Southern Dissent* (Urbana: University of Illinois Press, 1993); Jeffrey Ostler, *Prairie Populism: The Fate of Agrarian Radicalism in Kansas, Nebraska, and Iowa, 1880–1892* (Lawrence: University Press of Kansas, 1993); Stephen Cresswell, *Multiparty Politics in Mississippi, 1877–1902* (Jackson: University Press of Mississippi, 1995); Samuel L. Webb, *Two-Party Politics in the One-Party South: Alabama's Hill Country, 1874–1920* (Tuscaloosa: University of Alabama Press, 1997).

3. The one area where there is little new work is the Southern Farmers' Alliance. This is perhaps due to the superb literature that already exists on the Alliance. Instead, the new generation of scholars focuses on other issues, but all historians note the significance of the work, agenda, and leadership of the Alliance as part of the overall story of Populism. It is also important to note that there are eminent scholars at work on Populism in the American South; for example, Gregg Cantrell, Worth Robert Miller, Donna Barnes, and others are writing important monographs and they have produced some splendid new studies. This book focuses on scholars that came of age as historians toward the end of the 1990s. Thus, a new generation of historians of southern Populism is beginning to take shape, though it is not really a new school of research. Initially, much of the work appeared in journals, which is not surprising, but over the past five years or so, several new monographs have appeared that are leading to a new departure in the study of Southern Populism. Some of the new generation of scholars include the following: James L. Hunt, *Marion Butler and American Populism* (Chapel Hill: University of North Carolina Press, 2003); Joe Creech, *Righteous Indignation: Religion and the Populist Revolution* (Urbana: University of Illinois Press, 2006); Connie Lester, *Up From the Mudsills of Hell: The Farmers' Alliance, Populism, and Progressive Agriculture in Tennessee, 1870–1915* (Athens: University of Georgia Press, 2006); Joseph Gerteis, *Class and the Color Line: Interracial Class Coalitions in Knights of Labor and the Populist Movement* (Durham, NC: Duke University Press, 2007); Matthew Hild, *Greenbackers, Knights of Labor and Populists: Farmer-Labor Insurgency in the Late Nineteenth-Century South* (Athens: University of Georgia Press, 2007); James M. Beeby, *Revolt of the Tar Heels: The North Carolina Populist Movement, 1890–1901* (Jackson: University Press of Mississippi, 2008); and Omar H. Ali, *In the Lion's Mouth: Black Populism in the New South, 1886–1900* (Jackson: University Press of Mississippi, 2010).

Some important recent articles on southern Populism include James M. Beeby, "'Equal Rights to All and Special Privileges to None': Grass-roots Populism in North Carolina," *North Carolina Historical Review* 78 (2001): 156–187; Thomas A. Upchurch, "Why Populism Failed in Mississippi," *Journal of Mississippi History* 65 (2003): 249–276; Joseph Gerteis, "Populism, Race, and Political Interest in Virginia," *Social Science History* 27 (Summer 2003): 197–227; Omar H. Ali, "Independent Black Voices from the Late 19th Century: Black Populists and the Struggle against the Southern Democracy," *Souls:*

A Critical Journal of Black Politics, Culture, and Society 7 (Spring 2005): 4–18; Bruce E. Stewart, "The Urban-Rural Dynamic of the Southern Farmers' Alliance: Relations between Athens Merchants and Clarke County Farmers, 1888–1891," *Georgia Historical Quarterly* 89 (Summer 2005): 157–184; Omar H. Ali, "Standing Guard at the Door of Liberty: Black Populism in South Carolina, 1886–1897," *South Carolina Historical Magazine* 107 (2006): 190–203.

4. Regional studies of the South, Populism, third-party movements, and politics in the Gilded Age are noted in the first footnote. Other key works include J. Morgan Kousser, *The Shaping of Southern Politics: Suffrage Restriction and the Establishment of the One Party South, 1880–1910* (New Haven, CT: Yale University Press, 1974); Melton McLaurin, *The Knights of Labor in the South* (Westport, CT: Greenwood Press, 1978); Howard Rabinowitz, *Race Relations in the Urban South, 1865–1900* (New York: Oxford University Press, 1978); Bruce Palmer, *"Man Over Money": The Southern Populist Critique of American Capitalism* (Chapel Hill: University of North Carolina Press, 1980); Joel Williamson, *The Crucible of Race: Black-White Relations in the American South since Reconstruction* (New York: Oxford University Press, 1984); Theodore Mitchell, *Political Education in the Southern Farmers' Alliance, 1887–1900* (Madison: University of Wisconsin Press, 1987); William Link, *The Paradox of Southern Progressivism, 1880–1930* (Chapel Hill: University of North Carolina Press, 1992); Michael Perman, *The Struggle for Mastery: Disfranchisement in the South, 1888–1908* (Chapel Hill: University of North Carolina Press, 2001); Steven Hahn, *A Nation Under Our Feet: Black Political Struggles in the Rural South from Slavery to the Great Migration* (Cambridge, MA: The Balknap Press of Harvard University Press, 2003); Jarod Roll, *Spirit of Rebellion: Labor and Religion in the New Cotton South* (Urbana: University of Illinois Press, 2010). A regional study is Edward Ayers, *Promise of the New South: Life After Reconstruction* (New York: Oxford University Press, 1992).

5. The relationship between African Americans and the Populists and the role of black Populists has long vexed historians. Omar H. Ali's essay notes most of the key texts and articles that focus on issues of race and Populism. However, a good starting point is Gerald H. Gaither, *Blacks and the Populist Movement: Ballots and Bigotry in the New South* (Tuscaloosa: University of Alabama Press, 2005). This is a revised version of *Blacks and the Populist Party: Ballots and Bigotry in the New South* (University: University of Alabama Press, 1977). See also Gregg Cantrell, *Feeding the Wolf: John B. Rayner and the Politics of Race, 1850–1918* (Wheeling, IL: Harlan and Davidson, 2001); Jack Abramowitz, "The Negro in the Agrarian Revolt," *Agricultural History* 25 (1950) 89–95; Jack Abramowitz, "The Negro in the Populist Revolt," *Journal of Negro History* 38 (1954): 257–289; Robert Saunders, "Southern Populists and the Negro," *Journal of Negro History* 54 (1969): 240–261; Charles Crowe, "Tom Watson, Populists and Blacks Reconsidered," *Journal of Negro History* 55 (1970): 99–116; Lawrence Goodwyn, "Populist Dreams and Negro Rights: East Texas as a Case Study," *American Historical Review* 76 (1971): 1435–1456; William F. Holmes, "The Demise of the Colored Farmers' Alliance," *Journal of Southern History* 41 (1975): 187–200; Gregg Cantrell and D. S. Barton, "Texas Populists and the Failure of Biracial Politics," *Journal of Southern History* 55 (1989): 659–692; Gerteis, "Populism, Race, and Political Interest in Virginia"; Omar H. Ali, "Independent Black Voices from the Late 19th Century"; Omar H. Ali, "Standing Guard at the Door of Liberty."

6. The most recent analysis of the vision of Populism is the awarding-winning book by Charles Postel, *The Populist Vision* (New York: Oxford University Press, 2007). Postel's work focuses on the entire United States. However, he does include some analysis of the South. Despite a new generation of historians and the resurgence of interest in Populism, there is still no regionwide study of the People's Party in the South that focuses on how that party organized its political machinery, campaigned for office, aligned in places with African Americans and Republicans, and attempted to resist (and sometimes support) the forces of disfranchisement. In addition, there is no regionwide analysis of the role of gender within Populism and how women played a pivotal role within the Populist insurgency. One can only hope that these subjects will find their own historian in the near future.

POPULISM IN THE SOUTH REVISITED

"The Race Cry Doesn't Scare Us"... Or Does It?

POPULISM AND RACE IN GRANT PARISH, LOUISIANA

—JOEL SIPRESS

The publication, over seventy years ago, of C. Vann Woodward's epic biography of Georgia Populist Tom Watson made legend the story of the otherwise obscure Henry S. Doyle. Doyle, a young black preacher, was an active Populist and a zealous supporter of Watson. During Watson's bitter 1892 congressional reelection campaign, Doyle delivered over sixty campaign speeches on the Populist congressman's behalf. Watson's call for black and white to unite in a crusade for economic justice had provoked a torrent of racist demagogy from the conservative Democrats who dominated late nineteenth-century Georgia. By his outspoken support for Watson, Doyle repeatedly placed his own life in danger. Toward the end of the 1892 campaign, Doyle was threatened with lynching while passing through Watson's hometown of Thomson. The preacher fled to Watson for protection and obtained refuge in the congressman's home. Fearing for Doyle's life, Watson sent riders out on horseback to comb the countryside in search of assistance. All that night and the next day, hundreds of armed white Georgia farmers poured into Thomson. For two days and nights they stood guard over Doyle.[1]

The image of white Georgia farmers riding to the rescue of a black Populist has long haunted historians of the American South. More than any other incident of the period, this episode has come to symbolize the lost opportunities and forgotten possibilities of the late nineteenth century. During the Populist upheaval of the 1890s, Woodward famously argued, "Negroes and native whites achieved a greater comity of mind and harmony of political purpose than ever before or since." For those in search of a usable past, Woodward's portrait of Populism as an interracial movement of the poor demonstrated the possibilities of class-based politics even on the hostile cultural terrain of the South. The late nineteenth century, with its militant agrarian politics and its relative racial openness, formed a poignant counterpoint to the harsh racial segregation and class exploitation that followed. The era was, in the words of one historian of Populism, a moment of "democratic promise."[2]

Neither Woodward's rendering of the Doyle episode nor Populism's reputation for racial egalitarianism have stood the test of time. Despite their declarations of universal brotherhood, Populists for the most part failed to forge lasting interracial alliances. White Populists too often accepted the South's racial orthodoxy and too rarely proved willing to allow African Americans real power or a meaningful voice in the People's Party. The Georgia yeomen who rode armed to Thomson on that legendary October night were concerned more for their hero, Tom Watson, whose own life was rumored to be in danger, than they were for Henry S. Doyle. Charles Postel's assertion that white Populists failed to challenge "core beliefs in white supremacy and the master race ideology" sums up well the new historiographical consensus.[3]

Despite their starkly different conclusions, those in the Woodward camp and those critical of it both stand firmly within the tradition of post–World War Two race relations scholarship, a field defined by its focus on white racial attitudes and the degree to which those attitudes have deviated from American democratic norms. Studies of Populism and race have been concerned largely with the racial attitudes of white Populists and the ways that these attitudes shaped the Populist stance on issues of race. For those in the Woodward tradition, Populist outreach to African American voters and assertions of interracial solidarity serve as evidence of an incipient racial egalitarianism among white Populists. For critics, the dismissal of "social equality" by white Populists suggests a deeply rooted racial animus. Given the diverse and even contradictory evidence regarding the Populist racial stance, the dispute between the two historiographical camps often boils down to a series of subjective judgments of the degree to which white Populists deviated from an ideal standard of racial enlightenment.[4]

Relations among black and white, however, are shaped at least as much by the cultural and institutional terrain upon which individuals operate as they are by the particular racial attitudes of such individuals. This is especially true in the realm of party politics, a field in which actors must make careful strategic choices to maximize their electoral fortunes within a set of structural constraints that lay largely beyond their individual or collective control. White Populists sought political power on a cultural and institutional terrain that was deeply hostile to third-party reform efforts. It was a terrain that virtually required interracial cooperation while simultaneously placing steep barriers in its way. The first-past-the-post single-member district electoral system required Populists to seek broad and inclusive coalitions; a southern racial orthodoxy that equated interracial politics with race treason made such coalitions difficult to construct and even harder to sustain. Regardless of their individual racial attitudes, white Populists shared a pragmatic interest in building cross-racial political alliances, the pursuit of which required them to challenge elements of southern racial orthodoxy. At the same time, they faced enormous cultural and institutional barriers against such alliances. Populist inconsistencies on racial matters tell us little about the racial attitudes of individual white Populists. These inconsistencies, by contrast, do reveal the fundamental tension between the structural necessity of interracial Populist politics and the structural barriers against it.[5]

Nowhere are the structural imperatives and limits of cross-racial Populist politics more clear than in Grant Parish, Louisiana. Grant Parish was home to both a powerful Populist insurgency and a well-organized African American community with a history of autonomous political action. In the early 1890s, Populists in Grant Parish rejected the principle of white political solidarity, a centerpiece of southern racial orthodoxy, and called for an interracial coalition of the "laboring classes." Citing common economic grievances, white Populists actively solicited black participation in the People's Party. An assertion of shared economic interests, however, proved a weak foundation upon which to construct an interracial Populist reform coalition. While white Populists did form short-term alliances of convenience with their black neighbors, the Grant Parish People's Party itself remained a political vehicle of, by, and for smallholding white farmers. The case of Grant Parish reveals the factors that impelled white Populists to seek black allies, as well as the practical barriers that undermined those efforts.

Grant Parish lies astride Louisiana's Red River in the north-central part of the state. Created by Louisiana's Reconstruction legislature in 1869, the parish was named for Ulysses S. Grant, Republican president and hero of the Union war effort. Along the Red River in Grant lay a narrow band of fertile alluvial soil where, in the three decades prior to the Civil War, a small group of planter families had constructed a way of life based upon cotton and slavery. Having carved out great plantations from a vast wilderness emptied of its native population, these families were both pioneers and aristocrats. The wealthiest, Meredith and Mary Smith Calhoun, owned lands that stretched for seven miles along the Red River and held some thousand men, women, and children in bondage, making them among the nation's largest slave owners. To their south lived the son of a former Louisiana lieutenant governor. To the east lay the home of a former North Carolina congressman. One local planter was descended from the original commandant of the French Poste du Rapide, the earliest European settlement in the area. Another had risen from Irish immigrant roots to become a prominent lawyer, politician, and landowner.[6]

At the time of its founding, most of Grant's people and most of its wealth were found in the plantation belt. Beyond the plantations of the river valley, however, lay another Grant Parish. Here was found a vast forest of long-leaf pine and rolling hills peopled mainly by white family farmers. Sparsely populated, the hill country retained many of the characteristics of a frontier. The forest was a perfect home for white settlers who planted corn in the fertile creek bottoms and stocked the woods with domesticated hogs and cattle that were free to roam the open range. Stock thrived year round with little or no attention by grazing on the coarse grass that carpeted the pine forests and by feeding on the acorns that fell from the scrub oak that mixed among the pines along the creek bottoms and hill slopes. Hogs and cattle could be slaughtered either for home consumption or driven to the Red River where proprietors of pen boats purchased the animals for sale in New Orleans.[7]

Four years of tumultuous civil war brought sweeping changes to both the plantation belt and the hill country of Grant Parish. In the river valley, as Eric Foner writes, the demise of a social order resting upon the coercive authority of the individual master "threw open the most fundamental questions of economy, society, and polity."[8] The exact system of labor that would replace slavery remained in doubt for a number of years, until finally a combination of cash renting, sharecropping, and wage labor took root. Increasingly, the large landowners of the river valley began to view plantation agriculture simply as a jumping off point for a host of business ventures, ranging from marketing and finance to timbering and sawmilling. In the piney woods, where the wartime loss of livestock had dissolved the foundations of the antebellum economy, the social changes, though less visible, were in their own way equally profound. With meat, a traditional source of both subsistence and cash, in short supply, hill country farmers turned increasingly to cotton, the South's leading staple crop. As cotton prices entered their grueling postwar decline, piney woods farmers found themselves trapped in a deepening cycle of debt. Across the South, the transformations in plantation and upcountry life prompted a series of intense political and social struggles to shape the new order that would emerge from the ashes of the old. In Grant Parish, the close proximity of the plantation belt and the upcountry meant that these struggles would be played out in microcosm.[9]

During Reconstruction, former slaves and former masters fought bitterly for political control of Grant Parish. At the time of its creation in 1869, Grant Parish had a narrow black voting majority. This allowed an interracial group of radical Republicans to mobilize Grant's black population and claim the most important parish offices. In 1871, armed strife erupted between opponents and supporters of the radical officeholders. With the support of a local state militia unit (all black and under the command of an African American Civil War veteran) the radicals initially held the upper hand. In the spring of 1873 a disputed local election led to an armed confrontation at the parish courthouse in the village of Colfax. The battle that followed left roughly one hundred black men dead, most of them shot after they had surrendered, in what Eric Foner terms "the bloodiest single instance of racial carnage in the Reconstruction era."[10]

Though the Colfax Massacre of 1873 shattered local black military power, it nonetheless failed, in and of itself, to secure conservative rule in Grant Parish. The massacre, in fact, cast the parish into a period of economic and political chaos that threatened the very viability of the local plantation economy. Ultimately, conservatives abandoned the tactics of brute force and instead embraced electoral politics as a more effective path to secure local political power while restoring stability to the tumultuous parish. By the mid-1870s, the migration of smallholding farmers into the Grant Parish hill country had reversed the parish's demographic balance and created a narrow white voting majority. If the large landowners of the river valley and the smallholding farmers of the hill country could be united in a common electoral front, conservative rule could be established in Grant without a shot being fired. Out of this simple electoral calculus was born the politics of white supremacy.

"White supremacy," as practiced in Grant Parish, was more a political doctrine than a well-articulated political program. More than a slogan, "white supremacy" was a body of interrelated principles around which conservative defenders of elite interests sought to organize politics. At the heart of this doctrine was a simple proposition, that race is and always will be the fundamental social and political divide. White supremacists argued that southerners faced an inevitable choice between the competing forces of "white supremacy" and "negro domination." The preservation of white rule, they insisted, required the maintenance of white political solidarity. All who broke ranks were, by implication, race traitors. From an electoral point of view, calls to metaphoric race war served a simple strategic purpose—to unite and mobilize a diverse and divided white electorate against the Republican Party, particularly its radical wing.[11]

White supremacist politics first entered Grant Parish in 1874, through the vehicle of the "White Man's Party." The party, the brainchild of a group of conservatives in the nearby town of Alexandria, sought to rally backwoods farmers in central Louisiana against Republican rule through a direct racial appeal. As one party founder explained, "I believed then, sir, religiously, and I believe now that it was only possible to unite the white people of North Louisiana ... by appealing to their pride of race." Many white voters, especially those in the piney woods, had grown tired of politics. "They had their crops to make and gather and they did not care to lose the time going to barbecues, going to registration, and going to election when it did not amount to anything after all." The White Man's Party warned that black Republicans wished to "Africanize" the state and turn it into a "new San Domingo." Only racial unity, they argued, could prevent the subjugation of the white race.[12]

In the summer of 1874, Grant Parish conservatives endorsed the White Man's Party as an electoral vehicle for their local candidates in the upcoming fall elections. Accusing radical Republicans of introducing a racial line in politics, the conservatives declared themselves "an assembly of the Caucasian race" who "are not sorry they were born white, nor afraid to claim the legal rights of free born educated white citizens." Though claiming to speak for the entire white population of the parish, the party's slate of candidates leaned heavily in the favor of the large landowners of the river valley. The plantation belt tilt of the ticket proved to be the party's Achilles' heel. In the fall elections, an "independent" ticket with hill country ties split the white vote and deprived the White Man's Party of a clear-cut victory. Two years later, however, conservatives replayed the 1874 campaign under the banner of the Democratic Party and took control of the parish. For the next sixteen years, conservative Democrats, though continually opposed, dominated Grant Parish politics. White supremacy, with its insistence upon racial unity and implicit equation of political dissidence with race treason, remained their most potent political weapon against their opponents, both black and white.[13]

Once in power, Grant Parish's Democratic Party establishment reached an informal understanding with the parish's African American community that allowed for the continued exercise of black political and civil rights so long as black people did not openly challenge their social and economic subordination. The *Colfax Chronicle*, a mouthpiece for the Democratic establishment, summed up the terms of this agreement quite bluntly. "The negro is the equal of the white man in the eyes of the law," explained the *Chronicle*, "and no amount of swaggering can make the fact any less a fact. That he may be ten thousand times below the white man in the social scale, cuts no figure in the eyes of the law."[14] This accord, though perpetuating the fundamental inequalities of plantation life, allowed Grant Parish's black community to maintain its tradition of autonomous political action. While black voters did not participate electorally in numbers proportional to their share of the population, they did compose a significant bloc in local elections, particularly in the plantation belt where black voter turnout was generally large and enthusiastic. The Grant Parish Republican Party, with black leadership, a mostly black executive committee, and the near unanimous support of the black electorate, provided the African American community with an organized political voice. Though the Republicans lacked the numbers to elect black candidates to parish office, they were able to exert significant political influence through the strategy of bloc voting. While supporting Republican nominees for statewide and federal office, the Grant Parish Republican Party used its endorsement process to deliver black votes to local candidates who, regardless of partisan affiliation, were deemed sympathetic to black interests and who had a chance of winning.[15]

Despite its claims to represent the white race as a whole, the Grant Parish Democratic Party served primarily as a vehicle to advance the interests of the large landowning and commercial interests of the river valley, often at the expense of people in the hills. River valley Democrats controlled the party apparatus, monopolized patronage jobs and party nominations, and orchestrated the selection of delegates to state and district party conventions. Every Democratic candidate nominated for parish office between 1879 and 1888 resided in or around the two river valley towns of Colfax and Montgomery. A majority of the candidates (five out of nine) were planters or merchants. Not one was a smallholding farmer. Nearly 80 percent of delegates to state and district conventions selected by the Grant Parish Democratic Party between 1879 and 1888 lived in the river valley. Sixty-three percent were planters, merchants, or lawyers. Only 23 percent were smallholding farmers. The Democratic Party apparatus also controlled the parish police jury, Louisiana's equivalent of the county commission. Under an 1880 law, direct election of police jurors was abolished and replaced with gubernatorial appointment. While a majority of police jurors technically represented hill country wards, they owed their positions not to voters but to the governor and the party apparatus. As a consequence, residents of the river valley received the lion's share of policy jury patronage.[16]

A longstanding controversy surrounding Newton C. Blanchard, Grant Parish's representative to the United State Congress, revealed the political impotence of piney woods farmers within the Democratic Party. A wealthy Shreveport lawyer, Blanchard was disliked by smallholding farmers, both for his stands on the issues and his aristocratic pretensions, which included a penchant for traveling to Europe (ostensibly "for his health").[17] The congressman, though, was a favorite among local planters, as he was the stepbrother to one of the parish's largest landowning families. When he first sought the congressional seat in 1880, Blanchard's partisans in Grant packed the Democratic mass meeting that would choose the parish's delegates to the district nominating convention. Despite Blanchard's limited support in Grant, his supporters rammed through a pair of pro-Blanchard delegates. After hill country Democrats threatened to walk out, an anti-Blanchard man was narrowly elected to fill out the three-member delegation. The two Blanchard delegates from Grant Parish provided the congressman with his margin of victory at the district nominating convention.[18]

Blanchard's failure to oppose the infamous "Backbone Railroad" land grant, one of the great corporate giveaways of America's Gilded Age, earned him the enmity of piney woods farmers. The Backbone land grant provided robber baron Jay Gould's New Orleans and Pacific Railroad with nearly one million Louisiana acres, including roughly one hundred thousand acres in the Grant Parish hill country, miles from the railroad's proposed route. At a stroke, thousands of acres of public land that had been open to settlement were placed in private hands. Some farmers who had not yet received title to the land they had settled saw their home sites given away to Gould's railroad. Rejecting piney woods demands that he fight for the grant's forfeiture, Congressman Blanchard instead negotiated a compromise settlement with the railroad that allowed farmers who had settled prior to the date of the grant to purchase their land back from the railroad for price somewhat below the market rate, but far in excess of the cost to settle public lands. Nevertheless, despite grumbling in the piney woods and occasional talk of replacing Blanchard, the Democratic Party repeatedly renominated the congressman.[19]

The marginalization of piney woods voices within the Democratic Party fueled an "independent" political movement in the Grant Parish hills. The community of Big Creek, which had long nurtured a culture of political dissent, was a focal point for independent politics. In 1861, the Big Creek community opposed Louisiana's secession from the Union, and during the Red River campaign of 1862, one local resident organized and commanded a Unionist partisan company. After the war, Big Creek became one of the first communities in north Louisiana to organize a chapter of the Grange, a social and economic fraternity of farmers that reached its peak as a national movement in the early 1870s. Explained one Big Creek Granger, "The necessity of concerted action on the part of farmers to protect their interests from the abuses of monopolies, and corrupt legislation" had been "a subject of long consideration" in the community. Among the suggestions of this Granger was that the plantations of the nearby Red River Valley be subdivided and sold to the "honest workingman."[20] Among the most prominent of the independents was Big Creek's Benjamin F. Brian. A Louisiana native, Benjamin Brian settled at Big Creek in 1868, where he worked first as a blacksmith and wheelwright. Later he obtained a modest fifty-acre farm and also preached the Baptist faith. Brian was a perennial candidate for state senate, running independent campaigns for that post in every election between 1876 and 1888.[21]

By attacking the corruption of the existing parties, with occasional forays into inflationary monetary reforms that would offer relief to indebted farmers, Brian and the independents built a small but devoted following in the hills. Although piney woods voters overwhelmingly supported Democrats in statewide races, most split their tickets for local offices and proved especially willing to support independents from their own particular neighborhoods. By the 1880s, independents and Democrats were roughly evenly matched in the hill country in local races. While the Democrats' entire local ticket swept the piney woods in the 1879 election, in both 1884 and 1888 the hills split evenly between the Democratic and independent slates. Yet, with no more than about a third of piney woods voters ever willing to vote a straight independent ticket, hill country votes alone could not propel Brain and his allies to victory parish wide.[22]

The existence of a large and well-organized black electorate in Grant Parish provided the hill country independents with both their greatest political opportunity and their steepest political challenge. Recognizing that they could not be elected on the basis of white votes alone, the independents worked to forge an electoral coalition between hill country dissidents and black Republicans. A number of independents, including Benjamin Brian, had dabbled with Republicanism during Reconstruction, and a few had formal ties to the party. These personal connections, along with a shared antipathy to the river valley establishment, provided inroads with black activists. The Grant Parish Republican Party endorsed the independent slate in both 1878 and 1879, helping to propel Brian into the state senate from the district that included Grant in the latter year. (Due to the adoption of a new state constitution, Louisiana held state and local elections in both 1878 and 1879.)[23]

Though shared opposition to the river valley establishment had brought hill country dissidents and black Republicans together in a common cause, it did not bring them together as equals. While independent candidates typically received more black votes than white votes, not once did the independent slate include a black candidate for parish office. Nor did independent candidates openly address the fundamental social and economic inequalities of plantation life. The absence of black candidates on the independent ticket and the failure of white candidates to aggressively assert black interests reflected a simple structural reality; regardless of the political divisions among the white electorate, neither a black candidate nor a white candidate perceived as too closely allied with black interests could be elected in a white majority parish. Black Republicans thus took a subordinate role in their alliance with the hill country dissidents in the hopes that they could barter their votes for a more responsive parish government.

Building an interracial coalition of hill country and river valley voters required a delicate balancing act on the part of the independents. In the valley, they had to stress their Republican ties and commitment to black interests while in the hills they had to distance themselves from the Republicans and their black constituents. In 1878, the independent candidate for sheriff, a Civil War Unionist and longtime Republican from the piney woods, assured black voters that he remained loyal to the party despite running an independent campaign. That same year, a prominent black Republican who had served in the state legislature under Reconstruction urged support for the independent ticket as the only way to elect Republicans to office. In the hills, by contrast, independent candidates emphasized their nonpartisan status and argued against party-line voting. Benjamin Brian, despite running regularly with Republican support, described himself as an "independent Democrat." Speaking in the hills during the 1888 campaign, he declared that though both parties were corrupt, he believed that the Democrats represented "the wealth, intelligence, and virtue" of Louisiana's people. Brian claimed to always cooperate with Democrats on "questions of vital moment."[24]

Despite their best efforts, piney woods independents could never quite overcome persistent suspicions among many white voters that they were untrustworthy on the race issue, suspicions that the Democratic Party did its best to fan. In 1878, the *Colfax Chronicle* ominously reported that the independent candidates had attended what the paper termed a radical "council of war" held in "the wigwam of 'Fat' Tom Johnson," the portly black man who chaired the Grant Parish Republican Party. One Colfax Democrat warned against people "who pretend to be independent and say they go for the man and not party," but who, while all honest men are asleep, "are visiting the nightly meetings of dusky men ... In the hills they are good Democrats, but tired of party, and go for the man but with the dusky man, are simon-pure Republicans and despise all Democrats."[25] Democratic rhetoric remained remarkably constant for the next decade. "Our 'independent' candidates are in hot water," the *Chronicle* declared in 1888. "In the hills they have to explain that they are not Republicans, and in the bottoms they have to explain that they are not Democrats."[26] Democratic propagandists painted each election as an inevitable choice between Democrats and open or closeted Republicans. "Can you hesitate for one instant in choosing between the two parties," asked a Democratic handbill, "the one struggling to preserve and defend all that is best of our civilization, and the other endeavoring to array race against race?" The handbill left little doubt of the dire consequences of a Democratic defeat. "The memory of Easter Sunday 1873," it warned as it referenced the Colfax Massacre, "is too fresh in the minds of the people of the parish of Grant for them to rivet anew the shackles they that day struck off."[27]

The Democratic Party also did its best to plant the seeds of division between black Republicans and hill country independents. Even as they painted piney woods dissidents as racially disloyal, they simultaneously fanned black suspicions that the independents were racial opportunists. In 1878, a Democratic speaker warned a black audience that hill country Republicans and independents were unprincipled men. "These sort of fellows d——d the nigger in the hills and hugged him in the bottoms," he declared. A decade later, the *Chronicle* warned of "would-be pap-suckers who are perfectly willing to run on the Democratic, Republican, or Independent ticket, just so long as they have a ghost of show to get the chance of feeding at the public crib."[28] Though the Democrats were not able to shatter the Republican–hill country alliance, over time cracks did begin to appear.

Led by Charles H. Thomas, the president of the Grant Parish Republican Party, a group of black activists sought closer cooperation with the river valley establishment. Thomas hoped to win favors for black people by appealing to the Democratic establishment's paternalistic instincts. Upon receiving a gift of garden seeds from Democratic congressman Newton C. Blanchard, for instance, Thomas thanked both the congressman and the Democratic editor of the *Colfax Chronicle* for "all the good" they had done for the black race. In 1884, through Thomas's efforts, the Republican Party endorsed a mixed ticket of Democrats, Republicans, and independents.[29]

The rise and fall of state representative William P. Guynes illustrated the political tightrope that piney woods dissidents had to walk. Guynes, one of a handful of overt hill country Republicans, was elected state representative from Grant in 1884 in a tight three-way race, largely on basis of black support. Once in office, he worked to broaden his hill country constituency by pushing a proposal to relocate the Grant Parish courthouse to the piney woods. The idea of "courthouse removal" (as it was called) had longstanding bipartisan support in the hills. A centrally located courthouse, advocates argued, would be a convenience to people in the hills and would encourage the commercial development of the region. For one piney woods Democrat, courthouse removal was a simple matter of white rule, the bulk of the parish's white population lived in the hills so that is where the courthouse should lie. Another advocate, a self-described Greenbacker involved with independent politics, declared it a question of "justice, of equality and principle." In the spring of 1886, Guynes introduced, and had passed, legislation calling for a local referendum to relocate the courthouse to the hill country of eastern Grant Parish.[30]

With the white electorate split, black votes held the balance of power in the referendum. Guynes campaigned hard for removal among the black voters of the river valley, suggesting that it was a party measure that would break up the Colfax "ring." Guynes's standing among black Republicans was in decline, however. To gain leverage in the Democratic-controlled legislature, Guynes had made a number of significant political compromises, including joining the Democratic legislative caucus and voting to extend the governor's power to appoint police jurors, a measure that denied black residents representation on the police jury, even in the black majority First Ward. The night before the courthouse election, a mass meeting of black voters resolved unanimously to oppose removal. The next day, virtually every black voter in Grant Parish cast his ballot against the removal proposal. The measure went down to defeat by a wide margin.[31]

Although it ended in failure, the courthouse removal campaign did earn Guynes the gratitude of many in the piney woods. When he ran for reelection in 1888, he received nearly half of the hill country vote in a two-way race. His legislative compromises, though, had cost him much of his African American support. One in four black Republicans who cast ballots in 1888 either sat out the state representative race altogether or voted for Guynes's Democratic opponent. These black defections cost Guynes his reelection. Structural constraints had placed Guynes in a no-win political position. To secure reelection, particularly in a two-way race, Guynes had to expand his piney woods support. But in trying to deliver the goods to the hill country, he was forced to sacrifice the interests of his African American core constituency. In the end, Guynes was simply unable to balance the demands of the two groups. The Populist insurgents of the 1890s would face a similar set of challenges.[32]

The early 1890s witnessed a wave of electoral dissidence in the Grant Parish hills that far outstripped the independent politics of the 1880s, in both depth of support and degree of passion. At a state level, Louisiana Populism was relatively weak. Large segments of the state were virtually untouched by the Populist revolt, and the Louisiana People's Party failed to develop an effective statewide organization. In the piney woods of Grant Parish, however, and in the hill country of north-central Louisiana more generally, the Populist revolt was as intense as anywhere in the South. The north-central Louisiana hills were the birthplace of Louisiana Populism and remained its heartland until the demise of the People's Party in the late 1890s. In Grant Parish, and in its neighboring parishes, the People's Party was constructed from below with little support or guidance from a statewide organization.[33]

For most of the 1880s, white supremacy (with its insistence on the political centrality of race) had limited the spread of piney woods dissidence. Toward the end of the decade, though, the rise of the Louisiana Farmers' Union (an affiliate of the National Farmers' Alliance) placed issues of economic reform at the center of local politics and fueled the growth of agrarian radicalism in the Grant Parish hills. The Farmers' Union launched its first Grant Parish organizing drive in March 1887. Within two months, eight local chapters were established, and representatives from these eight chapters had organized a Grant Parish Farmers' Union (GPFU). By 1889, the union had 402 members (279 men and 123 women) organized into thirteen subordinate unions, located mostly in the piney woods. Two additional local chapters in Grant chose to affiliate with the Farmers' Union in neighboring Winn Parish. The Farmers' Union's program of cooperative marketing and purchasing, which promised to liberate farmers from a downward cycle of falling cotton prices and escalating debt, was particularly attractive to those in the piney woods that had come to depend upon cotton for their livelihood. During the 1887 season, local unions pursued individual purchasing agreements with particular furnishing merchants. In 1888, the GPFU negotiated a parish-wide purchasing agreement with a single furnishing merchant. By 1889, the GPFU had established a cooperative association to operate its own stores.[34]

By uniting piney woods farmers around a common cause, the GPFU began to dissolve existing political allegiances in the hill country. The union brought together Democrats, Republicans, and political independents without regard to party affiliation. The parish union's first president was a party-line Democrat, as were the vice president and treasurer. The GPFU's lecturer, by contrast, was a Greenbacker who had been active in independent politics and had helped lead the courthouse removal campaign. Piney woods Republican William P. Guynes served as the assistant lecturer. Benjamin F. Brian was elected president of the Big Creek Union. Other local unions were led by Democrats.[35]

The Farmers' Alliance movement also had the potential to forge new political links between black and white farmers in Grant Parish. Though restrictive policies limited membership in the Farmers' Union to white people, the late 1880s saw the emergence of a parallel Colored Farmers' Union in Grant Parish. The Colored Farmers' National Alliance (with which the Louisiana Colored Farmers' Union was affiliated) was technically independent of the white Alliance. Nevertheless, the two Alliances established collaborative relationships in a number of states, including Louisiana, as well as at the national level. In Louisiana, for instance, after first attempting to establish its own independent purchasing and marketing exchange, the Colored Farmers' Union contracted to purchase goods through the white union's statewide cooperative association. The Winn Parish Cooperative Association (which operated a union store in Grant Parish at the river town of Montgomery) went further by extending credit to landowning members of the Colored Alliance.[36]

In Grant, the Colored Farmers' Union first took root in those parts of the parish that lacked well-established black political and civic organizations. A small hill country community of black farmers organized a Colored Farmers' Union in 1888 under the auspices of the local white union. When the parish union was organized in the fall of 1889, three of the six officers elected were drawn from the ranks of the hill country's small black population. As the union cooperative movement expanded in scope, the Colored Farmers' Union spread into the plantations of the river valley. By 1890, residents of the river bottom made up the majority of the parish union's membership. Established black civic leaders, including Charles H. Thomas, the longtime chair of the Grant Parish Republican Party, became more active in the organization, and river bottom residents also took greater control of the parish union's leadership.[37]

In certain ways, the relationship between black and white farmers within the cooperative movement paralleled the relationship between hill country independents and black Republicans in parish politics. Though the cooperative movement brought black farmers from the river valley and white farmers from the hills together around a common cause, it did not bring them together as equals. The cooperatives served both black and white farmers, but black farmers had no voice in governing them. The Grant Parish Farmers' Union Cooperative Association was governed by a board of trustees elected by those affiliated locals of the white parish union that had purchased association stock. (Stock could only be purchased by affiliated union locals and not by individuals.) The exclusion of black farmers from the white parish union thus excluded black farmers from the cooperative association board. Black farmers were similarly excluded from governance of the state cooperative association, which also limited shareholding to local affiliates of the white Farmers' Union. In addition, the benefits of the cooperatives were limited mainly to those relatively few black farmers (landowners or renters) who controlled their own crop. The cooperatives offered little to the many renters whose crops were under the de facto control of local furnishing merchants and virtually nothing to those who worked for a wage as plantation laborers. Despite these limitations, a growing number of black farmers in Grant Parish accepted a subordinate position within the cooperative movement, as they had in the independent-Republican alliance, in hopes of reaping a degree of material benefit.[38]

While cooperative enterprise was at the heart of the Farmers' Union's appeal, the GPFU also became a forum for increasingly radical economic reform ideas. In October 1889, Thomas J. Guice, the state lecturer of the Louisiana Farmers' Union, delivered a lecture in Grant Parish on the topic of the agricultural crisis. Rejecting the view that low prices for farm commodities were a result of overproduction, Guice blamed falling prices on "the war between labor and capital." This war, Guice argued, was reducing farmers to the status of mere wage workers "who earn as much for their masters, as did the former chattel slaves." He warned farmers not to vacillate and temporize with bankers and speculators. "Eternal vigilance is the price of liberty," he concluded. Guice's fiery message elicited heartfelt applause.[39] As the Grant Parish Farmers' Union grew in size and influence, it came into increasing conflict with the river valley political establishment. The use of tax exemptions to promote railroad development, for instance, pitted the Farmers' Union against parish boosters. In 1889, the parish police jury (all of whose members served through gubernatorial appointment) aroused the ire of the union by approving an ordinance granting a ten-year tax exemption to any railroad that would cross the Red River in Grant Parish. After GPFU delegates voted unanimously to condemn the ordinance, which they saw as a giveaway to special interests, the police jury reversed itself. The following spring, despite continued union opposition, the police jury approved seven-year tax exemptions for two proposed rail lines. The irate members of one local farmers' union condemned the police jury's action on the grounds that it was "unjust to tax the laboring peoples and exempt railroads" and demanded that their ward's representative resign from the body.[40]

The impetus for the GPFU's final break with the Democratic Party was the National Farmers' Alliance proposal for a federal subtreasury program to provide low-interest government loans directly to farmers. The subtreasury plan, first presented publicly at the December 1889 convention of the National Farmers' Alliance, was the brainchild of Charles W. Macune, the president of the order. Under Macune's plan, the federal government would erect a public warehouse in every county in the country that produced at least $500,000 worth of agricultural commodities. Farmers who stored their products in these "subtreasuries" could borrow up to 80 percent of the value of the crop at a guaranteed low interest rate. By shifting agricultural credit from private to public hands, the subtreasury program promised to achieve what the cooperative movement had failed to do, to free farmers from the furnishing merchants who were the primary providers of credit in the cotton South. The subtreasury plan aroused enormous enthusiasm among the farmers of the Grant Parish piney woods. The secretary of one local Farmers' Union declared that the order's members would "hold to it with death-like grasp." "We will work for it, talk for it, write for it, and last but not least, we will vote for it," he added.[41]

In the summer of 1890, the GPFU joined with union activists across Louisiana's Fourth Congressional District in a failed attempt to deny renomination to incumbent Democratic congressman Newton

C. Blanchard, a firm opponent of the subtreasury plan. In response to Blanchard's renomination, the Winn Parish Farmers' Union issued a call for a special convention in the town of Nachitoches to select a Farmers' Union candidate to challenge Blanchard in the November election. An enthusiastic group of GPFU activists gathered shortly thereafter to choose a delegate to the Nachitoches convention. The *Colfax Chronicle* reported that the "so-called 'independent' element was out in force" at the meeting. In fact, the piney woods rebellion had spread far beyond the ranks of the traditional dissidents. Spurning the warnings of the *Chronicle*'s editor, who cautioned that an independent campaign would simply help the Republicans, the meeting voted overwhelmingly to support a Farmers' Union candidate. Just four of the roughly eighty men present voted no. Commitment to the reform agenda of the Farmers' Union had dissolved fears of Republican rule.[42]

The delegates to the Nachitoches convention nominated state union lecturer Thomas J. Guice for Congress and called upon all labor organizations of the district, including the Colored Farmers' Alliance, to support Guice's candidacy. By placing economic reform at the top of their political agenda and by making a direct appeal for black votes, Guice and his supporters had repudiated one of the central tenets of white supremacist politics, that race always comes first. The response of the Democratic establishment was immediate and fierce. Raising the specter of race treason, the *Colfax Chronicle* warned voters that Guice was a closet Republican. Thomas S. Adams, the president of the state Farmers' Union and Guice's superior in the organization, pressured him to withdraw. In October, the Rapides Parish Farmers' Union withdrew its endorsement. Guice finally bowed to the pressure and abandoned his candidacy, citing his unwillingness to "court negro Republican votes to oppose the best interests of the white people of the state."[43] Though the opposition of the Farmers' Union's state leadership had delayed temporarily the Populist revolt in Louisiana, the union farmers of Grant Parish had nonetheless made a decisive break with the Democratic Party.

In May 1891, over fourteen hundred delegates gathered in Cincinnati, Ohio, for the founding convention of the People's Party. Among the delegates was Hardy L. Brian, secretary of the Winn Parish Farmers' Union and son of veteran Grant Parish independent activist Benjamin F. Brian. Hardy Brian carried with him credentials as the official representative of the Farmers' Union's of Winn, Grant, Catahoula, and Vernon Parishes. Brian pronounced the era of racial politics to be over in the South. "The race cry doesn't scare us," he explained. "We find that we can manage the colored men in the Alliance very well, and we are not a bit frightened about negro supremacy."[44] Meanwhile, in Grant Parish, an itinerant teacher and preacher named L. A. Traylor, who the Alliancemen of Grant and Winn Parishes had contracted to administer a newly established Farmers' Union College near the town of Montgomery, began barnstorming the parish on behalf of the People's Party. A gathering of two hundred men and women hosted by the Ada and Tison unions unanimously endorsed the new party and invited the black people of the parish to "co-operate with us in our effort to free the country from plutocratic usurpation and tyranny."[45] Traylor also addressed a meeting of the Colored Farmers' Union, where his reform message was warmly received. The meeting, chaired by longtime Republican leader Charles H. Thomas, unanimously adopted a series of resolutions endorsing the People's Party, its platform, and pledging to support candidates for office nominated by the white Farmers' Union. This pledge, however, was conditioned upon the Farmers' Union breaking decisively with the Democratic Party. "Whereas it is currently reported that the Democratic party has invited the Farmers' alliance to hold white primaries, and go into convention with them, promising to give them all the offices," read one of the resolutions. "Be it resolved, that, should the white alliance allow themselves pulled into either of the old parties we will not support their candidate."[46]

In September 1891, a group of about forty Alliancemen gathered at Colfax to organize the Grant Parish People's Party and elect a party executive committee. The makeup of the executive committee revealed Populism in Grant Parish to be a grassroots movement of white smallholding farmers who had been radicalized by the Farmers' Union cooperative movement. Smallholding farmers, most of them Farmers' Union activists, made up over 80 percent of the committee membership. While prominent independents, such as Benjamin F. Brian, played a central role in organizing the local party, former Democrats made up a significant share of the executive committee. And, despite calls for interracial cooperation, the entire Populist parish executive committee was white.[47]

Although the Grant Parish People's Party was a creation of white hill country farmers, local Populists envisioned themselves building a movement of all who labored, regardless of race. Believing that both wealth and virtue derived from the physical production of tangible goods, Populists drew a sharp distinction between those who lived by their own labor and those who lived off the labor of others. Grant Parish Populists, though generally small proprietors who owned their own land, nonetheless numbered themselves among the "laboring class of people" and regularly referred to the Farmers' Alliance as a "labor organization." They drew a contrast between the "toiling millions" and those they termed "class of gentlemen" who, they argued, sat "upon the throne of their majesty, sucking the very life blood of this nation."[48] Believing that all who labored shared common materials interests, they saw no contradiction between calls for interracial solidarity and the exclusion of black men from leadership roles within the party. Indeed, they expected African American people to rally to Populist cause, and they drew hope from the cooperation achieved between the white Farmers' Union and its black counterpart. "There is a colord [sic] organization who constitute the majority of the republican voters in the state," explained one local Populist, "who are only waiting for an opportunity to support the peoples party."[49]

Seventy-eight delegates from seventeen parishes gathered in the town of Alexandria on October 2, 1891, for the founding convention of the Louisiana People's Party. Grant Parish's Benjamin F. Brian presided over the convention's preliminary organization and "expressed great satisfaction at seeing the 'independent' political action for which he has labored for the last fifteen years," the *Colfax Chronicle* reported. Grant Parish was solidly for the People's Party, Brian boasted. "Even the negroes had organized and were ready for it," he reported. While all official delegates were white, two black Alliancemen, including the superintendent of the state Colored Farmers' Union, were present and were admitted to the speakers' platform.[50] After endorsing the People's Party and adopting a party platform, the convention issued an address, "To the voters of the State of Louisiana, irrespective of Class, Color, or Past Political Affiliations." The address, coauthored by Benjamin Brian's son Hardy L. Brian, called upon black and white alike to abandon the politics of race and join together in a peaceful revolution of the "wealth producers."

> You, Colored Men, who in your natural exuberant gratitude to the Party that claimed the exclusive merit of freeing your race from the bonds of slavery, furnished the votes that have kept the Republicans in power ... you must feel that you have fully repaid all you owe them ... You must now realize that there is no hope of any further material benefit to you from that Republican party, and that, if you remain in it, you will continue to be the hewers of wood and the drawers of water in the future as you have been in the past.

Brian declared an end to the politics of white supremacy and its insistence upon white unity. "The Spectre of Negro Supremacy" had been used to keep white Democrats in "the toils of scheming Machine Politicians, as effectively as the Voudou is employed to terrify the credulous Negroes themselves," he wrote. "That Spectre can no longer be summoned."[51]

In October 1891, the Grant Parish People's Party hosted a grand barbecue and mass meeting at the Summerfield Union Hall to endorse the third-party move. The 750 men, women, and children in attendance, about one-third of whom were African American, were treated to rousing speeches and a sumptuous meal, served at separate tables for black and white. Evan Thomas, president of the Texas State Farmers' Alliance and a leading third-party advocate, spoke in favor of the People's Party and the subtreasury plan. The *Colfax Chronicle* reported an overabundance of food and indicated that much of the leftovers were carried home by black attendees in "wallets and baskets." The Summerfield barbecue was a living embodiment of the interracial movement that white Populists envisioned building, a movement in which black men were invited to participate and to share in the benefits but in which they would occupy a separate and subordinate position.[52]

Yet, despite the rapid spread of agrarian rebellion in the Grant Parish hills, the Populists of the 1890s faced the same structural dilemmas as had the piney woods dissidents of the 1880s. To compete successfully in the electoral arena, the Populists needed black support, but the more vigorously the People's Party pursued black voters, the more they opened themselves up to Democratic charges of race treason. The third-party move, the *Colfax Chronicle* ominously declared, had been concocted by the "pseudo Independent-Republican contingent." Another Democrat was even more explicit. "The third party plan is a dangerous entering wedge to split the Solid South, and defeat white supremacy."[53] White Populists sought to inoculate themselves from the race treason charge by excluding black men from leadership positions within the People's Party. The People's Party's racially exclusionary practices, however, made Populism a more difficult sell among African American voters and activists, particularly given the history of autonomous black political action in Grant Parish.

In the fall of 1891, Grant Parish Populists took a bold political gamble by inviting African American voters to participate in a primary election to choose a parish ticket for the following April's local elections. Far from cementing an interracial Populist alliance, as Populist leaders had hoped, the primary election marked the end of interracial Populism in Grant Parish.

Black voters, who made up just over half of the primary electorate, cast their ballots as a bloc and determined the makeup of the entire People's Party ticket. The handpicked choices of the Farmers' Union leadership, with the exception of state senate candidate Benjamin F. Brian, went down to defeat. A self-described "stalwart" Republican received the Populist nomination for state representative in a racially polarized race. Although all of victorious candidates were white, and most had garnered some degree of white support, the results shocked party leaders, who had expected black primary voters to defer to the candidate preferences of the white Farmers' Union.[54]

The primary election shook the People's Party "from center to circumference," reported Benjamin Brian's son Hardy.[55] Taken aback by the outcome, the Populist Party's parish executive committee delayed releasing the primary results for several weeks before finally certifying the victors. Local Democrats could hardly contain their glee at the Populist disarray. "The discontent of the Third Partyites over their late primaries in Grant Parish is amusing," cackled the *Colfax Chronicle*. "We have all along warned them of the power of the colored brethren when the whites divide their forces . . . Take your medicine friends; it's a pot of your own brewing."[56] A group of white Populists waged a campaign to repudiate the ticket and replace it with candidates more to their liking. Finally, just two weeks before the April 1892 elections, the Grant Parish People's Party reaffirmed its support for the primary winners. By then, however, the damage to the fragile trust between white and black Populists had been done.[57]

An undercurrent of racial tension also marred the Louisiana People's Party's February 1892 state nominating convention. Although Populists opened the convention to black men (at least 24 of the 171 delegates were African American), white delegates resisted the demands of some black Populists that the party's state ticket include an African American candidate. The names of two prominent black politicians, including a former superintendent of the Louisiana Colored Farmers' Union, were placed in nomination for the office of state treasurer. After a lengthy debate, both men withdrew under pressure from those, including some African American delegates, who argued that it was not the "proper time" for black men to run for office. The state platform adopted by the convention reflected the ambivalence of white Populists toward interracial politics. "The interests of the white and colored people of the South are identical," declared the platform. "Equal justice and fairness must be accorded to each." Expressions of interracial solidarity nevertheless coexisted with assumptions of black inferiority. The same platform that promised equal justice also warned that both black and white would suffer unless "the undisputed control of our government were assured to the intelligent and educated portion of the population"—words long euphemistic in Louisiana for white rule. The party, in effect, called for interracial solidarity, but under the leadership of white Populists.[58]

Louisiana's April 1892 state and local elections, in which voters could choose from among five gubernatorial tickets, was among the most complex and confusing in the state's history. A controversy surrounding the proposed rechartering of the Louisiana State Lottery split both Democrats and Republicans in the pro- and anti-lottery wings, each of which nominated a full slate of candidates for state office. For governor, the Populists nominated Robert L. Tannehill, the former sheriff of Winn Parish and a past treasurer of the state farmers' union. The Louisiana Farmers' Union, much to the disappointment of its Populist wing, allied with the anti-lottery Democrats, thus depriving the People's Party of a statewide infrastructure. In Grant Parish, the pro- and anti-lottery Democrats each fielded their own candidates, as did the Populists. The local Republican Party also split into pro- and anti-lottery wings, each of which endorsed a mixed ticket drawn from the local Democratic and Populist slates.[59]

The April 1892 elections shattered Democratic hegemony in Grant Parish and established the People's Party as its strongest electoral force. Populist gubernatorial candidate Robert L. Tannehill carried Grant with 42 percent of the vote, compared to a combined 29 percent for the two Democratic candidates and a similar 29 percent for the two Republicans. Populist state senatorial candidate Benjamin F. Brian won a convincing victory in the parish and was elected to represent the district that included Grant. Populists were also elected to the offices of state representative, parish clerk, and coroner. Just one Populist, sheriff candidate Henry B. Thompson, went down to defeat. Despite the controversies surrounding their local primary, Populists delivered the piney woods for their entire slate, in some cases by astounding margins. Tannehill received 81 percent of the vote in the hill country precincts while Brian gained a remarkable 88 percent. Sheriff candidate Henry B. Thompson, though receiving a minority of the white vote in the previous fall's Populist primary, carried the piney woods with 55 percent of ballots cast in a three-way race.[60]

The Populist victories, however, masked the failure of the Grant Parish People's Party to expand beyond its white piney woods base and into the plantations of the river valley. Robert L. Tannehill received just 6 percent of the vote in the parish's three black majority precincts and gained not one single vote in the Fairmount Precinct, which the *Colfax Chronicle* deemed "the negro stronghold in Grant." Instead, African American voters mainly cast their ballots for one of the two rival Republican state tickets in the field. Black voters largely shunned the People's Party's local ticket, which they themselves had helped to construct, in favor of the two mixed slates endorsed by the pro- and anti-lottery Republicans. Despite their massive margins in the hill country, Populist candidates remained heavily dependent upon Republican support, and Republican support was not always there. The victorious Populist candidates for state representative, parish clerk, and coroner had all received a Republican endorsement. By contrast, sheriff candidate Henry B. Thompson ran without Republican endorsement and went down to defeat, due largely to his poor showing in the black-majority precincts of the river valley.[61]

In Grant Parish, Populist sentiment remained confined almost entirely to the white voters of the piney woods. The same proved true statewide. As had been the case since the end of Reconstruction, Democratic force and fraud (particularly in the black majority precincts along the Mississippi and Red Rivers) prevented many African American voters from freely casting ballots. Among those black ballots that were freely cast, though, virtually none was cast for the People's Party ticket. Populist gubernatorial candidate Robert L. Tannehill gathered only 6 percent of the statewide vote, carried just four parishes, and received a majority of the vote in but two. The People's Party received little support beyond its core constituency of Farmers' Union radicals in the state's north-central hill country. Roughly two-thirds of Tannehill's total vote came from a set of ten contiguous parishes (including Grant) in the north-central part of the state. The Populists elected just one member, Grant Parish's Benjamin F. Brian, to the state senate and but three to the legislature's lower house. Populist dreams of an interracial reform movement of the "laboring classes" lay in ruins.[62]

Like the piney woods independents before them, the Populists of Grant Parish had failed to resolve the central structural dilemma facing agrarian rebels in the rural South, how to win black support without alienating their white voter base. Populists assumed that an agenda of economic reform and declarations of interracial solidarity would rally both black and white to the People's Party banner. The Populist reform agenda, however, offered little direct material benefit to the sharecroppers, tenant farmers, and agricultural laborers who made up the bulk of Grant Parish's black population. Populist professions of interracial solidarity were undercut by their insistence that black men accept a subordinate position within the party. White Populists asked black people to abandon a Republican Party that had served as a vehicle for autonomous black politics in Grant Parish ever since emancipation to accept a junior partnership in what was essentially a white piney woods movement. When, during the 1891 People's Party primary, black voters stepped beyond their subordinate role, white Populists recoiled with alarm. Black voters in Grant Parish returned to their traditional Republican loyalties and time-tested strategy of employing bloc voting to influence the outcome of local elections.

After the electoral disappointments of 1892, Louisiana Populists abandoned the effort to integrate African American voters directly into the People's Party. Nevertheless, the structural imperative to seek black support remained. Populists ceased to make direct appeals to black voters and instead pursued African American support through a series of fusion agreements with the Louisiana Republican Party. In 1896, for instance, the Populists and Republicans ran a joint ticket for state office comprised of members of both parties. In 1896, Grant Parish Populists campaigned energetically for Republican support, as did the Democrats, as both camps understood that the African American vote would be decisive to the outcome. Yet, if the structural imperative to seek black support remained, so too did the need for Populists to prove their white racial credentials. By 1894, the Louisiana People's Party (which just a few years earlier had urged black Louisianans to join the Populist cause and had seated black delegates at its state convention) had openly declared itself to be a "white man's party" and sought to allay white racial fears by playing to white stereotypes of black inferiority. "The negro does not want to 'dominate' anybody," wrote the *Louisiana Populist*, an official party organ founded in 1894. "He could not if he wanted to." In 1896, Grant Parish Populists challenged local Democrats to a "white primary," with the losing party's candidates to withdraw from the general election. The Democrats rejected this proposal, and both parties continued to campaign for Republican support. Local Republicans endorsed a mixture of Democratic and Populist candidates, as they had in 1892. The Republican endorsement again proved decisive in most local races, as it had four years earlier.[63]

So what were the racial attitudes of Grant Parish Populists? Unfortunately, we have little access to their inner thoughts. Some, like Benjamin F. Brian and the hill country independents, had long established political relationships with black Republican activists in the Grant Parish river bottom. This is at least suggestive of a worldview more egalitarian than the harsh white supremacist perspective that dominated southern political life in the post-Reconstruction period. Others, however, had been loyal Democrats and had only abandoned the self-proclaimed party of white supremacy when they came to see issues of economic reform as more important than issues of race. For them, the People's Party's halting and tentative moves toward interracial solidarity must surely have fostered discomfort and unease. Regardless, the party's stance on issues of race owed less to the attitudes of individual Populist activists than it did to the structural imperatives of southern politics. To win elections, Grant Parish Populists needed the support of black voters, hence the drive to build interracial alliances. If pursued on terms of equality, however, such partnerships risked alienating much of the white Populist voter base in the hill country. The result was a Populist racial stance that was ambiguous and at times contradictory.

At the turn of the century, disfranchisement radically changed the structural imperatives of southern politics. With black voters purged from the electorate, little incentive remained for white reform politicians to pursue cross-racial alliances. While racial liberalism (real or perceived) came with a price, championing white supremacy brought electoral benefits, particularly when the racial order appeared under threat. For historians like Woodward, who were products of the harsh Jim Crow era with its strict racial orthodoxy, the relative racial openness of late-nineteenth-century southern politics was both striking and surprising. Expressions of interracial solidarity and direct appeals for black votes by white politicians and party leaders, common features of late-nineteenth-century southern agrarian politics, were wholly alien to the lived experience of the Woodward generation. Struck by the contrast between their own experiences and those of an earlier generation, historians like Woodward often failed to appreciate the ambiguities and limitations of the interracial agrarian politics of the earlier era. And yet, something was indeed different about late-nineteenth-century southern politics. In the 1890s, black men in many parts of the South, including Grant Parish, still retained the right to vote. By 1900, they no longer did. And that structural reality, more than the racial attitudes of white politicians and activists, made all the difference in the practice of southern politics.[64]

Notes

1. C. Vann Woodward, *Tom Watson: Agrarian Rebel* (New York: Macmillan, 1938), 239–240. The Doyle episode also figures prominently in Omar H. Ali's account of black

Populism. Omar H. Ali, "Black Populism in the New South, 1886–1898" (Ph.D. diss., Columbia University, 2003), 123–125.

2. C. Vann Woodward, *The Strange Career of Jim Crow*, 3rd rev. ed. (New York: Oxford University Press, 1974), 64; Lawrence Goodwyn, *Democratic Promise: The Populist Moment in America* (New York: Oxford University Press, 1976). William Ivy Hair's classic study of post-Reconstruction Louisiana politics, *Bourbonism and Agrarian Protest: Louisiana Politics, 1877–1900* (Baton Rouge: Louisiana State University Press, 1969), falls very much within the Woodward tradition.

3. For pioneering critical views of Populist racial attitudes, see Robert Saunders, "Southern Populists and the Negro, 1893–1895," *Journal of Negro History* 54 (July 1969): 240–261; and Charles Crowe "Tom Watson, Populists, and Blacks Reconsidered," *Journal of Negro History* 55 (April 1970): 99–116. Barton C. Shaw provides a searing critique of the Georgia People's Party in *The Wool-Hat Boys: Georgia's Populist Party* (Baton Rouge: Louisiana State University Press, 1984). Charles Postel, *The Populist Vision* (New York: Oxford University Press, 2007), 19. Later in life, Woodward himself admitted that his egalitarian portrait of Watson and the Populists was overdrawn. C. Vann Woodward, *Thinking Back: The Perils of Writing History* (Baton Rouge: Louisiana State University Press, 1986), 36–37.

4. The foundational text of the race relations school is Gunnar Myrdal's classic study, *An American Dilemma: The Negro Problem and Modern Democracy* (New York: Harper and Row, 1944). Myrdal adopted a socio-psychological approach to the "negro problem," which he defined as a moral dilemma that pitted American principles against American prejudices. Among historians, the leading voice of the race relations school has been George M. Fredrickson. See, for example, *The Black Image in the White Mind: The Debate on Afro-American Character and Destiny, 1817–1914* (New York: Harper and Row, 1971). Reflecting back on his body of work, Fredrickson has stressed his concern with the "intellectual, cultural, and psychological roots of prejudice." Fredrickson, *The Arrogance of Race: Historical Perspectives on Slavery, Racism, and Social Inequality* (Hanover, NH: Wesleyan University Press, 1988), 4. Examinations of race and Populism that lie outside the race relations framework are limited largely to the handful of detailed studies of black Populists. See, for instance, Gregg Cantrell, *Kenneth and John B. Rayner and the Limits of Southern Dissent* (Urbana: University of Illinois Press, 1993), and Ali, "Black Populism in the New South."

5. The metaphor of an institutional and cultural "terrain" is taken from Barbara J. Fields, "Slavery, Race and Ideology in the United States of America," *New Left Review* 181 (May/June 1990), 113–114. The sociologist Donna Barnes provides an example of a structural approach to issues of Populism and race in her recently published work *The Louisiana Populist Movement* (Baton Rouge: Louisiana State University Press, 2011).

6. Glenn R. Conrad, ed., *A Dictionary of Louisiana Biography*, 2 vols. (New Orleans: Louisiana Historical Association, 1988), vol. 1, 42; *Biographical and Historical Memoirs of Louisiana*, 2 vols. (Chicago: Goodspeed Publishing Co., 1892), vol. 2, 497; G. M. G. Stafford, *The Wells Family of Louisiana and Allied Families* (Alexandria, LA: Standard Printing Company, 1991), 107; James Fair Hardin, *Northwestern Louisiana: A History of the Watershed of the Red River, 1714–1937*, 3 vols. (Louisville, KY: Historical Record Association, 1939), vol. 1, 451; *Biographical and Historical Memoirs of Northwest Louisiana* (Nashville: Southern Publishing Company, 1890), 506. The 1860 Federal Manuscript

Census lists fourteen plantation households in what would become Grant Parish. (A planter is defined as the owner of twenty or more slaves.) Setting aside the huge Calhoun operation, these plantation families owned an average of 69 slaves and 598 improved acres. Two farm operations in the area (with 17 and 15 slaves, respectively) fell short of the definition of plantation. There were no small farms in the future Grant Parish plantation belt. Federal Manuscript Census, 1860, Louisiana, Rapides Parish, Agricultural and Slave Schedules.

7. John Berton Gremillion, "Grant Parish" (Baton Rouge: Louisiana State Department of Education, n.d.), 6; Philip C. Cook, "The North Louisiana Upland Frontier: The First Three Decades," in *North Louisiana, Volume One: To 1865—Essays on the Region and Its History*, ed. B. H. Gilley (Ruston, LA: McGinty Trust Fund Publications, 1984), 24; Samuel H. Lockett, *Louisiana Like It Is: A Geographical and Topographical Description of the State* (Baton Rouge: Louisiana State University Press, 1969), 47, 75 (first printing of an 1874 manuscript); Thomas A. Caine, *Soil Survey of Winn Parish* (Washington, D.C.: Government Printing Office, 1909), 10; Milton Dunn, "History of Natchitoches, Louisiana," *Louisiana Historical Quarterly* 3 (January 1920), 32; Harley B. Bozeman, "Winn Parish as I Have Known It," Winn Parish *Enterprise*, January 8, 1959. Stockherding was a characteristic occupation along the entire backwoods Louisiana frontier. Cattle herds numbering in the hundreds were not uncommon in the early nineteenth century. John Lauren Harr, "The Ante-Bellum Southwest, 1815–1861" (Ph.D. diss., University of Chicago, 1941), 57, 196–199.

8. Eric Foner, *Nothing But Freedom: Emancipation and Its Legacy* (Baton Rouge: Louisiana State University Press, 1983).

9. For an analysis of the social and economic changes in postbellum Grant Parish, see Joel M. Sipress, "The Triumph of Reaction: Political Struggle in a New South Community, 1895–1898" (Ph.D. diss., The University of North Carolina at Chapel Hill, 1993). The average size of herds of swine in the piney woods of Grant Parish fell by 50 percent during the 1860s. Sipress, "The Triumph of Reaction," 381–382. Between the Union's scorched earth policy, forced requisitioning by both armies, and simple neglect, the South lost one-third of its stock of swine during the Civil War. Gavin Wright, *The Political Economy of the Cotton South: Households, Markets, and Wealth in the Nineteenth Century* (New York: W. W. Norton, 1978), 100, 164.

10. Eric Foner, *Reconstruction: America's Unfinished Revolution, 1863–1877* (New York: Harper and Row, 1988), 437. For accounts of the Colfax Massacre, see Joel M. Sipress, "From the Barrel of a Gun: The Politics of Murder in Grant Parish," *Louisiana History* 42 (Summer 2001): 303–321; Ted Tunnell, *Crucible of Reconstruction: War, Radicalism, and Race in Louisiana, 1862–1877* (Baton Rouge: Louisiana State University Press, 1984), 189–193; Charles Lane, *The Day Freedom Died: The Colfax Massacre, the Supreme Court, and the Betrayal of Reconstruction* (New York: Henry Holt and Company, 2008); Nicholas Lemann, *Redemption: The Last Battle of the Civil War* (New York: Farrar, Straus and Giroux, 2006), 3–29. Three white conservatives also perished in the battle.

11. Stephen Kantrowitz writes that "'White supremacy,' more than a slogan and less than a fact, was a social argument and a political program." Kantrowitz, *Ben Tillman and the Reconstruction of White Supremacy* (Chapel Hill: University of North Carolina Press, 2000), 2. To deem white supremacy a "program," though, is to suggest that the political goals of white supremacists were congruent with their public pronouncements. In fact,

as Kantrowitz himself recognizes, the public pronouncements of white supremacists often served to obfuscate their political goals. However, to deem white supremacy a slogan, as does Barbara Fields, is to minimize its concrete intellectual content. In the late-nineteenth-century South, "white supremacy" served as shorthand for a clearly defined set of political principles. Fields, "Slavery, Race and Ideology in the United States of America," 156. Although the roots of white supremacist doctrine can be found in antebellum pro-slavery and pro-secession arguments that linked white equality with black subordination, only with emancipation and black enfranchisement did white supremacy emerge full-blown as a tool of political mobilization. See, for instance, Jane Dailey's analysis of the rise of white supremacist politics among Virginia's conservatives in response to the interracial Readjuster movement. Jane Dailey, *Before Jim Crow: The Politics of Race in Postemancipation Virginia* (Chapel Hill: University of North Carolina Press, 2000), 77–102.

12. Testimony of Robert P. Hunter, *House Reports*, 43rd Cong., 2d Sess., No. 261, Pt. 3, 509.

13. *Alexandria Caucasian*, August 8, 1874; September 26, 1874. Election results from 1874 found in testimony of F. C. Zacharie, *House Reports*, 43rd Cong., 2d Sess., No. 261, Pt. 3, 41–42; and the *Alexandria Caucasian*, November 7, 1874. Results from 1876 are from the *Colfax Chronicle*, November 11, 1876.

14. *Colfax Chronicle*, March 22, 1879.

15. Taking the votes cast for the Republican state ticket as a rough approximation of the black vote, the percentage of total votes in Grant Parish cast by black voters ranged from a low of 22 percent in 1879 (a year of an unusually low black turnout) to a high of 41 percent in 1888 (a slight overestimate due to a number of white votes cast for the Republican ticket that year). *Colfax Chronicle*, December 6, 1879; May 5, 1888. According to the federal census, Grant Parish was 44 percent black in 1880 and 41 percent black in 1890. For accounts of the Republican endorsement process, see the *Colfax Chronicle*, October 26, 1878, and April 12, 1884. In addition to exercising their right to vote, black men also continued to serve on juries in Grant Parish, albeit in disproportionately low numbers, and held toe offices of constable and justice of the peace in the parish's black majority First Ward. Jury lists may be found throughout the 1880s in the *Colfax Chronicle*, as can election results for ward offices.

16. Nine individuals served as parish police jury clerk and parish treasurer (the two most important local patronage positions) during the 1880s. All seven who can be identified resided in the parish's two river valley wards. All but one were planters, merchants, or lawyers. All three of the decade's police jury presidents also hailed from the river valley. One was a merchant, the second a planter merchant, and the third a sawmill entrepreneur. Profiles of officeholders and activists are drawn from sources including the *Chronicle*, the federal manuscript census for 1870 and 1880, and *Biographical and Historical Memoirs of Northwest Louisiana* (Nashville: Southern Publishing Company, 1890). For details, see Sipress, "The Triumph of Reaction," 208–209, 390–394.

17. Hair, *Bourbonism and Agrarian Protest*, 206.

18. Blanchard's father's second wife had, during a previous marriage, given birth to Grant Parish planters Thomas, William, James, and Dennis Hickman. Melrose Collection, Scrapbook No. 1, 18, Cammie G. Henry Research Center, Watson Library, Northwestern State University of Louisiana. *Colfax Chronicle*, September 4, 1880; September 11, 1880.

19. *Colfax Chronicle*, November 24, 1883; July 5, 1884; July 19, 1884; July 17, 1886; August 7, 1886; *Winnfield Southern Sentinel*, May 14, 1886. For background on the Backbone Railroad land grant, see Hair, *Bourbonism and Agrarian Protest*, 49–51.

20. "Letter from Big Creek," *Alexandria* (La.) *Caucasian*, June 6, 1874.

21. At the time of secession Big Creek was contained within the Mill Creek precinct of Rapides Parish, which voted unanimously against secessionists in the January 1861 election for delegates to the state secession convention. *Alexandria* (La.) *Constitutional*, January 12, 1861. Big Creek resident William H. Willett organized a Unionist company in 1864 that was incorporated into the First Battalion, Louisiana Cavalry Scouts. D. E. Haynes, "A Thrilling Narrative of the Sufferings of Union Refugees and the Massacre of the Martyrs of Liberty of Western Louisiana" (Washington, 1866), 47; *Compiled Service Records of Volunteer Union Soldiers Who Served in Organizations from Louisiana* (Washington, D.C.: National Archives Microfilm Publications), roll 11; Obituary of Benjamin Franklin Brian, Nachitoches *Louisiana Populist*, November 6, 1896; Federal Manuscript Census, 1870, Grant Parish, Agricultural Schedule; Federal Manuscript Census, 1880, Grant Parish, Agricultural Schedule. *Colfax Chronicle*, October 28, 1876; November 9, 1878; December 6, 1879; May 3, 1884; May 5, 1888. Louisiana was one of a number of southern states that saw "independent" agrarian political movement in the immediate post-Reconstruction period. See, for instance, Hair, *Bourbonism and Agrarian Protest*, 60–82; Michael R. Hyman, *The Anti-Redeemers: Hill-Country Political Dissenters in the Lower South from Redemption to Populism* (Baton Rouge: Louisiana State University Press, 1990); and Dailey's study of the Virginia Readjuster movement in *Before Jim Crow*.

22. *Colfax Chronicle*, September 30, 1876; October 28, 1876; October 26, 1878; April 12, 1884; April 7, 1888. In 1878, Brian and the independents ran as a "Greenback" slate promising to fight for an inflationary monetary policy. An upper bound for the party-line Democratic vote may be calculated by adding together the lowest vote obtained by any Democratic candidate in each hill country precinct. By this method, the party line Democratic vote in the 1884 election was no more than 23 percent of the total hill country vote. The figure for the 1888 election is 28 percent. Using a similar method, no more than 16 percent voted straight independent in the 1884 election and no more than 35 percent did in 1888. The only independent to ever to carry the hills by a wide margin was Benjamin Brian, who received 64 percent of the piney woods vote in an 1888 race, which was still not enough, by itself, to win parish wide. Election results in the *Colfax Chronicle*, December 6, 1879; May 3, 1884; May 5, 1888.

23. As a Reconstruction police juror, Brian had cooperated with the Republicans who controlled the board. Minutes of the Grant Parish Police Jury, September 5, 1870, WPA Collection, Louisiana and Lower Mississippi Collections, Louisiana State University. His 1879 election to the state senate was something of a fluke. A factional dispute led a significant group of Democrats, particularly in neighboring Winn Parish, to vote for Brian. *Chronicle*, November 1, 1879; December 27, 1879; "A Reply to an Open Letter From J. H. Ringgold Addressed to the Voters of the 24th Senatorial District," J. H. Ringgold Letter, Louisiana and Lower Mississippi Collections, Louisiana State University.

24. *Colfax Chronicle*, September 7, 1878; September 28, 1878; Letter of Dick, *Colfax Chronicle*, July 10, 1876; *Colfax Chronicle*, July 6, 1878; October 25, 1879; April 7, 1888.

25. *Colfax Chronicle*, July 27, 1878; Letter of Principle, *Colfax Chronicle*, October 19, 1878.

26. *Colfax Chronicle*, April 14, 1888.

27. "An Address to the Voters of Grant Parish on the Political Issues Involved in the Present Campaign," Melrose Collection, Scrapbook No. 67, Cammie G. Henry Research Center, Watson Library, Northwestern State University of Louisiana.

28. *Colfax Chronicle*, October 12, 1878; March 10, 1888.

29. *Colfax Chronicle*, January 12, 1887; April 12, 1884. Ironically, Blanchard had been personally involved in the 1878 terror campaign that had broken the back of the Louisiana Republican Party. Blanchard was one of 120 conservatives indicted by a federal grand jury for participation in election fraud and violence during the 1878 campaign. The indictments were dropped after a federal trial produced a hung jury. Philip D. Uzee, "Republican Politics in Louisiana, 1877–1900" (Ph.D. diss., Louisiana State University, 1950), 49.

30. Letter of Raw Hide, *Colfax Chronicle*, June 19, 1886; letter of James A. Bradford, *Colfax Chronicle*, July 17, 1880; letter of G. H. Harvill, *Colfax Chronicle*, August 29, 1885; *Colfax Chronicle*, June 12, 1886. In 1884, Guynes received 39 percent of the total vote, including 16 percent of the vote in hill country precincts. The Democratic candidate and a hill country independent split the bulk of the white vote. *Colfax Chronicle*, May 3, 1884.

31. *Colfax Chronicle*, October 30, 1886; June 7, 1884; June 5, 1886; October 30, 1886; November 6, 1886. The courthouse removal proposal was defeated by a margin of 65 percent to 35 percent.

32. *Colfax Chronicle*, May 5, 1888. In 1888, Guynes ran 25 percent behind the Republican gubernatorial candidate in the three black majority precincts in Grant Parish. In 1884, by contrast, he ran just 6 percent behind the Republican gubernatorial candidate in the same three precincts.

33. For a discussion of the organizational weakness of the Louisiana People's Party, see Hair, *Bourbonism and Agrarian Protest*, 227–228. Lawrence Goodwyn also comments upon the relative weakness of Louisiana Populism in *Democratic Promise*, 333–334. Although Hair's work has long been the standard work on Louisiana Populism, Donna Barnes's work on Louisiana Populism provides a more detailed account of the People's Party movement in Louisiana. Donna Barnes, *The Louisiana Populist Movement: Mobilization, Political Opportunity, and Framing*.

34. *Colfax Chronicle*, March 5, 1887; June 4, 1887; July 16, 1887; March 17, 1888; January 12, 1889; July 13, 1889; September 14, 1889. The GPFU operated union stores at Colfax and at Pineville in neighboring Rapides Parish. The Pineville store was jointly operated by the GPFU and the Rapides Parish Farmers' Union. *Colfax Chronicle*, February 22, 1890; December 13, 1890. The Louisiana Farmers' Union was founded in August 1886 by a group of Lincoln Parish farmers. It affiliated with the National Farmers' Alliance in January 1887. Hair, *Bourbonism and Agrarian Protest*, 146–148; Robert C. McMath Jr., *Populist Vanguard: A History of the Southern Farmers' Alliance* (Chapel Hill: University of North Carolina Press, 1975), 34–35; Goodwyn, *Democratic Promise*, 90–91.

35. *Colfax Chronicle*, June 4, 1887; October 12, 1889; August 16, 1890.

36. *Washington National Economist*, December 14, 1889; January 25, 1890; "Charter and By-Laws of the Winn Parish Farmers' Union and Cooperative Association," Hardy L. Brian and Family Papers, Louisiana and Lower Mississippi Collections, Louisiana State University, Baton Rouge. At its December 1888 annual meeting, the National Farmers'

Alliance approved a resolution encouraging state and local affiliates to pursue cooperative relationships with the Colored Farmers' Alliance. *National Economist*, March 14, 1889. For discussions of the Colored Farmers' Alliance, see McMath, *Populist Vanguard*, 44–46, 52–53; Gerald H. Gaither, *Blacks and the Populist Movement: Ballots and Bigotry in the New South*, rev. ed. (Tuscaloosa: University of Alabama Press, 2005), 1–30, and Ali, "Black Populism in the New South," 72–122.

37. *Colfax Chronicle*, December 1, 1888; November 2, 1889; May 3, 1890. Membership statistics are based upon the amount of dues paid by each subordinate union to the parish union.

38. "Charter of the Farmers' Union Commercial Association of Grant Parish," *Colfax Chronicle*, September 14, 1889; "Charter of the Farmers' Union Commercial Association of Louisiana," *Colfax Chronicle*, October 6, 1888.

39. *Colfax Chronicle*, October 5, 1889.

40. *Colfax Chronicle*, July 20, 1889; October 12, 1889; October 19, 1889; April 12, 1890; April 19, 1890; "Resolutions from Indian Creek," *Colfax Chronicle*, June 7, 1890.

41. Letter of A. J. Dunn, *Colfax Chronicle*, September 6, 1890. For a discussion of the subtreasury plan and its political significance, see Goodwyn, *Democratic Promise*, 166–172; John D. Hicks, *The Populist Revolt: A History of the Farmers' Alliance and People's Party* (Minneapolis: University of Minnesota Press, 1931), 186–194.

42. Hair, *Bourbonism and Agrarian Protest*, 205–208; Colfax, *Chronicle*, August 23, 1890; August 30, 1890; September 20, 1890.

43. *Baton Rouge Daily Advocate*, October 5, 1890; *Colfax Chronicle*, October 4, 1890; October 11, 1890; October 25, 1890.

44. *Cincinnati Enquirer*, May 19, 1891; Hair, *Bourbonism and Agrarian Protest*, 211–212; *Colfax Chronicle*, July 11, 1891. Brian was one of two delegates from Louisiana to attend the Cincinnati convention.

45. *Colfax Chronicle*, July 18, 1891; July 4, 1891; August 1, 1891; November 14, 1891. *New Orleans Picayune*, September 19, 1891. Prior to coming to Grant, Traylor had lived in Sabine Parish, where he had been active in the Farmers' Union. Traylor had chaired the 1890 Natchitoches convention that had nominated Thomas J. Guice for Congress as a Farmers' Union candidate. *Baton Rouge Daily Advocate*, October 5, 1890.

46. *Colfax Chronicle*, August 8, 1891.

47. *Colfax Chronicle*, September 19, 1891. Members of the Populist executive committee are listed in the *Colfax Chronicle*, April 2, 1892. Of the twenty-five committee members, the occupations of twenty-three can be identified. Of these, nineteen (83 percent) were smallholding farmers (one of whom also worked as a country physician). Seventeen committee members (68 percent) can be identified as Farmers' Union activists. Ten committee members (40 percent) can be identified as former Democratic Party activists. Profiles of Populist activists are based upon the 1880 and 1900 Federal Manuscript Census (the 1890 Manuscript Census was destroyed by fire) and political coverage in the *Chronicle*.

48. Resolution of the Montgomery Farmers' Union, *Colfax Chronicle*, June 27, 1891; Letter of B. A. Fortson, *Colfax Chronicle*, June 20, 1891; Letter of B. A. Fortson, *Colfax Chronicle*, June 27, 1891; Letter of S. W. Lacroix, *Colfax Chronicle*, August 22, 1891. For discussion of the role of "producerism" in Populist thought, see Robert C. McMath Jr.,

American Populism: A Social History, 1877–1898 (New York: Hill and Wang, 1993), 51–53, and Bruce Palmer, *"Man Over Money": The Southern Populist Critique of American Capitalism* (Chapel Hill: University of North Carolina Press, 1980), 9–19.

49. Letter of S. W. Lacroix, *Colfax Chronicle*, September 12, 1891.

50. *Colfax Chronicle*, October 10, 1891; *New Orleans Picayune*, October 3, 1891; Hair, *Bourbonism and Agrarian Protest*, 217.

51. "Organization, Platform and Address of the People's Party," Hardy L. Brian and Family Papers, Louisiana and Lower Mississippi Collections, Louisiana State University, Baton Rouge.

52. *Colfax Chronicle*, October 17, 1891.

53. *Colfax Chronicle*, October 24, 1891; Letter of M. A. D., *Colfax Chronicle*, July 11, 1891.

54. Nachitoches *Louisiana Populist*, July 5, 1895; *Colfax Chronicle*, December 12, 1891; February 6, 1892.

55. Nachitoches *Louisiana Populist*, July 5, 1895.

56. *Colfax Chronicle*, December 12, 1891.

57. Nachitoches *Louisiana Populist*, July 5, 1895; *Colfax Chronicle*, December 12, 1891; March 5, 1892; April 2, 1892.

58. *New Orleans Times-Democrat*, February 18, 1892; February 19, 1892; Hair, *Bourbonism and Agrarian Protest*, 196, 222–223. Many historians, including both Woodward and Hair, have interpreted Populist assertions of an identity of interests between black and white as a challenge to the South's racial orthodoxy. Conservative paternalists, however, also argued that the interests of black and white were identical. In both cases, the assertion of an identity of interests was used to argue that black should defer political power to white.

59. For a discussion of the 1892 Louisiana state elections, see Hair, *Bourbonism and Agrarian Protest*, 215–226.

60. For election results, see the *Colfax Chronicle*, April 23, 1892. Brian received 60 percent of the vote parish wide. Benjamin Brian's son Hardy later recalled that, despite the primary controversy, Grant Parish Populists had rallied to their ticket "with a patriotism seldom equaled." Nachitoches *Louisiana Populist*, July 5, 1895.

61. *Colfax Chronicle*, February 20, 1892; March 5, 1892; March 19, 1892; April 2, 1892; April 16, 1892; May 9, 1892. Thompson received 33 percent of the parish-wide vote compared to 40 percent for victorious Democratic candidate Charles D. Kemp. (A rival Democratic candidate, Phillip Goode, received 27 percent.) Thompson received just 19 percent of the vote in the three black-majority precincts, compared to 45 percent for Kemp and 36 percent for Goode.

62. Hair, *Bourbonism and Agrarian Protest*, 225–226. For election results, see Lucia Elizabeth Daniel, "The Louisiana People's Party," *Louisiana Historical Quarterly* 26 (October 1943), 1126–1129.

63. *Colfax Chronicle*, February 1, 1896; February 15, 1896; March 7, 1896; March 28, 1896; January 11, 1896; January 25, 1896; April 4, 1896; April 25, 1896, May 9, 1896; *Louisiana Populist*, August 31, 1894; October 19, 1894; *Colfax Chronicle*, March 14, 1896. For a discussion of the 1896 Populist-Republican fusion campaign, see Hair, *Bourbonism and Agrarian Protest*, 248–267. The Populists and Republicans also reached a fusion agreement during the 1892 congressional elections. Hair, *Bourbonism and Agrarian Protest*, 229–230.

64. Woodward discusses the ways in the cultural context of Jim Crow shaped his views of southern history in *Thinking Back*, 36–37, 81–91. For classic examples of the benefits of racial fear mongering and the costs of racial liberalism in the Jim Crow South, see Dan T. Carter's account of the early career of George Wallace in *The Politics of Rage: George Wallace, the Origins of the New Conservatism, and the Transformation of American Politics* (New York: Simon and Schuster, 1995) and Julian M. Pleasants and Augustus Merrimon Burns's account of the 1950 U.S. Senate race between Frank Porter Graham and Willis Smith in *Frank Porter Graham and the 1950 Senate Race in North Carolina* (Chapel Hill: University of North Carolina Press, 1990). For an example of a twentieth-century reform politician who combined agrarian appeals with militant white supremacy, see Chester M. Morgan, *Redneck Liberal: Theodore G. Bilbo and the New Deal* (Baton Rouge: Louisiana State University Press, 1985).

"Workingmen's Democracy" in the Deep South

THE KNIGHTS OF LABOR IN GEORGIA POLITICS, 1884–1892

—MATTHEW HILD

During the past three decades historians have delved deeply into the political activities of the Noble and Holy Order of the Knights of Labor, the nation's largest labor organization during the turbulent "Gilded Age." As Leon Fink has explained, the Knights' entry into politics represented an attempt to inject "workingmen's democracy" into a national political landscape that was becoming increasingly dominated by the newly emerging "robber barons" of the corporate world. Along with the growing political power of big business came increased corruption and fraud in American elections and growing concern among the working classes that "republican institutions are not safe under such conditions."[1]

While increased corporate clout and the corruption of the electoral process undermined democracy across the United States during the late nineteenth century, no other part of the nation experienced as drastic a deterioration of "government of the people, by the people, for the people" as the Deep South. By the end of Reconstruction, control of this region lay firmly in the grip of an ironically named Democratic Party that represented the interests of planters and industrialists while crushing its opposition through corruption, fraud, and not infrequently violence. Although historians have paid less attention to the Knights' political activities in the Deep South than in other parts of the nation, the sadly unique character of post-Reconstruction politics in the heart of Dixie made these efforts particularly significant. For, as can be clearly seen in the case of Georgia, the "Empire State of the South," the Knights fought the South's entrenched "Bourbon Democracy" in near isolation between the mid-1880s and early

1890s. While the Knights' efforts not surprisingly failed, they nevertheless set a precedent and an agenda for advocates of "workingmen's democracy" for decades to come.[2]

For nearly two decades after the Civil War, Bourbon Democrats, Republicans, and Independent Democratic candidates all vied for political office and power in Georgia. The Republican Party began to fade in the state in the early 1870s, however, and, in the words of the historian Charles Wynes, was "on its last legs by 1876."[3] The Independent movement lasted longer; its best-known figure, William H. Felton of Bartow County, served as the United States congressman from northwest Georgia's Seventh District from 1875 to 1881. But by 1882, the Bourbon Democrats had closed ranks against the Independents, whose attempts at fusion with the Republicans in the late 1870s and early 1880s sealed their demise. Thus, for the time being, the Bourbon Democrats, so named by their Republican rivals who considered them to be "unreconstructed," exercised political dominance over the state. Not until 1892 would the People's (or Populist) Party present the next challenge to Democratic rule in Georgia.[4]

The Knights of Labor entered Georgia politics during this period of one-party dominance between the demise of the Independent movement and the rise of Populism. An organization of skilled and unskilled workers of virtually all sorts, male and female, white and black, urban and rural (including farmers and farm laborers); the Knights' meteoric career began in Philadelphia in 1869. The Order entered Georgia ten years later with the formation of a local assembly in Rome in the northwestern part of the state. This assembly lapsed one year later, but the Knights chartered more locals in Georgia during the early 1880s. By 1886, which turned out to be the year that the Knights' membership peaked in both Georgia and the nation, the organization encompassed 99 local assemblies in Georgia with at least 9,000 members. National Knights membership officially surpassed 700,000 that year, and may have actually reached one million as membership grew faster than it could be recorded. The Knights' heyday proved brief, however; lost strikes, employer and governmental repression, and internal conflicts combined to reduce the organization to a mere shadow of its former self by the early 1890s, not only in Georgia but across the United States.[5]

While the Knights of Labor waged many strikes and boycotts, including a boycott against the *Atlanta Constitution* that was started by the Atlanta Typographical Union and a strike in the Augusta cotton mills that involved some three thousand workers, the labor organization also put forth a platform of reform demands. Many of these demands could only be achieved through federal or state legislation; some of them, in fact, such as greenback monetary reform and land reform, would be reiterated in the platforms of the Southern Farmers' Alliance and the Populist Party. Thus it was not surprising that the Knights of Labor entered the political arena, despite the assertion of national Knights chieftain Terence V. Powderly in 1880 that "our Order is above politics."[6] This statement seemed disingenuous given that Powderly himself was serving as the Greenback-Labor mayor of Scranton, Pennsylvania, at the time. Moreover, his predecessor as the Order's Grand Master Workman, Uriah S. Stephens, had run unsuccessfully as a Greenback-Labor candidate for Congress in the district that included Philadelphia in 1878, and Powderly's successor, James R. Sovereign, served on the Populist National Executive Committee and established a Bryan Free Silver Campaign Labor Bureau in Chicago in 1896. From the time that the Knights of Labor became an important national organization in the mid-1880s until it faded from prominence in the early to mid-1890s, it always played a role in politics at the national level as well as the state and local levels in many parts of the United States. As the Order's shrinking membership base shifted from the nation's cities to the countryside in the 1890s, notes the historian Robert E. Weir, "much of the KOL ... [became] indistinguishable from Populism."[7]

According to Leon Fink, Knights of Labor political activity evolved through three phases: a national lobbying effort, which peaked between 1884 and 1886 with, among other accomplishments, the passage of a national anti-contract labor law and the establishment of the U.S. Bureau of Labor; "a grassroots entry into local politics" by the Knights in some two hundred cities and towns across the nation from 1885 to 1888; and the Knights' involvement in the farmer-led Populist movement from 1890 to 1894. Of these three phases, Fink identified the second as the "most significant," arguing that the unprecedented wave of independent labor tickets that the Knights sponsored in the mid- to late 1880s "may still stand as the American worker's single greatest push for political power," an assertion that certainly rings as true today as when Fink made it more than a quarter of a century ago.[8]

Although the timing unfolded somewhat differently than at the national level, the Knights of Labor engaged in all of these phases of political activity in Georgia between 1884 and 1892. At face value, these efforts produced negligible results. Little came of the Knights' lobbying efforts before the state legislature, the Knights' electoral victories in the state were few and far between, and little remained of the Knights in Georgia (or nationally) by the time that the Populist Party arrived on the political scene in the early 1890s. Nevertheless, the political activities of the Knights of Labor in Georgia left a greater legacy than their limited success would suggest. Even in failure, the Knights at least provided a means for challenging Bourbon Democratic dominance of the state at a time when there was no viable second (let alone third) party in Georgia. Moreover, in a number of cities and towns, the campaigns waged by the Knights helped lay the groundwork for greater success by later labor tickets or Populist tickets. In the early 1890s, some of the state's few remaining local assemblies of the Knights of Labor practically became Populist clubs. Finally, the lobbying efforts begun by the Knights before the state legislature would be continued by others after the Order's demise, slowly but surely producing some of the results that the Knights had sought regarding issues such as the convict lease system, child labor, the length of the workday, and the creation of a state bureau of labor statistics.

In Georgia, the Knights' "grassroots entry into local politics" preceded the organization's lobbying efforts before the state legislature, in part because the Knights needed to elect some representatives to the General Assembly to introduce and argue on behalf of the reform bills that they favored. In 1886, the Knights put forth candidates for the state House of Representatives in Bibb County (Macon), Chatham County (Savannah), and Richmond County (Augusta). The Knights also became involved in municipal politics in Atlanta and Savannah during the mid- to late 1880s.

In Savannah, where the Knights of Labor claimed about one thousand members in 1886, the organization derailed Bourbon Democratic domination of local politics more than once. On September 24, 1886, the Knights turned out *en masse* for a Chatham County Democratic Party convention at which the party chose candidates for the state house of representatives. As the *Savannah Morning News* noted with much chagrin, the labor organization "showed its hand and 'scooped in' the nominations for the Legislature with ease."[9] In addition to nominating all three of the party's legislative candidates, the Knights also succeeded in passing a set of resolutions at the meeting in the name of the local Democratic Party. These resolutions included demands for the establishment of a state bureau of labor statistics, the abolition of the contract labor system in all state and municipal works, the abolition of child labor in workshops, mines, and factories, state ownership of the Western and Atlantic Railroad, and the recognition by incorporation of labor unions and other workingmen's associations. While such resolutions were in keeping with the platform of the national Knights of Labor, they were hardly in keeping with that of the Georgia Democratic

Party. The *Morning News* commented that "the wisdom of a few of [the resolutions] is questionable" and described the Knights-nominated ticket as "not altogether satisfactory." The newspaper also suggested that Savannah's "regular Democracy" might in effect ignore or nullify the Knights' participation in the Democratic Party convention by nominating an "independent" ticket of its own nominees.[10]

On September 27, 1886, the "regular Democracy" took the newspaper's advice and renominated all three incumbent legislators in opposition to the ticket nominated by the Knights at the party's convention. The city's business community firmly supported the incumbents, and the *Morning News* published a letter to the editor claiming that many politically active Savannah Knights, including several who had attended the Democratic convention, were in fact Republicans. (The truth of this assertion is unclear, but it cannot be dismissed as mere partisan libel, as Republicans played an active and visible role in Knights of Labor politics in other southern states such as Arkansas and North Carolina.)[11] The newspaper also raised legitimate questions about why two of the Knights' three nominees were lawyers, when the Order's constitution barred lawyers from membership on the grounds that they were "social parasites."[12] While the *Morning News* was hardly impartial in its coverage of the campaign, it probably had a valid point about the incongruity of the Knights nominating lawyers; the only victorious candidate on the Knights' ticket, a lawyer and past state legislator named Phillip M. Russell, did not become a champion of legislation favored by the Knights. To add insult to injury, the internal dissension created among the Savannah Knights of Labor by this foray into electoral politics nearly destroyed the organization, which claimed fewer than four hundred members in the city by October 1887.[13]

Nevertheless, the Savannah Knights celebrated a surprising political victory in January 1889 when one of their own, a baker named John Schwarz, won election to the mayor's office. Schwarz was a Democratic alderman, but he ran for mayor on a ticket nominated by a disaffected group of Democrats who called themselves the Citizens' Club. Unfortunately for Schwarz (and the city at large), his two-year term suffered from a rash of major fires, which led carpenters and mechanics to pour into the city in search of construction work. Throughout the spring and summer of 1890 the *Journal of the Knights of Labor* (the Order's national journal) warned mechanics and laborers to stay away from Savannah, "as it is crowded with idle men." The *Journal* further explained, "There is no work to be had [in Savannah], money is scarce, and the outlook is gloomy and discouraging."[14]

Not surprisingly, Schwarz lost his bid for reelection in January 1891, and the Savannah Knights nearly disintegrated in the early 1890s. A leading Populist in nearby Screven County urged Terence V. Powderly to try to reorganize the Savannah Knights in July 1892 as a means of boosting the third party's strength, but when Savannah workingmen attended Populist Party meetings that summer, their employers soon drove them away by threatening to fire them.[15]

In Atlanta, by contrast, the Knights' political efforts produced less success at the ballot box but left a greater legacy for future working-class political influence. The state's largest city then as now, Atlanta also ranked as the stronghold of the Knights of Labor in Georgia. In mid-1886, according to official Knights of Labor records, Atlanta's District Assembly 105 represented nearly three thousand members. Between 1882 and 1886 the Knights organized fourteen local assemblies in Atlanta, at least two of which consisted entirely of African Americans. As elsewhere, the Knights organized skilled and unskilled workers in Atlanta. Specific types of workers who joined the Knights in Atlanta included telegraph operators, printers, carpenters, painters, railroad employees and car builders, and workers in cotton mills and other kinds of factories. The Atlanta Knights were also affiliated with a supposedly secret political organization known as the Mutual Aid Brotherhood, described by some historians as the "political arm" of the labor organization.[16]

The Knights of Labor became active in Atlanta politics in 1884. In the nonpartisan municipal campaign that year, the Knights initially joined the *Atlanta Constitution* and the city's business leaders in organizing a "Citizens' ticket" of reformers who pledged to clean up the scandal-ridden city government, a much-publicized concern in Atlanta politics at the time. But when the Citizens' ticket failed to include any workingmen, Knights of Labor leaders bolted and joined traditional Democrats in putting forth a "People's ticket" in the municipal elections. Unfortunately for the Knights, however, the only victorious People's candidate was the lawyer John Tyler Cooper, often cited in Atlanta newspapers as a member of the local Democratic ring, who was elected to the board of aldermen. Among the Knights of Labor included on the People's ticket, printer James G. Woodward lost his bid for a seat on the city council by 343 votes, but, like most other People's candidates, he carried the working-class Third and Fifth wards.[17]

For the next four years, the Knights of Labor continued to place candidates on People's tickets in Atlanta municipal elections, in conjunction with anti-prohibition forces outside the Order. (Prohibition loomed as a major issue in Atlanta politics during the mid- to late 1880s; the city was "dry" from 1885 to 1887.) The People's tickets consistently fell short of victory though. This failure stemmed in part from a lack of support from African American voters, who were repeatedly disappointed by the failure of the labor/anti-prohibition coalition to nominate any African American candidates. By 1891, the Mutual Aid Brotherhood had disappeared, and the last local assemblies of the Atlanta Knights of Labor apparently followed suit within two years.[18]

Nevertheless, even in failure, the political activities of the Knights of Labor in Atlanta left a mark upon city politics and paved the way for greater labor clout in future municipal elections. The career of James G. Woodward illustrates this point well. An active figure among the Atlanta Knights of Labor, Woodward ran unsuccessfully for a seat on the city council in 1884. He won a seat on the council two years later and was elected to the board of aldermen in 1888. In 1892 he ran for mayor as the candidate of the Industrial Legislative Council (also known as the Industrial Union Council), which consisted of committees from twenty-nine different Atlanta labor organizations, most of which were trade unions. Woodward lost in 1892, but he ran for mayor again in 1898 and won. His victory, in the words of one scholar, represented "a distinct recognition of the growing power of organized labor in Atlanta."[19] Woodward would serve four terms as mayor between 1899 and 1917. Known as "the working man's mayor," his accomplishments included the improvement of public schools for whites and blacks as well as increased efficiency and reduced waste and corruption in city government.[20]

In terms of engaging in direct conflict with employers, the Knights of Labor proved more active (albeit briefly) in Augusta than anywhere else in Georgia, and the Augusta Knights entered politics in 1886 amid the largest textile strike that the South had ever experienced, spurred by the low-wage scale in the mills. What began in July 1886 as a strike that closed two mills escalated into a lockout that closed the rest of the city's mills, leaving about three thousand mill hands out of work. Most of these mill hands joined the Knights of Labor (except children under eighteen, who were ineligible) at some point during this ordeal; by mid-August, the Knights membership in Augusta had reached three thousand.[21]

In mid-September, as the city's mills began hiring small numbers of nonunion strikebreakers, the Augusta Knights of Labor nominated two Independent candidates for the state house of representatives, one white (Griffen Gay) and one black (R. G. Cumming). But in a typical example of how partisan politics could play a divisive role within the supposedly nonpartisan Knights of Labor, the master workman (or leading officer) of the city's largest local assembly, the Reverend J. Simmions Meynardie, denounced the Knights' Independent ticket, which the *Augusta Chronicle* suggested was in fact a Republican ticket. Meynardie denied any connection between the Knights of Labor ticket and the Republican Party, but he urged Knights to vote instead for the Democratic candidates, particularly former county public school system superintendent Martin V. Calvin, whom he proclaimed "cordially endorses the principles of our Order."[22] Cumming ultimately dropped out of the race. In a four-man contest, Gay received 1,320 votes, while the three Richmond County candidates who won seats in the state house received between 1,920 and 3,050 votes. Gay made a strong showing, however, in the district that included Augusta's working-class Fifth Ward, inhabited by millworkers and farmers. This labor and farmer support for the Knights' candidate in the Fifth Ward would rematerialize for Populist leader Tom Watson in numerous congressional elections.[23]

The Knights of Labor reached an agreement with Augusta's mill owners (who had banded together in an organization called the Southern Manufacturers' Association) in November 1886, but the millworkers gained very little for their months of lost wages. Not surprisingly, Knights of Labor membership in Augusta fell rapidly, dropping below one thousand by the summer of 1887 and to fewer than five hundred by the summer after that. From the remnants of the shattered Knights, however, arose another labor organization in Augusta by mid-1888, an initially secret body that called itself the Independent Order of United Workingmen. Much like the Knights of Labor had done in Chatham County (Savannah) two years earlier, the United Workingmen attended a Richmond County Democratic Party meeting in July 1888 and dominated the proceedings, only to find their efforts denounced by the local press and counteracted by the "regular Democracy." The United Workingmen ultimately nominated an Independent candidate for one of Richmond County's three seats in the state house of representatives in the fall of 1888, but he fared poorly at the polls. The United Workingmen's candidate, however, former Knight of Labor Silas C. Reed Jr., became a local leader of the Populist Party several years later.[24]

As in other Georgia cities, the Knights of Labor also entered politics in Macon in 1886. Like their Savannah brethren, the Macon Knights attempted to wield influence through the Democratic Party. In doing so, however, the Macon Knights had a greater chance for success, for in Bibb County the Democrats chose their candidates for the Georgia House of

Representatives not through a nominating convention but rather through a primary election. This meant that Knights of Labor candidates seeking the Democratic nomination in Bibb County would not have to contend with the party machinations that derailed the efforts of Savannah Knights to work through the party.

The Knights' debut in Macon politics occurred on July 3, 1886, when James E. Schofield, the recording secretary of Local Assembly 7722, placed an announcement in the *Macon Daily Telegraph* that he would be a "working man's" candidate for the state house of representatives, subject to winning a position on the Democratic ticket in the party's primary on August 4. The fact that Schofield had joined several hundred other Macon residents in enrolling in the Knights of Labor earlier in the year underscores the organization's broad admission standards; while the thirty-eight-year-old Schofield was indeed a workingman, a machinist, he was also the junior partner in J. S. Schofield and Son Iron Works, a very prosperous local business. Unlike many leading Atlanta Knights, Schofield was also a self-avowed "temperance man," a stance that his opponents tried to use against him during the primary campaign.[25]

Another candidate in the Democratic primary also pledged to work for the interests of the Knights of Labor in return for their votes, even though he was not a Knight himself. This candidate, the fifty-four-year-old Colonel William A. Huff, perhaps saw the Knights as a means of regaining some lost political power and prestige. A city alderman at the time, Huff had served as Macon's mayor from 1870 to 1878 and had owned a once very successful wholesale grocery business that had failed and left him bankrupt. James E. Schofield assured Terence V. Powderly that Huff would "represent the K. of L." in the legislature.[26]

Huff and the politically inexperienced Schofield both secured positions on the Bibb County Democratic Party's three-man ticket for the Georgia House of Representatives. All three Democratic nominees coasted to victory in the general election in October 1886, which drew only about one-seventh of the turnout that the primary had. By then, the ambitious Schofield also had become the State Master Workman of the Georgia Knights of Labor.[27]

Upon taking office later that year, Schofield and Huff wasted little time in trying to advance the agenda of the Knights of Labor; indeed the session of 1886–1887 marked the beginning of the Knights' efforts at lobbying the Georgia General Assembly. Schofield and Huff formed the core of a small but persistent labor bloc in the state house of representatives that also included Martin V. Calvin and Charles Z. McCord of Augusta. Calvin, it will be recalled, had received the ringing endorsement of Augusta Knights leader J. Simmions Meynardie, while McCord, a lawyer whose office sat near those of several cotton mills on Broad Street, reportedly also benefited from Knights of Labor support at the polls. The Georgia Knights' legislative wish list, which this handful of representatives would introduce in the house, focused upon four goals: a ten-hour workday law, a child labor law, the creation of a state bureau of labor statistics, and the abolition of the state's notorious convict lease system. All of these goals reflected planks in the platform of the national Knights of Labor.[28]

The most controversial of these battles proved to be the campaign to abolish the convict lease. This effort actually began several months before the Knights' representatives even entered the legislature. In the spring of 1886 the old Independent warhorse (and future Populist) William H. Felton, by now a representative in the state house, read before the Georgia General Assembly an anti-convict lease resolution written by his wife, Rebecca Latimer Felton. This resolution, which carried the Woman's Christian Temperance Union's stamp of approval, called for an end to the convict lease system and the establishment of a state reformatory prison. Nothing came of the resolution, but the issue was revived in dramatic fashion in July 1886 when a mutiny by more than one hundred convict laborers at the Dade Coal Company in northwest Georgia shed light on the horrors of the convict lease system. When Schofield and Huff entered the state house later that year, they joined the Feltons in renewing the battle to end the convict lease. Huff introduced a bill that led to an investigation of the exploitative system. Ultimately, however, the combined efforts of the Knights, the WCTU, and the Feltons could not overcome the powerful interests that supported the convict lease, most notably Dade Coal Company owner and U.S. senator Joseph E. Brown. (Brown, along with Alfred H. Colquitt and John B. Gordon, played such a dominant role in Georgia politics from the 1870s to 1890 that the trio was dubbed the "Bourbon Triumvirate.") When the state legislature rejected convict lease reform in the fall of 1887, Huff publicly blamed fellow legislators who, he claimed, had succumbed to gifts from Brown such as free railroad passes, whiskey, and cigars. "Joe Brown tooted his horn," Huff fumed, "and you little fellows of the House are bowing to it."[29]

The Knights of Labor and the small house labor bloc also fell short in the rest of their goals after making an earnest fight for reform. Knights across the state participated in lobbying efforts, though; Knights of Labor petitions in support of a ten-hour workday bill that the state house of representatives debated in September 1887 came from all of the state's textile centers, drawing 1,500 signatures from Macon and 900 from Augusta. The Knights ultimately won a limited victory in this battle. In the fall of 1889 the state legislature reconsidered the ten-hour workday bill, once again prompting petitions from the Knights urging its passage. After the House Committee on Immigration and Labor raised the workday limit to eleven hours, the bill became law, although it lacked sufficient enforcement measures. Georgia Knights of Labor leaders realized, however, that their efforts before the state legislature had not been entirely in vain. As an Atlanta Knight informed Terence V. Powderly, the introduction of these labor bills "generated a healthy agitation, with that, many of us were satisfied for a beginning."[30]

The Knights of Labor faded into oblivion in Georgia (and practically everywhere else) during the early to mid-1890s, the result of lost strikes, failed political efforts, the blacklisting of members, racial strife, and defections to trade unions in the cities. Nevertheless, other organizations continued to fight the Knights' battles, including the Georgia Federation of Labor, which was formed in 1899. The Georgia General Assembly finally passed a ten-hour workday law for factories in 1911, and a child labor law three years later, although neither law included effective measures for enforcement. More meaningful fulfillment of the Knights' efforts came in 1908, when the state government finally abolished the miserable convict lease system, and in 1911, when the state established the Georgia Department of Labor, which more than met the Knights' goal of creating a state bureau of labor statistics.[31]

The Georgia Knights of Labor also participated in the third phase of Knights political activity identified by Leon Fink: involvement in the farmer-led Populist movement. In this phase, in fact, the Georgia Knights were ahead of the national trend. The Southern Farmers' Alliance, which played the largest role in forming the Populist Party, entered Georgia in 1887. The Alliance quickly became a large and powerful organization in the state, with 100,000 members by 1890. The organization established chapters in many small towns where the Knights already had formed local assemblies, as well as in many communities that the Knights never reached. As historians such as Robert McMath and Numan Bartley have noted, the Knights and the Alliance espoused similar values and reform programs, and by 1888 the two organizations were moving toward a coalition of sorts in Georgia. In northwest Georgia's Paulding County, after some initial wariness on the part of the Alliance, the farmer and labor organizations soon joined forces in an effort "to drag Mr. Monopoly from his high pinnacle and set him on the back seat for a generation or so, and let him earn his bread by the sweat of his brow," as local Knights leader James F. Foster put it. Specific plans of the Paulding County Knights-Alliance coalition included the possibility of jointly nominating a member of either organization for Congress that year, but the coalition lacked the influence to accomplish such a lofty goal. In the adjacent county to the east, Cobb County, a partnership between the Knights and the Alliance also began to develop in 1888. James C. Sanges, a carpenter and leading figure among the Cobb County Knights, ran for the Georgia House of Representatives in both 1886 and 1888, as a "Workingman's candidate" the first time and "the people's candidate" in his second campaign. He fell short in both elections, but in August 1888 the *Marietta Journal* reported with much indignation that Sanges had spoken at "'a grand rally'" in the small Cobb community of Post Oak, the purpose of which was supposedly "to consolidate the Farmers['] Alliance and the Knights of Labor, and to abuse the Democratic party, which they called rotten, in the absence of any worse word."[32] Sanges subsequently wrote a letter to the editor stating that he had spoken as a guest of the Farmers' Alliance with no intention of consolidating that organization with the Knights of Labor. Sanges clearly favored the idea of Alliance-Knights unity, however, and in June 1889 he reported in a letter to the Knights' national journal that the Georgia State Assembly of the Knights of Labor and the Georgia Farmers' Alliance had become allies.[33]

Five months later, a coalition between the Southern Farmers' Alliance and the national Knights of Labor began in Atlanta, when Terence V. Powderly invited Georgia Alliance leaders to address the Knights' annual national General Assembly convention. Powderly and the Alliance leaders all urged cooperation between the two organizations, and the Knights would subsequently participate in the series of conventions that led to the founding of the People's (or Populist) Party. Although the Knights' declining membership, which sank below 100,000 in 1892, limited the organization's usefulness to the Populists, the Knights clearly gave the third party support in Georgia. The historian Melton McLaurin has noted, for example, that "Knights in rural assemblies in Georgia ... expressed support [in 1892] for General James Weaver, the Populist presidential nominee."[34]

The case of Paulding County not only supports McLaurin's assertion but also shows that rural Georgia Knights did more for the Populist Party than merely support Weaver. The Paulding County Knights came out in support of Populism even before the county's first Populist convention. In August 1892, one month before that convention, James F. Foster informed the Knights' general secretary-treasurer, John W. Hayes, "we will vote for Weaver for President." Furthermore, he added, "I am satisfied we will elect everything in this fall's election." While Paulding County Knights sometimes proved negligent about attending their local assembly meetings, Foster reported, "when the signal is given for a political rally the laboring men of farms and factory join hands and march in unbroken columns to the [site] of action."[35] Foster's prediction proved accurate. The Populists swept Paulding County in the national, state, and county elections in the fall of 1892 and early the following year. The party's county ticket in 1892 included O. F. Brintle, who had just completed a term as the Knights' State Master Workman, for the position of surveyor. The Knights remained active in Paulding County at least as late as 1894, and the Populists followed their initial success in the county by "taking nearly every contest for the next three years."[36]

Little remained of the Knights of Labor in urban Georgia by 1892, but nevertheless a few signs point to some Knights' support for the Populists in the cities. In Atlanta, H. M. Cramer, a prominent Knights of Labor political activist since the mid-1880s, became the president of the city's People's Party Club No. 1.[37] In Augusta, Knights of Labor Local Assembly 5030–smaller but still intact six years after the failed textile strike–sent a glowing letter of support to Democratic-turned-Populist congressman Tom Watson in February 1892. The Knights commended Watson as "a champion for the workingman, both of city and country," and gave him their pledge "to sustain you to the utmost limit of our power." At about the same time, more than three hundred workers and farmers attended a meeting at the Knights of Labor Hall in Augusta's working-class Fifth Ward and offered similar praise and promises of support for Watson.[38] Earlier that month, Watson had introduced a bill that would have prohibited the use of Pinkerton guards as a private army, and after a bloody battle broke out between Pinkertons and striking steelworkers in Homestead, Pennsylvania, that summer, Watson again argued for the passage of legislation to outlaw the use of Pinkertons as strikebreakers. When his efforts failed, he suggested that "the campaign cry of the People's Party be 'remember Homestead.'"[39] Speaking before a reported crowd of four thousand in Augusta's Fifth Ward that fall, Watson directly appealed for workers' votes. "Don't take my word for it," he told his working-class audience, "that I have stood by you, but write to Powderly ... or any of your Knights of Labor men in this county."[40] While Democratic fraud in Richmond County, where

Watson lost by a margin that exceeded the number of registered voters, led to his defeat in the election of 1892, the official returns show that Watson drew 42 percent of the vote in Augusta's Fifth Ward, which probably means that he would have carried the ward in an honest election. In the Populist leader's next two congressional campaigns, in 1894 and 1895, he carried the Fifth Ward, although those elections too were marred by fraud. (The latter election occurred after the winner of the former, Democrat J. C. C. Black, agreed to resign and submit to another election, so obvious was the illegitimacy of his victory.)[41]

By 1894, the Knights of Labor had practically disappeared from Georgia. At face value, the organization accomplished relatively little in its political endeavors in the state. A handful of its candidates won election to the state house of representatives or to mayor's offices (Knights won mayoral elections in Albany [1887] and Hazlehurst [1891] as well as Savannah), but the Knights hardly posed a serious threat to the Bourbon Democrats' control of the state. Most of the Order's lobbying efforts before the state legislature failed. The Knights made some legitimate efforts at building a coalition with the Farmers' Alliance and supporting the Populist Party, but unfortunately for the Populists, by 1892 the Knights had practically disappeared in the urban settings where the third party was most desperate for support.[42]

Nevertheless, the political activities of the Knights of Labor in Georgia left more of a legacy than historians have acknowledged. Populist leaders who had courted the Knights and supported some of their causes continued to support labor reform in the early twentieth century. For example, Rebecca Latimer Felton, who battled alongside Knights of Labor representatives and her husband, William H. Felton, against the convict lease system in 1886–1887 (and who also fought alongside her husband in his unsuccessful campaign as a Populist congressional candidate in 1894), ultimately played a significant role in the abolition of the convict lease. Populists (or former Populists) also continued the Knights' battle against child labor; in 1902, Tom Watson spoke before the Georgia General Assembly in support of a child labor bill, albeit to no avail. (The bill's supporters in the legislature included Representative Seaborn Wright of Floyd County, the Populists' gubernatorial candidate in 1896.) Watson continued to win political support from factory workers; when he mounted an unsuccessful challenge in the Democratic primary election against Tenth District incumbent Carl Vinson in 1918, he once again carried Augusta's Fifth Ward. In other areas of the state as well where the Knights had contributed to the Populist movement, the Populist spirit remained alive well after the defeats of 1896 that essentially destroyed the party. In Paulding County, where the Knights had been in the vanguard of the Populist revolt, Tom Watson outpolled the Democratic and Republican candidates in his hopeless bid for the presidency in 1904 under the Populist banner.[43] Moreover, while the Knights' challenges to Bourbon Democratic domination in cities such as Augusta and Savannah during the latter half of the 1880s may appear to have been futile, without the Knights those organized protests may not have arisen at all. In Atlanta, the Knights' efforts in local politics laid the groundwork for significant labor clout in the years ahead. While the efforts of the Knights and their few representatives and allies in the state legislature to pass labor reform bills generally failed, they nevertheless sparked reform movements that others would carry into the Progressive Era with greater success. Even the few instances in which the Georgia Knights of Labor gave significant support to the Populist revolt suggested the possibility that working-class Georgians of farm and factory might vote together along class lines, an idea that would be revived in numerous political campaigns in twentieth-century Georgia.[44] In assessing the Knights' political legacy in the state, then, perhaps the last word should go to the Atlanta Knight of Labor and political activist H. M. Cramer: "[We] generated a healthy agitation, with that, many of us were satisfied for a beginning."[45]

Notes

1. Leon Fink, *Workingmen's Democracy: The Knights of Labor and American Politics* (Urbana: University of Illinois Press, 1983), (quote from the preamble to the constitution of the Knights of Labor, 4). On the growing political power of big business as well as increased corruption and fraud in American politics during the Gilded Age, see Mark Wahlgren Summers, *Party Games: Getting, Keeping, and Using Power in Gilded Age Politics* (Chapel Hill: University of North Carolina Press, 2004). On the Knights and politics, see, in addition to Fink, Melton A. McLaurin, *The Knights of Labor in the South* (Westport, CT: Greenwood Press, 1978); Richard J. Oestreicher, *Solidarity and Fragmentation: Working People and Class Consciousness in Detroit, 1875–1900* (Urbana: University of Illinois Press, 1986); David Brundage, *The Making of Western Labor Radicalism: Denver's Organized Workers, 1878–1905* (Urbana: University of Illinois Press, 1994); Matthew Hild, *Greenbackers, Knights of Labor, and Populists: Farmer-Labor Insurgency in the Late-Nineteenth-Century South* (Athens: University of Georgia Press, 2007).

2. On the dominance of the Democratic Party in the post-Reconstruction South, see Edward L. Ayers, *The Promise of the New South: Life after Reconstruction* (New York: Oxford University Press, 1992); Kenneth C. Barnes, *Who Killed John Clayton?: Political Violence and the Emergence of the New South, 1861–1893* (Durham, NC: Duke University

Press, 1998). Two studies that do examine the Knights' political activities in the Deep South are McLaurin, *Knights of Labor*, chap. 5, and Hild, *Greenbackers, Knights of Labor, and Populists*.

3. Charles E. Wynes, "The Politics of Reconstruction, Redemption, and Bourbonism," in *A History of Georgia*, ed. Kenneth Coleman, 2d ed. (Athens: University of Georgia Press, 1991), 207–224 (quote, 219).

4. Ibid., 217–222; Numan V. Bartley, *The Creation of Modern Georgia*, 2d ed. (Athens: University of Georgia Press, 1990), 119. The authoritative study of Felton and the Independent movement in Georgia is George L. Jones, "William H. Felton and the Independent Democratic Movement in Georgia, 1870–1890" (Ph.D. diss., University of Georgia, 1971). The most comprehensive study of Georgia politics during this period is Judson C. Ward Jr., "Georgia Under the Bourbon Democrats, 1872–1890" (Ph.D. diss., University of North Carolina at Chapel Hill, 1947). On Populism in Georgia, see Alex M. Arnett, *The Populist Movement in Georgia: A View of the "Agrarian Crusade" in the Light of Solid-South Politics* (New York: Columbia University, 1922); Barton C. Shaw, *The Wool-Hat Boys: Georgia's Populist Party* (Baton Rouge: Louisiana State University Press, 1984).

5. Norman J. Ware, *The Labor Movement in the United States, 1860–1895: A Study in Democracy* (New York: D. Appleton and Co., 1929; reprint, Gloucester, MA: Peter Smith, 1959), xi, 65–66, 68; Richard Oestreicher, "A Note on Knights of Labor Membership Statistics," *Labor History* 25 (Winter 1984): 106; Matthew G. Hild, "The Knights of Labor in Georgia" (M.A. thesis, University of Georgia, 1996), 7–8, 12–13, 107–108, 131, 146. Robert E. Weir, *Beyond Labor's Veil: The Culture of the Knights of Labor* (University Park: Pennsylvania State University Press, 1996), 12. The Knights of Labor officially dropped the words "Noble and Holy" from its title in 1882 in order to appease the Catholic Church (Ware, *Labor Movement*, 93), but the organization would still be often referred to by its original full title in the years that followed and by many historians ever since. On the decline of the Knights of Labor nationally after 1886, see Bruce Laurie, *Artisans into Workers: Labor in Nineteenth-Century America* (New York: Hill and Wang, 1989), 164–175; Craig Phelan, *Grand Master Workman: Terence Powderly and the Knights of Labor* (Westport, CT: Greenwood Press, 2000), 196–215, 227–258. On the Knights' decline in the South, McLaurin, *Knights of Labor*, chap. 9. On the Knights' decline in Georgia in particular, Hild, "The Knights of Labor in Georgia," 13–15, 42–43, 48–49, 67–70, 94–95, 101–102, 111, 127, 129–130, 138, 141; Hild, *Greenbackers, Knights of Labor, and Populists*, 176.

6. On Knights of Labor strikes and boycotts in Atlanta, Matthew Hild, "'A 'Flagrant and High-handed Outrage': The Knights of Labor and Skilled Workers in Atlanta, 1882–1886," *Atlanta History: A Journal of Georgia and the South* 43 (Fall 1999): 35–47. On the Augusta textile strike of 1886, Melton A. McLaurin, *Paternalism and Protest: Southern Cotton Mill Workers and Organized Labor, 1875–1905* (Westport, CT: Greenwood Publishing Corporation, 1971), 91–112; Merl E. Reed, "The Augusta Textile Mills and the Strike of 1886," *Labor History* 14 (Spring 1973): 228–246. For the Knights of Labor platform, see Ware, *Labor Movement*, 377–380. On the similarities between the platforms of the Knights and the Farmers' Alliance, see Robert C. McMath Jr., *American Populism: A Social History, 1877–1898* (New York: Hill and Wang, 1993), 79. For various national People's Party platforms, John D. Hicks, *The Populist Revolt: A History of the Farmers' Alliance and the People's Party* (Minneapolis: University of Minnesota Press, 1931; reprint,

Westport, CT: Greenwood Press, 1981), 433–444. The Terence V. Powderly quote is taken from the *Journal of United Labor*, May 15, 1880.

7. Phelan, *Grand Master Workman*, 33, 64–65; Gerald N. Grob, *Workers and Utopia: A Study of Ideological Conflict in the American Labor Movement, 1865–1900* (Evanston, IL: Northwestern University Press, 1961), 81; Hild, *Greenbackers, Knights of Labor, and Populists*, 191; Weir, *Beyond Labor's Veil*, 15, 126 (quote).

8. Fink, *Workingmen's Democracy*, 19 (first two quotes), 26 (third quote). Fink identified 189 American towns and cities where labor tickets ran between 1885 and 1888, which are listed in a table on pp. 28–29. The actual number, however, is higher. For Georgia, for example, Fink lists Macon as the only city or town where the Knights of Labor fielded a political ticket during this period, when in fact such tickets also ran in Athens, Atlanta, Augusta, Decatur, Marietta, and Savannah. Hild, *Greenbackers, Knights of Labor, and Populists*, 79–80, 90–94, 109; Eugene J. Watts, *The Social Bases of City Politics: Atlanta, 1865–1903* (Westport, CT: Greenwood Press, 1978), 17–18, 28; James M. Russell, *Atlanta, 1847–1890: City Building in the Old South and the New* (Baton Rouge: Louisiana State University Press, 1988), 211.

9. *Savannah Morning News*, September 25, 1886. The *Record of the Proceedings of the Tenth Regular Session of the General Assembly [of the Knights of Labor], Held at Richmond, Va., Oct. 4–20, 1886*, microfilm (Madison: State Historical Society of Wisconsin, 1950), 327, lists the membership of Savannah-based District Assembly 139 as 1,037 as of July 1, 1886. This figure most likely includes some local assemblies that were affiliated with D.A. 139 but were located outside the city of Savannah.

10. *Savannah Morning News*, September 25, 1886.

11. Ibid., September 26, 28, 29, 1886. For examples of Republicans playing roles in Knights of Labor politics in Arkansas and North Carolina, see Hild, *Greenbackers, Knights of Labor, and Populists*, 90; Melton McLaurin, "The Knights of Labor in North Carolina Politics," *North Carolina Historical Review* 49 (July 1972): 298–315.

12. Savannah *Morning News*, September 25, 30, 1886; *Constitution of the General Assembly, District Assemblies, and Local Assemblies of the Order of the Knights of Labor of America* (1885), 59, Terence Vincent Powderly Papers, microfilm edition (Glen Rock, NJ: Microfilming Corporation of America, 1974), reel 64 (quote). The *Morning News* also made much of the support given to the Knights' ticket by liquor dealers, who were also ineligible to join the Order, but it was not uncommon for anti-prohibitionists to align themselves with Knights of Labor municipal candidates.

13. Hild, "The Knights of Labor in Georgia," 87; Hild, *Greenbackers, Knights of Labor, and Populists*, 94. On the internal dissension created within the ranks of the Savannah Knights of Labor by their political activities in 1886, Hild, "The Knights of Labor in Georgia," 74–76, 81–82. The *Report of the General Secretary [of the Knights of Labor]* (1888), 4, Powderly Papers, reel 67, indicates that Savannah's D.A. 139 had 377 members in good standing as of October 1, 1887.

14. Hild, "The Knights of Labor in Georgia," 101; *Journal of the Knights of Labor*, March 20, April 17, 24, May 15, June 5, 26, July 10, 1890. The *Journal of United Labor* changed its name to the *Journal of the Knights of Labor* in December 1889.

15. *Savannah Morning News*, January 21, 1891; John W. Hayes to Powderly, June 27, 1890, Powderly Papers, reel 33; Hild, "The Knights of Labor in Georgia," 102; J. F. Brown to Powderly, July 4, 1892, Powderly Papers, reel 38; *Journal of the Knights of Labor*, September 1, 1892.

16. Jonathan Garlock, comp., *Guide to the Local Assemblies of the Knights of Labor* (Westport, CT: Greenwood Press, 1982), 52–59; H. M. Cramer to Powderly, July 13, 1889, Powderly Papers, reel 30; *Record of the Proceedings of the Special Session of the General Assembly [of the Knights of Labor], Held at Cleveland, O., May 25 to June 3, 1886*, microfilm, 76; Watts, *Social Bases of City Politics*, 17; Russell, *Atlanta, 1847–1890*, 211. The *Proceedings of the General Assembly, 1886*, 327, lists a membership figure of 2,827 for Atlanta's District Assembly 105 as of July 1, 1886; this figure includes some local assemblies outside of Atlanta. In March 1886 W. M. Harbin, state organizer of the Knights of Labor in Georgia, claimed that the Knights had "a membership of over four thousand [in Atlanta]. Perhaps over five thousand." *Atlanta Constitution*, March 14, 1886. Garlock lists two Atlanta local assemblies as consisting of African Americans; W. M. Harbin told a reporter in March 1886 that there were "four colored assemblies in Atlanta" (*Atlanta Constitution*, March 14, 1886). Later that year, however, the Knights of Labor revoked Harbin's organizing commission because he had organized local assemblies of African Americans "but failed to either make report or return fees for charters." *Journal of United Labor*, September 10, 1886.

17. Thomas M. Deaton, "James G. Woodward: The Working Man's Mayor," *Atlanta History: A Journal of Georgia and the South* 31 (Fall 1987): 12; Russell, *Atlanta, 1847–1890*, 207–209.

18. Russell, *Atlanta, 1847–1890*, 209–213; Watts, *Social Bases of City Politics*, 17, 28–29; Allison Dorsey, *To Build Our Lives Together: Community Formation in Black Atlanta, 1875–1906* (Athens: University of Georgia Press, 2004), 139–140; Gregory Mixon, *The Atlanta Riot: Race, Class, and Violence in a New South City* (Gainesville: University Press of Florida, 2005), 31; Joseph Gerteis, *Class and the Color Line: Interracial Class Coalition in the Knights of Labor and the Populist Movement* (Durham, NC: Duke University Press, 2007), 122–124; Garlock, comp., *Guide to the Local Assemblies*, 55.

19. Deaton, "James G. Woodward," 11–23; *Atlanta Constitution*, August 27, 1892; *Atlanta Journal*, November 14–15, 1892; Watts, *Social Bases of City Politics*, 18; Franklin M. Garrett, *Atlanta and Environs: A Chronicle of Its People and Events* (New York: Lewis Historical Publishing Company, 1954), II: 373 (quote).

20. Deaton, "James G. Woodward," 11–23.

21. McLaurin, *Paternalism and Protest*, 91–112; Reed, "Augusta Textile Mills," 228–246; Ware, *Labor Movement*, 382; *Journal of United Labor*, August 25, 1886.

22. *Augusta Chronicle*, September 15, October 2, 6 (quote), 7, 1886; Edward J. Cashin, *The Story of Augusta* (Augusta, GA: Richmond County Board of Education, 1980), 157–158. See also Julia M. Walsh, "'Horny-Handed Sons of Toil': Workers, Politics, and Religion in Augusta, Georgia, 1880–1910" (Ph.D. diss., University of Illinois at Urbana-Champaign, 1999), 263. For other examples of political activity causing division within the Knights of Labor, see McLaurin, *The Knights of Labor in the South*, 159; Gregory S. Kealey and Bryan D. Palmer, *Dreaming of What Might Be: The Knights of Labor in Ontario, 1880–1900* (Cambridge: Cambridge University Press, 1982), 248–249.

23. Walsh, "'Horny-Handed Sons of Toil,'" 264; *Atlanta Constitution*, October 7, 1886.

24. *Proceedings of the General Assembly of the Knights of Labor of America, Eleventh Regular Session. Held at Minneapolis, Minnesota, October 4 to 19, 1887*, microfilm, 1414; *Report of the General Secretary* (1888), 4; Hild, "The Knights of Labor in Georgia," 57–66; Walsh, "'Horny-Handed Sons of Toil,'" 267.

25. James E. Schofield to Powderly, August 6, 1886, Powderly Papers, reel 17; *Macon Daily Telegraph*, July 3, 1886; *Sholes' Directory of the City of Macon, July 1, 1878* (Macon, GA: A. E. Sholes, 1878), I: 201; Richard W. Iobst, *Civil War Macon: The History of a Confederate City* (Macon, GA: Mercer University Press, 1999), 444. Membership figures for the Knights of Labor in Macon are not available, so the membership of "several hundred" mentioned here is an estimate. For a listing of Knights of Labor local assemblies in Macon, see Garlock, comp., *Guide to the Local Assemblies*, 52.

26. Schofield to Powderly, August 6, 1886, Powderly Papers, reel 17; Ida Young, Julius Gholson, and Clara Nell Hargrove, *The History of Macon, Georgia, 1823–1949* (Macon, GA: Lyon, Marshall, and Brooks, 1950), 314, 347, 496; *Sholes' Directory of the City of Macon, 1878*, I: 149.

27. Schofield to Powderly, August 6, 1886, Powderly Papers, reel 17; *Macon Daily Telegraph*, August 5, October 7, 1886; *Atlanta Constitution*, October 7, 1886.

28. On McCord and his alleged support from the Knights in 1886, see *Sholes' Directory of the City of Augusta, 1886* (Augusta, GA: Chronicle Book and Job Rooms, 1886), 28–29, 47, 272; *Augusta Chronicle*, July 25, 1888. See Ware, *Labor Movement*, 377–380, for the Knights' platform. The platform called for "the reduction of the hours of labor to eight a day," but such a demand would have been impossibly optimistic in the late-nineteenth-century South.

29. Ward, "Georgia Under the Bourbon Democrats," 419, 422, 428; John E. Talmadge, *Rebecca Latimer Felton: Nine Stormy Decades* (Athens: University of Georgia Press, 1960), 86, 99; Harold E. Davis, *Henry Grady's New South: Atlanta, A Brave and Beautiful City* (Tuscaloosa: University of Alabama Press, 1990), 146–148; *Atlanta Constitution*, November 20, December 2, 1886, October 6 (quote), 7, 1887; Schofield to Powderly, December 31, 1886, Powderly Papers, reel 20. According to Talmadge, Rebecca Felton joined the WCTU in 1886 in order to "bring it into her crusade" against the convict lease (99). On the Bourbon Triumvirate, see also Matthew Hild, "Bourbon Triumvirate," *New Georgia Encyclopedia*, http://www.georgiaencyclopedia.org (accessed September 16, 2009).

30. Mercer G. Evans, "The History of the Organized Labor Movement in Georgia" (Ph.D. diss., University of Chicago, 1929), 410–416, 448–449, 573; *Augusta Chronicle*, September 15, 17, 1887, October 17, November 7, 1889; *Atlanta Constitution*, August 4, September 22, 1889, January 2, 1890; *Acts and Resolutions of the General Assembly of the State of Georgia, 1889* (Atlanta: Franklin Publishing House, 1890), 163–164; H. M. Cramer to Powderly, January 8, 1888, Powderly Papers, reel 24 (quote).

31. Evans, "Labor Movement in Georgia," 31, 416–418, 426, 580–581, 592; William F. Holmes, "Populism and Progressivism," in Coleman, ed., *History of Georgia*, 306; Bartley, *The Creation of Modern Georgia*, 155.

32. Fink, *Workingmen's Democracy*, 19; McMath, *American Populism*, 63, 79; Bartley, *The Creation of Modern Georgia*, 143; *Journal of United Labor*, June 16, 1888; Hild, "The Knights of Labor in Georgia," 134–135; *Record of the Proceedings of the General Assembly, Oct. 1886*, 323; *Marietta* (Ga.) *Journal*, September 9, October 14, 1886, August 2, 9 (quotes), October 11, 1888. On the Southern Farmers' Alliance as the chief organization behind the founding of the Populist Party, see Robert C. McMath Jr., *Populist Vanguard: A History of the Southern Farmers' Alliance* (Chapel Hill: University of North Carolina Press, 1975), esp. chaps. 7–8. On the rise of the Farmers' Alliance in Georgia, see McMath, *Populist Vanguard*, 41–43.

33. *Marietta* (Ga.) *Journal*, August 16, 1888; *Journal of United Labor*, June 20, 1889.

34. *Atlanta Constitution*, November 13–16, 1889; McLaurin, *Knights of Labor*, 176–179 (quote on 179); Oestreicher, "A Note on Knights of Labor Membership Statistics," 107.

35. James F. Foster to John W. Hayes, August 14, 1892, John William Hayes Papers, microfilm edition (Glen Rock, NJ: Microfilming Corporation of America, 1974), reel 8.

36. W. A. Foster Jr., with Thomas A. Scott, *Paulding County: Its People and Places* (Roswell, GA: W. H. Wolfe Associates, 1983), 238; *Dallas* (Ga.) *Paulding New Era*, November 18, 1892; *Journal of the Knights of Labor*, August 4, 1892; Steven Hahn, *The Roots of Southern Populism: Yeoman Farmers and the Transformation of the Georgia Upcountry, 1850–1890* (New York: Oxford University Press, 1983), 280–281 (quote). The *JKL* article, a report on the meeting of the Georgia Knights of Labor State Assembly, spells Brintle's last name as "Brintts," but this is undoubtedly an error. The editor or compositor must have misread "Brintle," written in longhand, as "Brintts." A letter from James C. Sanges in the *Journal of United Labor*, June 20, 1889, correctly spells Brintle's name, and mentions that he is from Roxana (Paulding County) and an officer in the Knights of Labor State Assembly.

37. Russell, *Atlanta, 1847–1890*, 209, 213; *People's Party Paper* (Atlanta), July 8, 1892.

38. *People's Party Paper*, February 25, 1892.

39. C. Vann Woodward, *Tom Watson: Agrarian Rebel* (New York: Macmillan, 1938), 203–207; *National Economist*, July 16, 1892 (quote).

40. Augusta *Revolution*, October 4, 1892, quoted in Walsh, "'Horny-Handed Sons of Toil,'" 299.

41. Woodward, *Tom Watson: Agrarian Rebel*, 241–242, 269–277; Walsh, "'Horny-Handed Sons of Toil,'" 316–319; Shaw, *The Wool-Hat Boys*, 117–118, 120–122; *People's Party Paper*, November 9, 1894; *Augusta Chronicle*, October 3, 1895. Watson contested his defeat in the October 1895 election, but without success.

42. Hild, *Greenbackers, Knights of Labor, and Populists*, 176. On the election of a Knight to the mayor's office in Albany, see McLaurin, *Knights of Labor*, 97; on Hazlehurst, see the *Journal of the Knights of Labor*, November 12, 1891.

43. Talmadge, *Rebecca Latimer Felton*, 86–89, 98–99; Shaw, *The Wool-Hat Boys*, 116, 120, 207–208; Woodward, *Tom Watson*, 373, 461–462; Hild, *Greenbackers, Knights of Labor, and Populists*, 214; Brewton (Ala.) *Laborer's Banner*, March 29, 1902; Foster with Scott, *Paulding County*, 240.

44. For example, when U.S. senator Hoke Smith of Georgia successfully ran for reelection in 1914, he and his campaign managers made overt appeals both to farmers and to organized labor. See Dewey W. Grantham Jr., *Hoke Smith and the Politics of the New South* (Baton Rouge: Louisiana State University Press, 1958), 271–272.

45. Cramer to Powderly, January 8, 1888, Powderly Papers, reel 24.

"Of Whom Shall the Third Party Be Composed?"

URBAN LABORERS AND THE ORIGINS OF THE PEOPLE'S PARTY IN DALLAS, TEXAS

—ALICIA E. RODRIQUEZ

In his influential *Origins of the New South*, C. Vann Woodward identified the building of a successful farmer-laborer coalition as a key Populist political strategy. Developing alliances between southern and western voters, and between white and black southerners, were also part of this strategy. Other scholars, including Robert C. McMath Jr. and Chester McArthur Destler, have highlighted the role that labor played in informing Populist political ideology, in party building, and in leadership. More recent studies have examined in greater depth labor's role, advancing the argument that though long overlooked, urban workers contributed significantly, in more than one way, to this national political and social movement that challenged the existing political parties. Despite the recognition of the fact that workers and their labor organizations were deeply involved in the Populist Party, few studies have explored the farmer-labor coalition at the local level. Case studies can shed light on how local events, combined with the backdrop of national events and episodes, prove powerful in motivating individuals to take action in hopes of changing the course of their lives.[1]

This examination of Populism explores the role of the workingmen of Dallas, Texas, in establishing the People's Party in the city and in organizing the statewide party. Dallas men involved in the city's labor movement laid the foundation for a new party, provided experienced leadership, shaped party ideology, and built the party's organizational network. In Dallas, urban laborers created an active and vocal branch of the party that contributed significantly to the development of the Populist movement in Texas. As urban laborers, they also came into conflict with their employers, and with city government, and in doing so encountered obstacles to enjoying life, leisure, and respect, while working in a rapidly changing industrial America. These men, who literally helped construct modern America and thus appreciated its promise, felt their futures lay not in a romantic vision of an agrarian past, but in the reality of the wonders being created before their eyes. Having left the farm, they became creatures of modern America even though they understood the conditions under which farmers toiled, and with them built an entity to advance reform. Thus, studying the role of labor in the People's Party challenges older interpretations of who the Populists were and why they became Populists, and it supports recent interpretations, which more thoroughly address the role of labor in the party. Examining workers' roles in creating a local branch of the party and contributing to the establishment of the larger Texas party challenges scholars to examine workers' involvement in the People's Party in other southern cities.[2]

Long before laborers organized a branch of the People's Party in Dallas, farmers and laborers had established a tradition of cooperation and mutual support. In the 1870s, farmers began organizing in response to the challenges of the new market economy. Local community-based alliances emerged, coalescing to form the Texas Farmers' Alliance in the 1880s. Battling scarce and high-priced credit, exorbitant railroad shipping rates, and unpredictable Mother Nature, these farmers eventually found common ground with the wage laborers, who confronted similar problems in the late-nineteenth-century economy.[3]

Farmers and laborers worked together during the labor unrest of the 1880s. By 1885, Texas ranked ninth nationally among those states with the greatest number of workers involved in strikes. Many of them were members of the Knights of Labor, which had founded a Dallas chapter in the spring of 1882. The Knights of Labor, with support from farmers, were involved in the successful March 1885 machinists' strike against the Gould system railroads. Other farmer-supported union actions against the railroads and other businesses followed, including the Great Southwest Strike of 1886, in which railroad workers from Dallas and Forth Worth paid a heavy price in job losses. Despite the strike's failure, laborers and Alliancemen were united by a shared sense of grievance against the economic interests that they felt exploited them.[4]

A glance at each organization's reform demands confirms the considerable ideological debt farmers owed to labor. In Texas, more prominently than in any other southern state, labor and farmer discontent came together to build the ideological and organizational foundations on which the Alliance constructed the third party. Past disappointments had mounted as the promises of change through legislation and from reform politicians went unfulfilled. Farmers had help elect James Hogg as a reform governor only to be disappointed. Labor's demands for improved working conditions and pay were not met with satisfaction. Thus, the elements of labor and farmer activism, and subsequent disappointment, came together in Texas. The influence that labor had on farmers is readily apparent; all but four out of fifteen of the Farmers' Alliance's famous 1886 Cleburne Demands, are virtually the same as those Terence Powderly put forth in the Knights of Labor's 1878 Reading, Pennsylvania, preamble.[5]

Both the Cleburne Demands and the Dallas Demands (1888) were essentially proto-Populist Party planks that illustrate the ideological relationship between labor unionists and Alliancemen. The Dallas Demands emerged from an 1888 Dallas meeting of the Texas Farmers' Alliance. J. M. Perdue, an author of the Cleburne Demands, chaired a committee to "enquire into the cause of industrial depression." The committee's radical report gave the greenback monetary theory its central place in Alliance politics.[6] Its twelve proposals, known as the "Dallas Demands," included abolishing the national banking system, authorizing the unlimited coinage of silver and gold, and the regulation of interstate commerce, interest rates, railroads, land policy, and the expenditure of public monies. Those termed the "producing classes," farmers and laborers, shared a non-Marxist class consciousness. They did not call for government ownership and control of business, but sought government regulation to protect the ability of the common man to provide for himself and his family, free of exploitation by business and capital. Agrarians and laborers developed their ideology and built their cooperative relationship as both groups faced increasing challenges resulting from the accelerating industrialization of the South.[7]

Dallas, during the Populist era, typified both the promise and the problems of the changing South. Founded in 1841, Dallas was one of the newest of the Old South cities. In the post-Reconstruction era, its emergence as a significant railroad hub and its growing manufacturing sector transformed it into a quintessential New South city. Dallas enjoyed economic prosperity as southern migrants seeking new lives and new opportunities made their way to the Lone Star State and the opportunities that its developing markets and industries presented. The city's boosters promoted Dallas as the South's "Queen City" and had much on which to base their claim. Between 1880 and 1890, Dallas's population quadrupled to 38,000. Few southern cities could match Dallas's up-and-coming position as the type of southern urban center promoted by New South booster Henry Grady, who had visited the city in 1888.[8]

During this period of Dallas's growth, the rise of Populism coincided with a rise of labor activism in the South, illustrative of the disillusionment and discontent experienced by the region's producing classes. Although rapid growth and industrialization benefited the city and its residents, it also brought new problems. Labor unrest, competing visions of the city's future, and disputes over who should lead it created tension among workers, capitalists, and civic leaders. The workingmen in Dallas battled business owners over wages, pay dates, and work hours, seeking legislative remedies at the local and state levels. They also demanded improved city services and efficient, honest government.[9]

By 1890, with farmer and labor discontent in Texas at a full boil, these producers achieved new levels of organization and cooperation. In 1889, Dallas trade and labor organizations called a meeting of workingmen from throughout the state. In July 1889, delegates from thirty-four Texas cities assembled in Dallas for what organizers called the "Eight-Hour Convention."[10] The delegates represented thirteen organizations, with the Texas Farmers' Alliance prominent among them. Representatives included five workingmen from Dallas. Of these, one served as the meeting's secretary and another as a member of the platform committee. An African American man, Melvin Wade, served on the five-member executive committee. Two of the Dallas delegates, including Wade, would become active members of the People's Party during the next decade.[11]

The Eight-Hour convention at Dallas resulted in the creation of the Texas State Federation of Labor and the adoption of a pro-labor, anti-big-business platform, which espoused the principle of equal rights to all and special privileges for none.[12] This Jeffersonian-Jacksonian promise of Americans' equality before the government became the rallying cry of late nineteenth-century reformers. Populists, in particular, recited the slogan as they sought to remind Americans how far actual political and social practice had strayed from principle. The Federation's platform echoed this promise as its planks called for measures that would create an honest, responsive government that would ensure fair treatment of wageworkers. Sounding very much like their Knights of Labor and Farmers' Alliance predecessors, the workers' platform also called for an eight-hour workday as a way to provide employment for more workers, to in turn better serve the nation's welfare. In addition, the platform advocated the adoption of the single tax to replace all existing taxes. Henry George's argument that this tax on the value of land would prevent monopolistic accumulation of land by a few at the expense of many, resonated with these workers. Revenue collected from the single tax, George argued, would benefit the greater good. The platform also demanded the repeal of the "National bank law and all other class laws," government ownership of the railways, telephones, and telegraphs, the abolition of the United States Senate and all state senates, the abolition of the grand jury system, the adoption of the Australian ballot to end the "[present] corruption and the damnable boodle system," and finally, the adoption of a lien law that would protect the economic interests of laborers. The Eight-Hour conventioneers appeared to be more radical than some of their predecessors in that they favored government ownership of railways and telephones, whereas preceding groups only wanted government regulation of these industries. Over time, however, they would temper their demands.[13]

In 1890, the leadership of the Eight-Hour convention's creature, the Texas State Federation of Labor, met in Fort Worth. A painter, P. H. Golden of Dallas, a native of New Orleans and the son of Irish Catholic immigrants who had migrated to Dallas in 1886 at the age of forty, served as the organization's vice president and acting president. He seems to have deliberately scheduled the meeting to occur after the state's Democratic and Republican conventions. The shrewd timing of the meeting allowed labor the opportunity to evaluate the proceedings of the conventions and the resulting party platforms. Golden's published call for the meeting read: "If our rights have been provided for [at the parties' conventions], very well, if not, we can say so." He stated: "We are not compelled to blindly follow as we have for years in the past." Sounding very much as if poised to form a third party, the call continued, "If we do not act independently the politicians will never respect us or grant us any concessions. We are not compelled to bow to any party. We must look for and demand the execution of principles in the future, instead of hopelessly following men and party."[14] While not yet throwing off the yoke of the two traditional parties, the Federation clearly issued a challenge to the Democrats and the Republicans.

Federation delegates issued a revised and expanded version of the July 1889 Dallas platform. Again, the platform favored an eight-hour day, but this time it specifically called for the eight-hour rule's application on state and municipal public works. The plank also called upon the state legislature to pass the eight-hour law. The organization moderated some of its earlier radicalism. For example, the Federation dropped its demand for the abolition of the United States Senate, and instead advocated a constitutional amendment allowing the direct election of U.S. senators (along with postmasters, the president, and vice president). Another plank demanded that the state of Texas adopt a law providing for binding arbitration of labor disputes between employers. The revised platform included planks pertaining to the adoption of state schoolbooks, the abolishment of the convict labor system, and a demand for a law that would make it a felony for Pinkertons or other policing agencies from outside of Texas to make arrests within the state without a special permit. Furthermore, the Federation called for the dissolution of the Texas Rangers, proposing that the Rangers' duties would be turned over to the sheriffs and local militias. Finally, the platform resolved that members of the Labor Federation would oppose "the election to offices by all honorable means, the election of any and all persons" who opposed their position on any issue.[15] The Federation's members were growing confident of their potential to exercise power. The Farmers' Alliance was doing the same. With a mutual interest in reform and a shared history of cooperation, if the two groups could unite, they could become a formidable pressure group in the name of reform.

As the Federation's leadership ramped up its reform rhetoric in the months leading up to the establishment of the People's Party in Dallas, city workingmen publicly expressed their grievances with local government and frustration with their inability to gain concessions from employers. In a December 1890 council meeting, the Dallas Board of Aldermen debated the eight- and nine-hour workday, after the Federation adopted a plank advocating the eight-hour workday.[16] One alderman proposed that "the city accept nine hours as a day's labor on all public works, in accordance with the recent action of union carpenters." While two aldermen supported the proposal, others argued vociferously against it, charging that the city had no right to pass such a resolution. Another charged that such overtures to labor "always come up on the eve on an election." Still another added that the resolution anticipated a strike, yet, he continued, "I don't see how the man on the street gang can strike."[17]

After some debate and accusations that those who favored limiting work hours did so for political gain, the council voted 10 to 9 to postpone discussion of the issue until May, well past the municipal elections scheduled for early April 1891. Of those who supported the motion to postpone the discussion, only one of the ten was up for reelection in the spring. It appears that those who did not have to think about an impending election were more likely to vote to postpone discussion of the issue. There is no record of labor's immediate reaction to the council's decision to postpone the discussion, but workingmen were not pleased.[18] Months later the discussion of the episode surfaced during a laborers' meeting. At that time workers directed their anger at the council for not supporting the measure. It also prompted some men to consider the possibility of a new party.[19]

On December 8, 1890, days after the council's decision on public works work hours, further evidence of the tension between labor and local government came to light. Members of the Dallas Central Eight-Hour Labor League expressed their interest in "petitioning the legislature to prohibit all municipalities from formulating and adopting charters for the government of the people before being adopted by a popular vote."[20] The interest in such a prohibition was precipitated by the council's discussion of proposed city charter amendments; proposals included allowing only taxpayers to vote on issues dealing with "expenditures of money or the assumption of debt," and that a poll tax be required to vote in elections.[21] Workers' discussions reveal that they, finding much not to like about the council's proceedings, wanted greater citizen power in matters of city government.[22]

The laborers believed that if the legislature adopted such a provision allowing for greater citizen oversight, the producing classes in Dallas would gain access to power and could shape a labor-friendly city charter. If lobbying and good will could not convince the council to act in labor's interest, perhaps state intervention could. While persuading the state legislature to take action would be a formidable task, political rhetoric demonstrates that workingmen were exploring all avenues by which to achieve reform and putting those in positions of power on notice.

Meanwhile, carpenter J. P. Diffey, the League's first vice president, actively collected signatures for a petition that asked the state legislature to adopt the Australian ballot. The petition also requested that the legislature submit to voters a constitutional amendment that would require all voters to register for participation in elections. Diffey explained to the press that the secret ballot "prevents the purchase of votes and the intimidation of voters. It [the petition] provides any one from being nearer to the polls than fifty feet, and the state prints the tickets, relieving the candidates from the expense."[23]

Voter intimidation was a feature of post-Reconstruction politics. A worker might feel pressured to vote the way his employer did, fearing punitive measures if he voted otherwise. Under the Australian system no one would know how the employee voted, and the fear of employer retaliation would disappear. Freedom from such intimidation would mean all voters, black and white, rich and poor, employer and employee, could cast their ballots freely. While the secret ballot might impose difficulties for illiterate voters, apparently laborers either did not recognize this drawback or they believed the reform was worth the risk. Having the state pay the cost of printing ballots would also benefit laborers. Wealthy candidates supported by business interests could easily afford printing costs. A laboring man's candidate, however, supported by men with little extra cash would have difficulty launching a successful campaign. Ballots printed at the state's expense would be one way to help level the political playing field. Such a measure might also help workingmen remove those members of the council they felt were hostile toward labor.[24]

The following week, on December 14, 1890, the Labor League met again to discuss their desire to gain a stronger voice in local government. Members discussed the city charter, arguing further for a charter developed with input from and approval by the citizens of Dallas. They did not want the charter to be solely a product of the council. Providing average citizens a greater role in formulating city policy was not the only issue on the minds of labor that day. P. H. Golden spoke strongly against the charter provision that dictated the qualifications that candidates for city office had to meet. The current charter required that candidates be property owners in the city of Dallas. This requirement, Golden said, served "to disfranchise the laborer."[25] Capable men without property did not have the opportunity to serve either their city or the interests of men in their class. The laborers' meetings, on which the local press recorded in great detail, often providing verbatim transcripts of the proceedings, reveal that Dallas workers were experiencing the same feelings of political alienation, discontent, and disrespect that their agrarian brethren had long suffered.

While the month of December 1890 witnessed a rise in local labor discontent, the Farmers' Alliance also entered a new phase of political development. Twenty-five states sent delegates to the meeting of the National Farmers' Alliance and Industrial Union (NFA&IU) in Ocala, Florida. In addition to the NFA&IU delegates, several other farmer and labor organizations sent observers. Alliance members went to the convention to discuss plans and a strategy for the 1892 election cycle. The meeting produced a new platform, which was overwhelmingly adopted by Alliance members who clamored for a third party. Many Alliancemen had previously expressed reluctance about moving away from simply engaging in lobbying and cooperative action, and into politics, but now they embraced the prospect of participating in partisan politics. The famous Ocala platform put forth demands familiar to both labor and agrarian organizations: stronger regulation of railroads, a graduated income tax, direct election of U.S. senators, and the subtreasury plan. With few changes, this platform would form the core of Populist ideology. While sectional tensions over policy issues at the Ocala meeting hurt the chances of a successful national political coalition emerging, the proceedings at the Ocala meeting seem to have energized Dallas laborers in their quest for reform.[26]

On January 4, 1891, at "quite a large meeting" of Federation laborers, workers discussed the recent Alliance activity and debated the prospect of a new third party. One prominent laboring man, "Brother" Robinson, declared that he had "got tired of being a [D]emocrat long ago."[27] In fact, he argued, neither party would serve as an agent for the reforms that the country desperately needed. Robinson continued:

> The people have been demanding a direct vote for president, and no party demands it; the people have been demanding unlimited coinage of silver and both parties oppose it; they demand the repeal of the specie resumption act; they demand governmental control of railroads, express, telegraphs and telephones, and both parties have continued to oppose it. They try to fail to notice these demands as far as possible. In order to take grounds against the people they fail to remember them.[28]

Another laborer, T. H. A. Spencer, a recent arrival from New York, affirmed the need for a third party. "We have been under the regime of the [R]epublican and [D]emocratic parties and we find that the country is suffering from great evils and the people are downtrodden by corrupt practices." Identifying himself as a Democrat disgusted with his party, he vowed, "it will be a cold day when I vote that ticket again." He continued, "The [A]lliance threatens both parties, it will destroy them eventually, and they deserve it."[29] These words were met with enthusiastic applause from the crowd of laborers. There stood labor, cheering the destruction of the Democratic and Republican parties. The speaker, who seemed "to carry the meeting by storm" raised the issues and concerns of the laboring men, and prodded them to think of the possibility and advantages of a third party, as the old parties were no longer effective.[30]

During the Eight-Hour Labor League meeting held at the Elm Street labor hall on January 11, 1891, Dallas workingmen debated the question, "Of Whom Shall the Third Party be Composed?"[31] A local express driver,

J. P. Robertson, argued that the time had come for a new party. The old parties, he said, "promised you everything you wanted, but went back on their word."³² Another laborer, a "Mr. Edmundson," registered that "there were enough dissatisfied laborers to compose a third party, who could at least hold a balance of power." A new third party was needed as "[t]he only differences between the two old parties was in the names."³³ One League member characterized the Democratic Party as an institution with such a long line of broken promises that it could not be trusted under any circumstances; he would "as soon trust a Benedict Arnold as to trust the old party any longer."³⁴ Recounting the city council's failure to pass an eight-hour workday ordinance for those employed on public works, Wade recalled, "When the eight hour law was before the council the city attorney had said that it was unconstitutional." But, he asked, "Was it unconstitutional for a laboring man to rest two hours?"³⁵ Closing the Sunday afternoon meeting on a note that tapped laborers' concerns, Melvin Wade, a black man who had served on the executive committee of the 1889 Eight-Hour Labor League, said, "Every man who had to work for his bread and meat ought to belong to the third party."³⁶ Wade, a former slave from Tennessee, was an active member of the Knights of Labor, and while he had initially been wary of joining the People's Party, over time he would become a significant figure in the Dallas People's Party, as well as in the state party as a Populist lecturer.³⁷

The meeting, the proceedings of which were published, identified nine speakers' thoughts that evening. Along with other labor meetings, these events suggest that Dallas laborers contemplated the promise for reform that a new political party might hold. They were dissatisfied with where they stood in relation to capital, and they saw others around them, such as farmers, who suffered the same lot. Yet third parties had come and gone in the past with little effect. Such political business was a risky venture. In addition, switching parties, particularly if it meant leaving the dominant Democratic Party, presented psychological obstacles and bore social consequences. Leaving a party to which one's Civil War and Reconstruction-era ancestors had belonged was not only difficult psychologically, but was also viewed negatively by the community in which one lived, interacted, and depended upon for one's livelihood. But, it seemed, there was no political organization to turn to for help, and there were many who had reason to unite for pursuit of economic advancement and social reform.³⁸

On January 18, 1891, the Dallas Labor League met in the Elm Street labor hall in what a news report's headlines pronounced "A RED HOT

MEETING."[39] Before the meeting came to order several members discussed the latest politics among themselves. Further reflecting the discontent with the two political parties and the growing acceptance of the idea of a third party, all those engaged in the conversation agreed that both the Republican and Democratic parties "should be scourged out of the temple."[40] As the meeting continued, the political rhetoric heated up. In registering his desire for a new party, one workingman who regularly spoke at Labor League meetings detailed the ills that plagued society and expressed support for the recently defeated Lodge Election Bill or the "Force" bill, as it was known in the South. This bill, if Congress had passed it, would have provided for the federal supervision of elections in the South. It was designed to eliminate the fraud and voter intimidation that ran rampant in southern elections. While most white southerners saw the bill as an onerous piece of legislation that would have allowed outsiders to pry into the South's affairs, this Dallas laborer "saw nothing wrong in a bill that forced people to behave themselves and give the voter a fair whack at an election." He continued, "I tell you unless something is done to alleviate such things there will more anarchists, aye, red-handed anarchists, in this country. I do not wonder that there are anarchists in this country; the wonder is there are not more of them."[41] Government supervision of federal elections, which had been despised by the white South during the Reconstruction era, was now being welcomed as a needed reform measure, even if white southerners in general rejected the Lodge Bill.[42]

As in previous meetings, laborers openly challenged the credibility of the two existing parties and welcomed the possibility of change under a new one. The discussions the workingmen held in the Elm Street labor hall revealed several things about labor and their desire for reform. The laboring men trusted in the promise of the current political system. They also believed, however, that industrial magnates, in collusion with the Democratic and Republican parties, had ignored the interests of the workingmen to the point of endangering the nation. But these workers did not wish to replace the current system of government with a new one; they were not socialists. The laborers of Dallas wished simply to bring honesty, fair play, and order to the democratic nation that they believed had drifted from the principles on which it was originally founded. In Dallas, an important southern transportation hub, as well as a commercial and industrial center, one of the South's relative few, workers were exposed every day to sweeping changes brought by technological innovations. They welcomed these changes but believed they should not come with a decline in workers' status. Thus, while the People's Party would come to serve the interest of farmers who experienced economic hard times or may have felt that they were being marginalized by the transformation of modern America, laborers also saw a chance to have their interests served by a third party. Laborers wanted economic, political, and social reform that resulted in respect and a fair chance for the producing classes. As the two traditional parties had long neglected the cries of the people in favor of serving the rich and powerful, the people needed an alternative vehicle for reform. This vehicle would be a third party, and the workingmen seemed ready to not only climb aboard, but also steer.[43]

Further frustration with the dominant Democratic Party is evidenced by the contentious April 1891 Dallas mayoral and city council election, in which an organization of independent voters challenged the entrenched Democrats. The election had pitted an incumbent, newly declared independent candidate favored by many workingmen, over the Democratic nominee. The incumbent had years earlier spoken of the Knights of Labor as "lawful and necessary to the well-being of society and to successful industry as the organization of capital."[44] Prior to the April municipal election, the local Democrats had held a convention and acted in a way that angered labor by striking from the platform's final form a plank that had been inserted at labor's request. It had read that "the city convicts shall not be employed on public works."[45] In response, a "prominent laborite" said that labor was "not at all pleased" with some of what had been heard at the convention. Of those who had advocated the plank's removal he said, "They seem to think that it is all right for convicts to be placed on public works in competition with honest labor. We don't."[46]

While the independent incumbent won reelection, workingmen perceived the Democratic Party's platform as hostile to labor, hence cultivating ill will toward the party. In addition, in the aftermath of the election, the state legislature decided to reduce the amount of bonds the city could issue. This action, which was viewed as punishment for bucking the Democratic Party's mayoral candidate, could affect labor by reducing the number of jobs for workingmen created by public works projects. Again, workers were finding more reasons to break from the party of their fathers.[47]

A failed strike also underscored labor's inability to bring about minimal concessions from those in power. On May 5, 1891, unskilled day laborers, who had been employed to excavate a bed for the Elm Street cable railway, went on strike. The workers claimed that when the cable railway company hired them, the company offered them a wage of $1.15 a day. They learned, however, that they would not be paid weekly: they would have to work until June 20 to receive their pay. If anyone wished to receive his pay before June 20, he could do so, provided that he agreed to accept a 10 percent discount on his time check. The change infuriated the workers. The strikers issued a circular on May 5, 1891, in which they argued that they could not provide for their families under the terms presented by the cable railway company. In response, they demanded a wage of $1.50 a day, payable every Saturday night, and the reduction of their workday from ten hours to nine. They walked off of the job after the company rejected their demands.[48]

The workers, led in part by men who would become members of the Dallas People's Party, organized to support the strike. In an effort to build support for their cause, they called a meeting to discuss the strike. Some four hundred men attended, including W. E. Farmer, past district master workman of the Knights of Labor, who addressed the crowd. While the meeting and the strike generated considerable interest among workingmen and attracted the city council and the mayor's attention, the movement was short lived.[49]

By mid-May support and enthusiasm began to wane. The mayor of Dallas had tried to broker a deal that laborers were willing to accept, but it appears that ultimately the cable railway company hired strikebreakers. The company had secured "a large work force" and construction "work was moving as though nothing had happened."[50] The Federation of Labor's executive committee, which had taken interest in the strike, announced that it would not call for a general strike of all the city's laborers, as had been speculated. Such an action would be "impracticable and impolite."[51] With organized labor's inability or unwillingness to take strong action by calling a general strike, and the railroad company's apparent ease with which it could find strikebreakers the cable railway workers' walkout was broken. With little solidarity apparent among workers, and no larger political body to support their cause, employers had no incentive to respond to labor's demands. If labor reforms were ever to come about in Dallas, interested and committed workers needed to look beyond the existing labor organizations.

Before the strike episode had played out, news arrived that a coalition of groups ready to move forward with formally establishing a third party would convene in Cincinnati, Ohio. Many historians consider this meeting the "beginning of the People's Party in the South."[52] Dallas laborers met to choose delegates to attend the May 19, 1891, National Union Conference and elected the president of the Dallas branch of the Federation of Labor, P. H. Golden, to serve as their delegate to the convention. In addition, they chose W. E. Farmer of the Knights of Labor to attend the convention as the Texas state delegate-at-large.⁵³

On May 21, 1891, headlines in the *Dallas Morning News* announced, "PEOPLE'S PARTY BORN—With a Whirlwind of Enthusiasm at Cincinnati."⁵⁴ In attendance were a number of prominent Texas radicals who had been laboring to jump start the reform movement in their state. By the end of the convention, the coalition largely adopted the Ocala platform and chose "People's Party of the United States" as its name.⁵⁵

Soon after the conference concluded, the Eight-Hour Labor League met to greet the returning delegates and hear the news from the third-party convention. The events that took place in Cincinnati were significant in facilitating the birth of the national People's Party, but the meeting also led Dallas workingmen to launch the People's Party in their city. The returning delegates and Dallas laborers organized a meeting that promised to lay out the details and meaning of the Cincinnati convention. There, the People's Party platform and the resolutions adopted at the convention would be explained. The *Morning News* proclaimed: "Speeches will be made and the [P]eople's party campaign in Dallas opened."⁵⁶ Circulars distributed throughout the city read:

> Let the people rule and prosper instead of unscrupulous monopolies now enthroned in governmental power by mercenary courthouse rings, old partisan leaders and Wall street speculators. Rally, rally fellow citizens at the city hall Thursday night, May 28, 1891, to inaugurate in Dallas, the chief city of Texas, the largest state in the union, the party of the people, by the people, for the people.⁵⁷

On the same day, the Federation of Labor president and Cincinnati delegate, P. H. Golden, announced that the Federation would hold a convention on July 3, 1891, in nearby Sulphur Springs. Golden called on "all subordinate branches of the Farmers' [A]lliance, Grange, Wheel, Knights of Labor, and labor organizations generally of Texas" to attend. In addition, he outlined the reforms demanded by labor, which he termed "not sweeping" but "essential to the welfare and happiness of our people." He closed his announcement, saying, "In inaugurating the people's movement it remains for you to say whether Texas shall lag behind in the procession or take her place in the ranks of the legions now forging onward to permanent and lasting victory."⁵⁸ The Federation and the new third party, which shared a leadership that included Golden and other local workingmen, were clearly preparing the ground for planting the seeds of the reform movement in Dallas.

The prospect of a powerful farmer-laborer coalition prompted at least one Democratic Party leader to take notice and preemptive action to co-opt the Populists. On May 23, 1891, former lieutenant governor and Democratic Party organizer Barnett Gibbs of Dallas came out swinging at the new party. The third-party's platform, Gibbs declared, was "too general and too long and embrac[ed] too many subjects to attract much support." He also criticized the subtreasury system, and added that he believed that the Democratic Party would "devise a system less expensive and more conservative than the sub-treasury." He added that "The Industrial classes [sic] are almost a unit in favor of a more elastic and less centralized system of finance; but most of them look to the [D]emocratic Party for relief in that direction. If this [finance] plank in the Cincinnati platform was more specific and conservative it would endanger [D]emocratic successes."[59]

When Gibbs addressed an audience in Lancaster, Texas, the following day, the subject of his speech was Democratic Party organization and the third-party threat. Addressing a crowd of some two hundred voters, the Democrats, he said, could "do more than any third party for the people."[60] In an effort to counter the People's Party's subtreasury plan, he sought to promote discussion of the "financial question" by offering a bill that would establish banks of circulation. Admonishing his party, Gibbs said that "If the [D]emocratic leaders who aspire to, or now enjoy the emoluments and honors of public office, don't do something besides throwing a few silver dollars into circulation to relieve the people of the money trust, they will be left after the next congress adjourns. The [D]emocratic party," he continued, "will have to shoot or give up the gun." As a warning to the Democratic Party, he added, "Party tradition and veneration won't go anymore. The [D]emocratic party can't be today what it was twenty-five years ago . . . people can change leaders . . . just like they swap horses."[61] Clearly, Gibbs recognized the potentially formidable threat posed by a political coalition comprised of workers and farmers. If these two groups could unite, the Texas Democratic Party would be in serious trouble.

Soon after, on May 28, 1891, Dallas workingmen held the inaugural meeting of the People's Party in their city. Situated in a vacant lot behind the Dallas city hall, the "well-attended" meeting featured patriotic paraphernalia and lively speakers championing the cause of common men. Visually reminding the crowd of its commitment to the promise of American ideals, "United States flags enfolded the platform and a hedge of them waved over its sides."⁶² The designated speakers, at least two of whom had regularly attended and participated in Labor League discussions about the third party, railed against the old parties for having ignored the calls for reforms that would ease the plight of the common man. The criticisms of the old parties and the arguments that had previously dominated Labor League meetings were now being brought to the public in an open-air meeting in the heart of Dallas. Local Populists moved forth to bring labor fully into the People's Party movement as Texas insurgents worked to establish themselves statewide.⁶³

In addition to laying out the reform agenda and articulating their reasons for bolting the old parties, the new Populists, who had publicly criticized Democratic Party stalwart Gibbs's banking plan in the days before the meeting, verbally attacked him at their inaugural meeting. The focus, however, was on the common man's plight and what the new party could do for him. Too long had workingmen suffered at the hands of the powerful and well connected, and now was the time for change.⁶⁴

Although it was "well attended," and despite its sharp political rhetoric, the meeting did not instantly generate a mass movement in the city, but it marked a turning point in Dallas's political history. The atmosphere was ripe for change. The April mayoral election left many workingmen disgusted with the Democratic Party. In addition, the city council had refused to discuss the possibility of an eight-hour workday on public works, and workingmen had recently been reminded of their lack of solidarity by the failed cable railway strike. These recent experiences, along with the emergence of a national party and discussions of the third-party movement taking place in Dallas and throughout the country, made the chance to be part of a formal, national reform party attractive.⁶⁵

The Eight-Hour Labor League, many of whose members now joined the People's Party, continued to meet and discuss Populist political philosophy and the subtreasury bill. Enthusiasm for the new party dominated the Labor League's discussions as the July 3, 1891, Sulphur Springs Federation of Labor meeting approached. Promoters billed the event as one that would change the course of history. James Fitzgerald, a Dallas laborer and acting secretary of the Federation, pronounced, "The Sulphur Springs convention will be one of the things of its kind to be remembered in Texas history, the woods being 'literally full of reformers,' down in eastern Texas. The laboring people of the state will be fully represented."⁶⁶ The enthusiasm with which the Dallas delegates had left Cincinnati had caught fire in Texas.

In the days before the convention, the press sought comment from those prominent men who would attend. On July 2, 1891, a reporter for the *Dallas Morning News* interviewed W. R. Lamb, of Bowie, Texas, en route to the convention. Lamb, the chairman of the national Executive Committee of the People's Party in Texas, also served as the president of the State Reform Press Association. When asked if the Texas Federation of Labor would declare its support of the People's Party at Sulphur Springs, Lamb said that he did not know, but expected the organization "to do so at some time in the near future."[67]

The next day, July 3, 1891, under a headline that read "DEMOCRATS SCARED UP," the *Dallas Morning News* reported that "The [D]emocrats of Sulphur Springs look upon the convention as nothing less than a section of the [P]eople's party, and are watching every move."[68] P. H. Golden denied that the convention was a political one, the report, however, noted that principles advocated by the People's Party were slated as topics for discussion at the meeting. In addition, the convention agenda convinced Sulphur Springs Democrats that the labor convention held a third-party motive. W. R. Lamb himself surveyed the crowd with respect to their third-party leanings. He fueled Democratic fears by announcing that he found the delegates solidly for the People's Party and the subtreasury.[69]

Despite concerns spreading among Sulphur Springs Democrats, Federation president P. H. Golden, for reasons unknown, tried to tamp down rumors. "This convention of the Federation of Labor," said Golden, "is not in any manner identified with the [P]eople's party in this or any other county." Even though his presidential address discussed many of the same topics raised in People's Party meetings, he claimed that the Federation was comprised of men of all political parties. "The fact that a great many members of the Federation," Golden continued, "and of various organizations embraced in it, have joined the [P]eople's party movement is because they have despaired from relief from them [the old parties] and have been convinced that it is useless to hope longer."[70] Whether or not the Federation met to officially serve as a forum for the third party, a gathering of so many Populist delegates served this purpose regardless of how observers and participants characterized it.

Among the keynote speakers who addressed the crowd was H. A. Spencer, an avowed Dallas Populist and a fixture at Dallas labor meetings, who had addressed the Populists during their inaugural meeting. In his address to the Federation, Spencer berated the old parties and their leadership but, perhaps in a final effort to gain concessions from the old parties, stopped just short of endorsing the People's Party. Indeed, the *Dallas Morning News* remarked, "The proceedings of the convention were not marked by the political tendencies which the [F]ederation generally gets credit for," but, it continued, "the outcroppings of dissatisfaction with the [D]emocrats and [R]epublican parties were too plain to be misunderstood."[71]

Democratic leadership worried about the potential that such a meeting could have on the political scene. One leading Democratic politician, after hearing the platform, remarked that "this order may not be a political one, but a serious effort on the part of labor organizations to put that platform into action would result in one of the most powerful political movements." The *Morning News* further observed that while many Federation delegates claimed that they were still allied with the old parties, these delegates were also willing to join "what they term the reform movement" unless the old parties made changes soon.[72]

Although the delegates publicly stated that the meeting was not political, it clearly was. Those who attended, as well as those who reported the event, were well aware of this fact. While third-party politics and the link between the Federation and the People's Party were downplayed by all convention-goers except for W. R. Lamb, who unequivocally spoke of the connection, the Federation's ties to the People's Party were indisputable. P. H. Golden, as well as H. A. Spencer, respectively the Federation president and a keynote speaker at the convention, were two of the leading players in the drive for the organization of the Dallas People's Party. James Fitzgerald, the secretary and treasurer of the Texas State Federation, played a critical role in the Dallas Populist Party, too. At least two of the three, Golden and Fitzgerald, had previous experience in organizing labor. Their political consciousnesses had likely developed over many years. During these years each must have witnessed disappointments while trying to achieve reform through the existing parties. Now, it seemed, while they would have liked the traditional parties to take up their causes, they knew they could not be trusted to do so.

In the aftermath of the Sulphur Springs meeting, the convention's proceedings, its platform, and the benefits of a third party figured prominently in Dallas Labor League discussions while labor leaders continued to press a reform agenda.[73] At one meeting, Fitzgerald raised before Democrats the third-party specter, when he complained, "Labor has long obsequiously done the will of the old parties; but if those parties wish to live they must now do the righteous will of the deeply wronged labor, or a new party, loyal to the toiling masses, will take possession of the government in the name of the industrial people of this great republic." Likening the Sulphur Springs labor platform to the Populists' Cincinnati platform, Fitzgerald said that those platforms "voice[d] the principles of reform, which the majority of the industrial voters of the United States in the ranks of toil believe in." He announced his belief that the laboring classes would "no longer make themselves a political nonentity by standing divided, but will form a great invincible army of reform to redeem the nation from misrule."[74] Perhaps Fitzgerald had hoped that the threat of a third party would move the Democrats to act on labor's behalf. At this early date in the Populist Party's history however, most Texas Democrats dismissed the third party as a serious challenge to its hold on power.

As labor continued its discussions and pushed its reform agenda, the Dallas County Farmers' Alliance and the Dallas Branch of the Federation of Labor were strengthened their relationship. In July, the Alliance invited "all branches of organized labor in the City of Dallas" to attend a picnic it would host just outside of the city. H. A. Spencer and P. H. Golden consented to speak at the celebration, while the Federation volunteered to hire a band to provide entertainment. Such joint events served to cement the bonds between the organizations.[75]

Another turning point in the party's establishment in Texas took place when the state Farmers' Alliance and the state People's Party scheduled overlapping meetings in August 1891 in Dallas; this caused a stir among Democratic partisans. The eyes of Texas were upon Dallas as observers contemplated the meaning of these virtually concurrent meetings. Observers anticipated the arrival of prominent third-party men who would speak at the convention. These included W. R. Lamb of Bowie, head of the Texas State People's Party, who in Cincinnati had been chosen as a member of the National Executive Committee of the People's Party. According to Lamb, one of the Populist convention's goals would be to adopt the platform outlined in Cincinnati and to define the state party's official position on other issues. In their attempt to strengthen the party throughout the state, the party also intended to establish regional, county, and district committees.[76]

The People's Party held its first Texas statewide convention, which was indeed "the founding meeting of the People's Party in the South," on August 17–19, 1891, in Dallas.[77] Lamb opened the meeting in the Dallas City Hall auditorium with as many as 150 people present. As his first act of official business, he appointed members to the committee on permanent organization and to the platform committee. Federation president P. H. Golden of Dallas sat on both committees. During the evening session of the convention, the delegates formally endorsed the national platform of the People's Party adopted in Cincinnati and added eleven more planks specific to the Texas party. After two days of meeting, the convention adjourned, and party leaders announced that they would reconvene in Fort Worth in February 1892.[78]

The Texas State Farmers' Alliance convention began on August 18, 1891, and its delegates shared the same headquarters, the Phoenix Hotel, as the People's Party delegates. Of the 2,000 delegates in attendance, 121 were sent by Texas County Alliances. Evan Jones, president of the Farmers' Alliance, presided over the convention, which was attended by prominent Alliancemen, including C. W. Macune and W. R. Lamb. Throughout the convention speculation concerning the relationship between the Alliance and the People's Party continued. The *Morning News* wrote "that four-fifths of the men now in Dallas as Alliance delegates have cast loose from the old parties and are going to try their political parties elsewhere may be accepted as fact."[79] The *Morning News* wondered, however, what percentage of their constituencies did the delegates with third-party leanings represent? Whatever wild speculation ran rampant in the press, the proceedings of the convention confirmed that the Alliance and the People's Party shared many members.[80]

Before the convention adjourned, delegates heard many anti-monopoly speeches that sounded much like those heard just days earlier at the People's Party convention. Some of the same faces and voices seen and heard at the Populist convention were now seen and heard at the Alliance meeting. And the principles and platforms endorsed and adopted likewise sounded remarkably similar. Reporters noted the congeniality among members of the two groups as they mixed in the hotel where delegates from both groups lodged. The "atmosphere [in the hotel] seemed laden with the essence of peace and brotherly love," one journalist reported. Leaders of the organizations "had a regular old-fashioned love feast." And, the reporter continued, it was well known that many members of the third party were prominent members of the Alliance. Certainly, Dallas laborers who founded the Dallas branch of the People's Party and who were in joint attendance at both conventions, were not far from officially joining political forces in the People's Party.[81]

While the Alliance and the People's Party members denied any collusion between the two organizations, the press suspected that a partnership was already underway. Elsewhere in Texas, meetings occurred that underscored the beginning of a shift in the political winds. In one editorial, the *Dallas Morning News* explained that "The demands of the People's party are such as to afford the prospect that it will attract the wage workers and farmers in large numbers." Whether the old parties recognized the People's Party threat so soon after its inception, the *Morning News* certainly did, or at least wanted the Democrats to take note of the political threat that the third party posed. The editorial continued, "What the men in public life now have to realize is that every candidate is required to answer yes or no to the People's party demands. Irrespective of the wisdom or unwisdom of the People's party platform, this requirement is a proper one."[82]

Despite the initial groundswell of enthusiasm, People's Party organization in Dallas stalled in 1892. P. H. Golden, who had spearheaded the third-party movement, left the party and resumed his affiliation with the Democrats and was later elected to political office. Golden became the object of scorn for the city's Populists, who viewed him as a traitor.[83] Without Golden's powerful leadership, the movement suffered. In 1893, however, by the time Dallas held its municipal election, the city's Populists had organized and began meeting weekly, as the old Dallas Central Eight-Hour Labor League transformed itself into the Dallas Central Populist Club, meeting in the city's Elm Street labor hall. They continued to espouse their political philosophies and worked to recruit new members to the organization. While never running a complete slate of candidates at the city level, the Populists supported party candidates for county offices and endorsed those candidates who ran for city office as nonpartisan independents, against Democratic Party nominees. In doing so, they claimed victory at the polls in Dallas. In addition, the Dallas Populists discussed and engaged in political action, with some serving important roles in the larger arena of state party politics.[84]

While never enjoying the political victory and reform its member sought, the state People's Party did enjoy some success in the coming years, before the national party collapsed in 1896, in essence, putting an end to the movement, and ending the regular meetings of the Dallas Populist Club in the Elm Street labor hall. The state party continued to nominate candidates for office, including Barnett Gibbs, the former People's Party critic, who ran as the gubernatorial candidate in 1898. He lost the election and by 1900 returned to the Democratic Party.[85] While a farmer-laborer coalition could not achieve long-term change at the national level, such a coalition did enjoy limited, short-term victories nationally, as recent scholars have shown. This examination of workers' involvement in People's Party organization building helps scholars appreciate the level of discontent of urban workers that led them to join a third party with agrarian and urban roots.

Thus, while the southern People's Party is generally recognized as a party organized by farmers, by the end of the summer of 1891, it was clear that Dallas laborers took the lead in establishing a branch of the party in their city, and in cooperation with the farmers, helped set the foundations of the state party.[86]

Notes

1. C. Vann Woodward, *Origins of the New South, 1877–1913* (Baton Rouge: Louisiana University Press, 1951), 252; Chester McArthur Destler, *American Radicalism, 1865–1901: Essays and Documents* (New London: Connecticut College Press, 1946); Robert C. McMath Jr., *American Populism: A Social History* (New York: Hill & Wang, 1993); Patricia Evridge Hill, *Dallas: Making of a Modern City* (Austin: University of Texas Press, 1996), 23–29. Evridge examines elements of the Populist-Labor coalition in Dallas, Texas, as party of a broader political and social history of the city. Gregg Cantrell and Kristopher B. Paschal, "Texas Populism at High Tide: Jerome C. Kearby and the Case of the Sixth Congressional District, 1894," *Southwestern Historical Quarterly* 109 (2005): 30–70, examines that congressional district that included Dallas County and argues that a successful farmer–labor coalition was being built there prior to the national party's collapse. Recent studies of Populism that include attention to labor's role include Matthew Hild, *Greenbackers, Knights of Labor, and Populists: Farm-Labor Insurgency in the Late-Nineteenth-Century South* (Athens: University of Georgia Press, 2007); Michael C. Pierce, "The Plow and The Hammer: Farmers, Organized Labor, and the People's Party in Ohio" (Ph.D. diss., Ohio State University, 1999); Charles Postel, *The Populist Vision* (New York: Oxford University Press, 2007). Studies that examine Populism and the role of labor in southern cities include Alicia E. Rodriguez, "Urban Populism: The People's Party in Dallas, Texas, 1887–1900" (Ph.D. diss., University of California, Santa Barbara, 1998); Julia M. Walsh, "'Horny-Handed Sons of Toil': Workers, Politics, and Religion in Augusta, Georgia, 1880–1910" (Ph.D. diss., University of Illinois at Urbana-Champaign, 1999).

2. Rodriquez, "Urban Populism," for broader treatment of the People's Party in Dallas. See John. D. Hicks, *The Populist Revolt: A History of the Farmers' Alliance and the People's Party* (Minneapolis: University of Minnesota Press, 1931); James Turner, "Understanding the Populists," *Journal of American History* 67 (September 1980): 354–373, for interpretations that focus on farmers' economic hardships and the isolation they experienced in modern America, respectively.

3. McMath, *American Populism*, 6–9; Hill, *Dallas*, 23–24, 26–37.

4. Lawrence Goodwyn, *Democratic Promise: The Populist Moment in America* (New York: Oxford University Press, 1976), 52, 286; Patricia Evridge Hill, "Origins of Modern Dallas" (Ph.D. diss., University of Texas, Dallas, 1990), 193; Alwyn Barr, *Reconstruction to Reform: Texas Politics, 1876–1906* (Austin: University of Texas Press, 1971), 109–110. Hild, *Greenbackers, Knights of Labor, and Populists*, 1–4; Ruth A. Allen, *The Great Southwest Strike* (Austin: University of Texas Press, 1942), 86–87, 90–91; Third Annual Report of the Commissioner of Labor, "Strikes and Lockouts, (1887)," 587. Figures for Dallas show

4,003 men employed by the Gould system before the strike. After the strike the number was 3,795. Of those employed after the strike, 495 new employees had been recruited from outside of Dallas. Of the 1,157 men in Dallas officially on strike, two-thirds of them, approximately 700, ended up losing their jobs. At least in later years, the Farmers' Alliance used the labor hall in Dallas for its meetings. *Southern Mercury*, January 1, 1891; American Federation of Labor, Dallas Branch meeting minutes. University of Texas, Arlington, Special Collections. AR5, Box 11, folder 2a, November 6, 1892.

5. Barr, *Reconstruction to Reform*, 110; McMath, *American Populism*, 79; Goodwyn, *Democratic Promise*, 234.

6. Winkler, *Platforms*, 268; Quoted in Goodwyn, *Democratic Promise*, 142.

7. Winkler, *Platforms*, 270–271.

8. Janice Lancaster, "Dallas and the Early Railroads" (M.A. thesis, Southern Methodist University, 1971), 21, 30; McMath, *American Populism*, 74; Kenneth W. Wheeler, *To Wear a City's Crown: The Beginnings of Urban Growth in Texas, 1836–1865* (Cambridge, MA: Harvard University Press, 1968), 161–166; John Stricklin Spratt, *The Road to Spindletop: Economic Change in Texas, 1875–1901* (Austin: University of Texas Press, 1955), 254–255, 282, 300; Henry Woodfin Grady, "Future of the Two Races: What the South Owes the Negro, and What His Place in Progress Should Be—The Wonderful Possibilities of the South," An Address of Hon. Henry W. Grady, of Atlanta, Georgia, Delivered at Dallas, Texas, October 27, 1888. Series title: Pamphlets on U.S. History and Politics. Holdings of University of California, Berkeley. See also Paul M. Gaston, *The New South Creed: A Study in Mythmaking* (New York: Knopf, 1970).

9. Woodward, *Origins*, 231; *Dallas Morning News*, May 6, 1891. The city had two main newspapers, the *Dallas Morning News*, a morning paper, and the *Dallas Times-Herald*, an afternoon paper. Thus, events and meetings occurring in the city were often reported the day they took place in the *Herald*, but not until the following day in the *Morning News*. Rodriquez, "Urban Populism" 52–55, 87–89, 93–94, 100–113.

10. Winkler, *Platforms*, 273; Barr, *Reconstruction to Reform*, 109.

11. Dallas *City Directory*, 1889–1890. Gregg Cantrell, *Feeding the Wolf: John B. Rayner & The Politics of Race, 1850–1918* (Wheeling, IL: Harlan Davidson, 2001), 36, 46; Goodwyn, *Democratic Promise*, 286. See also Rodriquez, "Urban Populism."

12. Winkler, *Platforms*, 274.

13. Ibid., 274–275.

14. *Southern Mercury*, July 24, 1890; *Memorial and Biographical History of Dallas County, Texas* (Chicago: Lewis Publishing Company, 1892), 939; Dallas *City Directory*, 1891–1892, 1893–1894.

15. *Dallas Morning News*, January 11, 1891.

16. Ibid., December 4, 1890.

17. Ibid.

18. Ibid.; Armstrong, "City of Dallas Mayors," 23–25, Dallas Public Library; *Dallas Morning News*, December 4, 1890; April 7, 1891.

19. *Dallas Morning News*, January 12, 1891.

20. Ibid., December 8, 1890.

21. *Dallas Daily Times-Herald*, December 9, 1890.

22. *Dallas Morning News*, December 8, 15, 1890.

23. Ibid.; Dallas *City Directory*, 1889–1890.

24. Often hailed as a great Progressive-era reform, the Australian or secret ballot posed danger of disfranchisement for illiterate voters. In addition, ballots printed by the southern state governments also proved effective tools at disfranchising voters. Perhaps Diffey was unaware of the potential drawbacks to the reforms for which he called. See J. Morgan Kousser, *The Shaping of Southern Politics* (New Haven, CT: Yale University Press, 1974), 51–60; Michael Perman, *Struggle for Mastery: Disfranchisement in the South, 1888–1908* (Chapel Hill: University of North Carolina Press, 2001), 19–21.

25. *Dallas Morning News*, December 15, 1890; Dallas City Charter, 1887, section 10; 1889, section 7.

26. McMath, *American Populism*, 140–141.

27. *Dallas Morning News*, January 5, 1891.

28. Ibid.; McMath, *American Populism*, 141–142. In later newspaper reports Spencer is referred to as H. A. Spencer. *Dallas Morning News*, May 29, 1891; July 4, 5, 20, 1891.

29. *Dallas Morning News*, January 5, 1891.

30. Ibid.

31. Ibid., January 12, 1891; Dallas *City Directory*, 1891–1892.

32. *Dallas Morning News*, January 12, 1891.

33. Ibid.

34. Ibid.

35. Ibid.

36. Ibid.

37. Goodwyn, *Democratic Promise*, 285–288. Wade regularly spoke at Labor League meetings and later became a regular speaker at People's Party Club meetings. Even after the national party collapsed in 1896, Wade remained hopeful of the party's future, claiming, "I'se a populist till I die." *Dallas Morning News*, November 26, 1896.

38. Goodwyn, *Democratic Promise*, 8–9; Woodward, *Origins*, 244; Edward L. Ayers, *The Promise of the New South: Life After Reconstruction* (New York: Oxford University Press, 1992). Ayers's chapter on Populism, 249–282, describes in detail the ridicule that third parties and those who joined them faced.

39. *Dallas Morning News*, January 19, 1891.

40. Ibid.

41. Ibid.

42. Gerald H. Gaither, *Blacks and the Populist Revolt: Ballots and Bigotry in the "New South"* (University: University of Alabama Press, 1977), 29–30; Woodward, *Origins*, 254–255; Kousser, *The Shaping of Southern Politics*, 29–31.

43. *Dallas Morning News*, February 28, 1891; *Dallas Times-Herald*, March 2, 1891; Hicks, *The Populist Revolt*, for the classic economic hard times interpretation, and Turner, "Understanding the Populists," for the isolation experienced by farmers. *Dallas Morning News*, March 9, 16, 23, 1891.

44. *Dallas Morning News*, March 30, 1887.

45. *Dallas Times-Herald*, February 7, 10, 1891.

46. Ibid., February 10, 1891.

47. *Dallas Morning News*, May 11, 1891; Alicia E. Rodriquez, "Disfranchisement in Dallas: Independent Party Challenges to Democratic Party in Dallas, Texas, 1891–1894," *Southwestern Historical Quarterly* 108 (2004): 43–64.

48. *Dallas Morning News*, May 6, 1891. The *Morning News* reprinted the text of the May 5, 1891, circular in its May 6, 1891, edition.
49. *Dallas Morning News*, May 6, 1891.
50. *Dallas Times-Herald*, May 18, 1891.
51. Ibid.
52. McMath, *American Populism*, 146.
53. *Dallas Morning News*, May 13, 1891; Dallas *City Directory*, 1891–1892.
54. *Dallas Morning News*, May 21, 1891.
55. McMath, *American Populism*, 144–146.
56. *Dallas Morning News*, May 25, 1891; McMath, *American Populism*, 145–146.
57. *Dallas Morning News*, May 27, 1891.
58. Ibid.
59. Ibid.
60. Ibid., May 24, 1891.
61. Ibid.
62. Ibid., May 29, 1891.
63. Ibid.
64. Ibid., May 24, 29, 1891.
65. *Dallas Morning News*, December 4, 1890, January 12, 1891; *Dallas Times-Herald*, May 18, 1891; *Dallas Morning News*, May 19, 1891.
66. *Dallas Morning News*, June 1, 1891; *Dallas Morning News*, June 17, 23, 25, 28, 29, 1891; *Dallas Times-Herald*, June 30, 1891.
67. *Dallas Morning News*, July 2, 1891.
68. Ibid.
69. Ibid., July 3, 1891.
70. Ibid., July 4, 1891.
71. Ibid.
72. Ibid., July 5, 1891.
73. Ibid., July 6, 13, 18, 20, 22, 27, 1891; *Dallas Times-Herald*, July 13, 1891.
74. *Dallas Morning News*, July 20, 1891.
75. Ibid.
76. *Dallas Times-Herald*, August 17, 1891; *Dallas Morning News*, August 17, 18, 19, 1891.
77. Goodwyn, *Democratic Promise*, 286–287.
78. *Dallas Times-Herald*, August 17, 1891; *Dallas Morning News*, August 18, 1891; *Dallas Morning News*, August 18, 19, 1891; Winkler, *Platforms*, 293–297.
79. *Dallas Morning News*, August 21, 1891.
80. Ibid., August 19, 21, 1891; *Dallas Times-Herald*, August 14, 15, 23, 1891.
81. *Dallas Morning News*, August 21, 22, 23, 1891; August 17, 18, 1891.
82. *Dallas Morning News*, August 28, 1891.
83. Ibid., August 6, 1892, and March 24, 1894.
84. Ibid., April 6, 1893; March 31, 1894; September 22, 1894; Cantrell and Paschal, "Texas Populism at High Tide," 30–70, discusses the campaign of Sixth Congressional District Populist candidate Jerome Kearby, a resident of Dallas. See also Rodriquez, "Urban Populism," for detailed treatment of the Dallas People's Party's activities after 1891.
85. Rodriquez, "Urban Populism," 371–372.

86. See endnote one for recent studies that examine the farmer-laborer elements of Populism. Ibid., 223, 258–260, 264–271, 315–366; *Dallas Morning News*, March, 10, 18, 24, 31, April 6, 1893.

Agrarian Rebel, Industrial Workers

TOM WATSON AND THE PROSPECTS OF
A FARMER-LABOR ALLIANCE

—MICHAEL PIERCE

By the time former Georgia congressman Thomas E. Watson ran for the nation's vice presidency on the People's (Populist) Party ticket in 1896, he had abandoned one of the core tenets of the party's founding, the idea that the party should unite all of the nation's producers of wealth. The party's 1892 Omaha platform had asserted, "the interests of rural and civic labor are the same; there [sic] enemies identical." But on the campaign trail in 1896, Watson conceived of the People's Party not as a national producerist party but as an agrarian and sectional one that united the farmers of the South with those from the West. In Lincoln, Nebraska, he insisted, "Relief must come from the South & the West. No hope from East & North." In Alma, Nebraska, Watson told those assembled that the "purpose of Populism" reflected the agrarian interests of those from the "South and the West." In Nashville, the People's Party standard-bearer portrayed the Populist movement as simply a revolt of farmers in the South and the West against the hegemony of the industrial East.[1]

Watson's abandonment of the idea that the People's Party should unite all of the nation's producers of wealth and his embrace of a more narrow Populist vision did not suddenly happen during the 1896 campaign. It had been coming slowly. As early as 1895, Watson began to distance himself from the Omaha platform with its eloquent identification of the party as a "union of the labor forces."[2] Instead, he called on the People's Party to embrace the agrarian reforms that the Southern Farmers' Alliance (National Farmers' Alliance and Industrial Union) demanded at Ocala in 1890. At the heart of Watson's evolving conception of the People's Party was his fear of the increasing influence of industrial workers and trade unionists, especially those from the Industrial Midwest, in party affairs. Rather than welcoming urban trade unionists into the People's Party, Watson, like other Populist leaders, took steps to alienate them.

Tom Watson's attempts (and those of other Populist leaders) to drive urban labor and trade unionists from the party challenge what has long been an article of faith among historians of Populism, that People's Party leaders would have welcomed the support of urban trade unionists, especially those associated with the American Federation of Labor (AFL). Until the 1990s, historians of Populism usually followed the lead of John Hicks, never examining the attitudes of organized labor except to quote AFL president Samuel Gompers, who in 1892 publicly derided the notion that the farmer-led party was "one in which the wage-workers will find their haven." Gompers went on, "Composed, as the People's Party is, mainly of *employing* farmers without any regard to the interests of the *employed* farmers of the country districts or the mechanics and laborers of the industrial centres, there must be a divergence of purposes, methods, and interests."[3] For some historians, the apparent refusal of urban trade unionists to join the People's Party was understandable. Lawrence Goodwyn, for instance, insists that the Omaha platform offered little of appeal to urban workers and that trade unionists did not participate in the Farmers' Alliance's "movement culture," which he saw as so essential to the success of the People's Party. Norman Pollack, however, lays the blame for the failure of the People's Party to forge an effective farmer-labor alliance "not with agrarians but with labor, especially its leadership." He goes on to state that the AFL "killed the farmer-labor movement" and "guaranteed the ultimate downfall of Populism."[4]

Since the 1990s, historians have started to look more closely at the relationship between organized workers and the People's Party, finding far more cooperation than the earlier studies suggested. Most of this work has focused on the activities of organized workers within specific localities or regions, and no region has received as much attention as the South. Building on the work of Daniel Letwin, Karen Shapiro, and Alicia Rodriquez, Matthew Hild has recast the way that historians understand southern Populism, finding widespread support for the People's Party among organized labor in the South, especially the Knights of Labor. Historians no longer attribute the failure of southern Populism to a lack of support from the labor movement or the inability to bridge the farmer-worker divide. This essay complicates the growing consensus. Leaders like Watson may have at times accepted the support of the relatively small number of organized workers within the South, men who could help win close elections at the local and state level and would always be relegated to secondary roles in party matters, but they did not feel the same way about trade unionists from the Industrial Midwest or other regions who joined the party, men who at times refused to play second fiddle to the party's agrarian leadership and did nothing to help southern or western Populists at the polls.[5]

Tom Watson entered Georgia politics rooted in an agrarian tradition that had denigrated northern industrial workers and their organizations since the antebellum era. Recalling the development of his political ideas, Watson declared, "I gloried in Bob Toombs."[6] Robert Toombs, who represented Georgia in the U.S. House of Representatives and Senate throughout the 1840s and 1850s, had been among the South's most articulate and vigorous defenders of the peculiar institution and the plantation system it sustained. Toombs insisted that the slave system was morally superior to the free labor systems found in the North and Great Britain, comparing the ordered agrarian society of the South to the anarchy and licentiousness brought about by ideas of freedom and equality in the North. Whereas the slaveholder saw to it that slaves were provided food, clothing, shelter, and moral guidance even in times of economic difficulties, the employer of free labor felt no such obligation to workers, laying them off in response to market conditions, working hard to reduce their wages below poverty levels, and stripping them of the independence and virtue necessary to be true citizens. Much as Watson would in the Populist era, Toombs viewed the "strikes and mobs and labor unions and combinations against employers" that characterized northern cities not as assertions of rights and citizenship but rather as evidence that industrialization had rendered workers unfit citizens and threats to the republic.[7]

After the Civil War, Toombs had little choice but to reconcile himself to the abolition of slavery, but he never gave up his agrarianism or his hostility toward corporations and the free labor system. Constructed in opposition to urban and industrial labor, Toombs's agrarianism became its most strident when he fought Georgia's apostles of "New South" industrialization like Henry Grady. Toombs wanted the South to continue to look to cotton to sustain its economic and moral order and avoid the "helter skelter scramble for wealth" that was beginning to make the region more closely resemble the North. By the time that Watson first encountered Toombs in the early 1880s, agrarianism had led Toombs to embrace what one biographer called "an early day Populism": railroad regulation, the elimination of class legislation, and laws to curb monopolies and the growth of corporations.[8]

At the start of the Populist era, Watson paid lip service to the idea that the movement should be an alliance of farmers and industrial workers. In

May 1891, he told a group of workingmen in Augusta, Georgia, "[T]he cause of labor is the same everywhere, whether in the fields or the factory, in railroads, mines, storehouses, or dockyards."[9] But Watson never thought that industrial workers and farmers were political equals. Sounding much like his mentor Toombs, Watson insisted that industrial workers, especially those in the urban North, were a degraded lot, dependent, unmanly, unable to fulfill the duties of citizenship, and thus easily manipulated by machine politicians, corporate despots, or radical demagogues. He explained to the readers of his newspaper, the *People's Party Paper*, how the existence of industrial workers threatened the nation's political system: "the bulldozing of working men has been one of the main reliances of the plutocracy in the North." Since industrial workers were powerless to free themselves from this coercion, farmers needed to move to the forefront to defend the republic. Likening industrial workers to antebellum slaves, a common trope among late-nineteenth-century labor reformers in the North but one that had a particular resonance in Georgia, Watson insisted that it was up to the farmers to stop ruthless capitalists from "fasten[ing] still more strongly the chains upon the industrial classes."[10]

Watson's early paternalism and condescension toward urban and industrial workers gave way to contempt and fear during his unsuccessful campaigns for Congress in 1892, 1894, and the special election of 1895. Watson entered these campaigns wary of the effects that factory workers, especially those in Augusta, the Tenth District's only industrial center, would have on the election. He warned in May 1892 of "threats [being] made [by] manufacturers employing large numbers of men that extra burdens would be laid upon those who dared to exercize [sic] the rights of free men and vote the People's party ticket."[11] Watson would later attribute each of his defeats to the bulldozing of factory and mill hands in Augusta, even though the historian Julia Walsh has demonstrated that Watson regularly carried the city's Fifth Ward, where most of these workers were concentrated. Never one to allow evidence to intrude upon his political ideas, Watson told the readers of his paper that his defeats provided evidence of the fact that the economic elite "control the voters in the cities and towns just as overseers used to control slave labor upon the plantations."[12]

Watson's fears of trade unionists and industrial workers grew after the Panic of 1893 set off a wave of labor and industrial unrest, particularly in the Industrial Midwest, that region bordered by the Great Lakes and the Ohio River. The unrest began in the late winter of 1894, when Jacob Coxey, a wealthy Ohio entrepreneur and monetary reformer who had been part of his state's delegation to the 1892 St. Louis convention that formally created the People's Party, announced plans for a march of unemployed men from Massillon, Ohio, to Washington, D.C., to demand congressional action to create jobs to help the nation's three to five million unemployed. Some 125 marchers strong, Coxey's "petition in boots" left Ohio on Easter Sunday, creating a media sensation far out of proportion to its modest size. Although the marchers were always peaceful and generally well behaved, as Coxey's contingent neared Washington and similar industrial armies were organized throughout the nation, fears of marauding bands of unemployed gripped the city. Many of the nation's leaders went into near hysterics. Several notable Populists, including William Peffer and William Allen, offered support to Coxey and his demands, but Watson refused to join them. The *People's Party Paper* brusquely declared that it did not "approve" of Coxey's proposal to have the federal government put people to work on roads and other public improvements. But the paper reserved most of its scorn for Coxey's method of lobbying Congress, calling the creation of an army of unemployed men "a vital mistake." Even after Coxey was arrested and imprisoned for twenty days for trying to speak on the steps of the Capitol building, Watson was unable to muster any sympathy or words of support, though he did use the occasions to criticize President Cleveland and the leaders of Congress for their actions.[13]

In late spring and early summer of 1894, Watson looked on in horror as the industrial unrest continued. This time it was led by a friend of Coxey, United Mine Workers of America (UMWA) president John McBride.[14] As thousands of the nation's factories shut in the wake of the Panic of 1893, the demand for bituminous coal dropped, causing market prices to fall and mine operators to abrogate wage scales they had signed with the UMWA. Hoping to create a shortage that would raise the market price of coal to the point at which the negotiated scales could be restored, the UMWA launched a strike with the support of some of the nation's largest mine operators. All but 24,000 of the nation's 184,000 coal miners joined the strike. Within a few weeks the market price of coal had risen to pre-panic levels, and the UMWA asked operators to reinstate the negotiated scales. The operators, some of whom were happy to continue selling their stockpiles at inflated prices, refused to do so. At this point, what had been a peaceful strike turned nasty, with miners and their allies in the American Railway Union (ARU) trying to stop shipments of scab coal by removing coal cars from trains and burning rail bridges at strategic points. The strike ultimately failed as hunger forced miners back to work at much reduced scales. Uninterested in the particulars of the strike and unable to express any sympathy for the miners, the *People's Party Paper* portrayed the episode simply as another example of industrial workers threatening the health of the republic. Watson's paper described the strikers as being "bent on destroying property, and preventing, through violence and terrorism, the filling of their places from the ranks of the hungry and unemployed."[15]

Watson's outrage at industrial workers and their unions reached its peak during the summer's Pullman strike and boycott. In response to declining orders for sleeping cars, the Pullman Company cut wages and raised the rents of its employees, who were obligated to live in company housing. These workers went on strike in May 1894, after negotiations to restore the wage cuts failed. As the strike wore on, Pullman strikers appealed to the ARU, and the Eugene V. Debs–led union announced that its members would boycott Pullman cars—that is, refuse to attach sleeping cars to trains or to operate trains with the sleeping cars already attached. The ARU's action precipitated a showdown with the railroad's trade association, the General Managers' Association (GMA), which intended to break both the boycott and the union. After the GMA's attempts to form a private security force to intimidate strikers failed, it began placing mail on Pullman cars, which gave United States attorney general Richard Olney a pretext to mobilize federal troops to squash the boycott. Meanwhile, a federal judge ordered the arrest of Eugene Debs for violating an injunction forbidding the union from interfering with the operations of the rail lines. Watson responded to these events much like he had the coal miners strike. He blamed the ARU for the episode and accused Eugene Debs of "paralyz[ing] the commerce of the country, incit[ing] insurrection, and redden[ing] the streets with innocent blood."[16]

The very events that provoked Watson's fears of industrial workers and trade unionists also transformed the People's Party in the Industrial Midwest as the men at the center of these upheavals, Coxey, McBride, and Debs, brought tens of thousands of workingmen into the Populist ranks. The People's Party had never attracted many of the farmers or workingmen of the Industrial Midwest, mostly because of the vibrancy of the two-party system in the region, but the strikes, boycotts, and arrests of 1894 convinced large numbers of the region's trade unions and labor federations that corporations had corrupted both major parties and that united political action through the People's Party offered the only salvation for the nation's workingmen. From the mine and steel towns of western Pennsylvania westward to the industrial cities of Illinois and Wisconsin, the People's Party became a workingman's party tied closely to urban labor federations as well as the UMWA and ARU.

Jacob Coxey and John McBride were at the forefront of labor's embrace of the Populist movement. In the wake of the nationwide coal strike and the Pullman boycott, McBride told Ohio trade unionists that capital's use of state militias, federal troops, and labor injunctions "allow only one kind of strike on the part of labor, and that strike must be with the ballot box." Since "it was evident that labor cannot hope for relief at the hands of either the Republican or Democratic party," McBride called for the formation of an Ohio labor party and scheduled its first meeting for the eve of the state's Populist convention in the hopes of affecting a merger. McBride's labor party, with support from every major urban labor federation in the state, issued a platform that emphasized the public ownership of monopolies. Using language that borrowed heavily from the Omaha platform, the trade unionists demanded that "the power of government, in other words, of the people, should be expanded (as in the case of the postal service) as rapidly and as far as the good sense of an intelligent people and the teachings of experience shall justify along the lines of collective ownership of all such means of production and distribution as the people may elect to operate." The next day, McBride easily convinced his old friend Jacob Coxey and other leaders of the Ohio People's Party to adopt the labor platform as their own, and the trade unionists became Populists.[17] Similar alliances were affected throughout in the region, all demanding some form of collective ownership of monopolies. In Illinois, journalist Henry Demarest Lloyd and machinist Tommy Morgan engineered the entrance of a large contingent of Chicago trade unionists into the People's Party. In Wisconsin, Milwaukee workingmen, led by Robert Schilling and Victor Berger, formed the core of the state's People's Party. In Michigan, only the opposition of Detroit trade unionists who were unwilling to endanger their alliance with Hazen Pingree (a Republican who endorsed much of the Populist platform) prevented that state's labor movement from formally endorsing the People's Party. In Indiana, ARU president Eugene Debs and UMWA vice president Phil Penna emerged as the most important Populist leaders.[18]

Labor's support led to dramatic increases in votes for the People's Party in the region. In 1894, Ohio Populists tripled their 1892 results with the largest increases in the industrial and mining areas. In Milwaukee, the vote jumped from about 1,296 (2.5 percent) in 1892 to 9,479 (19 percent) in 1894. In Chicago, support for the People's Party increased from about 2,000 (0.6 percent) voters in 1892 to close to 40,000 (12 percent) in 1894.

In Minneapolis, the Populists garnered 35 percent of the vote, and in the Twin Cities the party tallied almost as many votes in 1894 as the party had received in the whole state in 1892. Communities in the coal belt running from Western Pennsylvania through Illinois gave as much as 55 percent of the vote to the Populists. Henry Demarest Lloyd enthused, "the workingmen are rapidly coming to the conclusion to have nothing more to do with the old parties, that they will work with the People's Party."[19]

The large numbers of trade unions and labor federations endorsing political activism through the People's Party divided the membership of the AFL. As the *Chicago Tribune* explained,

> the greatest turmoil came with the Populist craze last election [1894] when a handful of designing ringsters in each of the larger bodies of trade unions tried to pledge their respective organizations to the Populist party. From the moment the scheme was broached there was a division. Lines were sharply drawn between the two factions. For want of a better name the new faction was called the "Socialists," while the men belonging to the conservative element, wishing their organizations to have nothing to do with politics, called themselves "strict trade unionists."[20]

The first showdown between the "Socialists" and the "strict trade unionists" came at the AFL's annual convention in December 1894. Although federation delegates refused to formally endorse partisan activity along the lines of Populism, they did ratify a platform that resembled the People's Party's and elected one of the "Socialists," John McBride, to the federation's presidency.[21]

Upon taking office, McBride insisted that the federation should help create a "union of labor men" that would "place a presidential candidate in the field" in 1896. McBride's language echoed the words of the People's Party's Omaha platform, which called the party a "union of labor forces," and his intent was unmistakable, he wanted to align the AFL with the People's Party. According to the *Cleveland Citizen*, McBride would spend a good part of his year in office advocating "in favor of independent political action along the lines of Populism." As he told Pittsburgh-area trade unionists, "If I had my way, there would be a labor party that would sweep all evils from the land."[22]

The rise of labor-Populism in the Industrial Midwest and within the American Federation of Labor increased tensions within the People's Party as three distinct factions emerged, each emphasizing different aspects of the Populist program and with different visions of the future of the party and the nation. The dominant faction—led by party chairman Herman Taubeneck and James Weaver, the party's 1892 presidential candidate—insisted that the party concentrate on the free and unlimited coinage of silver at a ratio of 16 to 1. Others, led by Tom Watson, stuck to the broad-gauged reform program of the Southern Farmers' Alliance—subtreasury plan, greenbacks, and free trade. Trade unionists and their allies from the Industrial Midwest and elsewhere emphasized government ownership of railroads, telegraphs, and other monopolies as the first step toward solving the nation's problems.

The first test of the strength of the three factions came at a conference called by party chairman Taubeneck at St. Louis for late December 1894. Although more people had voted for the People's Party in 1894 than ever before, Taubeneck and Weaver feared for the party's future and insisted that the party focus its platform on the free and unlimited coinage of silver at a ratio of 16 to 1. The Populists had not fared well on the Great Plains and Rocky Mountain West in the elections of 1894, losing gubernatorial offices in Colorado and Kansas and representation in state legislatures. Additionally, the American Bimetallic League's threat to create its own party devoted to the free coinage of silver had the potential of further eroding Populist support, and Weaver and Taubeneck worried that labor's increasing support for the party would taint it with radicalism and violence. To solve these problems, they argued that the party must trim the broad-based Omaha platform, getting rid of its most radical planks. To this end, Weaver and Taubeneck invited three hundred party activists to a conference in late December 1894 in St. Louis for the purported purpose of preparing for the 1896 campaign.[23]

Watson emerged as the most prominent opponent of the emphasis on free silver. He immediately opposed any attempt to trim the Omaha platform. Before the conference even began, Watson called Taubeneck's tactics "dangerous" and insisted, "The Omaha Platform constitutes our marching workers."[24] The *People's Party Paper* declared, "Don't monkey with our platform. Stand your ground like men, and fight for it until you die."[25] As C. Vann Woodward explained, "The genuine Populist of the South, the old-time Alliance man ... was never seriously befuddled by the free silver panacea."[26]

Taubeneck and Weaver's plan to use the St. Louis conference to trim the Omaha platform backfired. Taubeneck had not invited the "Socialists," but

Henry Demarest Lloyd and Jacob Coxey attended anyway determined to block what Lloyd saw as an attempt to "throw the radicals in the party overboard."[27] Lloyd arrived with a declaration written by former Illinois senator Lyman Trumbull that reaffirmed the broad-gauged demands of the Omaha platform and called for government ownership of all monopolies "affecting the public interest." Coxey arrived seeking to have his Good Roads and Non-Interest-Bearing Bonds Plan, a greenback/public works/gas and sewer socialism program, endorsed by the convention. At the convention, Lloyd and Coxey outmaneuvered the leadership at every turn, forcing the fight over the platform out of committee and onto the floor. In the end, the convention refused to trim the Omaha platform. Instead it adopted Trumbull's declaration and endorsed Coxey's plan. It was a complete victory for Lloyd, Coxey, and their trade union allies.[28]

Despite the setback at St. Louis, Taubeneck and the trimmers did not give up. They did, however, change tactics. Instead of extolling the virtues of silver, Taubeneck complained that "socialists" had "captured" the party and insisted that the emphasis on free silver was the only way to avoid "the destructive doctrines of the socialists."[29] Shortly thereafter, Taubeneck and the Populist members of Congress, except for Kansas senator William Peffer, signed a manifesto drafted by Weaver demanding that the party focus its energy on the silver question.[30] An editorial in the *National Watchman*, the closest thing the party had to an official organ, justified this action: "The time for Populism and Socialism to part has come.... Let us be conservative in order to secure the support of the businessmen, the professional men, and the well to do. These are elements we must use if ever success comes to our party. For every loud-voiced socialist who declares war on us, we will get a hundred of the conservative element of society."[31]

While Watson opposed Taubeneck and Weaver's attempts to focus on the free and unlimited coinage of silver, he shared their fears about the increasing influence of trade unionists in party affairs and the demands for greater government ownership of monopolies. Like other Populist leaders, Watson seemed to take satisfaction in the fact that the Populist vote in Chicago declined in the spring 1895 municipal elections. He would later write: "In Chicago, the hot bed of Socialism, Democrats and Republicans get all of the votes. The Populists are nowhere. And yet Chicago will send a red-hot delegation to our next National Convention 'demanding' that our Platform be further twisted to suit their radical ideas."[32]

Watson's growing fear of the labor movement and its increasing influence in the People's Party can be seen in a rambling and mostly incoherent article that appeared in the *People's Party Paper* on November 29, 1895. The article called attention to the split of the AFL into "two great divisions," those who wanted to transform the federation into a partisan organization and those who wanted to steer clear of partisan politics. It suggested that Eugene Debs, who was about to be released from prison, would attempt to reorganize the AFL's constituent unions along industrial rather than craft lines—much like the ARU and the UMWA, the two unions most closely identified with the Populist cause. Such a reorganization would "make it far easier" to transform the federation into a partisan organization. "It is understood," the article continued, "to be the purpose of the leaders to capture the machinery of the People's party."[33]

A month later, in December 1895, Jacob Coxey, organizer of an army of unemployed industrial workers, close ally of John McBride, one of the "Socialists" who had captured the 1894 St. Louis Convention, a rival of Watson's for a spot in the People's Party's 1896 ticket, ventured into Georgia as part of a southern speaking tour. Coxey had been busy since his arrest and twenty-day imprisonment in the late spring of 1894. That fall, he had run as a Populist for Congress, collecting over 25 percent of the vote in a district that included Akron, Canton, Massillon, and several smaller steel and mining towns. In the fall of 1895, Coxey ran for governor of Ohio on the People's Party's ticket, receiving over 50,000 votes, again mostly from urban and industrial areas. After this last defeat, Coxey hit the road, scheduling a series of speaking engagements across the country to tout his Good Roads and Non-Interest-Bearing Bond Plan and to better his chances for a spot on the national ticket in 1896.

Coxey's Good Roads and Non-Interest-Bearing Bond Plan was relatively simple, calling for federal financing of public works to end unemployment. Coxey wanted the national government to issue five hundred million dollars in bonds to state and local governments to be used for building roads and making public improvements such as power plants and sewer systems. The bonds, which would circulate as legal tender, and construction jobs that would pay $1.50 a day would stimulate other economic growth through improvements in infrastructure and an enlarged money supply. States and municipalities would repay the bonds with a 1 percent annual fee, the same rate that the government charged privately held national banks, over the course of twenty-five years. Coxey insisted that Congress should give states and cities wanting to create jobs the same terms that it gave bankers seeking corporate profit. Although his plan offered little direct aid to the nation's farmers, Coxey insisted that giving work to the unemployed would increase demand for food and fiber, thus spreading prosperity to the agricultural sector.³⁴

Coxey arrived in Atlanta in December 1895, just as the Georgia People's Party was convening its annual convention. There a local Knights of Labor leader, whom the *People's Party Paper* referred to as a "labor agitator," introduced a resolution inviting Coxey to address the gathering. The resolution passed, but Watson subsequently arranged to have the invitation withdrawn, telling reporters that Coxey "may not be [a Populist]. I have heard that he does claim to be a populist, but he is very much more pronounced than are southern populists. He has some extreme ideas." Such a response suggests that Watson considered Coxey and the trade union faction of the party he represented to be so outside of the Populist orthodoxy that they should be shunned and driven from the party.³⁵

During the convention and the subsequent acrimonious exchange with Coxey, Watson reiterated his fears that "socialists" were trying to take control of the People's Party and insisted that retreating from the Omaha platform was the only way to prevent such a takeover. At the heart of Watson's argument was his belief in a secret socialist plot, a plot in which Coxey was playing a central role: "Socialists have opened fire on us and are moving all of their secret machinery against us. They do not come manfully and say that they are socialists . . . . They . . . push the People's Party further and further, slyly but resolutely, until they got it committed to their own radical and vicious doctrines." Watson added that Georgia Populists had a duty to "open the eyes of the people to the stealthy approaches which the socialists are making to secure control of the People's Party."³⁶

The socialists must have begun plotting early because, according to Watson, "[at] Omaha the wording of one plank was altered to make it capable of being as construed into an attack on the private ownership of land." Despite the socialists' action, southern Populists had voted for candidates standing on the Omaha platform "believing that our [Ocala] platform had not been altered at Omaha." Since Georgia Populists did "not believe in Socialism with the collective ownership of land, homes, and pocketbooks," Watson argued that the only logical step was to dump the tainted Omaha platform and reembrace the one that the Southern Alliance drew up in Ocala in 1890.³⁷

After his confrontation with Coxey, Watson wrote Marion Butler boasting of his treatment of the Ohioan and reiterating his desire to steer the party clear of the trade union Populists and their allies from the Industrial Midwest: "[T]he Georgia Populists gave Coxey the cold shoulder and adopted the most conservative platform that the party has put forth. Speaking for myself, I do not hesitate to say that I will not go a step further toward Socialism and Radicalism than the Georgia platform goes. It is highly desirable, it seems to me, that those of us who favor this moderate and conservative course should begin to educate public sentiment in that line ... to the end that the extremists shall not control our next National Convention."[38] Butler's response to Watson has been lost, but in a subsequent letter Watson insisted that the two men "are in perfect accord" regarding Coxey and his allies. Watson also proposed that the North Carolinian take over the leadership of the party, since Taubeneck had proven unable to control Coxey, Lloyd, and the "Socialists." The party, Watson said, needed a chairman "who has nerve enough to rule with a rod of iron those hot-headed recalcitrants who want to load us down with extreme isms."[39]

Trade union Populists reacted angrily to Watson's attacks on Coxey. Eugene Debs and Henry Demarest Lloyd exchanged letters complaining of Watson's "tirade." Debs fumed, "I agree with you entirely that Mr. Watson has no rational conception of what 'Socialism' really is." The *Akron Advocate*, a workingman's paper, criticized Watson for his "criminal ignorance" and his efforts to "belittle" Ohio's Populists. Ralph Beaumont, a longtime leader of the Knights of Labor, insisted that Watson's intolerance was becoming detrimental to party—"nothing can be done if it is not done his way." The *Cleveland Citizen*, published by that city's Central Labor Union, denounced Watson's "sadly ignorant ... conception of socialism" and his "ridiculous tirades against the socialists in the People's party." At the root problem, the paper continued, is that "Mr. Watson is a lawyer" and thus has little sympathy for those who actually produce the wealth of the nation.[40]

As Taubeneck and Weaver continued their efforts in early 1896 to trim the Omaha platform, Watson and the midwestern labor-Populists briefly overcame their mutual distrust, forging an uneasy alliance built around opposition to both a platform based exclusively on the free coinage of silver and any sort of fusion with the Democrats. At the 1896 St. Louis convention, Watson-led southern Populists and the "Socialists" joined to protest the nomination of Democrat William Jennings Bryan, but by that time they knew that his nomination and some type of fusion were inevitable. As Henry Demarest Lloyd put it on the eve of the convention, "If we fuse, we are sunk; if we don't fuse, all the silver men will leave us for the more powerful Democrats."[41] As a sop to the southern Populists and in hopes of preventing the party from being completely swallowed by the Democrats, the convention nominated Watson for the vice presidency. Populists hoped that the Democrat's vice presidential nominee, Arthur Sewell, would step (or be pushed) aside for Watson, but this did not happen.

Throughout the fall, Watson, the only national figure campaigning under the People's Party's banner, redefined the Populist movement in a way that marginalized midwestern trade unionists and their allies. He abandoned the idea that the People's Party should attempt to unite all of the nation's producers of wealth. Instead, he articulated a vision of People's Party as a sectional and agrarian movement, one that brought together the farmers of the South and the West. In speech after speech, he hit on the same themes, "Relief must come from the South & the West. No hope from East & North"; "South & West must unite"; "Foundation of People's Party—Revolt of South & West"; "South & West against East & North." Part of this formulation was an effort to get Sewell bumped off the Democratic ticket, but it also reflected Watson's longstanding agrarianism, his faith in farmers and fears of industry and those it employed.[42]

Watson's reformulation of Populism as a sectional, agrarian movement made little strategic sense. Both presidential campaigns focused their attention on the Industrial Midwest, with Republican candidate William McKinley conceding much of the South and the West to Bryan, and Bryan assuming that McKinley would take the populous states of the industrial northeast. Only the broad swath running from Ohio to Wisconsin was really in play, and that is where the two major political parties devoted most of their resources. The chairman of the national People's Party Campaign Committee understood these dynamics and advised Watson to focus on the region, especially trade unionists in Illinois and Michigan. He optimistically explained, "Chicago has one hundred and thirty-four thousand Trade Unionists, and the man who gets this vote gets Chicago, and the man who carries Chicago will carry Illinois, and the man who carries Illinois will come very close to carrying the nation." Watson's response has been lost, but his hostility toward Chicago's trade unionists, in particular, and the region's industrial workers, more generally, has been established. Needless to say, he did not follow the advice. During the campaign, Watson limited his appearances to the agricultural states south of the Ohio River or west of the Mississippi, never venturing into Chicago or anywhere else in the Industrial Midwest to solicit votes for Bryan or the People's Party.[43] Watson did not want the region's trade unionists and urban workers in the People's Party, and he was not going to ask for their votes.

While Watson could turn his back on the workingmen of Chicago, Cleveland, and Milwaukee, he could hardly ignore industrial workers living in the South and the West, whose votes he hoped the party would need in the future. On Labor Day he spoke at a workingmen's picnic in Dallas, addressing industrial workers for the only time during the campaign. The historian Alicia Rodriquez has demonstrated that urban workingmen formed the backbone of the People's Party in Dallas and that the labor-led Populist movement presented a creditable challenge to the city's Democratic machine.⁴⁴ But Watson, ever the agrarian, could not bring himself to treat these Populist workingmen with the same respect that he reserved for farmers. Instead, he hectored them, lecturing them as though they were wayward children, neglectful, unruly, dependent, and in need of discipline, rather than voters who needed to be swayed by rational arguments or to have their enthusiasm roused. Wrongly assuming that those in the audience had voted overwhelmingly for the Democratic Party, Watson demanded that Dallas workingmen abide by an agreement that the leaders of the Knights of Labor made seven years earlier: "I am here today to remind you laboring men of the cities that you entered a contract with the laboring men of the country, and you ought to stand by it." Watson explained, "At St. Louis in 1889 seventeen labor organizations, representing the organized labor of the cities of this republic, met the western farmers and the southern farmers and signed an agreement that they would act together and vote together until the reforms demanded in the platform had been enacted." He scolded the workingmen for not living up to the agreement and insisted that they were morally obligated to vote for the People's Party. Watson wanted the votes of these workingmen, but he also wanted them to be quiet and do what the agrarian leaders of the People's Party told them to do.⁴⁵

Tom Watson was, as C. Vann Woodward so succinctly put it, an "agrarian rebel." His agrarianism, rooted in the ideas of Robert Toombs as well as Thomas Jefferson and John C. Calhoun, became the lens through which he viewed urban workingmen and their unions, both those in Augusta and those in the Industrial Midwest. These workingmen appeared to him as dependent, unmanly, unruly, without virtue, and, ultimately, dangerous to the republic; they were easily manipulated by both plutocrats and radical demagogues. Watson's actions—blaming workingmen for electoral defeats, criticizing striking miners and railroaders, fearing a secret plot to capture the party, insulting Jacob Coxey, abandoning the Omaha platform for the one drawn up at Ocala, rejecting the idea that the People's Party should unite all producers of wealth—make it clear that he did not consider workingmen to be suitable partners within the People's Party. As Watson wrote in early 1896, the differences between those he defined as real Populists and the trade unionists he called the "Socialists" were "vital and irreconcilable."[46] Thus Watson took steps to run them out of the party.

Watson was hardly alone among the traditional leaders of the Populist movement in his antipathy toward trade unionists. Marion Butler, Herman Taubeneck, and James Weaver also worked to push the "Socialists" out of the party. All of this calls into question not only the traditional historiographic argument that party leaders would have welcomed trade unionists into the party but also suggests that the party was much more fragile and unstable than historians have realized. By late 1894, three distinct factions of Populism had emerged, the free silverites led by Weaver and Taubeneck, broad-gaugers led by Watson, and the "Socialists" who called for government ownership of all monopolies affecting the public interest. By late 1895, this division had prompted the leaders of the two largest factions to repudiate the Omaha platform. At that time, only the "Socialists" were standing by the People's Party's founding principles. Thus, even before the fusion of 1896, the movement was already coming apart with fault lines that Watson considered to be "irreconcilable." The seeds of Populism's demise might have already been planted.

Notes

1. Notes for Lincoln, NE, speech, September 16, 1896; notes for Alma, NE, speech, September 17, 1896; notes for Nashville, TN, speech, October 23, 1896, folder 287, Thomas E. Watson Papers, Southern Historical Collection, Wilson Library, University of North Carolina, Chapel Hill, http://www.lib.unc.edu/dc/watson/ (accessed October 20, 2009).

2. The Omaha platform can be found at "The Omaha Platform: The Launching of the People's Party," http://historymatters.gmu.edu/d/5361/ (accessed March 19, 2010).

3. John D. Hicks, *The Populist Revolt: A History of the Farmers' Alliance and the People's Party* (Minneapolis: University of Minnesota Press, 1931), 115; Richard Hofstadter, *The Age of Reform: From Bryan to FDR* (New York: Knopf, 1955), 99; Samuel Gompers, "Organized Labor in the Campaign," *North American Review* 15 (July 1892): 91–96.

4. Lawrence Goodwyn, *Democratic Promise: The Populist Moment in America* (New York: Oxford University Press, 1976); Norman Pollack, *The Populist Response to Industrial America: Midwestern Populist Thought* (New York: Norton, 1966), 64–65.

5. Matthew Hild, *Greenbackers, Knights of Labor, and Populists: Farmer-Labor Insurgency in the Late-Nineteenth-Century South* (Athens: University of Georgia Press, 2007); Daniel Letwin, *The Challenge of Interracial Unionism: Alabama Coal Miners, 1878–1921* (Chapel Hill: University of North Carolina Press, 1998); Alicia E. Rodriquez, "Urban Populism: Challenges to Democratic Party Control in Dallas, Texas, 1887–1900" (Ph.D. diss., University of California at Santa Barbara, 1998); Karin A. Shapiro, *New South Rebellion: The Battle against Convict Labor in the Tennessee Coalfields, 1871–1896* (Chapel Hill: University of North Carolina Press, 1998).

6. C. Vann Woodward, *Tom Watson, Agrarian Rebel* (1938; reprint, New York: Oxford University Press, 1963), especially 39–40.

7. Ulrich Bonnell Phillips, *The Life of Robert Toombs* (New York: Macmillan, 1913), 155–166 (quotation, 163). Also see, Robert Toombs, Tremont Temple speech, January 24, 1856, reprinted in Alexander H. Stephens, *A Constitutional View of the Late War between the States: Its Causes, Character, Conduct, and Results* (Philadelphia: National Publishing, 1868), I: 625–647.

8. William Y. Thompson, *Robert Toombs of Georgia* (Baton Rouge: Louisiana State University Press, 1966), 266–248 (first quotation, 231; second, 236).

9. Thomas E. Watson, "Labor-day Address at Augusta, Georgia, May 1891," in *Life and Speeches of Thomas E. Watson* (Thomson, GA: Jeffersonian Publishing, 1911), 75.

10. *People's Party Paper*, May 13, 1892; second quotation cited in Julia Walsh, "'Horny-Handed Sons of Toil': Mill Workers, Populists, and the Press in Augusta, 1886–1894," *Georgia Historical Quarterly* 81 (Summer 1997): 311–344.

11. *People's Party Paper*, May 13, 1892.

12. Walsh, "Horny-Handed Sons of Toil"; *People's Party Paper*, October 18, 1895, cited in Robert Saunders, "The Transformation of Tom Watson," *Georgia Historical Quarterly* 54 (Fall 1970): 339–356 (quotation, 342). Saunders links Watson's preoccupation with Augusta's mill hands to his subsequent abandonment of the Omaha platform for the one formulated in Ocala. Sanders, though, argues that Watson's switch from Omaha to Ocala was part of an effort to win the support of workingmen, whom he assumed found the Omaha platform too radical.

13. *People's Party Paper*, April 13 ("approve"), May 11 ("vital mistake"), 1894. For more on Coxey's march, see Carlos Schwantes, *Coxey's Army: An American Odyssey* (1985; reprint, Moscow: University of Idaho Press, 1994); Michael Pierce, *Striking with the Ballot: Ohio Labor and the Populist Party* (DeKalb: Northern Illinois University Press, 2010), 164–168. For more on the Populist congressional delegation's support of Coxey, see Robert C. McMath Jr., *American Populism: A Social History, 1877–1898* (New York: Hill and Wang, 1993), 186–187.

14. Coxey and McBride were both from Massillon, Ohio. At the 1893 convention of the American Federation of Labor, McBride secured passage of a resolution supporting Coxey's Good Roads Plan, a greenbacks/public works program; Schwantes, *Coxey's Army*, 32.

15. Pierce, *Striking with the Ballot*, 156–163; *People's Party Paper*, June 15, 1894 (quotation).

16. Nick Salvatore, *Eugene V. Debs: Citizen and Socialist* (Urbana: University of Illinois Press, 1982); Almont Lindsey, *The Pullman Strike: A Story of a Unique Experiment and of a Great Labor Upheaval* (Chicago: University of Chicago Press, 1942); *People's Party Paper*, July 20, 1894.

17. *United Mine Workers Journal* (Columbus, Ohio), August 9, 23, 1894; *Columbus (Ohio) Dispatch*, August 14, 16, 1894.

18. Chester McArthur Destler, "Consummation of a Labor-Populist Alliance in Illinois, 1894," in *American Radicalism, 1865–1901* (1946; reprint, Chicago: Quadrangle Books, 1966), 162–174; Chester McArthur Destler, *Henry Demarest Lloyd and the Empire of Reform* (Philadelphia: University of Pennsylvania Press, 1963), 263–289; Caro Lloyd, *Henry Demarest Lloyd, 1847–1903, A Biography* (New York: G. P. Putnam and Sons, 1912),

244; Martin J. Klotsche, "The 'United Front' Populists," *Wisconsin Magazine of History* 20 (1937): 375–389; Roger E. Wyman, "Agrarian or Working-Class Radicalism? The Electoral Basis of Populism in Wisconsin," *Political Science Quarterly* 89 (Winter 1974–1975): 825–847; Salvatore, *Eugene V. Debs*, 147–160; Richard Jules Oestreicher, *Solidarity and Fragmentation: Working People and Class Consciousness in Detroit, 1875–1900* (Urbana: University of Illinois Press, 1986), 242.

19. Philip Foner, *History of the Labor Movement in the United States*, vol. 2, *From the Founding of the American Federation of Labor to the Emergence of American Imperialism* (New York: International Publishers, 1947), 325–326 (Lloyd quotation); *Report of the Ohio Secretary of State, 1894* (Columbus, 1895); Michael Nash, *Conflict and Accommodation: Coal Miners, Steel Workers, and Socialism, 1890–1920* (Westport, CT: Greenwood Press, 1982), 54–55. Although the percentage of voters casting ballots for the People's Party in the Industrial Midwest may seem small when compared to the numbers in the South or on the Great Plains, it should be pointed out that Populists in the Industrial Midwest competed in a vigorous two-party system. For an analysis of the ways in which the two-party system stifled third-party activism, see Jeffrey Ostler, *Prairie Populism: The Fate of Agrarian Radicalism in Kansas, Nebraska, and Iowa, 1880–1892* (Lawrence: University Press of Kansas, 1993).

20. *Chicago Tribune*, December 9, 1895.

21. *Chicago Tribune*, December 9, 1895; Michael Pierce, "The Populist President of the American Federation of Labor: The Career of John McBride, 1880–1895," *Labor History* 41 (Winter 2000): 5–24.

22. *National Labor Tribune* (Pittsburgh, Pennsylvania), January 10 (first quotation), October 31 (last quotation), *Cleveland Citizen*, November 16, 1895. Also see *New York Times*, January 2, 1895.

23. Chester McArthur Destler, "Free Silver vs. Collectivism: Disintegration of the Labor-Populist Alliance in Illinois," in *American Radicalism*, 227–228; *People's Party Paper*, December 14, 21, 1894; Frank L. McVey, "The Populist Movement," *Economic Studies* 1 (August 1896): 177; *American Non-Conformist* (Indianapolis), December 6, 1894.

24. *People's Party Paper*, December 14, 1894.

25. *People's Party Paper*, December 28, 1894.

26. Woodward, *Tom Watson*, 279.

27. Destler, "Free Silver vs. Collectivism," 229.

28. Destler, "Free Silver vs. Collectivism," 229–231; *American Non-Conformist*, January 3, 1895; *Chicago Tribune*, December 29, 30, 1894.

29. *American Non-Conformist*, February 21, 1895; *Cleveland* (Ohio) *Citizen*, February 16, 1895.

30. William Peffer, *Populism: Its Rise and Fall* (Lawrence: University Press of Kansas, 1992), 109–114; "Populist Manifesto—February 22, 1895," reprinted in McVey, "The Populist Movement," 201–202.

31. *National Watchman* (Washington, D.C.), February 22, 1895, reprinted in McVey, "The Populist Movement," 200–201. At the end of March 1895, Taubeneck assured the readers of the *New York World* that "The People's party at its next national convention will declare in favor of making the money question the 'great central idea'.... Those who desire to retard monetary reform by loading us down with other issues will, with the Socialists and Communists, go to the rear"; quoted in Peffer, *Populism*, 117–118.

32. *People's Party Paper*, November 15, 1895.

33. *People's Party Paper*, November 29, 1895.

34. Emery Bernard Howson, "Jacob Sechler Coxey: A Biography of a Monetary Reformer, 1854–1951" (Ph.D. diss., Ohio State University, 1973); Russell B. Nye, "Jacob Coxey," in *A Baker's Dozen: Thirteen Unusual Americans* (East Lansing: Michigan State University Press, 1956), 209–232; Schwantes, *Coxey's Army*, 37–40.

35. *People's Party Paper*, December 27, 1895; *Atlanta Constitution*, December 19, 20 (Watson quotation), 1895.

36. *People's Party Paper*, January 17, 1896. Other historians have noted Watson's confrontation with Coxey and his pronouncements on socialism, but they place them in different contexts and ignore Watson's belief that a conspiracy was afoot; Saunders, "The Transformation of Tom Watson, 1894-1895," 343–347; Shaw, *Wool-Hat Boys*, 171–173; Bruce Palmer, *"Man over Money": The Southern Populist Critique of American Capitalism* (Chapel Hill: University of North Carolina Press, 1980), 169–182.

37. *People's Party Paper*, December 27, 1895. Unlike the Omaha platform, the Ocala platform lacked a preamble proclaiming the unity of agrarian and industrial labor.

38. Thomas E. Watson to Marion Butler, December 23, 1895, Marion Butler Papers, Southern Historical Collection, Wilson Library, University of North Carolina, Chapel Hill (microfilm edition), reel 1. Georgia's 1895 Populist platform shed what Watson considered to be its most radical features—planks supporting the subtreasury system and abolition of alien landownership and the direct appeal to organized labor and industrial workers. Saunders, "Transformation of Tom Watson," 343–346.

39. Watson to Butler, December 28, 1895, Butler Papers.

40. Eugene V. Debs to Henry Demarest Lloyd, February 1, 1896, in *Gentle Rebel: Letters of Eugene Debs*, ed. James Robert Constantine (Urbana: University of Illinois Press, 1995), 23; *Sound Money* (Massillon, OH), January 7 (Akron quotation), 14 (Beaumont quotation), 1896; *Cleveland Citizen*, January 4, 1896.

41. Quoted in Caro Lloyd, *William Demarest Lloyd*, 1: 259.

42. See notes for speeches in folders 286–288, Watson Papers. For more on Watson's formulation of the People's Party as a sectional party, see Woodward, *Tom Watson, Agrarian Rebel*, 312–313.

43. George F. Washburn to Thomas E. Watson, September 3, 1896, folder 7, Watson Papers. Watson's campaign appearances in the late summer and fall of 1896 can be traced through the *People's Party Paper*. On the centrality of the Industrial Midwest in the 1896 campaign, see McMath, *American Populism*, 205.

44. Rodriquez, "Urban Populism," especially 258–314.

45. *Galveston Daily News*, September 8, 1896; Rodriquez, "Urban Populism," 359–360.

46. *People's Party Paper*, January 17, 1896.

"Hard Times Is the Cry"

DEBT IN POPULIST THOUGHT IN NORTH CAROLINA

—DAVID SILKENAT

Debt stood at the heart of the agrarian critique of American capitalist society. For Populists in North Carolina, across the South, and across the country, the problem of debt, both at the personal and communal level, was one of the primary issues that drove them to enter politics. Declining crop prices drove farmers to work harder every year in an attempt to pull themselves out of debt, only to find that the harvest yielded more bushels and less money than the year before. The resulting agrarian revolt challenged the existing political, social, and economic order in unprecedented ways. By the 1880s, farmers recognized that they could not combat their chronic indebtedness through individual effort; rather only collective political action could sufficiently reform the exploitive economic system.

Many white farmers in North Carolina concluded that their chronic indebtedness amounted to a form of slavery. One of North Carolina's most prominent agrarian reformers, Marion Butler, repeatedly compared the plight of the state's farmers to slaves. "For my own part," Butler argued, farmers' debts were "nothing less than a question of slavery or freedom."[1] Similarly, an elderly agrarian from Catawba County argued that "North Carolina is oppressed with debt and mortgages.... The people of this country have tasted liberty and they never will submit to be enslaved by a few. A revolution must come."[2] Samuel Archer, a farmer and Populist leader from Salisbury, claimed in 1896 that the Populist's stance against debt meant "freedom, not slavery; liberty not servitude."[3] Conversely, black farmers in North Carolina rarely compared debt to slavery, a surprising absence, not only because most black farmers were either born in or a generation removed from actual chattel slavery, but also because black farmers tended to be much more deeply mired in debt than their white neighbors, with far fewer opportunities to escape from the debt peonage of tenant farming.

This essay explores how North Carolina farmers understood the problem of debt in the final decades of the nineteenth century. It argues that black and white agrarians in North Carolina saw debt very differently. For instance, the ubiquity of the debt-slave metaphor among North Carolina's white agrarians and its near absence among black agrarians suggests that they approached debt from very different perspectives. White agrarians saw debt as a fundamental threat to their liberty and advocated for the creation of a new credit culture. They hoped to construct a new credit system that allowed farmers to have credit without social stigma, increased the role of the state in credit relationships, and reflected the economic realities of Gilded Age society. Black agrarians, however, were skeptical about debt reform measures such as the subtreasury plan or bimetallism advocated by white agrarians. While easing the crushing burden of debt experienced by black farmers in North Carolina was a political priority for black agrarians in the state, other issues, notably voting rights and election reform, remained higher priorities.[4]

Black and white agrarians drew upon decades of cultural and moral traditions about the meaning of debt. While black and white agrarians briefly came together in a political coalition, they brought with them two distinct interpretative schema about the social, cultural, moral, and financial meaning of debt. In comparing debt to slavery, for instance, Marion Butler was drawing upon more than a century of southern white rhetorical tradition. These differences created tension within the agrarian movement in North Carolina, divisions that undermined the movement's political effectiveness. To more fully understand how these different cultural traditions influenced Populist thought on debt, the first half of this essay examines how black and white North Carolinians understood debt between 1820 and 1880, arguing that race fundamentally shaped how debt was understood. The second half of this essay examines how these differences shaped the agrarian debate over debt in North Carolina.

For the purposes of this essay, the term "agrarian" refers to those who advocated a reform program intended to remedy the significant economic dislocation experienced by farmers in the final decades of the nineteenth century. Most white agrarians had some affiliation, officially or unofficially, with the North Carolina Farmers' Alliance. Many, but by no means all, later joined the Populist Party, while others stayed within the Democratic Party (or more rarely the Republican Party). Most black agrarians were members of the Black Farmers' Alliance, but remained politically affiliated with the Republican Party. The term "agrarian" will be used, therefore, as an umbrella term to refer to those who held a particular political philosophy rather than limiting it to members of one particular organization or political party. Because this essay focuses primarily on how North Carolina agrarians understood debt rather than the sometimes Byzantine history of agrarian politics, the following analysis of the agrarian movement in North Carolina will emphasize their public discourse on debt rather than the internecine battles that characterized the politics of the era.[5]

Throughout the nineteenth century, the structure of the southern agricultural economy meant that many of the region's residents, black and white, rich and poor, frequently went into debt. Three factors account for southerners' apparently perpetual indebtedness. First, because farmers could only expect to receive payment for their crops at harvest time, unexpected expenses, particularly in the summer months preceding the harvest, meant going into debt. Second, the limited amount of hard currency in circulation in the South both before and after the Civil War meant that most financial transactions had to be conducted on credit. Third, the South never developed a robust banking system, limiting the number of bank notes that served as economic lubrication elsewhere. One scholar has estimated that the cumulative effect of these factors meant that between two-thirds and three-quarters of all transactions in the antebellum South were conducted on the basis of credit; after the Civil War rates may have been even higher.[6]

North Carolinians employed a variety of strategies over the course of the nineteenth century to deal with the problem of debt in its social, cultural, and economic components. These strategies were not static; black and white North Carolinians changed how they understood and coped with debt depending on shifting economic conditions and social norms. Debt can be seen as both a financial instrument and as an intellectual and moral construct. The intent here is not to reinvent how scholars should think about various manifestations of debt, many of which have been thoroughly examined by economic historians, but rather to explore how these phenomena reveal cultural ideas about debt, and to observe how black and white North Carolinians' thoughts concerning debt changed over time.

Although debt of one form or another was ubiquitous throughout the South during the nineteenth century, indebtedness carried a significant social stigma for white North Carolinians during the antebellum period. Debt functioned as a fundamental threat to an individual's independence because it made the debtor assume a subordinate position to his creditor. Antebellum white southerners recoiled at the idea of dependence because they associated it with slavery. One of the distinguishing features of slaves, thought white southerners, was their subordination and dependence upon their master. Therefore, to enter into debt was to assume the position of a slave. While the metaphor comparing indebtedness to slavery was common throughout the United States during the nineteenth century, the symbol of the debt-slave was particularly palpable in the context of a slave society. As a result, most antebellum white North Carolinians sought to avoid indebtedness at all costs.[7]

At the same time, a desire for upward mobility and social standing often compelled white farmers to enter into debt. More than almost anything else, owning land and slaves demarcated social status in antebellum North Carolina. Tangible and visible, these forms of property offered antebellum white men access to the domain of mastery. To this end, they routinely violated the social prohibitions against debt in order to acquire these culturally and economically significant forms of property. Antebellum yeoman farmers often justified purchasing slaves on credit as a vehicle for social mobility. Indeed, buying slaves on credit was probably the greatest source of debt in the antebellum North Carolina and across the South. Antebellum white North Carolinians mediated the contradictory aspects of debt through the development of what anthropologists call a gift economy. Blurring distinctions between market and interpersonal transactions, gift-giving flourished in the antebellum white South because it functioned as needed credit without publicly making the recipient into a debtor. By engaging in reciprocal gift-giving, white North Carolinians created an informal credit system that simultaneously bound them horizontally and vertically in community and served a necessary economic role. This network of loans between white North Carolinians helped to create a system of mutual indebtedness that did not threaten to "enslave" its participants.[8]

Antebellum white North Carolinians did not, however, participate in this system indiscriminately. Instead, they established a socially sanctioned, informal set of rules that dictated to whom they could loan money and in what amounts, rules that one historian has described as an "etiquette of debt."[9] Although these rules varied from community to community and their interpretation was often determined by individual idiosyncrasies, they broadly required that participants in debtor-creditor relationships recognize each other as social peers, though not necessarily equals. Although planter-creditors maintained the façade of white male egalitarianism in their debtor-creditor relationships, poor white debtors recognized that their use of credit placed them in a subservient position and thereby threatened their liberty. For more than half of the antebellum white population in North Carolina who held little or no property, indebting themselves to their wealthier neighbors became the only way to sustain themselves. When the availability of credit contracted, these poor debtors suffered. In many cases, the calamity of their situation came not as much from their outstanding debts, but from their inability to tap into new sources of credit. Largely self-sustaining, at least compared to their postbellum descendents, poor white North Carolinians often needed to borrow money to pay their taxes. When hard times prevented them from borrowing, many poor farmers lost whatever property they owned in order to pay taxes in arrears. "A large majority of the people are farmers and are deeply in debt," farmers from Moore County wrote to the state legislature. "The consequence will be serious ... In vain have the people toiled laboured and economized. ... The property of the poore is rapidly passing into the hands of the rich—for a mere trifle."[10]

If poor whites suffered under the antebellum credit system, yeoman whites faired only slightly better. Even yeomen who wished to avoid debt could hardly avoid participating in local credit networks. Basil Armstrong Thomasson, a yeoman farmer and schoolteacher in Yadkin and Iredell counties, struggled throughout his life to balance his distaste of debt and the practical needs of his family. In January 1859, he noted in his diary that

> I've set in this year to get out of debt, and if we live and have health and strength enough to "push along, and keep moving," I think I'll come it. ... I must stop going in [debt] if I would get out. "Better to go to bed supperless," said Franklin, I think, "than get up in debt." Its [sic] bad to get up in debt, but I guess it would be well enough, generaly [sic], to go to bed supperless, or nearly so. We should eat to live, and not live to eat. O that I could govern myself in this matter of eating.[11]

The perils of debt were a reoccurring motif in Thomasson's diary. In one of his earliest entries, he notes that "I must curtail my expense and live on economy awhile." He was also critical of those who lived beyond their means, noting that "There is great danger of 'living too fast,' and most persons that buy on credit live in advance of their means," and "paying interest is bad business."[12]

Thomasson sought to avoid debt because he felt, in proper republican tradition, that debt threatened his independence. Many yeoman farmers in North Carolina continued to espouse the Jefferson ideal of the independent farmer, while they became increasingly embedded in the market economy. Like most yeoman farmers in the western Piedmont, Thomasson practiced a "safety first" model of agricultural production, growing most of his crops for his family's use rather than for the market. However, Thomasson's efforts do not necessarily indicate a rejection of the market economy, as Thomasson devoted a significant portion of his seventy-one-acre farm to tobacco, despite his personal repugnance to tobacco products. His forays in to the market, however, rarely netted Thomasson the kinds of returns that he desired. Thomasson's need for money pushed him into the local debt economy. Despite his efforts to the contrary, Thomasson relied upon local credit sources to meet his daily needs. He borrowed money from his neighbors, including local planters, and from shopkeepers. Thomasson became an integral part of a credit network based in kinship and social relationships, borrowing money from (and occasionally lending to) his social peers.[13]

North Carolina's black population, both slave and free, fell outside the gift economy credit system. Although scholars are increasingly recognizing the informal (and often illegal) economic relationships that transcended the color line during the antebellum period, the vast majority of these transactions were conducted via cash or barter. John Hope Franklin's seminal study of free blacks in antebellum North Carolina indicates that even under the best of conditions, free African Americans had difficulty securing credit. Planters were unwilling to grant credit to their black neighbors because doing so would effectively label them as an equal. Conversely, according to one fugitive slave, their inability to secure credit made slaves the preferred customers at antebellum general stores, as "The store-keepers are always ready to accommodate the slaves, who are frequently better customers than any white people; because the former always pay cash, whilst the latter almost always require credit."[14]

Although African Americans were largely excluded from local credit networks, enslaved North Carolinians suffered the heaviest costs when white debts went bad. Because debtors often used slave property as collateral or to settle debts, white debts often tore apart black families. Accounts of North Carolina slave life reveal that debt settlement was probably the most common reason why slave families were forcibly divided. Fugitive slave Moses Grandy described how his brother was abruptly clamped into irons and sold away from his family because "his master had failed; and he was sold towards paying the debts." Grandy's terse assessment concluded that "this is the usual treatment under such circumstances." Shortly thereafter, Grandy lost his wife because her owner found himself in debt. Near the end of his narrative, Grandy remarked that slave owners, "though they live in luxury, generally die in debt.... At the death of a proprietor, it commonly happens that his coloured people are sold towards paying his debts. So it must and will be with masters, while slavery continues."[15]

The experience of white North Carolinians during the Civil War fundamentally transformed their conception of debt. Their faith in the sanctity of the debtor-creditor relationship rapidly eroded as wartime economic conditions made predictable credit relations almost impossible. Rather than return to antebellum practices at the war's end, white North Carolinians struggled to construct a new conception of debt after 1865, reflecting postbellum economic and social conditions. Black North Carolinians experienced an equally radical reevaluation of the meaning of debt. Emancipation at the war's conclusion created the potential for many black North Carolinians to participate in white credit networks and to create credit networks and institutions of their own.[16]

Although a variety of factors contributed to economic dislocation during the Civil War, unprecedented levels of inflation did more than anything else to undermine white credit networks in North Carolina. Especially after 1863, the proliferation of Confederate paper money, coupled with myriad state currencies and widespread counterfeiting, and shortages of both consumer and agricultural goods resulted in hyperinflation in excess of 9,000 percent. By 1865, prices had risen so much that shoes in Wilmington sold for over $600 and wool overcoats for $1,500. Even in comparatively self-sufficient western counties, prices for foodstuffs increased dramatically, such that over the course of the war, the price of eggs increased 1,666 percent, flour 2,777 percent, and corn more than 3,000 percent.[17]

Under such conditions, even planters heavily invested in the gift economy realized the folly of lending money. Many creditors refused to accept Confederate currency, recognizing that its inflated value effectively negated the cost of the loan. North Carolina state treasurer and future governor Jonathan Worth found that he could not pay his personal debts with Confederate currency. In a letter dated August 1, 1863, Worth observed that he had more than enough money in Confederate currency to pay off his debts, but that none of his creditors would accept it. He concluded, "I am getting old and want to feel *out of debt* before I die."[18] Worth's difficulty in maintaining the antebellum system of credit reveals the extent to which the Civil War fundamentally challenged the gift economy in North Carolina.

The Confederate loss forced white North Carolinians to reassess the meaning of debt. Wartime conditions so decimated antebellum credit networks that they could not easily be resumed or reconstructed. Further, at the war's end, most white North Carolinians found themselves even more deeply in debt than they had been when the war began. For example, the McBee family of Lincoln County, North Carolina, emerged from the war more than twenty thousand dollars in debt, most of it from antebellum slave purchases. "I am perfectly satisfied in my own mind," wrote Alexander McBee to his brother Vardy, "that these debts will force me into Bankruptcy & that very soon."[19] Although their farm had survived the war unscathed, the loss of their slave property through emancipation meant that they now had to pay off debts on property they no longer owned. For the McBees and many other white families, the loss of their slave property meant the loss of almost half of their household wealth.[20]

This new conception of debt that emerged among white North Carolinians in the decades after the Civil War differed in two important respects from its antebellum precursor. First, it lacked the heavy moral overtones that characterized antebellum debt. To be sure, debt maintained certain negative connotations throughout the nineteenth century and beyond, but white North Carolinians increasingly thought and wrote about debt in pragmatic terms. Whereas antebellum white North Carolinians engaged in rhetorical feats to disguise their indebtedness, using the language of the gift economy, postbellum white North Carolinians routinely unmasked themselves as debtors. By thus exposing themselves as debtors, they created opportunities to recognize structural elements of the economy that maintained and exacerbated their indebtedness. This recognition that they belonged to a community of debtors prompted many North Carolinians to push for political and economic reform in the final decades of the nineteenth century.

The abolition of slavery contributed to the demise of the stigma that white North Carolinians pinned to debt. Without the pressing need to maintain the illusion of mastery, white North Carolinians became less attached to the idea that indebtedness implied dependence, and, by association, slavery. As the metaphor of the debt-slave lost its connection to actual chattel slavery, white North Carolinians found that they could contract debts without assuming the ideologically submissive position of a slave. The rhetorical value, however, of the debt-slave metaphor continued to touch a particular cultural chord among white North Carolinians and became one of the defining tropes of white Populist oratory.

For black North Carolinians, however, the debt-slave metaphor continued to have deep reverberations. Having secured their freedom in 1865,

African Americans avoided situations that resembled the exploitation they experienced in slavery. Some African Americans sought to avoid debt altogether because of the taint of dependence that it created. In September 1865, the *Journal of Freedom*, a black newspaper in Raleigh, urged it readers to "keep out of debt; work if possible, for men whom you esteem and trust; and each of you become land-holders so soon as you can without running into debt."[21] Although avoiding debt became a goal for many African Americans, the economic realities of the postwar South necessitated that they enter into credit relationships, most often with white landlords and shopkeepers. While debt never developed the social stigma among postbellum African Americans as it had among antebellum whites, they often imbued debt with moral connotations that no longer had much currency in the white community.

A second factor in the creation of a new postbellum conception of debt can be traced to the disappearance of antebellum social credit networks after the Civil War, replaced by more centralized models of credit in which many debtors owed money to an individual or entity. North Carolinians reconceived of debt in increasingly pecuniary terms, downplaying, although never entirely abandoning, its social aspects. The rapid modernization of the southern economy after 1865 pushed North Carolinians into novel credit relationships, most notably in the form of sharecropping, crop liens, and general stores. While sharecropping and crop liens represented labor arrangements as much as they did credit obligations, general stores represented the new credit system in its purest form. The proliferation of general stores after 1865 symbolized the rise of a new credit system, one simultaneously more formal, impersonal, and centralized than its predecessor.[22]

More than almost any other institution after the Civil War, general stores catered to a broad spectrum of southern society across lines of class, race, and gender. Selling a wide variety of products from groceries, whiskey, tobacco plugs, and dry goods to clothing, children's toys, farming implements, and patent medicines, general stores functioned as the primary locus of trade in most North Carolina communities. General stores also served a valuable social function where neighbors could congregate, exchange news, and socialize. In a cash-strapped economy, general stores also served as a central conduit for credit. Indeed, very few southerners could avoid routinely and repeatedly being indebted to general stores. An examination of general store account books from postbellum North Carolina indicates how the store centralized credit, tying community members from a range of backgrounds to a focal node. At the same time, these account books reveal how individual customers sought to mediate and control their indebtedness.[23]

Because of general stores' perceived prosperity, however, many North Carolinians came to resent them as parasites preying on the vulnerabilities of poor farmers. For men and women who toiled in the fields for hours under the sun, the apparent leisure enjoyed by general store keepers bred resentment. Many North Carolinians suspected that general store owners manipulated their account books to ensure that their customers remained indebted. According to George H. White, a black congressmen from Edgecombe County, and one of the most visible African American politicians during the "Fusionist" period, illiterate farmers suffered particularly from the tyranny of dishonest accounting, noting that "there is a great deal of fraud perpetrated on the ignorant; they keep no books, and in the fall the account is what the landlord and the storeman choose to make it."[24]

Some storekeepers sought to avoid the public animosity and other inherent problems in the general store system by functioning on a cash-only basis. The obvious drawback of this model was that it limited the amount of business that the store could entertain to the cash resources of its customers. The advantage of this model was that it could often offer lower prices than its credit-granting cousin because it did not have to factor credit costs into its prices. Cash stores also positioned themselves very differently in relation to their customers than credit-granting stores. Rather than assume the superior position of creditor, cash stores functioned as equals to their customers. This alternative social positioning reveals itself in the name that future Farmers' Alliance and Populist leader Leonidas L. Polk gave to the store he opened in Anson County the 1870s: "Farmer's Cheap Cash Store."[25]

To be sure, the cash store model rarely competed with credit stores in most communities. Of the more than four thousand general stores open in North Carolina in 1890, fewer than one in ten operated on a cash-only basis. The majority of these were in urban areas, where general stores often specialized. Besides Polk's Farmer's Cheap Cash Store, the most significant and important cash store in North Carolina was William Henry Belk's New York Racket Store in Monroe, the seat of Union County. Opened in 1888, Belk modeled his business on northern department stores. Unlike his credit-granting competitors, Belk offered a single cash price. "It was a new thing in our part of the county," Belk remembered. "I don't think anybody had ever tried it out down this way and mighty few anywhere." His friends warned him that such a scheme could not work, especially in a rural community like Monroe where most of his farmer-customers had little cash and were accustomed to purchasing on credit. To his friends' great surprise, the endeavor succeeded. Belk credited his success to the fact that his customers appreciated the feeling of shopping without the looming burden of debt. "When a fellow buys something and pays cash," Belk argued, "he just naturally feels good. He doesn't have that trade hanging over him." Belk's venture was so successful that he was able to open a second store in 1893, beginning the chain that would eventually evolve into the modern Belk's department store.[26]

The small number of general stores owned by African Americans often adopted the cash model. Located primarily in eastern North Carolina communities with high black populations, at least fifty-three black general stores between 1865 and 1879 generated enough business to attract the attention of northern credit agencies. Unfortunately, no business ledgers from black general stores have survived from nineteenth-century North Carolina, and therefore it is difficult to assess how credit practices differed in black and white general stores. The little anecdotal evidence suggests that black general store keepers were more conservative than their white counterparts in extending credit. For instance, in the 1890s, York Garrett's general store in Tarboro offered credit to fewer than half of its customers, all of whom were black.[27]

The failure of black general stores to offer credit hints at an ambivalence within the African American community over the entire idea of credit. Livingstone College president Reverend J. C. Price stood at one end of a wide spectrum of beliefs. Price argued that African Americans would be well served to borrow money from prominent whites. Not only would these loans help in the formation of black business, but they would also give that white community leader a financial and personal interest in their black debtors. The unstated implication of Price's argument was that a white creditor might protect a black debtor from dishonest merchants or even from racial violence. At the same time, Price urged black North Carolinians to demonstrate due diligence in paying off these debts. As John C. Dancy, a prominent black Republican and one of Price's protégés, noted in 1898, "The first test of a man's honesty is his disposition to pay his debts. If he seeks every possible excuse to avoid these it must be taken for granted the he lacks the essentials of true honesty."[28]

Many more black North Carolinians, however, saw with their own eyes that debt rarely resulted in "uplift" as Price suggested. Rather, debt had become just another form of slavery as black debtors perpetually found themselves unable to pay their debts. Many black North Carolinians argued that debt should be avoided at all costs, or if necessary only to other African Americans. Debt, some argued, was not only a poor financial situation, but also immoral. "DEBT," argued the *Christian Recorder*, a national black newspaper popular in North Carolina, "is an inexhaustible fountain of dishonesty.... Whoever runs in debt ... is A DISHONEST MAN."[29] Yet, regardless of what they felt about the idea of debt, black North Carolinians could not escape the practical reality that debt had become a necessary aspect of life for those at the bottom of the South's social and economic order. W. E. B. DuBois described black southerners' pervasive indebted condition in the *Souls of Black Folk* as "a pall of debt [that] hangs over the beautiful land; the merchants are in debt to the wholesalers, the planters are in debt to the merchants, the tenants owe the planters, and laborers bow and bend beneath the burden of it all."[30] DuBois's rival, Booker T. Washington, expressed a similar sentiment in 1888 when he observed that the "colored people on these plantations are held in a kind of slavery is in one sense as bad as the slavery of antebellum days." The poor black farmer's debt, Washington argued, "binds him, robs him of independence, allures him and winds him deeper and deeper in its meshes each year till he is lost and bewildered."[31]

The rise of general stores in postbellum North Carolina provides insight into the changing relationship between credit and community. Before the Civil War, credit and debt relationships functioned as *network*, linking myriad individuals together. Community members were expected to act both as creditors and debtors. General stores, however, centralized credit into a handful of institutions. Therefore, although most North Carolinians remained debtors as they always had, fewer and fewer of them had experience as creditors. They could no longer envision their debts as a component of community dynamics. Rather, debt had become a symptom of their economic dependence on storekeepers' credit.

Black and white North Carolinians' troubles with debt provided the primary impetus for the growth and politicization of the agrarian movement. As farmers recognized that their chronic indebtedness was the product of financial structures beyond their individual ability to combat, they increasingly sought through collective action to emancipate themselves from their debts. Yet, while black and white farmers shared many of the same financial problems, their different experiences with debt over the previous fifty years led them to think about debt differently. These divergent conceptions of the meaning and morality of debt created internal tension within the agrarian movement, contributing in part to the movement's inability to enact significant change in North Carolina. While this debate over debt was but one of many points of contention between white and black agrarians in North Carolina, it demonstrates how social and moral constructions developed over the previous half century undermined biracial agrarianism.

As in many other states, the agrarian revolt had its roots in the Grange. In the late 1870s, the Grange (officially the Patrons of Husbandry) became the first statewide organization with the specific purpose of improving the condition of farmers. Established in 1873, the Grange grew quickly in North Carolina; at its peak a decade later, the Grange had approximately 500 lodges and more than 15,000 members. A secret, fraternal organization, the Grange provided indebted farmers with a necessary social network, allowing them to see, perhaps for the first time, that their problems with debt were not individual and situational, but rather universal and chronic.[32]

Although numerically inferior to the Grange within North Carolina, the Knights of Labor also contributed significantly to how black and white agrarians understood debt. Unlike the Grange, which was a white-dominated organization, the Knights actively recruited both black and white farmworkers. Indeed, Knights' egalitarian ethos embraced the needs of workers, regardless of race, gender, and occupation. Entering the state in 1883, the Knights established dozens of local chapters with thousands of members by 1886. The Knights' proposed program of reforms, including railroad regulation, expanded public education, and anti-convict labor legislation, appealed to white and black farmers deeply mired in debt. Many white landholders, however, found the Knights threatening, not only because their proposals threatened them financially, but also because of the organization's biracial composition. By 1887, most whites left the Knights of Labor to join the newly formed Farmers' Association, effectively transforming the Knights into an African American organization, or in the words of one Oxford resident, "Nigger and Knight have become synonymous terms." By 1889, in large part due to white opposition and an association with radicalism, the Knights ceased to function as an effective organization.[33]

Although the apolitical Grange could help farmers identify the origins of their indebtedness, it could not provide them the needed political tools to effect change. Leonidas L. Polk recognized that farmers in North Carolina needed some vehicle outside the Grange to make their voices heard. His experience with the Farmer's Cheap Cash Store, as North Carolina's first agriculture commissioner from 1877 to 1880, and other ventures convinced him that their unremitting indebtedness financially crippled poor farmers to the extent that they could not resolve their debts on their own. In 1886, Polk established the *Progressive Farmer*, a newspaper intended not only to educate and inform farmers, but also to advocate and foment political action. Within a year, the *Progressive Farmer* had the largest circulation of any newspaper in the state. In 1887, Polk founded the North Carolina Farmers' Association, shortly thereafter to become the North Carolina Farmers' Alliance. Like his newspaper, Polk's insurgent agrarian organization experienced explosive growth. By August 1888, North Carolina hosted 1,018 subordinate Alliances in fifty-three counties, membership of 42,000; a year later, there were 1,816 subordinate Alliances in eighty-nine counties, and more than 72,000 members. Excluded from the white Alliance (along with lawyers, merchants, and atheists), black farmers formed a Colored Alliance in 1888, attracting more than 55,000 members by 1890, many of whom had previously been members of the Knights of Labor. Although the white and black Alliances pursued similar economic goals and maintained tenuous organizational ties, they never developed a fully biracial movement.[34]

From the beginning, North Carolina's Farmers' Alliance proposed an ambitious political program, including the creation of a state railroad commission, expanding educational opportunities for rural children, and reforming the convict leasing system. At the heart of their agenda, however, was a series of proposals to reduce the crushing burden of debt from the backs of North Carolina's farmers. Their three most significant proposals (the subtreasury plan, the abolition the state's homestead law, and a reduction in the maximum interest rate) each sought to create a new system of credit that would enable the state's farmers to liberate themselves from their debts. Indeed, many agrarians believed, in the words of agitator James Murdock, that "revolution demands the abolition of the credit system. . . . There can be no compromise with the present financial system. It must be destroyed root and branch."[35]

The cornerstone of the white Farmers' Alliance agenda, both nationally and in North Carolina, was an ambitious program known as the "subtreasury plan." The plan called for the federal government to build agricultural warehouses, known as "subtreasuries," in every county with more than half a million dollars in agricultural commodities per year. Farmers would be able to store nonperishable crops in these subtreasuries, waiting until crop prices rebounded from their harvest-time nadir. When farmers deposited their crops in the subtreasury, they would be able to borrow up to 80 percent of their value in treasury notes, paying only a nominal interest rate until they removed the crops for sale.[36]

White agrarians argued that the subtreasury plan would relieve at least some of the burden from the backs of indebted farmers in two ways. First, it promised that farmers would receive higher prices for their crops. By allowing farmers to choose when to sell, rather than forcing them to sell during the harvest, when the market was glutted, the subtreasury plan would permit farmers to benefit from the higher off-season crop prices that middlemen and speculators usually reaped. Indeed, many agrarians hoped that the subtreasury plan would effectively remove this entire parasitic class. Second, the subtreasury plan would create a flexible and expanded currency, inducing the inflationary pressures that would effectively reduce the relative size of farmers' debts. Unlike the hyperinflated Confederate currency, however, agrarians argued that the treasury notes issued by the subtreasuries would be a legitimate currency expansion because their volume would be proportional to agricultural production; in their eyes the only legitimate source of wealth. "We take the position," argued Leonidas Polk in the *Progressive Farmer*, "that no country can prosper when the farming industry does not prosper. That is the foundation of all prosperity. That is the producer of wealth; the others are simply manipulators who turn one thing already in existence into another, enhancing its value by converting it."[37]

Although the subtreasury plan originated in Texas, North Carolina agrarians became some of its most vocal proponents. Elias Carr, who became president of the North Carolina Alliance when Polk became president of the national Alliance, said of the subtreasury plan, "The one thing needful in the present financial condition of the people is a debt-paying system of finance in comparison with which all other questions sink into utter insignificance."[38] In 1891, Leonidas L. Polk argued that currency expansion by means of the subtreasury plan was "the great and paramount issue now before the American people."[39] Although North Carolina agrarians favored inflationary monetary policy, they for the most part rejected the Greenback panacea that high inflation rates would effectively erase their debts. Instead, they advocated that a moderately inflated currency would create parity now absent in creditor-debtor relationships. The object, according to the *Caucasian*, was an "honest dollar" that respected the needs of creditors and debtors alike.[40]

White agrarians also blamed North Carolina's homestead law for exacerbating poor farmers' credit problem. Originally passed in 1859 and significantly expanded several times after the Civil War, North Carolina's homestead law, like similar measures across the South, was intended to protect insolvent debtors from losing all of their property by excluding certain forms of property from debt suits. One unforeseen consequence, however, of this exclusion was that creditors demanded that farmers pay higher interest rates to compensate for their reduced collateral. "I believe," argued J. J. Goldston, an elderly Chatham County farmer, that "the homestead law has been one of the main causes of the indebtedness of the average farmer."[41] A landlord from Cleveland Country agreed. "One of our needs is the removal of the homestead law or greatly reducing it," he argued in 1887. "Take away the homestead and make people honest and responsible for their debts."[42] So too did a farmer from Harnett County, employing very similar language: "Repeal the homestead law and make all honest debts collectible. Enact such laws as will tend to the restoration of confidence between all classes of trade."[43]

Agrarians also argued that the state should restrict maximum interest rates. "Interest hangs on like grim death to a dead pig," concluded an editorial in the Salisbury *Carolina Watchman*, using language familiar to its agrarian readers. "The increase of wealth in this country is not more than three percent; so if Shylock gets more than that in the shape of interest, it is only a question of time when he will have all the wealth of the country. Usury must go!"[44] They proposed that the state reduce the maximum rate of interest from 8 percent to 6 percent and crack down on business practices, such as general stores' dual price system, that bypassed usury laws.

Indeed, many white agrarians concluded that any form of interest amounted to usury and was, therefore, immoral. Usury, claimed one North Carolina Populist in 1896, was "the most gigantic power for the subjection of industrial humanity that has ever appeared on earth."[45] Many white agrarians believed that creditors artificially employed distinctions between usury and interest to justify their exploitation of indebted farmers. "By changing the name from usury to interest," argued Farmers' Alliance president Marion Butler, somewhat tongue-in-cheek, "good people escape the penalty of disobedience to the Biblical injunction while they gather the fruit of their brother's toil."[46] Agrarians' opposition to interest grew naturally out of their belief in the labor theory of value. Farmers, agrarians believed, earned their money through physical and mental toil. Creditors who profited through interest, on the contrary, did not labor, and therefore their profits must be dishonest. "What do they [creditors] produce?" asked the *Caucasian*, Marion Butler's agrarian newspaper. "What do they distribute? What moral right have they to cumber the earth?"[47]

Many white agrarians concluded that any form of credit should be avoided and that a pure-cash system ought to replace it. For some, this rejection of credit was a moral matter as much as it was one of personal and political economy. James Murdock, an essayist for the *Progressive Farmer*, claimed that credit encouraged "recklessness in buying" and "rascality and laziness." The solution, according to Murdock, was a system of "pay as you go."[48] To be sure, most agrarians realized that, as a practical matter, a credit-free economy was impossible. Debt and farming had become so intermeshed in the minds of many North Carolinians that few could envision an alternative system. "The credit system of farming," claimed the *Tarboro Farmers Advocate* in 1891, "has become so habitual to many of our farmers as to be second nature, and they do not believe they could live under any other system."[49]

The relationship between debt and race proved to be a thorn in the side of the agrarian movement. Most white agrarians recognized that black farmers also suffered from debts they could not pay, prompting agrarian leader Marion Butler to conclude "what is good for a white laborer in the South . . . is equally good for a colored laborer."[50] Indeed, most white agrarians recognized that black farmers had even more difficulty in paying their debts than their white neighbors. According to a white mechanic from Hyde County in 1887, compared to whites, "black laborers [are] very poor: they are always in debt."[51] They also understood that the support of a black electoral majority in some eastern counties would be necessary for any statewide agrarian reform movement. However, they rejected the idea of a completely biracial organization, always keeping black agrarians at arm's length. Whatever parallels they drew between their plight and those of their black neighbors, most white agrarians supported white supremacy and rejected racial egalitarianism. This racial ambivalence manifested itself in an 1892 *Progressive Farmer* editorial: "Whatever hurts the white farmer or mechanic injures the colored farmer or mechanic. Naturally they should not be arrayed against each other . . . but the fact remains that the Anglo Saxons must rule this country and we believe all honest, intelligent negroes know the importance of this."[52]

Black agrarians recognized that their problems with debt were not identical to those of white agrarians. Because the vast majority of black agrarians did not own their own land but toiled as tenants, sharecroppers, or wage laborers, their relationship to debt differed in significant ways from their white counterparts, many of whom owned their farms. Therefore, although black agrarians desired many of the same goals as white agrarians, they did not necessarily advocate the same political measures to attain those goals. They recognized, for instance, that abolishing the homestead exemption would only expand credit for those who owned their land. Similarly, they understood that the subtreasury plan would not profit farmers who worked for wages and they were skeptical of its benefits for tenant farmers and sharecroppers. Conversely, black agrarians were consistently frustrated by white agrarians' refusal to advocate for the reform of the Landlord-Tenant Act of 1875, which granted landlords first lien on crops and criminalized the removal of crops without the landlord's authorization.[53]

The white Farmers' Alliance demonstrated considerable success in electing favorable candidates to the North Carolina General Assembly. By 1891, 110 of 170 members of the General Assembly were Alliancemen, most of whom were Democrats. Yet, despite their numerical superiority, the Alliance had difficulty in transforming this legislative majority into the envisioned economic reforms. A measure to reduce the maximum interest rate introduced by Allianceman Willis R. Williams of Pitt County, for instance, died in the Judiciary Committee despite widespread public support. The Alliance's failure to enact more meaningful change can be attributed to two main causes. First, many of the most devoted Alliancemen in the state legislature were political neophytes. Elected in large measure because they were farmers and not lawyers or professional politicians, their inexperience with the legislative process handicapped their effort to enact the Alliance agenda. Second, although the Farmers' Alliance had at least the nominal support of a majority of the legislators, it did not have the support of the majority Democratic Party. Non-Alliance ("Straight-Out") Democrats wielded enough political influence to keep the Alliance program in check.[54]

Even though the Alliance failed to enact meaningful change in debt's legal parameters, many local chapters of the Farmers' Alliance found that they could take steps to reduce their debts and lessen their dependence on credit. They saw cooperative purchasing as an alternative to the credit monopoly enjoyed by rural general stores. Such collective endeavors, they hoped, would remove farmers from the crushing seasonal burden of debt. Some initial forays into collective purchasing were moderately successful. For instance, the Bethany Alliance in northern Davidson County arranged a collective purchase of fertilizer in September 1889. Although such efforts enabled farmers to bypass the local general store temporarily, it did not absolve them of the fundamental credit crisis. When farmers attempted to escalate their collective purchasing power into exchange stores as a collective alternative to general stores, they usually failed. For instance, the

Mt. Sylvan Alliance in northern Durham County voted to create such a store in 1889 and started to collect money in 1890. The store, however, never opened. The Jamestown Alliance in Davie County did only slightly better, opening a small store in Mocksville. It, however, closed eighteen months later. The failure of exchange stores to become a meaningful alternative to general stores helped to convince many agrarians that debt reform within the existing political-economic paradigms would be almost impossible.[55]

Despite the robust efforts of thousands of North Carolina Alliancemen, financial conditions did not improve significantly. If anything, between 1887 and 1892, North Carolina farmers faced deeper and deeper levels of debt. "Farmers in my county have hard times," complained one Montgomery County farmer in 1891. "Farm products are so low and goods so high that the farmers can't make both ends meet. I would be glad if some remedy could be found for it. I am a farmer myself, and own a good farm, and work hard, but I am in debt at this time, and I do not see how I can help myself."[56] A petition from the Farmers' Alliance of Chatham County to the North Carolina General Assembly claimed that "there is very little money in the hands of the farmers. Almost every farmer is depressed; many are disheartened; labor is unremunerative . . . They are gradually but steadily becoming poorer and poorer every year."[57]

By 1892, many North Carolina agrarians had come to the conclusion that existing political leaders and institutions could not or would not act decisively to address the growing debt-burden under which many farmers labored. White agrarians seemed particularly incensed with Democratic politicians who had pledged solidarity with Alliance goals but failed to act decisively to enact their agenda. Senator Zebulon Vance was a particular source of frustration and ire. "Nine-tenths of the people in this State are carrying a burden of debt," wrote A. D. Taylor to Vance in July 1890. "I can not believe you will turn a deaf ear to their cry at this the time of their extremity."[58] That same month, Vance received a disheartening letter from Eugene Beddingfield, the secretary of the North Carolina state Farmers' Alliance: "The people are very restless. We are on the verge of a revolution. God grant it may be bloodless . . . You cannot stand before the tide if it turns in your direction. No living power can withstand it."[59] In what many agrarians saw as a particular act of betrayal, Vance sponsored a subtreasury bill in 1890, largely to placate Polk, but conspicuously failed to do anything to secure its passage.[60]

The Vance affair fundamentally divided the agrarian movement in North Carolina. Some, like Leonidas L. Polk, decided that only a new political party, the People's Party, could adequately address the farmers' need for radical reform. Others concluded that reform could happen only within the context of the Democratic Party and that any third party would result in a Republican victory at the polls, an election that potentially threatened white supremacy. A few, most notably Marion Butler, initially endorsed this latter course of action, only to later embrace Populism. This division spelled the end of the Farmers' Alliance as an effective political entity within North Carolina, as agrarians divided over how best to pursue their agenda.[61]

Unfortunately for North Carolina Populists, the creation of their party began inauspiciously when Leonidas L. Polk died unexpectedly in June 1892. Widely considered as a potential presidential candidate, Polk's death sent the new party into disarray. Although they carried only three counties in 1892, North Carolina Populists recognized that the Democratic Party no longer had an electoral majority. Joining forces with Republicans in 1894, Populists formed a coalition ticket (though maintaining separate organizational hierarchies) for the 1894 election that handily defeated the Democrats, gaining control over both houses of the general assembly. This bipartisan coalition reflected the biracial nature of the agrarian movement, with the majority of white agrarians joining the Populist Party, while most black agrarians stayed in the Republican Party.[62]

Although usually referred to as the Fusion movement, the alliance between Populists and Republicans was founded more on their mutual hatred of Democrats and their desire for political power rather than a common agenda or political philosophy. Ideological differences between Populists and Republicans on economic questions consistently threatened this marriage of convenience. Unlike their new Populist bedfellows, Republicans, particularly white Republicans, strongly rejected bimetallism (which by 1894 had replaced the subtreasury plan as the Populists' preferred inflationary measure), and opposed measures to reduce the maximum legal interest rate and abolish the homestead law. Black Republicans, who composed approximately two-thirds of the party in North Carolina, were not as hostile as white Republicans to bimetallism, though they rarely endorsed it with enthusiasm. Although the Fusion legislature enacted a number of meaningful reforms, particularly in democratizing the state's election law, decentralizing county government, and improving education funding, they failed to enact most of the Populists' core debt-relief program.[63]

Despite its centrality in the Populist Party's formation and ideology, debt-relief legislation was rarely considered by the North Carolina General Assembly during its two sessions under "Fusionist" control. Recognizing that their Republican allies did not share in the economic vision, Populists introduced only two significant pieces of debt-relief legislation. In the first session, the "Fusion" legislature in 1895 successfully passed a measure to restrict interest rates to 6 percent. The historian Allen Trelease's roll-call analysis of fourteen votes taken on this bill indicates that Populists and black Republicans supported it resoundingly, 96.8 and 93.6 percent respectively, while only 14 percent of Democrats supported it. The Republicans, Trelease argues, voted for this bill largely to secure Populist support for their election reform proposal rather than the interest bill's merits. According to the *News and Observer*, the Republicans, if left to their own devices, would have voted against any measuring lowering the maximum interest rate.[64]

In the second legislative session, the Populists proposed a bill in 1897 to prevent discrimination against silver as a legal tender. Here the Populists found that the Republicans abandoned them completely, with only 2.4 percent of Republicans voting for silver in four roll-call votes. Further, Republicans successfully added a crippling amendment to the measure, requiring that debts contracted in one form of money be repaid in the same kind of money. Thus gutted, the bill died, opposed by nearly all Democrats, most Populists, and approximately half of Republicans. These two measures indicate the extent to which "Fusion" politics effectively undercut North Carolina Populists in their efforts to bring about meaningful debt reform.[65]

In the end, the Populists' failure was more political than ideological. Although Fusion temporarily placed Populists in a position of political power, their coalition with Republicans was inherently unstable. The Democrats' white supremacy campaign of 1898 effectively exploited this political weakness, frightening white votes with tales of black domination and dissuading black voters through threatened and actual violence. Yet, despite this political failure, North Carolina's agrarian movement represented the culmination of three decades of cultural and intellectual transformation about the meaning, economics, and morality of debt. In the thirty years that separated the end of the Civil War and the "Fusionist" legislature of 1895, black and white North Carolinians considered and reconsidered the role that debt would play in their lives.[66]

Historians have categorized the Populists variously as petty backward-looking reactionaries, pragmatic reformers, agrarian capitalists, innovative proto-progressives, radical democratic egalitarians, and socialists. Their stance on debt, at least as manifested in North Carolina, indicates that most agrarians, white and black alike, wanted to be liberated from their debts, to have a clean slate, and to have an opportunity to lead productive lives unburdened by debt. They did not manifest a desire to return to informal antebellum credit networks, but envisioned a new credit system that incorporated significant government intervention and supervision. Their policies on debt support Charles Postel's assertion that Populists were fundamentally modern in their outlook, presenting an "alternative modernity suitable to their own interests." However, North Carolina agrarians did not speak with one voice about how to establish this modern credit system, as black and white agrarians espoused subtle, but significant differences in their understanding of the moral, social, and political implications of debt and credit. These differences helped to undermine their fragile political coalition, resulting in the reestablishment of white Democratic rule in the state.[67]

Black and white agrarians across the South struggled with how to reconcile a long history of racial animosity and cultural differences with their immediate political goals, including how to reform credit systems to better meet the needs of farmers in an industrial economy. What made the agrarian reformers in North Carolina different from their counterparts in other southern states was that they briefly held political power and thereby exposed racial divisions inherit in Fusion politics. While the issue of debt was only one of many issues that split white and black agrarians, it reveals a significant fissure at the intersection of economics, politics, culture, morality, and race.

Notes

1. Undated speech, Marion Butler Papers, Southern Historical Collection, Wilson Library, University of North Carolina, Chapel Hill.

2. Annual Reports, North Carolina Bureau of Labor Statistics (1890), 35.

3. *Progressive Farmer*, June 23, 1896.

4. Black Populism remains significantly understudied. My understanding of Black Populism in North Carolina draws heavily from Omar H. Ali, "Black Populism in the New South, 1886–1898" (Ph.D. diss., Columbia University, 2003), 197–201.

5. The agrarian movement has a robust historiographical tradition. Of particular note, see John D. Hicks, *The Populist Revolt: A History of the Farmers' Alliance and the People's Party* (Minneapolis: University of Minnesota Press, 1931); C. Vann Woodward, *Origins of the New South, 1877–1913* (Baton Rouge: Louisiana State University Press, 1951); Richard Hofstadter, *The Age of Reform, from Bryan to F.D.R.* (New York: Random House, 1955); Lawrence Goodwyn, *Democratic Promise: The Populist Moment in America* (New York: Oxford University Press, 1976); Steven Hahn, *The Roots of Southern Populism:*

Yeoman Farmers and the Transformation of the Georgia Upcountry, 1850–1890 (New York: Oxford University Press, 1985); Robert C. McMath Jr., *Populist Vanguard: A History of the Southern Farmers' Alliance* (Chapel Hill: University of North Carolina Press, 1975); Charles Postel, *The Populist Vision* (New York: Oxford University Press, 2007); James M. Beeby, *Revolt of the Tar Heels: The North Carolina Populist Movement, 1890–1901* (Jackson: University Press of Mississippi, 2008).

6. Eugene Genovese, *The Political Economy of Slavery* (Middletown, CT: Wesleyan University Press, 1988), 19–24; Larry Schweikart, "Southern Banks and Economic Growth in the Antebellum Period: A Reassessment," *Journal of Southern History* 53 (1986): 589–610; Thomas Govan, "Banking and the Credit System in Georgia, 1810–1860," *Journal of Southern History* 4 (1935): 164–184; Roger Ransom and Richard Sutch, *One Kind of Freedom: The Economic Consequences of Emancipation* (Cambridge: Cambridge University Press, 2001), 110–116; William A. Blair, *A Historical Sketch of Banking in North Carolina* (New York: Bradford Rhodes, 1899); Lewis Atherton, "The Problem of Credit Rating in the Ante-Bellum South," *Journal of Southern History* 12 (1946): 534.

7. For an assessment of the debt-slave metaphor, see Bruce Mann, *Republic of Debtors: Bankruptcy in the Age of American Independence* (Cambridge, MA: Harvard University Press, 2002), 131; Edward Balleisen, *Navigating Failure: Bankruptcy and Commercial Society in Antebellum America* (Chapel Hill: University of North Carolina Press, 2001), 165–167; and Scott Sandage, *Born Losers: A History of Failure in America* (Cambridge, MA: Harvard University Press, 2005), 193–194.

8. Richard H. Kilbourne, *Debt, Investment, Slaves: Credit Relations in East Feliciana Parish, Louisiana, 1825–1885* (Tuscaloosa: University of Alabama Press, 1995), 3, 50–55. Kilbourne argues that although the majority of slave transactions were conducted on a cash basis, those interested in buying slaves often borrowed money to finance the purchase. Also see Ariela J. Gross, *Double Character: Slavery and Mastery in the Antebellum Southern Courtroom* (Princeton, NJ: Princeton University Press, 2000), 32. For the gift economy in the antebellum South, see Kenneth S. Greenberg, *Honor and Slavery* (Princeton, NJ: Princeton University Press, 1996), 51–86. The central works in anthropology on gift culture are Marcel Mauss, *The Gift: The Form and Reason for Exchange in Archaic Societies*, trans. W. D. Halls (New York: Norton, 1990), and Lewis Hyde, *The Gift: Imagination and the Erotic Life of Property* (New York: Vintage, 1979).

9. T. H. Breen, *Tobacco Culture: The Mentality of the Great Tidewater Planters on the Eve of Revolution* (Princeton, NJ: Princeton University Press, 1985), 93–95.

10. Charles C. Bolton, *Poor Whites of the Antebellum South: Tenants and Laborers in Central North Carolina and Northeast Mississippi* (Durham, NC: Duke University Press, 1994), 24.

11. Paul D. Escott, *North Carolina Yeoman: The Diary of Basil Armstrong Thomasson, 1853–1862* (Athens: University of Georgia Press, 1996), 229.

12. The term yeoman is used to describe those white North Carolinians who owned their own land and owned very few or no slaves, occupying a significant position in white society between poor whites and planters. Historians have offered important distinctions between yeoman, plain folk, common whites, poor whites, and nonslaveholding whites, though disentangling their conflicting definitions of these groups can prove difficult. See Samuel C Hyde Jr., "Plain Folk Yeomanry in the Antebellum South," in *A Companion to the American South*, ed. John B. Boles (Malden, MA: Blackwell, 2002), 139–154; Bill

Cecil-Fronsman, *Common Whites: Class and Culture in Antebellum North Carolina* (Lexington: University Press of Kentucky, 1992); Hahn, *The Roots of Southern Populism*; Escott, *North Carolina Yeoman*, 56, 70.

13. Paul D. Escott, "Yeoman Independence and the Market: Social Status and Economic Development in Antebellum North Carolina," *North Carolina Historical Review* 61 (1989): 275–300; Hahn, *The Roots of Southern Populism*, 85; Drew R. McCoy, *The Elusive Republic: Political Economy in Jeffersonian America* (Chapel Hill: University of North Carolina Press, 1980); Cecil-Fronsman, *Common Whites*, 102; Escott, "Yeoman Independence and the Market," 282; Gavin Wright, *Political Economy of the Cotton South* (New York: Norton, 1978), 63; Escott, *North Carolina Yeoman*, 263.

14. Jeff Forret, *Race Relations at the Margins: Slaves and Poor Whites in the Antebellum Southern Countryside* (Baton Rouge: Louisiana State University Press, 2006), 74–114; Timothy J. Lockley, "Trading Encounters between Non-Elite Whites and African-Americans in Savannah, 1790–1860," *Journal of Southern History* 66 (2000): 47–76; Joseph P. Reidy, "Obligation and Right: Patterns of Labor, Subsistence, and Exchange in the Cotton Belt of Georgia, 1790–1860," in *Cultivation and Culture: Labor and the Shaping of Slave Life in the Americas*, ed. Ira Berlin and Philip D. Morgan (Charlottesville: University of Virginia Press, 1993), 138–154; Dylan C. Penningroth, *The Claims of Kinfolk: African American Property in the Nineteenth-Century South* (Chapel Hill: University of North Carolina Press, 2003), 45–78; John Hope Franklin, *The Free Negro in North Carolina, 1790–1860* (Chapel Hill: University of North Carolina Press, 1943), 89–90, 162. Some South Carolina and Louisiana planters facilitated a pseudo-credit system, serving as factors for their slaves' surplus production or offering credit at plantation stores. I have not been able to identify a similar practice among slave owners in North Carolina. John Campbell, "As 'A Kind of Freeman'?: Slaves' Market-Related Activities in the South Carolina Up Country," in *Cultivation and Culture: Labor and the Shape of Slave Life in the Americas*, ed. Ira Berlin and Philip D. Morgan, 265–270; Roderick A. McDonald, "Independent Economic Production By Slaves on Antebellum Louisiana Sugar Plantations," in *Cultivation and Culture: Labor and the Shape of Slave Life in the Americas*, ed. Ira Berlin and Philip D. Morgan, 295–299; Charles Ball, *Slavery in the United States* (New York: John S. Taylor, 1837), 191–192; Dylan C. Penningroth, *The Claims of Kinfolk: African American Property in the Nineteenth-Century South* (Chapel Hill: University of North Carolina Press, 2003), 66; Steven Hahn, *A Nation Under Our Feet: Black Political Struggles in the Rural South from Slavery to the Great Migration* (Cambridge: Belknap Press, 2003), 28.

15. Moses Grandy, *Narrative of the Life of Moses Grandy*, ed. Andreá N. Williams, in *North Carolina Slave Narratives*, ed. William L. Andrews (Chapel Hill: University of North Carolina Press, 2003), 162, 180.

16. On the transformative effect of the Civil War on African Americans in North Carolina and in the South more broadly, see Eric Foner, *Reconstruction: America's Unfinished Revolution, 1863–1877* (New York: Harper & Row, 1988); Hahn, *A Nation Under Our Feet*; Leon Litwack, *Been in the Storm So Long: The Aftermath of Slavery* (New York: Knopf, 1979).

17. The exact rate of inflation in the Confederacy depends in large measure on geographical location and the commodities used as indexes. The most complete study of inflation in the Confederacy is Eugene M. Lerner, "Money, Prices, and Wages in the Confederacy, 1861–1865," in *The Economic Impact of the American Civil War*, ed. Ralph

Andreano (Cambridge: Shenkman Publishing, 1962), 11–40. Also see Mark Thornton and Robert B. Ekelund, *Tariffs, Blockades, and Inflation: The Economics of the Civil War* (Wilmington, DE: Scholarly Resources, 2004), 59–80; John C. Inscoe and Gordon B. McKinney, *The Heart of Confederate Appalachia: Western North Carolina in the Civil War* (Chapel Hill: University of North Carolina Press, 2000), 174–175.

18. Jonathan Worth to Alfred Brown, August 1, 1863, in Joseph Grégorie de Roulhac Hamilton, ed., *The Correspondence of Jonathan Worth* (Raleigh, NC: Edwards & Broughton, 1909): I: 248.

19. Alexander McBee to Vardy A. McBee, March 10, 1867, McBee Family Papers, Southern Historical Collection, Wilson Library, University of North Carolina, Chapel Hill.

20. Richard Kilbourne calculates that slaves represented 45.8 percent of total wealth in the Cotton South. See Kilbourne, *Debt, Investment, Slaves,* 8, 75.

21. *Journal of Freedom*, September 30, 1865.

22. C. Vann Woodward, *Origins of the New South, 1877–1913* (Baton Rouge: Louisiana State University Press, 1951), 291–320; Roger L. Ransom and Richard Sutch, *One Kind of Freedom: The Economic Consequences of Emancipation* (Cambridge: Cambridge University Press, 2001); Jonathan Wiener, *Social Origins of the New South: Alabama, 1860–1910* (Baton Rouge: Louisiana State University Press, 1978); Gavin Wright, *Old South, New South: Revolutions in the Southern Economy since the Civil War* (Baton Rouge: Louisiana State University Press, 1996); Harold D. Woodman, *New South, New Law: The Legal Foundations of Credit and Labor Relations in the Postbellum Agricultural South* (Baton Rouge: Louisiana State University Press, 1995); Joseph P. Reidy, "Economic Consequences of the Civil War and Reconstruction," in *A Companion to the American South,* ed. John B. Boles (Malden, MA: Blackwell, 2002), 303–317.

23. Thomas D. Clark, *Pills, Petticoats, and Plows: The Southern Country Store* (Indianapolis: Bobbs-Merrill, 1944); Edward L. Ayers, *The Promise of the New South: Life After Reconstruction* (New York: Oxford University Press, 1992), 83–86.

24. Testimony of George H. White, *Report of the Industrial Commission* (Washington, D.C.: Government Printing Office, 1901), X: 4.19

25. Stuart Noblin, *Leonidas Lafayette Polk: Agrarian Crusader* (Chapel Hill: University of North Carolina Press, 1949), 78; Deborah Beckel, "Roots of Reform: The Origins of Populism and Progressivism as Manifest in Relationships Among Reformers in Raleigh, North Carolina, 1850–1905" (Ph.D. diss., Emory University, 1998), 184–194; Ayers, *The Promise of the New South,* 223.

26. LeGette Blythe, *William Henry Belk: Merchant of the South* (Chapel Hill: University of North Carolina Press, 1950), 38–46; Ayers, *The Promise of the New South,* 95–96.

27. Robert C. Kenzer, *Enterprising Southerners: Black Economic Success in North Carolina, 1865–1915* (Charlottesville: University of Virginia Press, 1989), 37–42, 59–60.

28. Leon Litwack, *Trouble in Mind: Black Southerners in the Age of Jim Crow* (New York: Vintage, 1998), 80; *AMEZ Quarterly Review* (April 1898): 81.

29. "Debt," *Christian Recorder*, February 6, 1873.

30. W. E. B. DuBois, *The Souls of Black Folk* (Chicago: A. C. McClure, 1903), 154.

31. Louis R. Harlan, ed., *Booker T. Washington Papers* (Urbana: University of Illinois Press, 1972), II: 503. Also see Pete Daniel, *The Shadow of Slavery: Peonage in the South, 1901–1969* (Urbana: University of Illinois Press, 1972), ix. On Washington's economic

thought, see Peter A. Coclanis, "What Made Booker Wash(ington)? The Wizard of Tuskegee in Economic Context" in *Booker T. Washington and Black Progress: Up From Slavery 100 Years Later*, ed. W. Fitzhugh Brundage (Gainesville: University of Florida Press, 2003), 81–106.

32. Lala Carr Steelman, *The North Carolina Farmers' Alliance: A Political History, 1887-1893* (Greenville: East Carolina University Publications, 1985), 10; Helen G. Edmonds, *The Negro and Fusion Politics in North Carolina, 1894–1901* (Chapel Hill: University of North Carolina Press, 1951), 23.

33. Matthew Hild, *Greenbackers, Knights of Labor, and Populists: Farmer-Labor Insurgency in the Late-Nineteenth-Century South* (Athens: University of Georgia Press, 2007), 93–98, 100–102; Laura Edwards, *Gendered Strife and Confusion: The Political Culture of Reconstruction* (Urbana: University of Illinois Press, 1997), 218–254; Melton McLaurin, "The Knights of Labor in North Carolina Politics," *North Carolina Historical Review* 49 (July 1972): 298–315; Robert C. McMath Jr., "Southern White Farmers and the Organization of Black Farm Workers: A North Carolina Document," *Labor History* 18 (Winter 1977): 115–119.

34. Steelman, *The North Carolina Farmers' Alliance*, 9–17, 21; Noblin, *Leonidas Lafayette Polk*, 150–207; McMath, *Populist Vanguard*, 38–40; Ayers, *The Promise of the New South*, 223–224; Frenise A. Logan, *The Negro in North Carolina, 1876–1894* (Chapel Hill: University of North Carolina Press, 1964), 84.

35. *Progressive Farmer*, December 8, 15, 1891.

36. McMath, *Populist Vanguard*, 90–91; Goodwyn, *Democratic Promise*, 166–169; Ayers, *The Promise of the New South*, 239.

37. *Progressive Farmer*, September 17, 1889.

38. Steelman, *The North Carolina Farmers' Alliance*, 81.

39. Bruce Palmer, *"Man Over Money": The Southern Populist Critique of American Capitalism* (Chapel Hill: University of North Carolina Press, 1980), 94.

40. Although Texan C. W. Macune usually gets credit for originating the subtreasury plan, John Hicks argued that he may have gotten the idea from an article written by North Carolinian Henry Skinner. John D. Hicks, "The Sub-Treasury Plan: A Forgotten Plan for the Relief of Agriculture," *Mississippi Valley Historical Review* 15 (1928), 359; *Caucasian*, April 11, 1895; Palmer, *"Man Over Money,"* 84.

41. Annual Reports, North Carolina Bureau for Labor Statistics (1895), 189.

42. Annual Reports, North Carolina Bureau of Labor Statistics (1887), 91.

43. Annual Reports, North Carolina Bureau of Labor Statistics (1893), 64.

44. Salisbury *Carolina Watchman*, August 20, 1891.

45. *Progressive Farmer*, June 23, 1896.

46. *Caucasian*, August 31, 1893.

47. Palmer, *"Man Over Money,"* 89; *Caucasian*, November 16, 1893.

48. *Progressive Farmer*, December 8, 1891.

49. Palmer, *"Man Over Money,"* 92–93; *Tarboro Farmers Advocate*, June 3, 1891.

50. James L. Hunt, *Marion Butler and American Populism* (Chapel Hill: University of North Carolina Press, 2003), 62.

51. Annual Reports, North Carolina Bureau of Labor Statistics (1887), 38.

52. *Progressive Farmer*, July 26, 1892; Eric Anderson, *Race and Politics in North Carolina, 1872–1901: The Black Second* (Baton Rouge: Louisiana State University Press, 1981).

53. Craig M. Thurtell, "The Fusion Insurgency in North Carolina: Origins to Ascendancy, 1876–1896" (Ph.D. diss., Columbia University, 1998), 23, 94; Woodman, *New South—New Law*, 51–54, 74.

54. Steelman, *The North Carolina Farmers' Alliance*, 125, 162.

55. Robert C. McMath Jr., "Agrarian Protest at the Forks of the Creek: Three Subordinate Farmers' Alliances in North Carolina," *North Carolina Historical Review* 51 (1974): 41–63. Although the vast majority of cooperative stores failed, a notable exception was the Farmers' Alliance Store of Siler City, which, as of December 1999, remained open for business. See Bruce E. Baker, "The Farmers' Alliance Store of Siler City, North Carolina, 1888–1999," unpublished seminar paper, December 1999, in the possession of North Carolina Collection, Wilson Library, University of North Carolina, Chapel Hill.

56. Annual Reports, North Carolina Bureau of Labor Statistics (1891), 68.

57. Hugh T. Lefler, *North Carolina History Told by Contemporaries* (Chapel Hill: University of North Carolina Press, 1965), 379.

58. Thurtell, "The Fusion Insurgency in North Carolina," 109.

59. Alan B. Bromberg, "'The Worst Muddle Ever Seen in N.C. Politics': The Farmers' Alliance, the Subtreasury, and Zeb Vance," *North Carolina Historical Review* 56 (1979): 28.

60. Vance evidently believed that the subtreasury plan was unconstitutional. Bromberg, "'The Worst Muddle Ever Seen in N.C. Politics,'" 19–40; Steelman, *The North Carolina Farmers' Alliance*, 66–81.

61. Hunt, *Marion Butler and American Populism*, 40–48; Steelman, *The North Carolina Farmers' Alliance*, 182–211; Beeby, *Revolt of the Tar Heels*, 10–48.

62. Beeby, *Revolt of the Tar Heels*, 59–84.

63. Ali, "Black Populism in the New South," 196–201. One significant exception to the Republican opposition to bimetallism was Republican (and former Greenbacker) governor Daniel L. Russell. See Jeffrey J. Crow and Robert F. Durden, *Maverick Republican in the Old North State: A Political Biography of Daniel L. Russell* (Baton Rouge: Louisiana State University Press, 1977).

64. *Public Laws of North Carolina* (1895), chap. 69. Trelease argues that white Republicans lukewarmly supported the measure, fearing that it would drive credit from the state. Allen W. Trelease, "The Fusion Legislatures of 1895 and 1897: A Roll-Call Analysis of the North Carolina House of Representatives," *North Carolina Historical Review* 57 (1980): 294. Also see Beeby, *Revolt of the Tar Heels*, 114–115; Thurtell, "The Fusion Insurgency in North Carolina," 256.

65. Trelease, "The Fusion Legislatures of 1895 and 1897," 294–295.

66. On the white supremacy campaign of 1898, see Robert H. Wooley, "Race and Politics: The Evolution of the White Supremacy Campaign of 1898 in North Carolina" (Ph.D. diss., University of North Carolina at Chapel Hill, 1977); Michael Perman, *Struggle for Mastery: Disfranchisement in the South, 1888–1908* (Chapel Hill: University of North Carolina Press, 2001); Anderson, *Race and Politics in North Carolina 1872–1901*; David S. Cecelski and Timothy B. Tyson, eds., *Democracy Betrayed: The Wilmington Race Riot and Its Legacy* (Chapel Hill: University of North Carolina Press, 1998); Beeby, *Revolt of the Tar Heels*; Edmonds, *The Negro and Fusion Politics in North Carolina*.

67. Postel, *The Populist Vision*, 4.

Reconceptualizing Black Populism in the New South

—OMAR H. ALI

> As members of the Colored Farmers' Alliance we avowed that we were going to vote with and for the man or party that will secure for the farmer or laboring man his just rights.
> —J. L. MOORE, letter to the editor, *National Economist*, March 7, 1891

The Reverend John L. Moore was among a number of key black Populist leaders directing southern African Americans to take independent political action in the early 1890s. The black minister, who served as superintendent of the Colored Farmers' Alliance in Florida in 1891, argued that for African Americans to regain their civil and political rights, black voters would need to support candidates (including non-Republican candidates) who supported reforming the electoral process. In response to attacks on African Americans for their endorsement of legislation that would allow federal supervision of elections in the South, Moore published a letter to the editor (initially appearing in a Jacksonville newspaper and then reprinted, with much broader circulation, in the *National Economist* newspaper). The letter not only denounced election fraud in the region but "ask[s] Congress to protect the ballot-box."[1] The controversy into which Moore entered centered on the Lodge Election Bill, a congressional bill whose sponsors sought to redress Democratic voting fraud in the South, such as ballot stuffing and miscounting of votes. The proposed legislation stipulated that in districts with five hundred people or more, if at least fifty of its citizens signed a petition attesting to fraudulent electoral activity, the federal government could be brought in.[2]

African Americans had united strongly in favor of the proposed bill, named after its Massachusetts Republican sponsor, Henry Cabot Lodge. And while the legislation technically only applied to federal elections, the bill would, in fact, impinge upon state and local elections. Not surprisingly, the bill ignited fierce opposition in the southern white press, whose editors and writers variously called it "the Force Bill."[3] Democrats across the South rallied to prevent a "repetition of the destructive rule of ignorant negroes and unscrupulous whites"—a reference to the era of Reconstruction, purportedly a time of massive corruption, even unholy "Negro domination." Southern Democrats needed to take a strong stance, and quickly, against the challenge to white rule. As the *Greensboro Daily Democrat* made plain, the Democratic Party was "a white man's party, organized to maintain white supremacy." The Lodge Bill passed the House, but was defeated in the Senate by southern Democrats. Challenges to white supremacy would not be tolerated.[4]

Moore's letter in support of black political rights and the diversification of black electoral options (that is, not being solely tied to the Republican Party) was written as much in defiance of Democratic rule in the South as it was in favor of a new independent political strategy among leaders of the black Populist movement. A minister of the African Methodist Episcopalian Church in Crescent City, Moore was elected superintendent of the Putnam County Colored Farmers' Alliance in 1889 and soon assumed statewide leadership of the organization. He helped found the Florida People's Party, on whose state executive committee he served for two years, and became a national delegate to the series of conventions leading up to the formation of the national People's Party in 1892—the most powerful threat to Democratic authority in the South.

Moore was part of a growing chorus of black Populist leaders in his call for independent action. Others included William H. Warwick of Virginia, the Reverend Walter A. Pattillo of North Carolina, Henry Sebastian Doyle of Georgia, George Washington Murray of South Carolina, and John B. Rayner of Texas. Each of these leaders pursued one or a combination of independent electoral tactics: building third parties, working in fusion or cooperation with Republicans, or simply running insurgent campaigns when other options were not possible in a county or state. Like Moore, most of these leaders also came out of the ranks of the Colored Farmers' Alliance.[5]

While mention of the Colored Farmers' Alliance repeatedly comes up in the scholarly literature on the Populist movement, until recently, little else was actually known about the organization. As Charles Dew notes in his "Critical Essay on Recent Works" in the 1995 edition of C. Vann Woodward's classic *Origins of the New South*, there is a dearth of research and analysis on the black organization. The history of the Colored Farmers' Alliance, asserted Dew, "is obviously in need of additional primary investigation."[6] I decided to look into the history of the Colored Farmers' Alliance and broadened the scope of my research to include African Americans in the Populist movement as a whole. My approach was regionwide. I read across a range of scholarly articles, books, dissertations, and papers on Populism while delving into primary sources.

Working from New York City and then at the Southern Historical Collection at the University of North Carolina, Chapel Hill, I began plowing through sources from the 1880s and 1890s. However, the more I looked at African Americans and their organizations, the more I began seeing a disconnect between the lives of rural African Americans in the New South and how black people were being characterized by scholars of Populism.[7] The evidence, in the form of newspaper accounts, legal testimonies, and letters, among other fragmentary sources, suggested something very different to me. It appeared as though African Americans had been engaged in a series of interconnected organizations that were separate and distinct from those of their white counterparts.[8] But was there a case to be made for a new perspective of African Americans and Populism? Was there such a thing as "Black Populism" as a movement unto itself, independent of the white-led Populist movement?

Three assumptions appeared to be guiding the scholarship on African Americans and Populism: First, African Americans and their organizations were offshoots of Populism; second, "Black Populists" were limited to African Americans solely affiliated with the People's Party; and third, African Americans operated principally under white leadership. Scholars, it seems, had too closely followed the words of white Populists in their descriptions and analyses of African Americans. Statements, such as the one made in an 1890 editorial appearing in the North Carolina *Progressive Farmer* that African Americans have "always [functioned with] the aid of white leaders" would become the standard academic view.[9]

Although the term "Black Populism" was used by scholars as early as the 1940s, first appearing in a master's thesis by Douglass Perry in 1945 entitled "Black Populism: The Negro in the People's Party in Texas," the perspective offered was that of white Populists bringing African Americans into *their* organizations, under *their* leadership.[10] Such a perspective would ultimately position African Americans in scholarly discourse as pawns of southern white men's efforts to gain or retain power. The notion, however, seemed antithetical to what I was reading (or perhaps *how* I was reading).

The overwhelming amount of scholarship assumed rural black southerners in the post-Reconstruction era as victims: what existed were white leaders (Democrats, Republicans, and Populists alike) and their object of manipulation were black people; the views of African American leaders—that is, analyzed and described from the perspective of rural African Americans' strategic political and economic interests—was virtually nonexistent. In other words, the epistemological approach and framing of African Americans *in* Populism would exclude the ontological existence of African Americans as anything other than subservient and attached to the white Populist movement at both the individual level and organizationally.[11]

With few exceptions, it remains the case that when historians, political scientists, and other scholars refer to "Black Populism" they are either implicitly or explicitly referring to African Americans in a movement understood to be fundamentally white in both its composition and leadership. However, given the *de facto* segregated institutional arrangements in the New South (before the advent of *de jure* segregation; that is, Jim Crow), if African Americans were going to challenge the authorities who ruled over them, would they not have had to organize themselves independently, as had those who organized the southern black churches, fraternal orders, and benevolent associations of the same period?

Rather than try to fit southern African Americans and their organizations into preexisting categories of what may be considered *white* Populism, I began to develop a concept of black Populism as a regional movement with its own historical integrity. The framework that I formulated became my doctoral dissertation in 2003, entitled "Black Populism in the New South, 1886–1898." It was completed the same year that Steven Hahn published *A Nation Under Our Feet: Black Political Struggles in the Rural South from Slavery to the Great Migration.*[12] Hahn's study, combined with others since, most notably Charles Postel's *The Populist Vision*, in which he acknowledges "two Populisms, black and white," along with Gerald Gaither's revised *Blacks and the Populist Revolt* (renamed *Blacks and the Populist Movement*); Matthew Hild's *Greenbackers, Knights of Labor, and Populists*; James Beeby's *Revolt of the Tar Heels*; and Joseph Gerteis's *Class and the Color Line*, indicate a new and growing academic consensus: southern African Americans in the post-Reconstruction era were not only actively organizing against (not simply victims of) Democratic rule but asserted themselves by developing their own lines of independent political organizing.[13]

As early as 1938, Girard T. Bryant implied that African Americans were independent of the white Populist movement; he titled the fifth chapter of his master's thesis "Colored Populism." But with the exception of Helen Edmonds's 1951 study on "fusion politics" in North Carolina, a notion of African Americans as independent appears to have been buried, not to reappear for nearly forty years. Gerald Gaither's 1977 publication *Blacks and the Populist Revolt* would make a major contribution to the subject of African Americans and Populism. Yet Gaither's detailed study, which throughout *suggests*, indeed offers proof of, black independence from white organizations, does not make the distinction between the two movements explicit. (The connector "and" in the title of his book indicates separation between African Americans and the Populist movement; it does not mean black independence *per se*).[14]

Another decade and a half would pass before Edward Ayers would note in his 1992 study *The Promise of the New South* that "Blacks [of the Colored Farmers' Alliance] ... did not think they could count on white fairness; they saw themselves as a group self-consciously opposed to whites, willing to organize for its members' protection," suggesting the black movement's independence.[15] Eight years later, Patrick Dickson would make a strong case for the independent origins and development of the Colored Farmers' Alliance in his master's thesis, "Out of the Lion's Mouth." Dickson's thesis, however, does not delve into black Populism after 1891. Regardless, such implicit and explicit perspectives of African Americans as independent, shifting away from the dominant scholarly view of African Americans and their organizations as "little more than an appendage [of the white-led Populist organizations]," as John D. Hicks wrote in his history of Populism in 1931, would remain the decidedly minority view—that is, until more recently.[16]

As has been the case with other periods in American history in which black political agency has had to be reconstructed (i.e., the slave revolts and conspiracies of the colonial era, the work of black abolitionists in the first half of the nineteenth century, and the role of black soldiers during the Civil War), the quarter century following Reconstruction has required new research and reconsideration regarding African Americans in the South. American history textbooks continue to reflect the older view, giving the overall impression that African Americans were politically passive in the decades following Reconstruction. But the more recent scholarship is making clear that far from being passive in the years following Reconstruction, black men and women took great measures, and, at times, at great costs, to carry out a variety of tactics to advance the political and economic interests of their communities.[17]

Beginning in the late 1870s, African Americans built new black institutions, or strengthened existing ones. Black Freemasons, originating in the Northeast, formed across the South, assuming political functions. As Corey Walker describes:

> African American appropriation of Freemasonry was a crucial component in a complex political struggle that did not dichotomize the political and cultural ... African American Freemasonry was part of a larger political strategy—what can be termed the "politics of culture"—that employed various cultural formations in an ever-expanding arsenal of political weapons designed to aid African Americans in articulating their discontent with a political system that marginalized their political choices and opportunities.[18]

Other fraternal orders of the late 1870s and early 1880s included the Colored Granges in Texas and Tennessee, the United Order of True Reformers and the Grand United Order of Good Samaritans in Virginia, and the National Order of Mosaic Templars of America in Arkansas. Michael Gomez has also noted the continuation of uniquely African-derived orders such as the Sande and Poro in the coastal Carolinas and Georgia. Likewise, a variety of "benevolent associations" were established in the period with chapters across the South. These included the United Friends Association, the Union Band of Brothers and Sisters, and the all-female United Daughters of Ham.[19]

Far more extensive than these associations, however, were the black Baptist and African Methodist Episcopalian churches that formed broad networks of support. The black churches, the "womb" of black society, as C. Eric Lincoln described, would serve as the primary bases in the development of black political action.[20] Along with benevolent associations and various mutual aid groups, black churches were essential for the stability and sustenance of African American communities in the post-Reconstruction period. Fraternal orders and benevolent associations (whose memberships often overlapped) usually met in black churches, as was the case with one AME church in Abbeville, South Carolina, which held meetings of the Colored Farmers' Alliance. As Orville Vernon Burton describes, "Independent black churches offered an opportunity to meet together away from the constant scrutiny of whites ... Rural churches housed such Afro-American institutions as the Masonic lodges, benevolent societies, burial organizations ... and sponsored schools, fairs, and social gatherings."[21] Black churches provided other vital support in the community: care for the sick and for orphans, loans for those without credit, funding to help cover funeral expenses, and pensions for widows.

Together with benevolent associations and male and female orders, the black churches were natural organizational springboards for what became black Populism. The Reverends Moore, Doyle, and Pattillo, ministers of either AME or black Baptist churches, were members of benevolent associations who then pursued the development of third-party politics. They would exemplify the breadth of black Populist organizing during the last two decades of the nineteenth century. Pattillo, for instance, represented the Colored Farmers' Alliance on the credentials committee of a national political conference held in St. Louis bringing together a number of reform organizations. The position was of considerable authority, reflecting not only Pattillo's prominence in the independent movement but his leadership role in the development of the national People's Party.[22]

Beginning in 1886 and continuing through 1900, African Americans built their own movement for economic and political reform: black Populism. The independent black movement, comprised of black farmers, sharecroppers, and agrarian workers, neither mirrored nor derived from the parallel white-based, white-led Populist movement, although it did share in common certain demands. Black Populists maintained their own organizations, put forward their own leaders, and developed their own set of tactics. They distinguished themselves from the white movement by demanding nondiscriminatory legislation, an end to separate-coach laws, higher wages for black workers, better credit for black farmers (along with lower interest rates on loans), an end to the convict lease system, the inclusion of black jurors in court cases involving black defendants, and federal support and oversight regarding public education and the electoral process (in the form of the Blair Education Bill and the Lodge Election Bill).[23]

During the two decades following Reconstruction, black Populism would assume different organizational forms and names (not unlike the modern civil rights movement, which encompassed, among other organizations, the National Association for the Advancement of Colored People, the Women's Political Council, the Southern Christian Leadership Conference, the Congress for Racial Equality, the Student Nonviolent Coordinating Committee, and a range of black churches). Although black agrarian groups had been established in some parts of the South before the mid-1880s, and notable black electoral participation continued beyond the late 1890s, for instance, a "Negro Alliance" had been formed in Prairie County,

Arkansas, as early as 1882, and African Americans in North Carolina's Second Congressional District remained active in the electoral arena beyond 1900, black Populism consisted of a specific period of discernible movement-building activities across the region.[24]

While leaving the South (that is, "voting with one's feet") or working with the Democratic Party were also strategies employed by African Americans during the period, black Populists, such as Moore, distinguished themselves by challenging Democratic rule, and therefore white supremacy. In addition to launching independent and insurgent campaigns against the Democratic Party, black Populists established farming exchanges, raised money for schools, published newspapers, led boycotts and strikes, and lobbied for political reforms. Within half a decade, the number of people actively participating in the movement grew into the tens of thousands. Exact numbers are impossible to verify since organizational membership lists were almost never made for fear of reprisal from white authorities should they be discovered, as was the case in Pitt County, North Carolina, during the fall of 1889 when a black chapter of the Knights of Labor was infiltrated.[25]

During the fall of 1889, black farm workers in Pitt County were in the process of organizing an assembly when a local white planter, John Bryan Grimes, a member of the Farmers' Alliance (and a Democrat), discovered their activities. In violation of the white Alliance's own policy against labor espionage, Grimes paid one of his black workers, George Freeman, to infiltrate a black Knights' assembly in Greenville, where more than a dozen African American men and women had been secretly holding meetings in a church. In September 1889, Freeman was paid to spy on the group. He applied for membership to the assembly and a late-night meeting was arranged to debate his application; two doorkeepers, Gale Moon and Elli Hardee, secured the church's entrance. Freeman was deemed suspect. The assembly's principal leader, Reverend Grimes Jr., along with Romeo Telfair, who served as president, believed that Freeman had ulterior motives. Both opposed Freeman's membership, as would another member, Sam Perry. Appeals were then made by the treasurer, Warren Jayson, and fellow member Henry Allen, who supported Freeman's application. The debate apparently carried on until 2 a.m., when Freeman's application was finally rejected by a full vote of the assembly, including two female colleagues, Phoebe Cobb and Fanny Glass, the latter also known as "the queen." Unfortunately, no further documents have surfaced to shed light on what became of the black assembly. But here we catch a glimpse of the Knights' structure and the kinds of precautionary measures that African Americans took to ensure their organization's existence.[26]

From what can be culled from existing records black Populism took shape in 1886 with the emergence of a cluster of organizations, including the southern branch of the Knights of Labor, the Colored Farmers' Alliance, the Colored Agricultural Wheels, the Cooperative Workers of America, and the Colored Farmers' Union. But as Gaither notes, the work of African Americans creating organizations for reform was not "a sudden political aberration but the culmination of a pattern of agrarian protest that had existed at least since Reconstruction."[27] The creation of formal organizations in 1886 therefore serves as an approximation of the starting point of the regionwide movement; it does not mean that movement-building efforts were not already underway. By the early 1890s, black Populists, whose participants had been up to this point largely engaged in the formation of farming cooperatives, instruction to improve agricultural techniques, demanding higher wages for agrarian workers, and lobbying state and federal government for economic reforms, increasingly placed their energies and resources in electoral initiatives. African Americans established third parties alongside white Populists, ran insurgent and independent candidates for office, and created fusion and coalitional campaigns. Divisions within the independent black movement, however, existed. Disputes, which primarily arose over specific tactics, tended to fall along class lines. In the early 1890s, small black landowners opposed the use of strikes by black agrarian laborers, for instance. Additionally, in areas where there was already a relatively strong black Republican presence, there was disagreement over whether or not a third party should be formed or supported. In addition to working with white independents—that is, those who were either politically unaffiliated or members of the People's Party (or the Union Labor Party)—black Populists selectively did work with the Republican Party as would, most prominently, George Washington Murray, a Colored Farmers' Alliance leader from South Carolina who was elected to Congress in 1893 via the Republican Party and became the leading voice in the fight to oppose black disenfranchisement in the state.[28] In some states where there was a viable People's Party, as in Georgia, African Americans selectively supported white Populist candidates for office.

During the fall of 1892, the young black minister Reverend Henry S. Doyle, a former Republican who worked with the Prohibition Party, set out to build the People's Party. He delivered over sixty speeches to black and white Georgians on behalf of Democrat-turned-Populist Tom Watson. In a campaign wracked with violence, at least fifteen African Americans were killed while scores of others were physically threatened and intimidated. Two African Americans, Anthony Wilson and Anton Graves, also took to the stump on behalf of the People's Party that year.[29] The logic of black and white voters joining forces against the Democratic Party based upon a common economic plight was as compelling as it was controversial in Georgia and elsewhere in the South. African Americans cheered Watson when he spoke at campaign rallies about shared economic interests among black and white southerners. However, African Americans also challenged Watson's picture of an equally shared plight. Addressing a People's Party convention in the summer of 1892, another Watson, a black Populist from Texas (his first name is not listed in the record), declared "it is now useless to tell you my interest is yours and yours mine," pointing to the very real socioeconomic and political differences among most black and white southerners, the former being predominantly landless sharecroppers and agrarian workers, while the latter tended to be farmers and often with black tenants or workers financially dependent upon them.[30] The differences in perspectives help point to the differences between the black and white movements.

As black Populism had expanded across the region between 1886 and 1891, it met different kinds of resistance, and from a variety of sources. Not only did individual white planters, merchants, landlords, and employers oppose the movement (sometimes through brutal force, as in the Leflore County Massacre of 1889 in Mississippi in retaliation for the Colored Farmers' Alliance boycott of a white-owned store), but political resistance also came from wealthier and more established African Americans, mostly tied to the Republican Party. Such black Republican leaders disapproved of black Populists directly challenging Democrats in the electoral arena by aligning with white independents.[31] Most black Republican leaders were vehemently opposed to a third-party strategy; they either did not trust white independents with whom black Populists were aligning themselves electorally, or they were simply invested in maintaining whatever degree of political authority they continued to enjoy in isolated parts of the South. In June 1892, for example, when the Reverend George W. Gaines suggested that it would be strategically wiser to vote for the "alliance party" (that is, the People's Party) the North Carolina Republican attorney Albion Tourgée (who later argued the landmark case of *Plessy v. Ferguson*) fired back, "I cannot imagine anything more perilous to the colored citizen."[32] The door to third-party politics among African Americans would not be closed, however:

two years later, under the leadership of black independents, the Republican and People's parties ran a cooperative campaign in North Carolina and briefly wrested power from the Democratic Party in the state legislature, where they instituted several key political reforms (notably, the restoration of home-county rule, the appearance of party insignias on ballots so that illiterate voters were not manipulated, and ensuring that all political parties were represented by election judges at the polls). Still other strategies were pursued among black leaders. For instance, some African Americans would support Democratic gubernatorial candidates over either Republican or Populist candidates, as in Alabama in 1893 and Georgia and Texas in 1896, with the hope of gaining or retaining limited political patronage.[33]

Black Populism, as an independent movement seeking to open up the political process through third-party politics, fusion, and cooperative campaigns with Republicans, began to buckle in 1896. White Populist and establishment black Republican leaders who had temporarily allied themselves with black Populists turned away or were driven apart through a combination of scare tactics and practical realities that made it increasingly clear that black and white electoral alliances could no longer be sustained in the face of growing legislation disenfranchising black voters (either in the form of poll taxes or amendments to state constitutions). The "Mississippi Plan" of black disfranchisement was followed by South Carolina in 1895 and Louisiana in 1898; other southern states followed soon thereafter.[34] By 1900, in the face of fierce opposition, propaganda campaigns, political intimidation, physical assaults on rank-and-file activists, and targeted assassinations of leaders, the movement collapsed. More isolated challenges by black Populists to the Democratic Party continued for several years (as in parts of east Texas), but black Populism as a regionwide movement had effectively been destroyed by the Democratic Party and its paramilitary adjuncts, including the revival of "Red Shirt companies" and the formation of associations of the White Man's Union.[35]

A new perspective, supported by new research, has begun to establish black Populism as a movement unto itself. This has taken place alongside ongoing efforts to analyze the role of African Americans *in* the Populist movement. The latter analyses have become more prominent in the overall literature on Populism since the mid-twentieth century, mostly as part of efforts by scholars to demonstrate the labor solidarity that existed between black and white southerners. In the 1950s, C. Vann Woodward, whose scholarship continues to serve as the model, if not starting point of New South history, popularized the idea that white Populists were sympathetic toward

African Americans.[36] His perspective, however, remained distinctly that of the white Populists and their movement. While Woodward did note in his *Origins of the New South* that "there is considerable evidence of independence among the Negroes," he would later make plain in *The Burden of Southern History* that Populism was a "native *white* political movement" [emphasis added].[37] Following Woodward, historians such as Norman Pollack, Walter Nugent, and Lawrence Goodwyn pointed to the relative openness of the white Populist movement, its democratic tenets, and the unusual (although not unprecedented) "biracial" coalitions in which white Populists participated. Still, the perspective was that of white Populists. As Goodwyn notes, "while much of [the Colored Alliance's] evolution was traceable to the actions of black people, its origins were a result of white radicalism."[38]

Like Woodward, many subsequent scholars of the New South, while more attentive to black political agency, continued to relegate African Americans to the periphery of Populism.[39] Such scholars identified black-white Populist coalitions as having occurred *within* the white movement when in fact they were tactical alliances forged *between* two separate strands of Populism, each with its own organizations, leaders, tactics, and perspectives. Indeed, it is only when black Populism is viewed as an autonomous movement, having a relationship to white Populism but independent from it, that it becomes possible to more fully understand the formation and character of the coalitions in which rural black and white southerners joined forces, as temporary as they were. The latest generation of scholars on the New South has begun to turn the tide in the overall historiography of the New South toward a far greater appreciation of African American political activity.

The conceptual problem of black Populism not having been viewed as a movement unto itself, as reflected in the work of historians up through the turn of the twenty-first century, is compounded by the paucity of primary sources detailing black Populist activities, organizations, leaders, and ideas. The particular difficulties confronted by black Populists in organizing their movement required covert actions. Consequently, we are left with piecemeal evidence of specific members, the details of their numbers, and the structures of their organizations. As Goodwyn has aptly noted, the actions of these African Americans has been "shrouded in mystery."[40] In addition to membership lists of black Populist organizations not having been kept, financial records, correspondence, diaries, and minutes of meetings are largely unavailable either because they were destroyed, or, as part of precautionary measures, rarely committed to paper. What does exist are remnants, oral histories passed down over the course of several generations, the words of African Americans and their organization's white spokespersons that appear in white Populist newspapers, and a few other written records. Most of the records that survive are mostly known through other contemporary sources, providing key insights into black Populism, but also limiting the scope of our knowledge about the movement.

New documents may very well be uncovered to shed further light on Black Populism. In the course of my own research on the Reverend Walter A. Pattillo, I came across an original photograph of the black Populist leader in the files of a black orphanage which he had helped to establish in Oxford, North Carolina; I gathered oral history from his great-grandson, Walter H. Pattillo Jr., a retired professor of biology (one among a number of interviews I conducted with descendents of black Populists); and a letter written by Pattillo in 1899 was passed along to me by a local archivist in the years since I first did archival work in the town near where the minister lived. The letter came from a descendent of one of Pattillo's neighbors in Granville County, Mrs. Julia Gregory, the widow of Dr. F. R. Gregory, a physician. Mrs. Gregory's family had carefully kept the letter of condolence sent by Pattillo soon after her husband passed away. The letter, along with family oral history, helps to give some insight into Pattillo's strong relationship with members of the white community, even as he built independent black-based institutions.[41]

In 2004, Gaither and Adams compiled a valuable annotated bibliography of primary and secondary sources as related to black Populism.[42] The bibliography could now include at least a dozen additional works that have since been published. These works entail a sentence here, or a name there, that can add to the rich and complex stories of black Populists and their collective movement; Marszalek's 2006 biography of George Washington Murray, for instance, provides a detailed account of the life of one of the movement's most prominent leaders. By the number of inquiries I have received since completing my 2003 dissertation, I am optimistic that other scholars will continue to build upon the history offered in existing studies. Postel's acclaimed *The Populist Vision*, affirming two separate Populisms, lends considerable weight to there being an independent black movement worthy of study and consideration. My own work has sought to establish a framework for students and scholars to view and perhaps further pursue the subject of black Populism themselves. To be sure, such future investigators will quickly discover that there are multiple paths to begin (or continue in) their research and hopefully help to further advance our collective understanding of the largest independent black movement in the South prior to the modern civil rights movement.

Notes

1. J. L. Moore, letter to the editor, *National Economist*, March 7, 1891.

2. United States representative Henry Cabot Lodge of Massachusetts introduced the bill on June 26, 1890. See *Congressional Record*, 51st Congress, Session 1; 5789–5793; 6538–6545; 6851; 6869.

3. See "What the Force Bill Means," a cartoon by C. De Grimm that was posted on large sheets in the South by the National Democratic Committee appearing in *Review of Reviews*, November 1892, reproduced in John D. Hicks, *The Populist Revolt: A History of the Farmers' Alliances and the People's Party* (Minneapolis: University of Minnesota Press, 1931), 252; Charles Postel, *The Populist Vision* (New York: Oxford University Press, 2007), 178–179.

4. Gerald H. Gaither, *Blacks and the Populist Movement: Ballots and Bigotry in the New South* (Tuscaloosa: University of Alabama Press, 2005), 56.

5. Omar H. Ali, *In the Lion's Mouth: Black Populism in the New South, 1886–1900* (Jackson: University Press of Mississippi, 2010); Gaither, *Blacks and the Populist Movement.*

6. C. Vann Woodward, *Origins of the New South, 1877–1913* (Baton Rouge: Louisiana State University Press, 1951), 542–543.

7. The classic history of the period is C. Vann Woodward's *Origins of the New South*, first published in 1951. Since Woodward, the most comprehensive history of the New South was published by Edward L. Ayers in his *The Promise of the New South: Life After Reconstruction* (New York: Oxford University Press, 1992).

8. Primary sources on the movement appear as reprints of newspaper articles in *The National Economist*, such as Moore's letter to the editor. These reprints also include selections from the *National Alliance* newspaper, the principal newspaper of the Colored Farmers' Alliance (which has been lost or not yet found). Other primary sources, such as legal testimonies, come from contested election cases, for instance in North Carolina in the mid-1890s. See, for instance, James M. Beeby, *Revolt of the Tar Heels: The North Carolina Populist Movement, 1890–1901* (Jackson: University Press of Mississippi, 2008). There are also a few letters, primarily from white Populist leaders discussing African Americans, to draw upon. Finally there is the brief history of the Colored Farmers' Alliance offered by its general superintendent Richard M. Humphrey in a book printed in 1892 and the Congressional Record, which contains speeches made by Colored Alliance leader George Washington Murray when he served in the House.

9. *Progressive Farmer*, August 26, 1890; Joe Creech, *Righteous Indignation: Religion and the Populist Revolution* (Urbana: University of Illinois Press, 2006), 196, n. 12.

10. Douglass Geraldyne Perry, "Black Populism: The Negro in the People's Party in Texas" (M.S. thesis, Prairie View A & M University, Texas, 1945).

11. This approach and framing appears throughout the scholarly literature on Populism. A recent expression of this appears in the description of the Colored Farmers'

Alliance as "the auxiliary of the all-white Farmers' Alliance." See Walter Edgar, ed., *The South Carolina Encyclopedia* (Columbia: University of South Carolina Press, 2006), 654.

12. Omar H. Ali, "Black Populism in the New South, 1886–1898" (Ph.D. diss., Columbia University, 2003); Steven Hahn, *A Nation Under Our Feet: Black Political Struggles in the Rural South from Slavery to the Great Migration* (Cambridge, MA: Harvard University Press, 2003).

13. Postel, *The Populist Vision*, 174, 202; Gaither, *Blacks and the Populist Movement*; Beeby, *Revolt of the Tar Heels*; Connie L. Lester, *Up From the Mudsills of Hell: The Farmers' Alliance, Populism, and Progressive Agriculture in Tennessee, 1870–1915* (Athens: University of Georgia Press, 2006); Matthew Hild, *Greenbackers, Knights of Labor, and Populists: Farmer-Labor Insurgency in the Late-Nineteenth-Century South* (Athens: University of Georgia Press, 2007); Joseph Gerteis, *Class and the Color Line: Interracial Class Coalition in the Knights of Labor and the Populist Movement* (Durham, NC: Duke University Press, 2007).

14. Girard T. Bryant, "The Populist Movement and the Negro" (M.A. thesis, University of Kansas, Lawrence, 1938), 53–66; Helen Edmonds, *The Negro and Fusion Politics in North Carolina, 1894–1901* (Chapel Hill: University of North Carolina Press, 1951); Gaither, *Blacks and the Populist Movement*.

15. Ayers, *The Promise of the New South*, 257.

16. Patrick J. Dickson, "Out of the Lion's Mouth: The Colored Farmers' Alliance in the New South, 1886–1892" (M.P.S. thesis, Cornell University, 2000), 24; Hicks, *The Populist Revolt*, 115. Since Bryant, there have been only four other full-length regional studies detailing the role of African Americans in Populism: Jack Abramowitz's 1950 Columbia University doctoral dissertation, "Accommodation and Militancy in Negro Life, 1876–1916"; William Gnatz's 1961 University of Chicago master's thesis, "The Negro and the Populist Movement in the South"; Gerald Gaither's *Blacks and the Populist Revolt*, based on his 1972 University of Tennessee doctoral dissertation; and my 2003 Columbia University doctoral dissertation. Among the state-based studies and shorter treatments of the subject there are five master's theses, seventeen articles in academic journals, and individual chapters in six academic books. There are over one dozen short articles, books, essays, and papers that reference the work of the Colored Alliance and other black Populist organizations. For instance, there is Ronald Yanosky's illuminating paper, "The Colored Farmers' Alliance and the Single Tax," delivered in Chicago at the 1992 Annual Meeting of the Organization of American Historians, which discusses the differences between the black and white Alliances regarding the issue of private property. To date there are only two biographies of black Populist leaders: Gregg Cantrell's *Feeding the Wolf: John B. Rayner and the Politics of Race, 1850–1918* (Wheeling, IL: Harlan Davidson, 2001), and John F. Marszalek's *A Black Congressman in the Age of Jim Crow: South Carolina's George Washington Murray* (Gainesville: University Press of Florida, 2006). See Ali, "Black Populism in the New South, 1886–1898," 11–12, n. 23, n. 24, for further details on the historiography of black Populism.

17. Exceptions to this are American history textbooks such as Eric Foner's *Give Me Liberty! An American History* (New York: W. W. Norton & Co., 2009) or African American history-focused textbooks, such as Darlene Clark Hine's *African Americans: A Concise History* (Upper Saddle, NJ: Pearson Education, 2006).

18. Corey D. B. Walker, *A Noble Fight: African American Freemasonry and the Struggle for Democracy in America* (Urbana: University of Illinois Press, 2008), 178.

19. Ayers, *The Promise of the New South*, 70; Nancy F. Cott, *No Small Courage: A History of Women in the United States* (New York: Oxford University Press, 2004), 296; C. A. Spencer, "Black Benevolent Societies and the Development of Black Insurance Companies in Nineteenth-Century Alabama," *Phylon* 46 (1985), 254; William Edward Spriggs, "The Virginia Colored Farmers' Alliance: A Case Study of Race and Class Identity," *Journal of Negro History* 64 (Summer 1979), 203–204; Michael A. Gomez, *Exchanging Our Country Marks: The Transformation of African Identities in the Colonial and Antebellum South* (Chapel Hill: University of North Carolina Press, 1998), 93–101.

20. C. Eric Lincoln and Lawrence H. Mamiya, *The Black Church in the African American Experience* (Durham, NC: Duke University Press, 1990), 17.

21. Orville Vernon Burton, *In My Father's House Are Many Mansions: Family and Community in Edgefield, South Carolina* (Chapel Hill: University of North Carolina, 1985), 242, 406, n. 69.

22. See Omar H. Ali, *In the Balance of Power: Independent Black Politics and Third-Party Movements in the United States* (Athens: Ohio University Press, 2008), 74–100.

23. The Blair Education Bill, sponsored by New Hampshire Republican senator Henry W. Blair in the mid-1880s, called for federal support for public education and, like the Lodge Bill, was strongly endorsed by the Colored Farmers' Alliance. See Daniel W. Crofts, "The Black Response to the Blair Education Bill," *Journal of Southern History* 37 (February 1971): 41–65.

24. Roy V. Scott, "Milton George and the Farmer's Alliance Movement," *Mississippi Valley Historical Review* 45 (June 1958), 107, n. 59; Bernice R. Fine, "Agrarian Reform and the Texas Negro Farmers, 1886–1896" (M.A. thesis, North Texas State University, 1971), 81–82; Theodore Saloutos, *Farmer Movements in the South, 1865–1933* (Berkeley and Los Angeles: University of California Press, 1960), 79; Eric Anderson, *Race and Politics in North Carolina, 1872–1901: The Black Second* (Baton Rouge: Louisiana State University Press, 1981), 331–342. Black Populism also took place in parts of the Midwest, including Missouri and Kansas, states where African Americans had recently migrated from the South.

25. The Colored Farmers' Alliance alone claimed over one million members in 1891. See Richard M. Humphrey, "History of the Colored Farmers' National Alliance and Co-Operative Union," in *The Farmer's Alliance History and Agricultural Digest*, ed. Nelson A. Dunning (Washington, D.C.: Alliance Publishing Co., 1891), 290.

26. Robert C. McMath Jr., "Southern White Farmers and the Organization of Black Farm Workers: A North Carolina Document," *Labor History* 18 (Winter 1977): 118–119.

27. Gaither, *Blacks and the Populist Movement*, 48.

28. Omar H. Ali, "Standing Guard at the Door of Liberty: Black Populism in South Carolina, 1886–1897," *South Carolina Historical Magazine* 107 (July 2006): 190–203.

29. Wilson had previously served as a Republican state legislator (and was later reelected to Georgia's assembly with the backing of the People's Party); see William Gnatz, "The Negro and the Populist Movement in the South" (M.A. thesis, University of Chicago, 1961), 83, 119.

30. *Southern Mercury*, June 30, 1892.

31. William F. Holmes, "The Leflore County Massacre and the Demise of the Colored Farmer's Alliance," *Phylon* 34 (September 1973): 267–274; Ali, *In the Balance of Power*, 76–86.

32. Albion W. Tourgée Papers, Johns Hopkins University, microfilm items 6341, 6350, Reel 30, Rev. George Washington Gaines to Albion W. Tourgée, and response (June 22 and June 24, 1892); Mark Elliot of the University of North Carolina, Greensboro, was kind enough to pass along some of his research regarding Tourgée's opposition to the third-party strategy. See Mark Elliot, *Color-Blind Justice: Albion Tourgée and the Quest for Racial Equality from the Civil War to* Plessy v. Ferguson (New York: Oxford University Press, 2006), 255.

33. Ali, *In the Balance of Power*, 95.

34. Michael Perman, *Struggle for Mastery: Disfranchisement in the South, 1888–1908* (Chapel Hill: University of North Carolina Press, 2001), 73–74, 88–90.

35. Omar H. Ali, "Independent Black Voices from the Late 19th Century: Black Populists and the Struggle Against the Southern Democracy," *Souls: A Critical Journal of Black Politics, Culture, and Society* 7 (Spring 2005): 13–15; Ayers, *The Promise of the New South*, 301; Lawrence C. Goodwyn, "Populist Dreams and Negro Rights: East Texas as a Case Study," *American Historical Review* 76 (1971): 1438, 1440.

36. Woodward, *Origins of the New* South, 1951.

37. C. Vann Woodward, *The Burden of Southern History* (Baton Rouge: Louisiana State University Press, 1993), 157; Woodward, *Origins of the New South*, 192.

38. Norman Pollack, *The Populist Response to Industrial America* (Cambridge, MA: Harvard University Press, 1962); Walter T. K. Nugent, *The Tolerant Populists: Kansas Populism and Nativism* (Chicago: University of Chicago Press, 1963); Lawrence C. Goodwyn, "The Populist Response to Black America," in *Democratic Promise: The Populist Moment in America* (New York: Oxford University Press, 1976). See also Charles Crowe, "Tom Watson, Populists, and Blacks Reconsidered," *Journal of Negro History* 60 (April 1970): 99–116; Robert Saunders, "Southern Populists and the Negro, 1893–1895," *Journal of Negro History* 54 (July 1969): 240–261.

39. Goodwyn, *Democratic Promise*, 118.

40. Goodwyn, *Democratic Promise*, 122.

41. Fann Montague of the Richard H. Thornton Library in Oxford, North Carolina, sent me a copy of this letter, dated March 27, 1899.

42. Anthony J. Adam and Gerald H. Gaither, *Black Populism in the United States: An Annotated Bibliography* (Westport, CT: Praeger, 2004).

Creating a New South

THE POLITICAL CULTURE OF DEEP SOUTH POPULISM

—LEWIE REECE

For white southerners of the 1890s, the need for white supremacy was as obvious as breathing. Nevertheless, for such an all-encompassing frame of reference, the slightest danger to the social order could suggest a possibility of the destruction of the racial status quo. White Populists of the 1890s fully shared the racial worldview that defined their history prior to their separation from the Democratic Party in 1892. This was even more the case in the Deep South, where African Americans were either a majority of the population or a very large minority in all of these states. Nevertheless, when Populists emerged as a distinct alternative to the Democratic Party, they made genuine efforts to receive African American support. This was more than simply an example of political opportunism (although both Georgia Populist Tom Watson and Alabama Jeffersonian Reuben Kolb were certainly guilty of that charge) for Populists also sought to craft public policies that would benefit the African American community. Moreover, over time Populism in the Deep South emerged as a challenge to the racial and political order within the region. Of course, considerable variation existed within this pattern. For example, in Mississippi, Populism was nearly a lily-white movement, but certainly that was not the case in Alabama, Louisiana, and Georgia. Conceding the limitations of race, southern Populism reveals a "forgotten alternative" to white supremacy that had defined southern identity for centuries. The failure of Populists and Republicans to stem the new racial order of the disfranchisement era ought not to obscure their desire to create a more just and humane society.

The Southern Farmers' Alliance's origins can be traced back to the early 1870s where farmers founded the original organization in Lampasas County, Texas. It soon spread to the rest of the state, although it remained a precarious organization throughout the 1880s. Its original purpose was very similar to many agricultural self-help groups that sought to pool their resources. By the mid-1880s it had a significant membership but was also highly factionalized over disagreements about the role that the state alliance should play in politics. It appeared that this disagreement would lead to a split into rival organizations, but Charles W. Macune, who was elected chair of the state executive committee in 1886, was able to bring both groups together. Having accomplished this objective, Macune then sought an active program of expansion into the South and the plains states. The advantage of such a program was that it would bring new members into an organization frequently starved for money, but it also eventually transformed the purpose of the order. Macune's first step was to form an alliance with the Louisiana Farmers' Union, which had been active as an agricultural organization in that state since the early 1880s. This merger was augmented with a similar consolidation with the Agricultural Wheel, which also agreed to adopt the all-white rule of the Texas Alliance. In 1887, these activities were followed with the sending out of a variety of local organizers who began to plant the alliance throughout the South. In some cases Alliance organizers were already present without official recognition from the Texas Alliance. The response throughout the Deep South was electric.[1]

The agreement between the Louisiana Farmers' Union and the new Farmers' Alliance led to an immediate expansion of the new organization within the Pelican State in 1887. Equally emphatic was the response in Mississippi, where Alliance lecturer S. O. Daws led a team of six lecturers into the state within the same year. Within a few weeks Daws planted sub-alliances in the state, and by 1890, approximately 80,000 farmers had joined the organization. The response was equally well received in Alabama, where the first alliances were formed by 1886, although complicated by the large presence of the Agricultural Wheel in the northern part of the state. Nevertheless, by 1890, the Alliance in Alabama was one of the strongest in the country, only passed in sheer numbers by Texas. The Alliance grew more slowly in Georgia, but even so a range of alliances at the county level were established by 1887, and by the end of that year a statewide organization was in place. Once the formal organization was established, white farmers joined in large numbers, and by 1890, there were more than 100,000 Alliancemen in the state. What was revealed in this pattern was a rapid expansion of the organization within the space of a few years. Such growth reflected not only the ability of the organizers, but the fact that local people throughout the South saw the Alliance as a remarkable opportunity. The key message that attracted farmers was the economic advantages of cooperative farming. Important selling points were cooperative economic entities such as cooperative stores, cotton warehouses, and ginning facilities. These efforts to pool economic resources did have an immediate impact as one historian of the Georgia Alliance estimates that in 1889, Georgia farmers saved $200,000 on fertilizer costs alone. However, such activities often lacked enough working capital to survive in the long term, and at the county level, these types of activities ultimately failed. At least for the Deep South it seems especially dubious that these short-lived enterprises, seemingly often on the verge of collapse, helped to create a "movement culture" that led directly to Populism. Instead, a more likely explanation would be the reform critique that was fostered within the Alliance.[2]

The fall of 1889 marked the formation of the National Farmers' Alliance and Industrial Union. Members of the Northern Alliance and the Southern Farmers' Alliance agreed to a joint meeting and merger in St. Louis. There, they agreed upon a platform of seven basic demands, calling for a fairly dramatic restructuring of the American economic system: the abolition of national banks, the substitution of legal tender treasury notes, the free and unlimited coinage of silver, the issuing of paper money, limits on economic speculation, and government ownership of transportation and communication. Another major development in St. Louis was the election of Leonidas L. Polk, the North Carolina editor of the *Progressive Farmer*. Polk defeated Macune, who did not support a political role for the Alliance. Yet, if the events in St. Louis put the Alliance on the way to radical political action, more problematic was the membership of the order. Perhaps because the Alliance grew so rapidly, many members did not share the same understanding of political economy and thus the meaning of the Alliance was almost immediately called into question. Some joined the Alliance because they shared a belief in their economic principles, while others were deeply committed to the status quo and found it politically convenient. While very large planters seem to have avoided the Alliance, many planters did join the organization with a clear conscience. Their sense was that the Alliance was less a political organization and more an association of farmers that was closely tied to the Democratic Party. Additionally, many Democrats joined the order out of a desire to either control the organization or because they found it politically convenient. Such tension would remain a source of political discord for the next two and a half years. Even as late as 1892 some members of the Alliance were still hopeful that the organization would turn away from third-party action. The limitations of

Alliance radicalism was also revealed in their expressing the racial orthodoxy of the white South.[3]

The Farmers' Alliance in the South was a reflection of the social milieu of the white South in the latter part of the nineteenth century. Moreover, with the exception of those that came into the Alliance out of an anti-Democratic Party experience, most members had no real experience with African Americans as political equals. Their racial worldview was therefore that of your basic southern Democrat in the Deep South, being all but consumed with the need for white supremacy and viewing with contempt the aspirations of the African American community. This is clearly revealed in a series of essays that N. A. Dunning published as propaganda materials for the Farmers' Alliance in 1891. While many of the essays in this volume simply repeated the standard platitudes about the dangers of sectionalism, the racist diatribe authored by J. H. Turner reflects an entirely different character. As a former slaveholder, much of Turner's positive rhetoric toward African Americans had a paternalist flavor, reflecting in some ways the kind of arguments phrased in the antebellum era. Turner began with a lengthy indictment of Reconstruction, in which he argued that African Americans had in many ways been promised forty acres and a mule and had been little more than the slaves of Carpetbaggers. The white slaveholding class had no choice but to dislike African Americans for "the white people of the South ignored him politically and hated him, because he followed those he knew were the enemies of good government."[4] Since the Democrats had returned to power, Turner argued, the record had changed, and African Americans had made good progress. He repeated the frequent myth that white southerners believed that African Americans did not pay tax to support public education, when in fact these schools were substantially under funded. But Turner also went a step further toward the end of his essay with a long indictment of newspaper accounts of racial violence, especially of the well-known acts of political violence against African Americans. These, Turner maintained, had never taken place, except for perhaps two or three somewhere. Claims of roots were a wild exaggeration for "no one took part except a few worthless negroes, who generally work by day at some public work, and a few drunken white men, who lounge around the street corners and whittle good boxes."[5] While the tenor of the other essays was not as strident as Turner, they shared a similar tone. The frequent denunciations of sectionalism were in fact the complaint of the Democratic South against efforts of the federal government to enforce the right to vote. It was emblematic of the general attitude of the white Alliance members on matters of race. This was not all that surprising considering that African Americans could not join the Alliance, participated only as onlookers at public events, and were marginalized as much as possible. Overcoming this stereotypical frame of reference would demonstrate an important shift in the Populist experience, although some could never overcome their prejudice. This way of thinking about African Americans as a group of people was also reflected in the way that white Alliance members thought about the subordinate African American organization, the Colored Farmers' Alliance.[6]

The Colored Farmers' Alliance development was an audacious story of advancement, just like that of the larger white organization, the Farmers' Alliance. The two were separate and autonomous organizations, although clearly the Colored Farmers' Alliance was considered by whites to have an inferior place within the movement. Much like the Farmers' Alliance in 1886, the Colored Farmers' Alliance started first in Texas and then spread quickly throughout the rest of the South. It stressed the importance of African American self-help, focused on economic rather than political issues, and in many cases was led by black ministers who largely advocated an accommodationist approach on the part of the African American community; that is, a political leadership style that sought negotiation and compromise, and focused on self-help and economic development, rather than political activism. Nevertheless, at the same time many members of the Colored Farmers' Alliance defense of the ballot and civil rights belied some of their rhetoric about racial and sectional controversy. However, it should be noted that most African Americans who joined the Colored Farmers' Alliance did so because they believed it could improve their economic standing, in this sense much of the same attraction that had led white farmers into the Farmers' Alliance. The two groups, however, were not entirely compatible, and this reflected the difference between an organization composed of farm workers and one dominated by the small- and medium-sized planters. Complicating the difficulties of the Colored Farmers' Alliance was the leadership of R. M. Humphrey, a white Baptist minister, who served as its president. As a minister, Humphrey had been involved in a range of Social Gospel activity that brought him into contact with the black community in Texas. Nevertheless, Humphrey had a disdainful view of African American achievement, although it was masked by a well-meaning conservative paternalism. In the Dunning collection of essays, Humphrey offered a brief history of the Colored Farmers' Alliance. In describing the difficulties confronting the Colored Farmers' Alliance, Humphrey noted the difficulties in developing people whose long experience with slavery had "become increasingly besotted and ignorant."⁷ Nevertheless, the Colored Farmers' Alliance had by its conduct brought an end to those who had feared a coming race war. What had been a deteriorating relationship between whites and African Americans had been arrested by the emergence of the two alliances. The Colored Farmers' Alliance in this sense revealed the possibility of racial harmony, in which African Americans would be removed as a political threat. It is highly doubtful that the membership of the Colored Farmers' Alliance shared Humphrey's agenda. Certainly, J. W. Carter, the spokesman of the Georgia Colored Alliance, was no accommodationist. He even went so far as to address the Georgia legislature and argued against the passage of segregated railroad cars in 1891. This example of political activism reveals as well that the Colored Farmers' Alliance had not completely abandoned the political realm. It was more than simply economic interest that had brought African Americans into the order, and their interests were not always compatible with the Southern Farmers' Alliance. Indeed, close relationships between the two Alliances were not always possible, and at the local level some white sub-alliances were frequently hostile. The two Alliances came into conflict over the desire of African American workers to strike for higher pay.⁸

The emergence of the Colored Farmers' Alliance occurred during a sustained period of African American activism throughout the plantation areas of the South. In some cases one could see a direct linkage to the Colored Farmers' Alliance, while in others it was other agricultural workers who were trying to organize workers for better pay and improved working conditions. In 1887, these tensions were revealed in an attempt by rural African Americans to strike for higher wages in southern Louisiana. The Knights of Labor had organized among African American workers in the heart of the sugar industry in Louisiana, and after negotiations for a modest increase in wages went nowhere black workers went on strike. Local planters used white workers in the place of black workers, began massive evictions of the black workers, and in areas where whites were the numerical minority, the air was filled with considerable tension. The conflict reached its eventual conclusion when, on November 21–23, 1887, the state militia fired on black workers, and with this massive use of force, crushed efforts at unionization. For southern whites, this event was not simply disconcerting; it also reminded leaders how precarious white rule was in the region. As long as the Colored Farmers' Alliance was controlled by southern whites, it was viewed as a fairly innocuous organization that could be tolerated. But in this environment, the very act of organizing itself was now called into question. For example, in 1889, when James Crumwell attempted to organize the local Colored Farmers' Alliance in LeFlore County, Mississippi, he raised the ire of local merchants and planters. Convinced this was part of an orchestrated campaign of incipient revolution, local planters struck savagely and murdered more than twenty-five people, including lynching four of the leaders. These events belied the suggestion that the Alliance was ushering in a new harmonious political order. The very ability of the Alliance to control the political environment was also dubious, for the election results in 1890 were certainly mixed.[9]

The muddled condition of the Farmers' Alliance was certainly revealed by the 1890 elections throughout the Deep South. The new governor of Georgia, William Northen, was ostensibly a member of the Alliance, but in fact it was more a case of empty rhetoric than anything else. The new Alliance legislature in Georgia showed how easily conservative Democrats joined the order when they elected the reactionary John B. Gordon to another term in the U.S. Senate. In Alabama, Alliance supporters were at first optimistic about the possibilities of political change. A key recruit to the movement was Reuben Kolb, the state commissioner of agriculture. Kolb informed Leonidas L. Polk that he believed he could be elected governor "if the farmers will unite to a man on me."[10] Yet, Kolb was aware of the limitations of the Alliance's power in Alabama politics. He knew he could not run simply as a farmers' candidate because the elite controlled the Alabama Democratic Party and they were determined to stop Kolb's advancement to the governorship. Engaging in strong-arm tactics at the Democratic Party convention, the planters managed to squeeze enough votes to elect Thomas Jones instead. These events should have made it clear that any notion that the Alliance was the Democratic Party was untrue. But instead, Alliance members were still optimistic that the war inside the party would ultimately be successful. The majority of members were in no mood to consider the possibility of third-party action, and this southern dominated movement also wanted to establish their racial orthodoxy.[11]

The meeting of the Alliance, in Ocala, Florida, in December 1890, was important in a number of different respects. Flush with what they considered to be a victory in the southern state elections, the Alliance was able to put off the decision regarding third-party politics for an additional two years. The Alliance reaffirmed the key elements of the agenda agreed to in St. Louis. A significant change, however, was a provision calling for the creation of the subtreasury. This was in many ways the brainchild of Charles

Macune, and it called for the federal government to create warehouses that could store certain key agricultural goods. Farmers could deposit crops that could be resold at a later time, and could borrow against the principle of the crop, paying only a small amount of interest and modest storage fees. This proposal, made during the 1890s, was one of the key differences that would eventually separate the Populists from their political opponents. It would also be a source of considerable discord within the Alliance throughout the Deep South. The final key provision would be of prime significance. It was a resolution introduced by William S. McAlister, a delegate from Mississippi. At this time Congress was in the process of debating the merits of a Federal Election Bill that mandated federal control over congressional and presidential elections. Its principal purpose was to guarantee the right to vote to African American and white political minorities. McAlister's resolution denounced what was termed a radical revolution in the election process that would be "fatal to the autonomy of the states." Moreover, the resolution urged senators to "employ all fair and legal means to defeat this unpatriotic measure, which can result in nothing but evil to our common and beloved country."[12] That such a resolution passed with hardly any significant opposition reveals the racial views of southern delegates, and northern delegates' limited commitment to civil rights. It was hardly the kind of decision that would endear the Alliance to African Americans, who were desperate to see this legislation enacted. The bill's eventual defeat by a filibuster in the Senate was a major setback for the cause of civil rights, and Congress would not seriously consider such legislation for another century. But the hopes and expectation of the Alliance would be dashed in the coming year.[13]

The coming year would expose the limitations of both the Alliance itself and the nature of race relations between the Southern Farmers' Alliance and the Colored Farmers' Alliance. The state legislatures did not usher in a range of reforms as had been expected, but instead proved a disappointment to the Alliance. Not only did the legislatures oppose the subtreasury, but far from ushering in significant economic reform, they proved to be just as conservative as previous legislatures. Moreover, the subtreasury itself became a major subject of debate within the Democratic Party, and it was an issue that the Alliance essentially lost. While not all southern Democrats were as rigid as those in Mississippi, where opposition to the subtreasury became a test of Democratic loyalty, all were just as firmly opposed to the proposal. Alliance leader Leonidas L. Polk hoped that the Democratic Congress would take concrete steps toward enacting the subtreasury. But instead Congress made no real effort to enact it, and Polk thus became increasingly alienated from the Democratic Party. For those who belonged to the Alliance, this became a moment of decision. Yet, many who belonged to the Alliance found the increasing movement toward the third party a betrayal of the nonpartisan goal of the organization. In Mississippi, for example, William S. McAlister and his supporters were essentially excommunicated from the state Alliance when they refused to support the subtreasury. The real loser in this process was the Alliance because as a result of disappointment in the state legislature of 1891, and the dispute over the subtreasury, its membership declined. The Colored Farmers' Alliance also reached the end of its journey. The events in LeFlore County were but a precursor, and when the national organization agreed to support the labor dispute between Arkansas cotton workers and planters, it effectively ended their efforts. As with similar events in Louisiana and Mississippi, planters refused to countenance an organization that was part of an effort for plantation workers to strike for higher wages. Refusing to negotiate with their workers, planters in the Arkansas delta responded with a massive assertion of force, which crushed this movement and led to the death of fifteen people and the arrest of another six. Nor had white members of the Alliance come to the assistance of their sister organization in the Colored Farmers' Alliance. Instead, Polk revealed the way in which the Alliance was a planter-dominated institution when he said it was not in the financial interest of planters to pay more than fifty cents a day to workers. Polk's journal, the *Progressive Farmer,* went a step further in arguing that it would be better to leave the cotton unpicked rather than to accept the demands of plantation workers. The Alliance and the Colored Farmers' Alliance had essentially both died.[14]

The process of creating a functioning third party in the Deep South was not a simple one. Even after the preliminary convention of the new Populist Party, held in February 1892, elements within the Alliance and the Democratic Party tried to check the development of the new party. Most members of the Alliance simply could not endure independent action, fearful that the destruction of the Democratic Party would lead to African American political equality. Some members of the Alliance were so completely alienated by the Democratic Party's response to the reform agenda, that they were determined to launch the new party. Among their number was Leonidas L. Polk, who would not countenance any suggestion of working within the Democratic Party again. Polk confided to a friend that he doubted that there was "any power on earth can prevent independent action."[15] Nevertheless, desperate Democrats were prepared to promise nearly anything to get Populists in the South to return to the party fold. Democrats were not serious but were simply determined to hold as many of their voters as possible. One of the more prominent Alliance supporters who refused to countenance third-party action was Lon Livingston of Georgia. Livingston had played a prominent role in the affairs of the Alliance and had even been the more radical alternative to the more conservative Alliance candidate, William Northen, for the Georgia governorship in 1890. However, Livingston decided to withdraw and run for Congress instead, and for the next two years he fought valiantly against the formation of a third party. While Livingston managed to hold many Georgia members of the Alliance in the Democratic Party, he clearly failed to prevent the emergence of a third party in the state. Moreover, Livingston also alienated many of the more radical members of the state Alliance. One Populist suggested to Polk that Livingston was a "scoundrel, a traitor, and any thing that is corrupt."[16] These feelings reflect not simply political alienation, but that the Populist Party was now a reality. Having a third party was one thing; it was quite another to be a viable party and to resolve the difficulties of race when it was such a central issue. This was clearly revealed in Louisiana, where the Populists fought their first statewide campaign in the Deep South.[17]

The difficulties that the Louisiana Populists faced in the 1892 election are a reminder that the national or regional issues of the Alliance were not always primary. For more than a decade, the defining issue of Louisiana politics was the state lottery, widely viewed as totally corrupt. The factional divide within the Democratic Party was essentially between pro- and anti-lottery Democrats, with urban Democrats largely supportive of the lottery, and the planter faction of the Democratic Party opposed. Of course, these differences were not entirely rigid, but the two Democratic groupings separated so substantially that they ran rival candidates, although the official nominee, Murphy Foster, was from the anti-lottery faction. Anti-lottery Democrats also entered into an electoral pact with the Farmers' Alliance, or at least with the more conservative leadership offered by Thomas Adams, who served as president. Adams was offered the Democratic nomination, but declined and agreed instead to run for secretary of state on the Democratic ticket. This was unacceptable to the more radical members of the Alliance, many of whom had roots in independent third-party action that went back to the Independents and the Greenback Party. As a result, in Louisiana it was not the subtreasury, third-party action, or anything else that led to revolt, but the state lottery and the politics of the Democratic Party.

Complicating the byzantine twists of Louisiana politics was division within the state Republican Party, between the more moderate faction led by former governor Henry Warmoth and the pro-civil rights wing led by former senator William Kellogg. In this state election there were two Democratic tickets, two Republican tickets, the conservative members of the Alliance joining the planter faction of the Democratic Party, and lastly, the Populists.[18]

Louisiana Populists met in Alexandria and nominated a state ticket. A small number of African Americans were present at the preliminary state convention as delegates. Charles Roxborough and L. D. Laurent, two prominent African American Populists, were nominated for secretary of state but they declined and agreed to serve as members of the state executive committee. In the official call of the state People's Party, some general statements were made to African Americans. Some Populists claimed that the interests of African Americans and whites were identical, and promised to administer the law with racial neutrality. Moreover, Louisiana Populists insisted it was pointless for African Americans to vote Republican as they could not win. African Americans would also certainly have understood the racial code in the call for government to be run by the intelligent and educated. Despite the hopes of Louisiana Populists, the results were disastrous. Murphy Foster and the anti-lottery faction of Democrats defeated their pro-lottery opponents, but the Populist campaign was never competitive. The Populist state ticket finished fifth, with approximately 9,000 votes. The Populists carried only four parishes in the northern part of the state and elected only four members of the state legislature. Polk was correct to note that in Louisiana you had one Democratic faction "arming themselves with Winchester rifles to shoot the other faction."[19] But the disorder and chaos had not helped Populists at all, and the 40,000 Republican votes for the two state tickets revealed the relative strength of the opposition parties in the state. The lesson of the campaign was clear to Louisiana Populists. If they truly wished to win, they needed to do better in the southern part of the state, home to the highest concentration of African Americans. Victory in Louisiana depended on Populists and Republicans working together, regardless of their differences on economic policy. Within months, Populists and Republicans indeed formed an electoral coalition in the state. The Louisiana election, however, took place in the infancy of the party's development and growth. By the summer of 1892, Populists were well on their way to forming a national structure, and assembling a national ticket.[20]

Following the decision to form a third party, it was expected that Leonidas L. Polk would be the Populists' presidential nominee of 1892. However, shortly before the national convention was held, Polk fell seriously ill and died very suddenly. Despite Polk's death, Populists remained hopeful about the presidential election. Among their number was Joseph Manning, one of the founders of Alabama Populism, and certainly the moral center of the movement within the state. Writing decades after the passing of Populism, Manning noted, "Here was a convention of the masses of the people from every section of the country. Not another, before or since, distinctly representative of the rank and file of the people of America."[21] Sectional balance was still maintained with the nomination of James Weaver of Iowa for president and James Field of Virginia for vice president. The party platform reaffirmed the Ocala demands and articulated the reform agenda of the new Populist Party. Among the more intriguing provisions of the party platform was a promise of a "free ballot and a fair count in all elections," although without federal intervention.[22] How exactly that was to be achieved in the southern states was unclear, but especially in the Deep South, Populists sought to mollify the concerns of southern whites about a new Federal Election Bill. With the national convention concluded, the next step was the state conventions in Alabama and Georgia to select a state ticket. After this the campaigns could begin in earnest, although with the trend of national opinion favoring the Democrats it would be a difficult environment for the Populists. The Alabama state elections would therefore be a critical test.[23]

Alabama politics was not as complicated as the situation that bedeviled Louisiana Populists. Nevertheless, Reuben Kolb and an independent alternative complicated efforts of Alabama Populists to present a united front against the Democratic Party. Kolb had deep roots in the Democratic Party going back to the 1874 election where he had been active in the violent overthrow that ended Reconstruction in the state. Prior to the emergence of the Alliance, Kolb was an active orthodox Democrat, with a substantial agricultural constituency. He had attempted to win the Democratic nomination in 1890, where he had been fended off by black belt elites. While Kolb in two contentious state election races made overtures for African American support, it frequently was little more than appeals for black votes. Moreover, as the state commissioner of agriculture, Kolb was a proponent of what Brazilian historians have referred to as "whitening"—that is, using immigration as a way to change the racial composition of the society. Kolb's efforts had largely failed, but the state's black population certainly remembered Kolb's position. Technically, Kolb had never truly left the Democratic Party, since he had formed the Jeffersonian Democratic Party to contest the

1892 election and claimed to be the true Democratic Party in the state. Populists, under the leadership of Joseph Manning, were much more racially egalitarian than the Jeffersonian Democrats led by Kolb, and on economic issues they aligned with the national party. Manning was totally devoid of racial prejudice and proved it by selecting an African American as a delegate to the party's national convention in Omaha in 1892. Manning would also prove especially adept at forging an electoral coalition between the Jeffersonian Democrats, his own Populists, and the state's Republican Party. A unified effort between the three forces would make a vibrant alternative to the Alabama Democratic Party in 1892.[24]

Democrats quickly found themselves under siege from a vigorous coalition campaign in the 1892 election. The revolt against the Democratic Party in the white areas of the state in northern Alabama was very intense. It reflected what had been decades of frustration on the part of Independents, Greenbackers, Republicans, and now Populists against an organized structure of persecution. Kolb's supporters actively recruited African Americans to participate as recruiters for the campaign and to introduce Kolb at public events, and African Americans were well represented at public meetings. In one public address, Peyton Bowman, who served as Kolb's campaign manager, urged African Americans to stand up for their race and to vote for a free ballot and a fair count. That is not to say that all of Kolb's supporters were advocates of racial equality. It is also true that the Kolb campaign at times accused the administration of failing to enforce the color line. Both Jeffersonian and Populist newspapers and speakers used racial slurs, and Kolb's campaign affirmed rather than attacked white supremacy. At the same time, they sought to preserve the rights of African Americans to vote and participate freely in the political process, while the Democrats tried to restrict that very right. The election results were quite close, but ultimately the election returns revealed a narrow Democratic victory of approximately 10,000 votes. Kolb ran strongly in the northern part of the state, but in the reported returns claimed massive majorities in the black belt in southern Alabama. Throughout the campaign Democrats had gone to the trouble to form African American clubs for Jones, and some claimed that they had used abundant amounts of money to secure victory. In both Alabama and Georgia close election results seemed to reveal African American Democratic support, but such evidence seems dubious and contrived.[25]

There can be little doubt that some African Americans tied and connected to the Democratic Party formed clubs to articulate the election of Thomas G. Jones as governor. However, the degree to which African

American voters divided between Kolb and Jones is obscured by the depth of fraud perpetrated in the black belt of southern Alabama. While a number of votes were claimed to be cast for Jones by election officials, their validity as a statistical measurement seems dubious. Individuals also seem to have written Jones claiming that for certain sums of money they could control the black vote in their individual county. These claims were often asserted every two years, and this raises some questions as to their validity. Additionally, the letters contain hearsay, in which individuals claimed they had heard, or it was commonly understood, that African Americans were bribed, volunteered, or in other ways, were marshaled for the Democratic ticket. What one does not have is any clear sign that African Americans had a massive interest in voting the Democratic ticket. Whites, however, claimed that African Americans eagerly voted the Democratic ticket, but that is not quite the same thing. Moreover, as soon as the legislature assembled, the first thing the Democratic legislature did was to pass a draconian suffrage restriction bill. That was hardly the gesture of confident Democrats convinced that they had assembled a new biracial coalition that would be able to govern the state. Conversely, in his memoirs, Manning suggested, "Why buy an election? The black belt system made that a non-essential."[26] In Manning's view then, what had happened was that Democratic election officials had used African American voters as an excuse to massage election returns. Election officials controlled the voting box, they threw out those votes they didn't want, and using the African American population in their counties as an excuse placed enough ballots in the box to manufacture a majority against Kolb. Manning suggested that the lesson Populists should gather from these returns was that the issue of "free speech, a fair vote and a honest count had been, through the developments of this conflict, made paramount to all else." The experience of Alabama would be replicated in the contests to come.[27]

Electoral alliances in many ways were the rule in Alabama, but a different pattern was followed in Georgia. Populists in the state were not interested in an alliance with Republicans, although they were certainly helped by not having a competing ticket. Populists in Georgia also had the difficulty of having to overcome their personal history. Many members of the Georgia Populist Party had once belonged to the Ku Klux Klan during Reconstruction, had been critical of African American efforts at becoming landowners, and were ardent defenders of the racial status quo. As African American Republican William Pledger sarcastically noted of Georgia Populists, they were "the men who have lynched the colored people in the past;

the men who have shot and robbed the colored people; the men who precipitated the 'Camilla Riot' years ago and who marshaled the red shirter and the night riders."[28] Similarly, Democratic newspaper editor Ellen Dortch joyously wrote questions that African Americans could ask Populist candidates for the state legislature in her native Franklin County. White Populists were thus asked to explain their past history, and this suggests that African Americans were not simply political pawns in the process. Their answers were probably satisfactory, because Populists carried the county in the elections of 1892. Populists in Georgia did make a determined effort to reach out to the local African American community. While affirming the basic principles of white supremacy, they repudiated lynching, called for African Americans to protect their right to vote, and denounced the convict lease system that unfairly targeted black prisoners. African Americans also participated in a variety of different ways within the party as activists, delegates to state conventions, and in a multitude of campaign support activities. Additionally, in Congressman Tom Watson, the Populists had someone who sought to marry Populist economic thought with an effort to garner black votes.[29]

Tom Watson may be one of the greatest conundrums about southern Populism. Beyond all doubt, he was the region's most noticeable national political figure, and in many ways Watson only reluctantly surrendered his commitment to Populism, or at least as he understood its principles. Watson inherited a substantial plantation in McDuffie County and came from the agrarian wing of the Democratic Party. Prior to the emergence of the Alliance, little about him suggested anything different than your average planter of the Democratic power structure. However, with the Alliance, Watson emerged as one of its strongest proponents, and, in 1890, he was elected to a term in Congress as a Democrat. When the Alliance divided, Watson went with the new party and was its unquestioned leader within the state. Watson's support for Populism was centered in an urgent desire to remedy the economic inequalities that hindered the economic development of the South. A persistent foe of entrenched corporate power, Watson had come to believe that the Democratic Party was too corrupt to be reformed. After Populism had for all intents and purposes died, Watson backtracked from many of his statements about racial equality and became not only an ardent negrophobe, but a vicious anti-Semite and anti-Catholic as well. Nevertheless, the message that Watson offered African Americans from 1892 to 1896 was one of political and economic equality. The essence of Watson's argument was that the economic interests of African Americans were the same as those of whites in rural areas, what some historians of Populism have referred to as the union of producers, a working-class solidarity that would make what united blacks and whites more important than their color. "Why is not the Colored Tenant open to the conviction that he is in the same boat as the white tenant; the colored laborer with the white laborer?"[30] However, perhaps the most important element of Populism for an African American audience was not economic theories, but their affirmation of the right to vote. Watson's advocacy in this regard was also couched around several qualifications: his denunciation of social equality, his opposition to federal protection of the right to vote, and his highly paternalistic invocation of planters knowing what was in the black self-interest. In a state where African Americans made up such a large percentage of the voting population, this created the possibilities of a true revolution.[31]

A more accurate nature of the relationship between African Americans and whites is revealed at the county and local level. While statewide, the Populist leadership distanced themselves from electoral alliances, at the county level, close relationships between blacks and whites were a fact. The very suddenness of the Populist effort meant that in many ways interracial cooperation would be stronger in 1894. Nevertheless, the surge of African American support worried Democrats who then aggressively sought to check the Populist insurgency. For example, political meetings held by Populists were broken up either through interruption of speakers, throwing of eggs, or brawls between competing supporters. Populists were not entirely blameless, for at times they were inclined to target African Americans whom they believed might vote Democratic. The Democrats did not stop at violence, however, but moved toward a series of efforts at economic coercion, threatening schoolteachers, farm laborers, and the economic interests of the vulnerable. William Wyne, the Democratic chair of Wilkes County, Georgia, made this explicit with a circular to plantation owners in the days before the 1892 state election. Wyne suggested that it was vital for planters to "bring to bear the power which your situation gives you over tenant laborers."[32] Wyne argued that if the Populists won, it would mean that the dangerous enemy would control the plantation. According to Wyne, this would mean that the biracial alliance would control the "regulation or control of rents, wages of laborers, regulation of hours of work, & at certain times of year strikes." In this frenzied environment, it was not at all a surprise that Democrats began an intense racial crackdown. Among their targets was H. S. Doyle, a young African American minister, who had served as a speaker and campaigner for the Populist ticket. Democratic authorities arrested Doyle in Augusta, but his release was secured by the prominent black Republican Judson Lyons, along with another black minister. Doyle was soon brought to Tom Watson's home for safekeeping. Watson refused to allow Doyle in the house, but instead hid him in a nearby shed, after a local African American supporter informed Watson that the Democrats wished Doyle lynched. Watson prevailed on local white Populists to come as a squad of defense for his home, although later some who came maintained they had not known it was to defend an African American man. But the lesson that Watson drew from such an event was "that the humblest white man and the poorest colored man in the Tenth district is as much an object of our care as the proudest leader we have got." None of these examples of interracial cooperation could change Democratic control of the election boxes, and the Democrats engaged in massive fraud to hold the governorship of Georgia and to defeat Watson as well. This pattern was duplicated in the presidential and congressional races, and it can hardly be a surprise that Populists drew the lesson that a free ballot and a fair count were paramount issues. The Georgia experience was replicated in the fall elections of 1892 for the presidency and congressional races in the rest of the Deep South as well.[33]

Despite the Populists' hopes in the Deep South, the results of the 1892 presidential election were disappointing. In Mississippi, disfranchisement removed African American and poor white voters from the electoral rolls, with the result that Populists had no hope of carrying or even being able to compete statewide. Weaver managed to carry a few counties in Mississippi, but had little support except for the hill country of Mississippi. Georgia Populists refused an alliance with the Republicans, and as a result finished third, well behind the Democrats. In Louisiana, closer relationships with the state Republicans meant Populists agreed on a division of the congressional races and to vote for the reelection of Benjamin Harrison in November. However, in Alabama that pattern was reversed when Republicans agreed to throw their support behind Weaver, and the Populists thus gained their best share of the popular vote in the South. The congressional races revealed substantial Populist support in various congressional districts of the Deep South, especially when Populists secured agreements with Republicans at either the state or local level. In many districts, Democrats felt they had no choice but to manufacture election returns to achieve victory. Nevertheless, even one Mississippi Democrat acknowledged privately that the races were much closer than at first they might appear. One result of these developments was to reshape how Populists thought of their campaigns and what they hoped to achieve. While economic change remained an important goal, the Populists focused on the need for honest elections. In doing so the relationships between Populists and Republicans grew stronger over time.[34]

A Democratic victory created a multitude of problems for the Democratic Party in the Deep South. It was one thing to use appeals to white supremacy and to see Populists as merely the Republican Party in a new form. However, once conservative Democrats were actually governing they reminded voters of the way Democrats were part of the status quo. At the national level this was especially the case when President Grover Cleveland pushed for the repeal of the Silver Purchase Act. As a result this led to a surge of bimetallists into the Populist movement in the two years preceding the 1894 state elections. That did not mean the Populists decreased their efforts to attract African American voters, and in many ways Populism reached its radical high tide in 1894, and not 1892. Just as before, Populists made a determined effort to win the state elections that year. Once again the election returns had such a fraudulent character that Democrats engaged in voter fraud. Democrats were unapologetic about the need to engage in fraud. When the historian Alex Arnett researched his book on Populism in Georgia, he had the opportunity to interview one of the Democratic election officials who had engaged in massive fraud. This anonymous official in Sylvania, Georgia, was vigorous in his defense of the necessity for the Democratic uses of power, "We *had* to do it! The Populists would have ruined the country!" Similar pronouncements were common throughout the whole Deep South, except for Mississippi where disfranchisement made fraud unnecessary. That being said, despite fraud, Populists united with African Americans did not secure victories.[35]

Black voters provided the critical constituency to allow Populists to take over county government in Carroll County, Georgia. In Taliaferro County, Georgia, local Populists established an interracial committee that operated until 1898 and made real efforts to ensure that local government treated African Americans fairly. Where Populists had power in rural Louisiana, they made efforts to ensure that blacks could serve as jurors and that the criminal justice system did not treat African Americans unfairly. Mississippi appears an exception in this regard, where a whitecapping movement took shape with considerable Populist support, and African Americans who sought to become landowners, improve their economic standing, or better their lives were directly attacked. Additionally, in both Louisiana and Georgia, Populists and Republicans formally contested congressional results to win seats. Especially methodical in this approach were the joint efforts of Populists and Republicans to document the electoral results at the congressional level.[36]

These issues had a palpable impact in Alabama, for example, where Populists and Republicans seethed after Kolb's defeat in 1892. It is testimony to the degree of Democratic fright, that almost immediately the Alabama legislature passed the Sayre Election Law that sought to restrict the right to vote. One of the election law's provisions was that a voter had only five minutes to cast his ballot. However, such measures did not prevent a massive turnout of voters in the state and congressional elections of 1894. But once again Democratic control of the election boxes prevented Kolb from winning. This time, however, Populists and Republicans marched on the capitol, created their own state militia, and seemed almost prepared to overthrow the state government. This was too radical an action for Kolb, however, and in the end the movement petered out. Nevertheless, Populist and Republican success at documenting the actual number of votes cast was successfully used at election time. In Selma, Alabama, despite a return of more than 2,000 Democratic votes, Manning and his supporters proved that only 767 votes were cast. Manning noted that when William Aldrich, the Republican congressional candidate, went to Dallas County in Alabama, he was "pounced upon and severely beaten by his opponent." Such measures were also time consuming, expensive, and required constant effort to move forward contests, which had to be explained before congressmen who often had a limited understanding of southern elections. The process of collecting evidence could be unfair, and southern Democrats would use all their advantages to delay and hinder an accurate result. When Rebecca Felton prosecuted the contest for her husband, William Felton, who had run as a Populist in Georgia, she was given just five minutes at one hearing to make her case. After fraud was used in Augusta to defeat Tom Watson in 1894, the victorious Democrat agreed to resign and allow for a new special election. However, the new special election did not take place for another seven months, and when it did take place it was as fraudulent as previous campaigns. While that was certainly frustrating, the success in seating a congressman in Alabama spoke to a renewed commitment of the Populists. The nature of these challenges, however, had an impact on the shaping and reshaping of the way Populists thought about the nature of southern politics.[37]

The state elections of 1896 were a critical crossroads for Deep South Populism. Within Georgia there can be little doubt that Populists grew closer ties with their African American allies. An interesting example of this was a letter to the *People's Party Paper* in the months before the state election. C. H. Ellington had served as the temporary chair at Omaha during the first Populist national convention. Ellington was so disgusted with Democratic fraud that he was in favor of "fusing with any party who are enemies of these ballot box stuffers and election manipulators." The Populist slogan in the coming campaign should be, "*Honest Elections, Honest Count, Home Rule.*"[38] Ellington's point of view, however, was not shared by Tom Watson, who by 1895 began to urge Populists to pivot to the right. Watson distanced himself not simply from African Americans, but urged that any discussion of the subtreasury or the more radical economic positions of Populism be either discarded or at least heavily watered down. The fact that Populists were so willing to move away from such an important constituency is striking considering the successes of many white Populists with African Americans. It is also not so surprising that African Americans withheld their support for the Populist ticket, although exceptions obviously took place at the local level. Late in the campaign of 1896, John Cunningham, the Populist chair of the state campaign, did make a last-minute effort to gain African American votes. Cunningham urged that every white Populist in the state should "make secure the vote of at least one colored voter and the victory is ours." Nevertheless, the Populist gubernatorial candidate in 1896 ran substantially behind what the party had achieved in African American areas two years before.[39]

Conversely, Louisiana Populists were on the verge of what may be the closest any Deep South Populist Party came to political power at the state level. Louisiana Democrats faced a multitude of problems as they attempted to fend off the Populist-Republican alliance. By the spring of 1896, sugar planters were restive against a Democratic Party whose reduction of tariff rates seemed to challenge their economic interests. Additionally, the Democratic machine that had long governed New Orleans, since the demise of Reconstruction, led to a nonpartisan citizens' movement that was in open revolt against the Democratic establishment. To make the situation worse for the ruling elite, they nervously picked this very moment to push for the disfranchisement of poor whites and African Americans. Disfranchisement raised concerns about losing the right to vote, which when combined with the economic downturn, brought a unity of purpose among anti-Democratic forces in the state. Sugar planters feared African Americans, city reformers interested in good government, and white Populists from the northern part of the state as separate elements of a political coalition that could be a substantial majority of the population. Unlike the election of 1892, in 1896 Populists and Republicans agreed on a unified ticket, with Republican John Pharr running a vigorous campaign. Democrats reacted with violence and economic coercion, and used their control of the counting process to manufacture the desired result. Republican Henry Warmoth ran for a seat in the Louisiana House of Representatives and his letter of contest demonstrates the extent to which Democrats tried to perpetuate their power. Warmoth noted that at one box some 396 votes were reported as being cast, despite it being an area that had only recently suffered a cyclone and drought, and hardly anyone now resided in the area. In other cases, Democrats fired at African Americans determined to vote Republican. Democrats refused to certify results when the returns went against them, and armed men prevented an election at one precinct. "Men who were dead and men who moved away and men who were absent were voted at this poll," Warmoth noted of another precinct where dubious returns were presented.[40] Perhaps the only positive development from the election was that Democrats backtracked in their support of disfranchisement. Much like Alabama in 1894, there was a moment in Louisiana where the violent overthrow of the state government seemed a real possibility. However, any possibility of military action had to be considered in light of the fact that the Democrats had more guns and the trained resources of the state militia. City reformers abandoned the Populists and Republicans on the question of an investigation into the election results, so the contests all ended quietly. Moreover, once Democrats secured the 1896 election, they soon returned to efforts to purge the electoral rolls and enshrine their power. The returns of 1896 were but a last sign of Populism's vibrancy as the tension between northern and southern Populists would be revealed over the presidential nomination.[41]

The coinage of silver at the ratio of 16 to 1 was an important part of the Populist platform from the beginning of the party. It was, however, never a central part of the appeal of Populism, especially in the Deep South. Nevertheless, by 1895 the coinage of silver was an effective way to make Populism a national movement that could draw disaffected silver Democrats and Republicans into the organization. However, in 1896, the strategy failed as the Democrats embraced silver, too, and nominated silver advocate William Jennings Bryan for president. This left Populists with the choice of either nominating someone else or joining forces with the Bryan campaign. It was not an easy choice, and it also revealed important fault lines within Populism itself. Populists from the plains states and rocky mountain region that had long been allies of the Democratic Party quickly endorsed Bryan. Southern Populists, with some notable exceptions mainly in the Upper

South, were aligned with the mid-roaders who opposed any effort at what was described as fusion. Populists in the Deep South were not opposed to electoral alliances with other parties, this was especially true for Louisiana and Alabama, but close affiliation with the Democratic Party meant political death. The compromise solution made by the Populist convention was to accept Bryan, but to insist on Tom Watson as the vice presidential choice. Initially, Populists were hopeful that Watson would replace Democrat Arthur Sewall, but when that did not happen the difficult question of how to negotiate a fair division of the electoral vote for the Populists was raised. For Deep South Populists this demonstrated an increasing alienation from the national party.[42]

Those who opposed a coalition with Bryan and the silver Democrats have been frequently described as the Midroaders; that is, those who preferred to stand in the middle of the road and avoid fusion. But little attention focused on the perspective of the Midroaders in the Deep South, with the exception of those in Georgia who aligned themselves with Watson. But when one examines the attitude of Deep South Populists what becomes clear is deep opposition to Bryan's election. There were exceptions, as Jeffersonian Democrat Kolb came out not only for Bryan, but for the state to cast its vote for the Democratic ticket. Deep South Populists also did not see these issues in the same way. Populists in Alabama made a determined effort to win their state election shortly after the national convention, but Watson refused to campaign for them because the Alabama Populist alliance with Republicans would "embarrass me greatly."[43] This spoke to what would be a consistent pattern with Tom Watson in which he saw himself not so much as representing the whole interests of the party, but rather engaged in a petulant campaign of his own selfish interests. Yet, some southern Populists did think of larger principles. For example, Arkansas Populist W. S. Morgan, whose roots in agrarian reform went back to the Agricultural Wheel, was deeply disgusted by the nomination of Bryan. The plains states that had insisted on Bryan's nomination by the Populists were only interested in a "wild rush for the hog."[44] Similarly, one Arkansas Populist noted that in his state, party members refused to vote in his local community after the nomination of Bryan. Over time, these feelings only grew more intense. A. A. Gunby, an important Louisiana Populist leader, warned Senator Marion Butler, chair of the Populist Party, that "we must keep in the middle of the Road or perish."[45]

By early September 1896 it was still unclear whether or not Bryan would even consent to the Populist nomination. Alabama congressman

Milford Howard, an ardent opponent of fusion in any form, grew incensed at Bryan's delay. "For a great party with almost two million voters we occupy a most humiliating position as bow the knee before the Democratic throne," Howard suggested to Senator Marion Butler.[46] Eventually, in mid-September, Bryan accepted the Populist nomination, although he made no efforts to give Populists a fair share of fusion. Many Deep South Populists viewed the whole question with complete indifference. This was especially true in Louisiana, where with the exception of some enthusiasts of silver such as J. A. Tetts, the bulk of the party was completely hostile to Bryan. Disdain for the Democratic ticket ran so deep that Butler had to order Louisiana Populists to accept the offer. A. A. Gunby suggested that Marion Butler failed to realize "how intensely our people hate the democrats who have robbed & insulted and oppressed them for years in this state."[47] Events were equally complicated in Alabama, where the state Populists reached an agreement with the state's Democrats. However, that agreement did not change the feelings of many dissidents. Manning refused to countenance any continued negotiations with Democrats over an electoral ticket. When the Populists acceded to the nomination of Bryan, Manning concluded that Populism was dead and instead joined the Republican Party. That fall, one of the founders of the Alabama Populist Party cast a ballot for Republican presidential candidate William McKinley. He was not alone.[48]

Although Populist opponents of the Midroaders asserted that they would all support the Republican ticket, the record was in fact mixed. Despite the disdain Louisiana Populists felt for the ticket, they either voted for Bryan or stayed home. Those areas that had shown considerable Populist support in the 1892 election did not see any noticeable Republican votes. For example, Winn Parish, which voted for Benjamin Harrison by a 2–1 margin in 1892, cast only thirteen votes for McKinley. Disfranchisement had effectively destroyed the Republican Party in Mississippi, and no noticeable gain in Republican votes was present in that state either. The pattern was quite different in Alabama and Georgia, where the McKinley vote included numerous Populist votes. Notable shifts included Blount County where Benjamin Harrison received 16 percent of the vote in 1888, Cleveland was narrowly chosen over Weaver in 1892, and McKinley won 51 percent of the votes cast in 1896. In many other counties in areas of Populist strength, the Republican ticket showed considerable gains. This was a mild change compared to what took place in Georgia. It was the best performance of the Republican presidential ticket in Georgia since 1872, with much of the growth due to the fact that Populists in the state cast their ballots for McKinley. Seven counties in Georgia carried by Weaver in 1892 were won by McKinley four years later. These counties were Columbia, Johnson, McDuffie, Oconee, Taliaferro, Warren, and Washington. As with Alabama, many centers of Populist strength showed substantial growth for the Republican ticket as well. McDuffie County was an interesting case in point. The home county of Tom Watson cast 71 percent of their ballots for McKinley, whose economic policies could not have been more different from Watson. In Taliaferro County where Populists and African Americans had forged a relationship, their persistent interracial cooperation reached another accord as white Populists rejected Bryan. McKinley received nearly 40 percent of the two-party vote and had his best performance by far in any southern state. Motivation in this sense is difficult to discern for Deep South Populists, for few Populists before the election would see it in their public interest to avow that they would vote the Republican ticket. However, it is dubious that this was just about revenge or a desire to get back at national Populists. A more likely explanation would be that the alliances that had been forged by whites and African Americans were deeply offended by the nomination of Bryan. After all, Bryan was an apologist for disfranchisement, a defender of lynching, and an ardent proponent of racial segregation. While the majority of white Populists could look past that record, a minority obviously felt differently. For those white southern Populists whose consciousness had been touched by their movement it was simply unthinkable to vote for Bryan.[49]

Populists had suffered from their association with Bryan in the 1896 election in every conceivable way. The election was an emotionally traumatic event that undermined national unity within the party. If southern Populists could have had the luxury of rebuilding, in time they might have been able to repair the movement. But Democrats moved quickly in both Louisiana and Alabama to complete the disfranchisement of both African Americans and poor whites. This loss of the right to vote came on the heels of a decade of defeat, and while Populists and Republicans fought with desperate tenacity, their resistance was at times muted. Mississippi completed the disfranchisement process before the agrarian revolt took shape and disfranchisement became a key factor in the weakness of Populism within the state. The coming of disfranchisement was more complicated in Georgia as it was not completed until 1906 when the Populist Party was but a shell of its previous existence. Tom Watson completed his move to the right by not only endorsing disfranchisement, but by being a focal point of support for the removal of the vote from poor voters who had previously been his supporters. Watson became a political kingmaker in the state Democratic Party, a forceful advocate of hostility to immigrants, Catholics, and Jews, spewing an especially virulent racism. The passage of disfranchisement did not mark the complete end of resistance as African Americans entered the courts to challenge the stripping of the right to vote in Louisiana, Mississippi, and Alabama. In contrast, for reasons that are not entirely clear, Populists played no observable role in these court challenges. However, the Supreme Court gave these legal efforts to combat disfranchisement short shrift, and in the most cursory of matters upheld the new electoral measures that stripped the ballot from thousands of voters. Moreover, these measures achieved their principal purpose of securing the power of planter and business elites, and crippling the political opposition in the southern states. Populism in the Deep South was in many ways legislated out of existence.[50]

Although southern Populists did not advocate racial equality, the movement dramatically expanded the ability to defend African Americans' right to vote in the Deep South. This was a substantial accomplishment. Yes, there were clear limits to what southern Populists were prepared to offer African Americans. In many cases Populists did not embrace the inclusion of African Americans as equals in the society. Reading Populist newspapers it is also easy to find racial slurs, attacking Democrats for being insincere advocates of white supremacy, and for being hypocritical in their relations with African Americans. Nevertheless, Populists were prepared to offer African Americans the important principle of equal political citizenship, and even someone as racist as Tom Watson defended the African American right to vote and to participate in the political process. The degree to which African Americans participated in the public work of the party varied considerably. But in the case of Alabama, Georgia, and Louisiana, a relatively consistent pattern of African American participation was evident. It should always be kept in mind that the vast majority of African Americans remained committed Republicans, and being able to cooperate with Populists was more a goal than to participate in Populist Party affairs. The Mississippi party, on the contrary, seemed almost completely indifferent to the concerns of African Americans, although they certainly were prepared to offer African Americans more than the hostility they received from the Democratic Party. If Watson ultimately capitulated to racism and became an ardent negrophobe and proponent of disfranchisement, we should consider the other patterns as well. After disfranchisement, many white Populists chose to join the Republican Party in the Deep South. Manning maintained his commitment to racial equality all of his life. After joining the Republican Party, former Alabama Populist Warren Reese fought disfranchisement and aggressively prosecuted peonage cases against the planter elite in Alabama. For many Populists who became Republicans, their experience with Populism forced them to radically reconsider their racial views.[51]

Notes

1. Edward L. Ayers, *The Promise of the New South: Life After Reconstruction* (New York: Oxford University Press, 1992), 216–218; N. A. Dunning, *The Farmers' Alliance History and Agricultural Digest* (1891; reprint, New York: Arno Press, 1975), 218–224; William I. Hair, *Bourbonism and Agrarian Protest: Louisiana Politics, 1877–1900* (Baton Rouge: Louisiana State University Press, 1969), 142–154; John D. Hicks, *The Populist Revolt: A History of the Farmers' Alliance and the People's Party* (1931; reprint, Lincoln: University of Nebraska Press, 1961), 96–113; Robert C. McMath Jr., *Populist Vanguard: A History of the Southern Farmers' Alliance* (Chapel Hill: University of North Carolina Press, 1975), 33–34; Robert C. McMath Jr., *American Populism: A Social History, 1877–1898* (New York: Hill and Wang, 1992), 78–82.

2. Alex M. Arnett, *The Populist Movement in Georgia* (New York: Longmans Green, 1922), 79–81; Ayers, *Promise of the New South*, 220–222; Dunning, *Farmers' Alliance*, 227–237; Hair, *Bourbonism and Agrarian Protest*, 154–157; Matthew Hild, *Greenbackers, Knights of Labor, and Populists: Farmer-Labor Insurgency in the Late-Nineteenth-Century South* (Athens: University of Georgia Press, 2007), 99, 103–104; McMath, *Populist Vanguard*, 33–43, 46–56. For a slightly different view of this process which emphasizes cooperative farming as creating a movement culture, see Lawrence Goodwyn, *Democratic Promise: The Populist Moment in America* (New York: Oxford University Press, 1976), 83–153.

3. St. Louis Demands, December 1889, in *A Populist Reader: Selections from the Works of American Populist Leaders*, ed. George Tindall (New York: Harper Torchbooks, 1966), 75–77; Ayers, *Promise of the New South*, 222–223, 230; Stuart Noblin, *Leonidas Lafayette Polk: Agrarian Crusader* (Chapel Hill: University of North Carolina Press, 1949), 201–228; McMath, *Populist Vanguard*, 40, 66–70; William W. Rogers Sr., *The One-Gallused Rebellion Agrarianism in Alabama, 1865–1896* (1970; reprint, Tuscaloosa: University of Alabama Press, 2001), 132–140; William F. Holmes, "The Southern Farmers' Alliance: The Georgia Experience," *Georgia Historical Quarterly* (hereinafter cited as *GHQ*) 72 (1988): 627–652.

4. J. H. Turner, "The Race Problem," 272–279, but also see the more racially neutral L. L. Polk, "Sectionalism and the Alliance," 249–253, and L. F. Livingston, "The Needs of the South," 284–287, which are all in Dunning, *Farmers' Alliance History*; Gerald H. Gaither, *Black and the Populist Revolt: Ballots and Bigotry in the "New South"* (University: University of Alabama Press, 1977), 17–18; Charles L. Flynn Jr., *White Land, Black Labor: Caste and Class in Late-Nineteenth-Century Georgia* (Baton Rouge: Louisiana State University Press, 1983), 176–183. Despite focusing on the Progressive era and its usefulness for white southern attitudes about African American education is Louis R. Harlan, *Separate and Unequal: Public School Campaigns and Racism in the Southern Seaboard States, 1901–1915* (1958; reprint, New York: Atheneum, 1968); McMath, *Populist Vanguard*,

44, 46; Theodore Mitchell, *Political Education in the Southern Farmers' Alliance, 1887-1900* (Madison: University of Wisconsin Press, 1987), 48-49, 74-77; Charles Postel, *The Populist Vision* (New York: Oxford University Press, 2007), 40-41, 59, 183.

5. Turner, "The Race Problem," 272-279.

6. Turner, "The Race Problem," 272-279; Polk, "Sectionalism and the Alliance," 249-253; Livingston, "The Needs of the South," 284-287; Flynn, *White Land, Black Labor,* 176-183; McMath, *Populist Vanguard,* 44, 46; Mitchell, *Political Education,* 48-49, 74-77; Postel, *The Populist Vision,* 40-41, 59, 183.

7. R. M. Humphrey, "History of the Colored Farmers' National Co-Operative and National Union," in Dunning, *Farmers' Alliance,* 288-292; Gaither, *Blacks and the Populist Revolt,* 1-20; Mitchell, *Political Education,* 153-154; Donald L. Grant, *The Way it Was in the South: The Black Experience in Georgia* (Athens: University of Georgia Press, 2001), 173-175; McMath, *American Populism: A Social History,* 92-94; Karl Rodabaugh, "The Prelude to Populism in Alabama," *Alabama Historical Quarterly* (hereinafter cited as *ALHQ*) 43 (1981): 111-152.

8. R. M. Humphrey, "History of the Colored Farmers' National Co-Operative and National Union," in Dunning, *Farmers' Alliance,* 288-292; Gaither, *Blacks and the Populist Revolt,* 1-20, 63; Mitchell, *Political Education,* 153-154; Grant, *The Way it Was in the South,* 173-175; McMath, *American Populism,* 92-94; Postel, *Populist Vision,* 58; Clarence A. Bacote, "Negro Proscriptions, Protests, and Proposed Solutions in Georgia, 1880-1908," *Journal of Southern History* (hereafter *JSH*) 25 (1959): 471-498; William F. Holmes, "The Demise of the Colored Farmers' Alliance," *JSH* 41 (1975): 187-200; Holmes, "Georgia Experience," 649-651; Rodabaugh, "The Prelude to Populism in Alabama," 111-152.

9. Ayers, *Promise of the New South,* 235-237; Gaither, *Blacks and the Populist Revolt,* 15-16; Hair, *Bourbonism and Agrarian Protest,* 177-185; J. William Harris, *Deep Souths: Delta, Piedmont, and Sea Island Society in the Age of Segregation* (Baltimore, MD: Johns Hopkins University Press, 2001), 111; McMath, *American Populism,* 98-99; John C. Rodrigue, *Reconstruction in the Cane Fields: From Slavery to Free Labor in Louisiana's Sugar Parishes, 1862-1890* (Baton Rouge: Louisiana State University Press, 2001), 183-191; Holmes, "Demise of the Colored Farmers' Alliance," 187-200; Rebecca J. Scott, "'Stubborn and Disposed to Stand Their Ground': Black Militia, Sugar Workers, and the Dynamics of Collective Action, 1863-1887," *Slavery and Abolition* 20 (1999): 103-126.

10. R. F. Kolb to L. L. Polk, June 6, 1889, L. L. Polk Papers, Southern Historical Collection, University of North Carolina, Chapel Hill; Arnett, *Populist Movement in Georgia,* 102-120; Ayers, *Promise of the New South,* 240-248; Samuel L. Webb, *Two-Party Politics in the One-Party South: Alabama's Hill Country, 1874-1920* (Tuscaloosa: University of Alabama Press, 1997), 98-99; William F. Holmes, "The Southern Farmers' Alliance and the Georgia Senatorial Election of 1890," *JSH* 50 (1984), 197-224; Karl Rodabaugh, "The Alliance in Politics: The Alabama Gubernatorial Election of 1890," *ALHQ* 36 (1974): 54-80.

11. Ayers, *Promise of the New South,* 240-248; Webb, *Two-Party Politics,* 98-99; Karl Rodabaugh, "The Alliance in Politics: The Alabama Gubernatorial Election of 1890," *ALHQ* 36 (1974): 54-80.

12. The text of the McAlister resolution can be found in Dunning, *Farmers' Alliance,* 153-154; Ayers, *Promise of the New South,* 239-240; Gaither, *Blacks and the Populist Revolt,* 20-22. A different view of Ocala can be found in Goodwyn, *Democratic Promise,* 225-232.

13. Omar H. Ali, *In the Balance of Power: Independent Black Politics and Third-Party Movements in the United States* (Athens: University of Ohio Press, 2008), 81; Ayers, *Promise of the New South*, 239-240; Gaither, *Blacks and the Populist Revolt*, 22-25; Goodwyn, *Democratic Promise*, 225-232.

14. L. L. Polk to J. W. Denmark, December 5, 1891, Polk Papers; Ayers, *Promise of the New South*, 250-261; Gaither, *Black Ballots*, 16; Goodwyn, *Democratic Promise*, 213-272; Noblin, *Polk*, 245-276; Mitchell, *Political Education*, 154-155; Postel, *Populist Vision*, 173-183; C. Vann Woodward, *Origins of the New South, 1877-1913* (Baton Rouge: Louisiana State University Press, 1951), 235-243; Lewis N. Wynne, *The Continuity of Cotton: Planter Politics in Georgia, 1865-1892* (Macon, GA: Mercer University Press, 1986), 180-183; William F. Holmes, "The Arkansas Cotton Pickers Strike of 1891 and the Demise of the Colored Farmers' Alliance," *Arkansas Historical Quarterly* 32 (1973): 107-119; William F. Holmes, "The Georgia Alliance Legislature," *GHQ* 68 (1984): 479-515; Thomas A. Upchurch, "Why Populism Failed in Mississippi," *Journal of Mississippi History* 65 (2003): 249-276.

15. L. L. Polk to John D. Thorne, March 29, 1892, Marion Butler Papers, Southern Historical Collection, Wilson Library, University of North Carolina, Chapel Hill; L. L. Polk to J. W. Denmark, February 8, 1892, Polk Papers; Goodwyn, *Democratic Promise*, 248-272; Noblin, *Polk*, 278-280.

16. H. D. Hutcheson to L. L. Polk, April 25, 1892, H. H. Boyce to L. L. Polk, April 4, 1892, H. H. Boyce to L. L. Polk, April 15, 1892, H. D. Hutcheson to L. L. Polk, April 15, 1892, Polk Papers; Arnett, *Populist Movement in Georgia*, 101-112; Goodwyn, *Democratic Promise*, 248-272; Barton C. Shaw, *The Wool-Hat Boys: Georgia's Populist Party* (Baton Rouge: Louisiana State University Press, 1984), 26-55; C. Vann Woodward, *Tom Watson: Agrarian Rebel* (1938; reprint, New York: Oxford University Press, 1975), 180-189.

17. Ali, *Balance of Power*, 83-85; Gaither, *Blacks and the Populist Revolt*, 35-46; Goodwyn, *Democratic Promise*, 248-272.

18. John R. Kemp, ed., *Martin Behrman of New Orleans: Memoirs of a City Boss* (Baton Rouge: Louisiana State University Press, 1977), 13-15; Richard N. Current, *Those Terrible Carpetbaggers: A Reinterpretation* (New York: Oxford University Press, 1988), 418-419; Hair, *Bourbonism and Agrarian Protest*, 215-221; Henry C. Dethloff, "The Alliance and the Lottery: Farmers Try for the Sweepstakes," *Louisiana History* (hereinafter cited as *LH*) 6 (1965): 141-159.

19. L. L. Polk to J. W. Denmark, February 8, 1892, Polk Papers; Gaither, *Blacks and the Populist Revolt*, 115-116; Kemp, *Behrman*, 16. The language from the initial address of Louisiana Populists can be found in Norman Pollack, ed., *The Populist Mind* (Indianapolis: Bobbs-Merrill, 1967), 385-386; Hair, *Bourbonism and Agrarian Protest*, 222-229; Perry H. Howard, *Political Tendencies in Louisiana, 1812-1952* (Baton Rouge: Louisiana State University Press, 1957), 93-98.

20. Hair, *Bourbonism and Agrarian Protest*, 228-229; Howard, *Political Tendencies in Louisiana*, 93-98.

21. Joseph C. Manning, *Fadeout of Populism* (New York: T. A. Hebbons, 1928), 27-35; Ayers, *Promise of the New South*, 260-261.

22. Manning, *Fadeout of Populism*, 27-35; Tindall, *Populist Reader*, 90-96; Ali, *Balance of Power*, 84; Ayers, *Promise of the New South*, 260-261; Gaither, *Blacks and the Populist Revolt*, 44-46.

23. Ayers, *Promise of the New South*, 261–269.

24. Gaither, *Blacks and the Populist Revolt*, 105–107; Bruce Palmer, *"Man Over Money": The Southern Populist Critique of American Populism* (Chapel Hill: University of North Carolina Press, 1980), 54, 154–163; Rogers, *One-Gallused Rebellion*, 99–101, 193–216; Webb, *Two-Party Politics*, 92–109. For Brazilian historical treatments of whitening, see Thomas E. Skidmore, *Black Into White: Race and Nationality in Brazilian Thought* (Durham, NC: Duke University Press, 1993); Emilia Viotti da Costa, *The Brazilian Empire: Myths and Histories* (Chicago: University of Chicago Press, 1985). Katharine M. Pruett and John D. Fair, "Promoting a New South: Immigration, Racism, and 'Alabama on Wheels,'" *Agricultural History* 66 (1992): 19–41; Jerrell H. Shofner and William W. Rogers, "Joseph C. Manning: Militant Agrarian, Enduring Populist," *ALHQ* 29 (1967): 7–38.

25. Gaither, *Blacks and the Populist Revolt*, 106–107; Rogers, *One-Gallused Rebellion*, 217–230; Webb, *Two-Party Politics*, 106–109; Leah R. Atkins, "Populism in Alabama: Reuben F. Kolb and the Appeals to Minority Groups," *ALHQ* 32 (1970): 167–180; Wayne Flynt and William W. Rogers, "Reform Oratory in Alabama, 1890–1896," *Southern Speech Journal* 29 (1963): 94–106; Karl Rodabaugh, "'Kolbites' Versus Bourbons: The Alabama Gubernatorial Election of 1892," *ALHQ* 37 (1975): 275–321; Charles G. Summersell, "The Alabama Governor's Race in 1892," *Alabama Review* (hereinafter cited as *AR*) 8 (1955): 5–35.

26. Manning, *Fadeout of Populism*, 25–26. The question of African American voting and the Democratic victory is summarized by Rogers, *One-Gallused Rebellion*, 216–222; but also useful is Gaither, *Blacks and the Populist Revolt*, 107.

27. Manning, *Fadeout of Populism*, 25–26.

28. Pledger quote in Steven Hahn, *A Nation Under Our Feet: Black Political Struggles in the Rural South, from Slavery to the Great Migration* (Cambridge, MA: Belknap Press of Harvard University Press, 2003), 432; also see 432–435 for the difficulties African Americans in Georgia would have had voting Populist; Gaither, *Blacks and the Populist Revolt*, 96–98; Shaw, *Wool-Hat Boys*, 57–67; Bruce I. Kimmel, "The Political Sociology of Third Parties in the United States: A Comparative Study of the Third Parties in Minnesota, North Carolina, and Georgia" (Ph.D. diss., Columbia University, 1981), 154–157.

29. Shaw, *Wool-Hat Boys*, 57–67; Harris, *Deep Souths*, 91–107; Kimmel, "The Political Sociology of Third Parties," 160–162; William F. Holmes, "Ellen Dortch and the Farmers' Alliance," *GHQ* 69 (1985): 149–172; Gaither, *Blacks and the Populist Revolt*, 97.

30. A range of Watson's statements during the 1892 campaign can be found in Pollack, *Populist Mind*, 360–380; Grant, *The Way it Was in the South*, 176–177; Palmer, *"Man Over Money,"* 51–61, 169–172; Theodore Saloutos, *Farmer Movements in the South, 1865–1933* (Lincoln: University of Nebraska Press, 1964), 131–133; T. Harry Williams, *Romance and Realism in Southern Politics* (Athens: University of Georgia Press, 1961), 52–54; Woodward, *Tom Watson*, 216–235; Charles Crowe, "Tom Watson, Populists, and Blacks Reconsidered," *Journal of Negro History* 55 (1970): 99–116; Eugene R. Fingerhut, "Tom Watson, Blacks, and Southern Reform," *GHQ* 60 (1976): 324–343; Bertram Wyatt-Brown, "Tom Watson Revisited," *JSH* 68 (2002): 3–30.

31. Gaither, *Blacks and the Populist Revolt*, 96–97; Palmer, *"Man Over Money,"* 51–61, 169–172; Williams, *Romance and Realism*, 52–54; Crowe, "Tom Watson, Populists, and Blacks," 99–116: Fingerhut, "Tom Watson, Blacks, and Southern Reform," 324–343; Wyatt-Brown, "Tom Watson Revisited," 3–30.

32. William Wyne to Democratic Farmers and Employers of Labor in Wilkes County, September 8, 1892, Thomas E. Watson Papers, Digital Collection, Southern Historical Collection, Wilson Library, University of North Carolina at Chapel Hill.

33. William Wyne to Democratic Farmers and Employers of Labor in Wilkes County, September 8, 1892, Thomas E. Watson Papers; Watson's account of the Doyle affair is in Pollack, *Populist Mind*, 380–385; Kimmel, "The Political Sociology of Third Parties," 157–163; Shaw, *Wool-Hat Boys*, 67–101; Woodward, *Tom Watson*, 235–243.

34. W. P. Guyness to H. C. Warmoth, July 16, 1892, A. S. Badger to Thomas H. Carter, July 25, 1892, Charles Foster to H. C. Warmoth, September 26, 1892, Henry C. Warmoth Papers, Southern Historical Collection, Wilson Library, University of North Carolina, Chapel Hill; Stephen Cresswell, *Multiparty Politics in Mississippi, 1877–1902* (Jackson: University Press of Mississippi, 1995), 114–125; Hair, *Bourbonism and Agrarian Protest*, 229–233; Kirwan, *Revolt of the Rednecks*, 94–96; Webb, *Two-Party Politics*, 110–113; Upchurch, "Why Populism Failed."

35. Quote in Arnett, *Populist Movement in Georgia*, 183–184; Cresswell, *Multiparty Politics*, 126–155; Grant, *The Way it Was in the South*, 178–179; Hair, *Bourbonism and Agrarian Protest*, 234–246; Kirwan, *Revolt of the Rednecks*, 96–101; Shaw, *Wool-Hat Boys*, 102–120; Woodward, *Watson*, 265–271; Kimmel, "Sociology of Third Parties," 165–175; Robert Saunders, "Southern Populists and the Negro, 1893–1895," *Journal of Negro History* 54 (1969): 240–261; Upchurch, "Why Populism Failed."

36. James C. Bonner, *Georgia's Last Frontier: The Development of Carroll County* (Athens: University of Georgia Press, 1971), 150–151; William F. Holmes, "Populism in Black Belt Georgia," *GHQ* 83 (1999): 242–266; William F. Holmes, "Whitecapping in Mississippi: Agrarian Violence in the Populist Era," *Mid-America* 55 (1973): 134–148; Michael J. Pfeifer, "Lynching and Criminal Justice in South Louisiana, 1878–1930," *LH* 40 (1999): 155–177.

37. Manning, *Fadeout of Populism*, 48–49; J. C. C. Black to T. E. Watson, March 27, 1895, Watson Papers; Rebecca Felton, *"My Memoirs of Georgia Politics"* (Atlanta: Index Printing, 1911), 654–677; William H. Skaggs, *The Southern Oligarchy* (New York: Devin-Adair, 1924), 122–125; Robert D. Ward and William W. Rogers, *Labor Revolt in Alabama: The Great Strike of 1894* (University: University of Alabama Press, 1965), 122–129; Webb, *Two-Party Politics*, 131–144; Woodward, *Tom Watson*, 270–277; David A. Bagwell, "The 'Magical Process': The Sayre Election Law of 1893," *AR* 25 (1972): 83–104; D. Alan Harris, "Campaigning in the Bloody Seventh: The Election of 1894 in the Seventh Congressional District," *AR* 27 (1974): 127–138; Terence H. Nolan, "William Henry Skaggs and the Reform Challenge of 1894," *ALHQ* 33 (1971): 117–134; Paul M. Pruitt Jr., "A Changing of the Guard: Joseph C. Manning and Populist Strategy in the Fall of 1894," *ALHQ* 40 (1978): 20–36.

38. C. H. Ellington to *People's Party Paper*, April 2, 1896, Watson Papers.

39. John D. Cunningham Circular, September 5, 1896, Butler Papers; Palmer, "*Man Over Money*," 174–182; Shaw, *Wool-Hat Boys*, 32–33, 55, 149–157; Robert Saunders, "Transformation of Tom Watson, 1894–1895," *GHQ* 54 (1970): 339–356.

40. H. C. Warmoth to John Dymond, May 9, 1896, Warmoth Papers; Hair, *Bourbonism and Agrarian Protest*, 245–267; Edward F. Haas, "John Fitzpatrick and Democratic Political Continuity, 1896–1899," *LH* 22 (1981): 7–30; Raymond O. Nussbaum, "'The Ring is Smashed!': The New Orleans Municipal Election of 1896," *LH* 17 (1976): 283–297; Matthew J. Schott, "Progressives Against Democracy: Electoral Reform in Louisiana, 1894–1921,"

LH 22 (1979): 247–260; Philip D. Uzee, "The Republican Party in the Louisiana Election of 1896," *LH* 2 (1961): 332–344.

41. Hair, *Bourbonism and Agrarian Protest*, 264–271; Michael Perman, *Struggle for Mastery: Disfranchisement in the South, 1888–1908* (Chapel Hill: University of North Carolina Press, 2001), 132–135; Schott, "Progressives Against Democracy," 247–260.

42. Robert F. Durden, *The Climax of Populism: The Election of 1896* (1965; reprint, Westport, CT: Greenwood Press, 1981), 1–85; Goodwyn, *Democratic Promise*, 387–492; James L. Hunt, *Marion Butler and American Populism* (Chapel Hill: University of North Carolina Press, 2003), 92–115; Woodward, *Tom Watson*, 278–318.

43. Thomas E. Watson to Marion Butler, July 28, 1896, R. F. Kolb to Marion Butler, October 20, 1896, Butler Papers.

44. W. S. Morgan to Marion Butler, August 5, 1896, Butler Papers; Durden, *Climax of Populism*, 45–125; Goodwyn, *Democratic Promise*, 498–507; Woodward, *Tom Watson*, 302–331.

45. A. A. Gunby to Marion Butler, August 31, 1896, T. B. Bickley to Marion Butler, August 7, 1896, T. G. McRaven to Marion Butler, August 10, 1896, Butler Papers; Goodwyn, *Democratic Promise*, 498–507.

46. M. W. Howard to Marion Butler, August 31, 1896, Butler Papers; Webb, *Two-Party Politics*, 144–145.

47. A. A. Gunby to Marion Butler, October 11, 1896, D. C. Scarborough to Marion Butler, September 4, 1896, C. C. Post to Marion Butler, September 7, 1896, D. C. Scarborough to Marion Butler, September 15, 1896, Marion Butler to H. L. Brian, September 18, 1896, Ben H. Peabody to Marion Butler, September 27, 1896, J. A. Tetts to Marion Butler, October 3, 1896, J. M. Clay to Marion Butler, October 12, 1896, J. T. Howell to Marion Butler, October 22, 1896, Butler Papers; Hair, *Bourbonism and Agrarian Protest*, 270–271. A slightly different interpretation of Bryan is in Durden, *Climax of Populism*, 72–88.

48. R. F. Kolb to Marion Butler, October 20, 1896, Butler Papers; Webb, *Two-Party Politics*, 144–154.

49. My interpretation in this paragraph is based on an examination of the county election returns. For the 1892 elections, Burnham, *Presidential Ballots, 1892*; for the 1896 elections, Edgar E. Robinson, *The Presidential Vote, 1896–1932* (Stanford: Stanford University Press, 1947); Shaw, *Wool-Hat Boys*, 160–161; Webb, *Two-Party Politics*, 144–154; Taliaffero County was the model black belt county of Georgia Populism in Holmes, "Populism in Black Belt Georgia."

50. Alexander M. Bickel and Benno Schmitt, *The Judiciary and Responsible Government, 1910–1921* (New York: Macmillan, 1984); Cresswell, *Multiparty Politics*, 152–155, 189–190; Hair, *Bourbonism and Agrarian Protest*, 271–279; J. Morgan Kousser, *The Shaping of Southern Politics: Suffrage Restriction and the Shaping of the One-Party South, 1880–1910* (New Haven, CT: Yale University Press, 1974); Perman, *Struggle for Mastery*, 70–90, 124–147, 173–194, 281–298; Webb, *Two-Party Politics*, 169–174; Woodward, *Tom Watson*, 370–486; Crowe, "Tom Watson, Populists, and Blacks," 99–116; Fingerhut, "Tom Watson, Blacks, and Southern Reform," 324–343; Russell Korobkin, "The Politics of Disfranchisement in Georgia," *GHQ* 74 (1990): 20–58; Robert M. Saunders, "The Transformation of Tom Watson," 339–356; Upchurch, "Why Populism Failed," 249–276; Wyatt-Brown, "Tom Watson Revisited," 3–30.

51. W. S. Reese to William E. Chandler, June 28, 1903, Joseph C. Manning to W. E. Chandler, December 25, 1903, William E. Chandler Papers, Library of Congress; Paul M. Pruitt Jr., "Defender of the Voteless: Joseph C. Manning Views the Disfranchisement Era in Alabama," *ALHQ* 43 (1981): 171–185; Upchurch, "Why Populism Failed," 249–276; Samuel L. Webb, "From Independents to Populists to Progressive Republicans: The Case of Chilton County, Alabama, 1880–1920," *JSH* 59 (1993): 707–736.

"[T]he Angels from Heaven Had Come Down and Wiped Their Names off the Registration Books"

THE DEMISE OF GRASSROOTS POPULISM
IN NORTH CAROLINA

—JAMES M. BEEBY

In the November congressional election of 1900, John C. McMillan, the U.S. postmaster at Teacheys in Duplin County, North Carolina, went to vote in the last election fought by the Populists in the Old North State. In addition to his military record, McMillan, a captain and Civil War veteran, had a long political resume. He was a former member of the North Carolina state legislature and chairman of the Duplin County Board of Education, and he also served as a justice of the peace. From all accounts, he was one of the most respected men in his area and one of the largest property owners in Teacheys. But as a Populist he faced opposition from conservative Democrats in the Old North State. Before the special August election of 1900, McMillan said, "I was told by a Red Shirt Democrat in person to my face, that if I did not stop canvassing and making speeches that I would ride my life out before I knew it." But, noted McMillan, the federal election of November in Duplin was as calm as the state election held three months earlier, in which voters approved the notorious constitutional amendment disfranchising black voters. One Democrat at the August election quipped to McMillan that it was so quiet "we ought to have a preacher here to preach for us." But that quiet was uneasy, McMillan testified, and the African American vote was severely depressed at both elections: "[I]t was the quiet that prevails in a wreck train when the wrecker stands, with his pistols in his hands and cries, 'Hands up' and robs them of their possession and rights."[1]

In Duplin, McMillan observed, some voters did not to go to the polls in either the August or November elections, and because many African Americans were not allowed to register or to vote in August, they assumed they would not be allowed to vote in November. Other voters, both black and white, were "afraid to go and attempt to vote, as they thought it would be dangerous." Some voters doubted that their ballots would be "counted as they cast them," and Populists in the area lacked confidence in the "election machinery." McMillan did not share these sentiments; he was confident and determined to cast his vote. However, when he entered the polling place, he noticed only one election judge at the polling boxes as he cast his ballot for Populist John E. Fowler. McMillan argued that the election in his district was not fair because there was no Populist representation on the election board and because the so-called Republican representative, a Mr. Laner, was a man known to have voted for the Democratic ticket. Earlier in the year, according to McMillan, Laner had tried unsuccessfully to get McMillan to sign a petition that contained the names of known Red Shirt Democrats. On the day of the election, the Democrats and Laner (a closeted Democrat) refused to let any voters watch the vote tally.[2]

The story of Captain John McMillan and other local Populists are rare in the historical literature. Few left sources, such as diaries and letters; thus historians must piece together what they can about local political activism during a time of heightened racial tensions and significant electoral stakes. It is very difficult to find information on grassroots Populism during the waning years of the movement, especially after 1898, when it was clear to all but dyed-in-the-wool Populists that there was no hope for the party. The election of 1896, internal bickering, and the move toward disfranchisement sounded the death knell for Populists. Only in a few isolated sections of the South, where local leaders worked diligently or a strong newspaper remained, did the People's Party survive the Democratic revival, and even in these areas survival was short lived. Historians of southern Populism have found it difficult to explain the reasons why white small farmers in the South continued to remain Populists during the party's twilight hours, at a time of increased political violence, vehement racist rhetoric, and white supremacy that tested the resolve of rank-and-file members.[3] Some recent studies of southern politics have focused on the grassroots Populist movement. Historians have examined the complex nature of cooperation politics between Populists and Republicans; tensions between whites and blacks during the tumultuous decade of the 1890s, resulting in the wholesale disfranchisement of African Americans and some poor whites; and the emergence of a legalized structure of Jim Crow. Analyzing contested election cases of U.S. congressional races is vital for understanding the political culture of the Gilded Age and allows a more sophisticated understanding of grassroots Populism in the South. This essay will examine the workings of the Populist Party in the Old North State, focusing on the internal politics of cooperation between Populists and Republicans in the congressional election of 1900 in North Carolina, the last active campaign for Populists.[4]

To help shed light on the political landscape and culture of local party politics, in this essay I will analyze the contested election case, brought in 1900, of *John E. Fowler (Populist) vs. Charles R. Thomas (Democrat)* of the Third Congressional District. I will explore how the Red Shirts and their Democratic supporters politically threatened and physically intimidated Populists and Republicans and committed violence and fraud at the polls. It will emphasize how African Americans persisted in their efforts to vote in the congressional race, even after the passage of the disfranchisement amendment in the summer. Populists and Republicans faced problems in the fall election as they reeled from the crushing blows at the polls in 1898 and 1900. Although the Populists were doomed, their story reminds us of how they tried to maintain a democracy and a competitive electoral system despite the mounting odds and virulent racial emotionalism. In addition, one can see the beginnings of a political realignment, with many Populists in the district moving toward the Republican Party. However, Populists were still unable to defeat the resurgent Democrats, even in the Third Congressional District, the bastion of power for Marion Butler. In the immediate post-disfranchisement South, Populists continued to organize and hope for victory, and the voices of local people, black and white, merit attention from historians.[5]

The political landscape of North Carolina was extremely complex throughout the 1890s. Members of the Populist Party, led by reformers and grassroots activists, had aligned themselves with Republicans and African Americans to smash the hegemony of the Democratic Party in 1894. From 1894 to 1897, North Carolina witnessed nothing short of a political revolution, as the reformers liberalized the state elections laws, passed a whole host of reform legislation in the state assembly, and elected hundreds of local, state, and federal officeholders. Among them were numerous black officials. In the face of this political transformation, a frightened and desperate Democratic Party seized on tensions within the reform-minded coalition. In the now-infamous white supremacy campaign of 1898, party members campaigned on the interlocking themes of race and protection of the purity of white women to smash Populists' and Republicans' hopes for victory in the November election. Using outright violence, intimidation, and appeals to emotion, Democrats won a landslide victory that culminated in the Wilmington "riot" of 1898. Now in the ascendancy, Democrats moved to disfranchise African Americans, destroy the reformist Populist Party, neuter the Republican Party, and therefore turn the Old North State into a one-party state, controlled by the Democratic Party. The anti-Democratic forces were nearly destroyed in the aftermath of the August 1900 suffrage amendment election; however, a few pockets of opposition remained. Republicans held on in the mountains of the West, and a few areas of Populist strength remained in the East, particularly around Sampson County, home of out-going Populist U.S. senator Marion Butler. However, these areas were small and the opportunities for a political renaissance were minuscule at best.[6]

At the local level, the Third Congressional District had witnessed an earlier contested election in 1894, and by 1900, it was the last remaining stronghold of the People's Party in the state. Populist leader Marion Butler was determined to fight off the Democrats, despite the overwhelming odds against a Populist political revival. The Third Congressional District lay in the eastern section of North Carolina and encompassed the counties of Bladen, Craven, Cumberland, Duplin, Jones, Moore, Onslow, and Sampson. Craven County was a majority black county, and some counties were Populist strongholds throughout the 1890s. For example, Sampson County was home to several leading Populists including former U.S. congressman John E. Fowler. Cyrus Thompson, the Populist secretary of state, hailed from Onslow County. Duplin County was also a fertile ground for Populism. It is not surprising that the Third Congressional District was politically active during the Populist insurgency of the 1890s.

In 1892, Democrats held onto the district, partly because of a split in the anti-Democratic forces. In 1894, Cyrus Thompson narrowly lost the district to a Democrat, even after a protracted contested election case. The Populists made amends in 1896, when Fowler, a close confident of Marion Butler, won a landslide victory in the district, after securing the support of Republicans (Fowler won by 5,433 votes over the Democratic candidate, Frank Thompson). However, this was the high tide of the Populist support. Tensions between the Populist and Republican cooperationists over the U.S. senatorship in 1897; the issue of silver and the state election of 1896; and the Democrats' virulent white supremacy campaign of 1898 signaled the decline of the People's Party in the Third Congressional District. Fowler lost in 1898 by just 189 votes, as Democrats annihilated their political opponents in one of the most vicious campaigns in the Old North State's history. Many commentators suspected that Democrats stole the 1898 election through violence (Fowler's vote plummeted by over two thousand votes and the Democratic vote increased by almost four thousand votes).[7]

After the Third Congressional District (and the rest of the state) voted for the suffrage amendment to disfranchise African Americans in 1900, the Populists withered away. However, in one last gasp, Populists attempted a retrenchment in the Third Congressional District by running Fowler. At first Democrats cheered as Fowler again lost. According to the official count, Democrat Charles R. Thomas received 13,541 votes to Populist (with Republican support) John E. Fowler's 11,632, or a majority of 1,909 votes. The Democrats were overjoyed as they celebrated almost total control of the state and the congressional delegation. However, after Marion Butler received scores of reports alleging fraud and intimidation, Populists decided to contest the election in the Third District. On December 27, 1900, candidate John E. Fowler served upon Charles R. Thomas a notice of contest.[8]

There is scant information on the state congressional elections of 1900; the contested election testimony, which this essay will closely examine, is the only detailed source on local politics from that period. From the testimony, it is clear that five factors were at work in the November election and that the Populists, despite terminal decline, wanted to win back one congressional district and perhaps stem the tide of virulent racism and the emergence of a one-party state.

First, the Red Shirts attempted to intimidate voters, both black and white, thus depressing the typical vote in the November election. In many cases they succeeded. The Red Shirts were bands of armed men who rode around the rural areas and towns of eastern North Carolina intimidating the local population and attempting to depress the African American, Republican, and Populist vote. According to one historian, the Red Shirts first appeared in North Carolina in Fayetteville on October 21, 1898. Unlike the Ku Klux Klan, the Red Shirts did not hide their identity. The quasi-paramilitary organization attracted all classes, including some of the wealthiest members of the Democratic Party, and were very active around election time. They subverted the democratic process, killed some opponents, and scared the living daylights out of rural folk. In 1900, the Red Shirts targeted both black and white leaders, particularly Populist speakers in the eastern section of the district in the county of Duplin, as well as rank-and-file black voters.[9]

A second factor at work was that despite Red Shirt intimidation, many African Americans, from the black leadership down to the illiterate African American voter in the countryside, continued to vote and endeavored to maintain their civil rights as they registered, voted, and organized. This is significant in and of itself. Third, despite the political problems and the twilight hours for democracy, in the Third Congressional District, at least, Populists and Republicans worked together to defeat the Democrats. The district had a strong local leadership, a nationally prominent senator, Marion Butler, and bad political blood dating back to 1892. Fourth, Populists tried to maintain their grassroots organization throughout the November election, with precinct captains, ticket workers, poll-box workers, and local party officials to ensure a high turnout at the polls, a complete organization of the black vote, and a fair count. Throughout the testimony many Populists expressed disgust with the nature of the election and the outright fraudulent activities committed by Democrats. Fifth, Democrats used all manner of subterfuge to commit voting fraud, from refusing to register black voters to throwing tickets on the floor during the count. For a short time, the Populists maintained the party's organization and attempted to gain electoral success.[10]

Many Populists felt certain that the Democrats had stolen the election. The only way to legally prove this was to contest a congressional election because the state government was in the hands of the Democrats. Therefore, the onus fell on ex-congressman John E. Fowler. Fowler was born in Clinton, Sampson County, in 1866. He was educated in the common schools of his home county, then attended Salem Academy and later Wake Forest College. Fowler read law at the University of North Carolina in Chapel Hill and was thereafter admitted to the bar. In 1892, he left the Democratic Party and joined the Populists, becoming a local leader and confidant of Populist leader Marion Butler. In the cooperation victory of 1894, he was elected to the state senate for the Fourteenth District, which included Sampson, Harnett, and Bladen counties. He was the youngest Populist in the state legislature at just twenty-eight years of age. He impressed many with his hard work, diligence, and determination to effect policy changes. In 1896, he ran for Congress and won the Third Congressional seat. He was just thirty years old when he began serving as a U.S. congressman. His ascendancy seemed to herald the rise of new politicians and a new way of life for North Carolina. But as the Populists waned, so did Fowler's career. In 1898, he lost his reelection bid during the virulent white supremacy campaign. But Fowler remained a Populist, closely connected with Butler. In 1900 he endeavored to win back the congressional seat.[11]

Testimony from African Americans and white voters clearly illustrate that the Red Shirts and Democrats succeeded in scaring off scores of black voters in both the August and November elections, which in turn depressed the vote for Populist John Fowler in November. Although this is well established, there is little information on how voters were intimidated in the eastern section of North Carolina after the August election and at the local level. The fact that intimidation and violence persisted after the election demonstrates that Populists continued to oppose Democratic power; and Democrats worried that their opponents would recover politically. Red Shirts often targeted African Americans in the eastern section of the state, particularly Duplin County. That the Red Shirts made no attempt to hide their identity further illustrates their contempt for law and order; it also reveals that they were strongly supported by Democrats and local officials, who abhorred black voting. After an inflammatory speech from Democratic gubernatorial candidate Charles B. Aycock in Kenansville on July 26, 1900, a company of Red Shirts led by Dr. Arthur rode from Kenansville toward Magnolia, shooting indiscriminately into the air. According to the Populist organizer A. J. Ward, this gang of Red Shirts fired over thirty times at a group of African Americans in the countryside, about two miles from Magnolia. After the firing subsided and the Red Shirts departed, Ward found the frightened group of African Americans hiding in a cotton patch. In Ward's damning statement of events, he admonished Aycock as a Red Shirt governor, annoying the attorney representing the Charles R. Thomas, the contestee. The lawyer countered by arguing that Aycock was not wearing a red shirt and therefore was not a Red Shirt governor. A. J. Ward refused to back down from his position and continued to indict Aycock as a Red Shirt governor:

> He has a Red Shirt crowd with him and a Red Shirt parade from Warsaw to Kenansville, wherever he came from. I judge by his talking to the crowd of Red Shirt men as he did that he was in deep sympathy with them. He said the "Ku Klux" were for a purpose and they accomplished it, and the "Red Shirts" are for a purpose and I think they will accomplish it.[12]

Populists were disgusted with the racist frenzy, violence, and intimidation that notable politicians, including Charles Aycock and Furnifold Simmons, chairman of the Democratic Party and author of the disfranchisement amendment, masterminded in the August election. These Populists, despite the odds, continued to work for fair elections.[13]

Moses Judge, a fifty-three-year-old Republican from Cyprus Creek, Duplin County, concurred that the Red Shirts "produced a good deal of excitement, and they [African Americans] were scared to go to the polls." Judge also avowed in his testimony that on election day, one Red Shirt, a Mr. Southerland, wore a red shirt and carried a gun as he went up to vote. Judge was not allowed to vote in the November election because poll workers said he could not prove his age on the day of the election.[14] Some African Americans were so afraid that they fled their homes in the weeks before the election. For example, Dave Kennedy, an African American voter in Duplin, testified that he hid in Grove Swamp, along with his brother and a friend, in fear of his life. The prospect of poisonous snakes, mosquito bites, and general discomfort was preferable to a band of marauding Red Shirts.[15] In Warsaw precinct, Ivey Blount recalled that he witnessed what looked like an army of Red Shirts shooting at houses. The wife of John Thomson, Blount testified, came to his home and "was wet up to her knees, and said she had lain out all night; she was scratched with briars, and that put a scare on me and I didn't go to the election; I did go back in the November election and voted but I was afraid."[16] Such reports were typical, and as a consequence, the black vote markedly declined.

Red Shirts focused on intimidating white and black leaders. If they could scare off the leaders, they rightly discerned that the Populist and Republican organizations, already in decline, would capitulate. One of the most infamous examples occurred again in Duplin County. Abe Middleton, a notable black leader and a former Republican county chairman, as well as a member of the state executive committee, found himself the target of Red Shirt ire. Although Middleton did not speak publicly or canvass in the election campaign in 1900, he was still the lightning rod for many Democratic and Red Shirt threats. They probably could not believe that such a prominent leader in the black community was not organizing and rounding up the sizable black vote. On the night before the August election, Middleton testified that there was a lot of shooting around his home in Kenansville, more than normal, within sixty-five to seventy-five yards of his house. On the day of the election, Middleton received word that an eighteen-inch "pasteboard coffin" was placed in his garden, a popular form of intimidation against Populists and Republicans at this time. Although he ignored the threatening news, Middleton was quite angry about it, perhaps because his wife found the coffin, and apparently Middleton retorted on hearing the news, "what the devil do I care about that coffin. I don't care about that, for when I am trying to do right and behave myself then can't be treated right what in devil do I care about the coffin."[17] However, many members of the black community did not ignore the incident and crowded around the black leader's home to get a glimpse of the coffin that "read 'Abe Middleton. At rest.'" Middleton noted that several other black leaders had also found coffins in their gardens. This was corroborated by Lafayette Hussy, who testified that Red Shirts and Democrats often used pasteboard coffins to intimidate black leaders and voters. Democrats and Red Shirts reasoned that if they could demoralize the black leaders they could successfully depress the black vote.[18]

In case intimidation did not work, Democrats made certain that African Americans could not register or vote. After passage of the disfranchisement amendment, African Americans continued their efforts to vote, but in Duplin, Craven, and Cumberland counties, many failed in their attempts. In the majority black county of Craven, a large number of African American voters were denied registration, particularly in James City, a predominantly black area of that county. For example, Whittington Spear, a fifty-six-year-old African American voter in Thurman Precinct, could not register to vote because he could not prove his age to the satisfaction of the Democratic registrar. Spear testified he would have voted for the Populist candidate, Fowler.[19] Jobb Grimes, a forty-six-year-old black voter, gave similar testimony, "I went to register and give my name and age, and he [the Democratic registrar] refused because I didn't have anyone to identify me, and he said I would have to get two men to identify me or else I couldn't register, and them I had to get were men he knowed and I couldn't get them."[20] Mac Oden, a forty-nine-year-old black voter, who had worked for the registrar's father over the previous two years, was also not allowed to register because he could not find two people to swear his age. Oden refused to give in lightly to Registrar Vinson and pushed for his constitutional rights, and in his words "worried him [Vinson] a good deal 'cause it was something I had been here a long time in this place here, and I knowed I was bona fide registered . . . I just worried him as long as he stood there, and at last he told me he was not going to do it anyhow."[21] Oden resisted in vain, but it is interesting to note that a black man, at the height of Red Shirt violence and in a time of terrible race relations, attempted to stand up for his rights in the face of a hostile white Democratic official.[22]

The contested election testimony is the only existing detailed source that illustrates conclusively that African Americans continued in their attempts to register and vote in the congressional and presidential election of 1900, despite the passage of the disfranchisement amendment in the summer and the continued obstruction of Democrats. It is also clear that many African Americans, particularly in heavily black areas such as James City, were repeatedly barred from registering. That African Americans testified in open hearings about Democratic and Red Shirt attempts to curtail voting illustrates that they were determined to use legal and political means to preserve their civil rights. However, many African Americans feared speaking publicly about these incidents after such a tumultuous few months. An interesting piece of testimony from Edward Dixon Sr., a father deacon of the First Colored Baptist Church in Warsaw, is notable in this regard. Dixon admitted that he was afraid to testify all he knew in court because "I am here in a place I feel that I have no protection." Fowler's lawyer directly pushed this issue, and Dixon gave a succinct answer: "Q. Are the colored people afraid to testify to all they know before this court in this investigation through fear? A. The answer is yes. Q. Are you afraid to testify all you know? A. Yes, sir; I am."[23]

Such testimony demonstrates both the success of the Red Shirts and the corrupt local politics at work during the racist Democratic campaigns; it also illustrates that some African Americans were determined to testify in open hearings on at least some of the details of intimidation and fraud. The testimony also delineates the ways in which Populists attempted to rally the black vote in the November election. Populist leaders worked with local Republican and black leaders to register black voters and often donated their time and money to defend African American voters in the courtroom. Of course, a Populist candidate stood to benefit if the contested election case proved successful, but only if it could be clearly shown that disenfranchised black voters intended to vote for a Populist and not a Republican candidate.[24]

Although the congressional election took place in November, Fowler and his lawyer spent a lot of time focusing on the August election and the conditions surrounding the campaign, registration, and voting. There are probably several reasons for this. First, Fowler attempted to show that the tactics used by the Red Shirts and Democrats depressed the normal level of registration and voting among white and black voters. Many Populists and Republicans were unable to vote in either election; thus the November election, Fowler argued, was not legitimate. Second, Fowler wanted to embarrass and give a political black eye to the recently elected Democratic governor, Charles Aycock. Aycock was a closeted Red Shirt, Fowler claimed, whose fiery speeches inflamed white supremacist passions and inspired much of the violence in the eastern part of North Carolina. In addition, the Populists sought to prove that other Democratic leaders help instigate the intimidation and violence. Populists wanted to broadcast to the nation that political liberty was dead in North Carolina. Third, Fowler wanted to illustrate that rampant registration fraud in the August election discouraged many voters from trying to register for the November election or from attending the polls. Fourth, Fowler aimed to demonstrate that scores of voters, who were prevented from voting or whose votes were not counted in the August election, did not expect a full and fair count in the November election. Fowler warned Butler that the situation was critical in the summer election: "Our folks down here will not have a dog's showing. The democrats have made arrangements to steal as they have never have before." Fowler argued that all of these elements indicated that he was the legitimate victor in 1900.[25]

Local Populists were determined to maintain their organization and work hard at the polls to stop the effects of the disfranchisement amendment, even amid the muddy political waters surrounding the November elections. Many believed that their well-oiled party machinery would help them succeed, despite the overwhelming odds in the 1900 election campaign. In Sampson County, Fowler worked on election day distributing tickets to voters. He also tried to keep an eye on the nature of the vote, the number of people denied the right to vote, and the count at the end of the day. It was rumored that the Democratic election judges would throw out Populist votes. W. H. Pope in north Clinton worked as a Populist judge, giving up his whole day to see that the election was fair. R. D. Carr, a local Populist leader in Kenansville, Duplin County, and justice of the peace and postmaster at Xenia, admitted that he worked in every campaign for Populists. Peter Fisher in Bern precinct in Craven County worked hard to give out Populist tickets all day. He, along with fellow activist L. W. Ham, saw themselves as "the special ones to give out the tickets." In the same county, William R. Dixon, a thirty-six-year-old Populist, worked tirelessly in Jasper Precinct to distribute tickets all day long. Many Populists retained strong partisan feelings, even though the party was in terminal decline. For example, J. W. Mallard stated that he was a Populist, and "I expect to be one of the last ones, too."[26] Dr. Virgil N. Seawall of Duplin County stated that he had been a Populist "sometime before the party was organized, I suspect" and that he had also canvassed for the Farmers' Alliance.[27] Edward Wagoner, a fifty-six-year-old Populist from Bern Precinct in Craven County, voted for Fowler and noted, "That was my choice, because he was a Third Party man, and I considered that next to my faith."[28] O. L. Ward continued to work hard as a Populist leader, despite the problems facing the party. In Cumberland County, A. A. McCaskill also worked all day in Cross Creeks Number Two Precinct, to keep a poll book and work for the cooperationists. Duncan C. Downing served as an assistant manager of the "Fusion Party," which entailed distributing literature and keeping the headquarters apprised of the situation in the county. Downing worked diligently and also gave out tickets on the day of the election.

Despite the physical risks and heated political campaign, some Populists and Republicans continued to organize at the local level. In Duplin County, a local Populist activist, J. B. Winders, apparently risked his life in trying to register African Americans to vote. According to B. L. Blackmore, some Democrats claimed that Mr. Winders "would be killed" if he tried organizing.[29] Many Populists gave up trying to vote in the November election. According to J. T. Wilkins, chairman of the county commission in Duplin County, in his district of Rose Hill there was a light vote in November because "the methods used by the Democrats prior to and during the August election caused the drop off.... The Populists and Republicans were disgusted with the methods used in the campaign and regarded it as useless to go out and vote."[30]

Not all Populists in Rose Hill agreed. One local Populist leader, C. C. Vann, the Populist candidate for sheriff in Rose Hill Township in Duplin County, worked very hard to get voters registered and he personally appeared before the Democratic registrar to help with the process. According to Vann, the registrar claimed that "he would register them, but that he had promised not to do it, and it was the last day of registration and he didn't want to do it then on that day so that everybody would know it."[31] Clearly it was not just anti-Democrats who were intimidated. But Vann pressed on and got some voters registered. Friendly relations and solid reputations occasionally carried the day in small-town North Carolina. When Vann testified as a rebuttal witness, he disagreed with Democrats who testified that the election was quiet, orderly, fair and free from intimidation. Vann argued, "I can't say that it was free from intimidation, if not allowing men to register and vote is intimidation. I know of some men not allowed to register and vote in the November election, white Populists and colored Republicans."[32]

A great deal of the contested election testimony concerns claims and counter-claims of election fraud and was not tied directly with intimidation. Democrats saw that black and white voters, both Populists and Republicans, continued their efforts to vote, even after disfranchisement. Worried over losing the election in the Third District, Democrats engaged extensively in fraud. The Populists' accusations of wrong-doing fall into several categories. First, Populist and Republican voters could not register during the summer, nor were they allowed to vote in August; thus they did not try to vote in November. For example, Frank Faison of south Clinton in Sampson County did not vote in November because there was some problem with proving his age in August, so "I didn't think it worth while to go back."[33] A. J. Ward noted similar actions in Rock Fish Precinct in Duplin County. He testified that many black voters "deprived of voting in the August election did not vote in the November election" because many thought they could not vote in the next election.[34] Still others were not allowed to register for the election in November. For example, in Warsaw Precinct, Democrats prevented as many as forty men from registering to vote. In Kinston, P. H. Bright wrote to Populist leader Hal Ayer that the registrars "are acting outrageously in the matter of registering negroes. Not more than a third who apply are allowed to register." There are dozens of other examples of similar shenanigans at registration.[35]

A second form of alleged fraud occurred on the day of the election, when voters who believed they had registered properly were not allowed to vote. The reasons given by the Democratic judges of election ran the gamut; a voter could not prove his age, could not prove his residency, had a problem with his registration, had committed a crime or some local issue was at work. For example, in Sampson County, W. N. Bass could not vote in the Herring Precinct because Democrats said "that my wife had left me and that wouldn't let me vote."[36] Some witnesses for the contestee expressed racist views. One piece of questioning illustrates this point very well. John A. Gavin, clerk of the superior court for Duplin County, was asked by Thomas's lawyer, "Isn't the average colored boy or colored man hard to identify, compared to white men?" to which Gavin replied, "It is more difficult to prove their age and they move about more than white people." The contestee then asked, "Isn't the average colored man more unscrupulous about the obligations of an oath than a white man?" And, Gavin concurred: "I would suppose so."[37] Democrats used these racist attitudes to explain why blacks voted in such low numbers.[38]

Populists also argued that the election machinery was in the hands of Democrats. This frequently meant there was no Populist or Republican recommended election judge at the election site. In addition, many of the cooperationist judges that were in attendance were cherry picked by Democrats. In heavily black areas, most were African Americans, some of whom were not in good standing with the local black community. A Democratic registrar in Friendship Precinct, Duplin County, admitted that the registration books were not open because they had not arrived in time. R. D. Carr in Kenansville noted that Republicans and Populists did not offer any black judges because "It was claimed to be a white man's fight, and we were asking for white men on the board."[39] Clearly, the opponents of the Democrats did not want to open themselves up to charges of promulgating black power. O. L. Ward, the chairman of the Populist Party executive committee in Duplin, furnished a list of Populist election judges for each precinct in the county (not just one name). At first, the election board refused to take the names and appoint any Populists at all, but then decided to take the list to consider the names and "probably" appoint them. Ward testified that "they did not appoint them."[40]

A fourth form of election fraud allegedly occurred after the voting took place. Fowler charged that Democrats refused to let Populist or Republican leaders watch the count and thus illegally threw out hundreds of votes for him all across the congressional district. For example, Fowler asked but was not allowed to see the vote count in north Clinton. After he asked a second time to see the count, the Democratic judge of election, O. H. Giddens, became angry, according to Fowler, and vowed, "I be d——d if any one shall go in and see them counted." Giddens stated, "He said you have all accused me of cheating and now I am going to cheat."[41] With two-thirds of the vote already counted, Giddens finally allowed a Mr. J. J. Matthis to observe the vote count for the remaining votes, but only then from the outside through a window. The only Populist allowed inside was busy tallying the vote and was unable to observe the count. J. J. Matthis, corroborating Fowler's testimony, said he knew that voters were allowed by law to see the vote, but that Giddens refused and that the Democrat used offensive language twice. According to Matthis, "Mr. Gidden's said he intended to count them right, but since they doubted him he will be * * * if he wasn't then going to cheat." A worried lawyer for Thomas argued that Giddens was joking, but Matthis scoffed, "He didn't seem that he was in a condition to be jocular much."[42]

Jessie Basnight, a senior local Populist leader in Thurman Precinct and chairman of the Populist executive committee, worked in conjunction with Robert Hancock, Republican chairman of the executive committee, on election day to ensure a fair count. Basnight and Hancock carefully monitored the day's activities and cited many voting irregularities, including registration problems. They testified that one Democrat refused to allow some African Americans to vote, even though they had registered.

The Democrat claimed that "the angels from Heaven had come down and wiped their names off the registration book; that they could not vote."[43] Hancock observed Democratic officials taking tickets from the voters and putting them in the wrong boxes; those boxes, he said, were changed throughout the day, and only Democrats were allowed inside to monitor the vote. During the count, according to Basnight and Hancock, Fowler tickets were thrown on the floor. Similar events occurred in Cumberland County. Frank Carr, chairman of the Populist Party executive committee, testified that the election board did not appoint the Populist judges and that neither the Populist or Republican parties supported those who were appointed. John B. Williams testified that in the Newton Grove Precinct in Sampson County, the registrar and all the judges were Democrats. The contested election testimony convinced Populists that the election was not fair, and it is clear that it was a well-coordinated attempt to keep the Populist vote light.[44]

Because of the extensive hearings and testimony in the contested election case and the slow pace of the proceedings, the congressional committee did not rule on the disputed 1900 election until 1902. In the Third Congressional District contested election case, John E. Fowler and his attorney William Clark failed to prove that Democrats had stolen the election through various forms of fraud and violence. Rep. M. E. Olmstead, from the Committee on Elections, Number 2, issued a brief four-page report to the U.S. Congress on April 9, 1902, explaining the committee's judgment. The committee acknowledged that in several districts of Craven County the election officers were all Democrats, or in some cases Republicans who were not recommended by the Republican executive committee. The committee saw "evidence of considerable irregularity in some parts of the county." But in several "unattacked" districts, the committee found no electoral problems at all, thus ruling that it could not throw out the entire county because of the problems in a few districts.

In Duplin County, the committee acknowledged that the Red Shirts sought "by public demonstration with guns and pistols, to terrorize and intimidate Republicans and Populists and prevent them from voting." But the committee disagreed with Fowler that such tactics were employed across the entire county, arguing "There is little or no evidence that the terrorization and intimidation in August had any material effect upon the Congressional vote in November." That statement contradicts witnesses' claims under oath that intimidation was widespread, and many refrained from voting out of fear. Although the committee did agree with Fowler that several Populists and Republicans were appointed without the recommendation of the aforesaid parties, the committee could not find "any evidence that they worked or voted against the contestant." Just as in Craven County, the committee refused to throw out the entire vote in Duplin County. In a bizarre twist, however, the committee acknowledged that in some Craven County districts "there is some evidence of carelessness and irregularity, and probably fraud in the conduct of the election and counting and return of the votes." But, the committee argued, some Republicans were dissatisfied with the Populist Fowler and voted for Thomas. In the end, the committee ruled, "we find that the frauds and irregularities shown are not sufficient to overturn" the contestee's election. The committee concluded that John E. Fowler was not entitled to take the seat in the House of Representatives, and Charles R. Thomas was duly elected U.S. congressman from the Third Congressional District. Fowler and his attorney clearly had difficulty convincing a congressional committee that the election was stolen, and the committee apparently failed to consider the political and racial turmoil of the 1890s in its decision.[45]

The testimony of rank-and-file Populists in the Third Congressional District contested election case points out several key issues in the waning days of the Populist insurgency. First, the Democrats and Red Shirts worked to prevent a fair and democratic election in the fall of 1900. In many places they succeeded, even though the congressional committee did not overturn the result. Second, in the face of massive fraud, intimidation, threats, and violence, both African American and white voters tried to stand up for what they believed, vote for the candidate they supported, and resist the white supremacy juggernaut driven by Charles Aycock and other Democrats. The voters clearly cared deeply about their civil rights, the future of the state, and the survival of the Populist and Republican parties. Third, the surviving evidence of local organizing, with small-town leaders and precinct captains battling away to get out the vote, illustrates how deeply the rank-and-file supported the tenets of the Populist Party, even in its twilight hours, and worked with the Republicans. Politics mattered to these activists and many risked personal injury, social ostracism, and economic hardship to work for the Populists. The testimony in this case indicates African American voters strongly supported the Populists in these endeavors. Finally, the political maneuvering in the Third District reveals the state's political realignment, as some Populist voters began to shift toward the Republican Party.

By the spring of 1902, the Populist Party was dead in North Carolina, strangled by the white supremacy campaign of 1898, marauding bands of Red Shirts threatening whites and African Americans throughout the eastern section of the state, and the wholesale disfranchisement of African Americans and some poor whites. At the national level, the rise of William Jennings Bryan doomed the national Populist Party. In addition, internal bickering between Populists and Republicans in North Carolina from 1896 until 1900 exacerbated the problems. Thus although the decision of the committee on elections obviously disappointed old-time Populists leaders such as Marion Butler, John Fowler, Cyrus Thompson, and their Republican allies, most of the rank-and-file Populists and African American voters had either given up on the electoral process or they no longer had the opportunity to vote. The eastern section of the state turned Democrat, particularly with the demise of the black vote, but Sampson County, led by Marion Butler, became an active Republican stronghold with heavily Populist tendencies. Throughout the state, the Republican Party, now without the African American support, fought hard to win three congressional seats in 1908. The party also claimed minor victories in the state legislature and benefited from patronage positions in the federal government. At the state level, however, Democrats held the vast majority of offices and had a monopoly on power. Populists did join Republicans to push a new Progressive-era set of policies and programs, but that is a story for another time.

In North Carolina's congressional elections of 1900, political parties realigned once again, excluding African Americans. Many voters, however, were determined to resist the policies of a conservative white-supremacy Democratic new world order, epitomized by Charles B. Aycock and Furnifold Simmons. Cooperation politics in North Carolina, and in the South, was over, the noble and home-grown interracial political experiment dead. Progressive politics and major political alliances between whites and blacks would have to wait until the civil rights movement of the 1960s.[46]

Notes

1. *Contested Election Case of John E. Fowler vs. Charles R. Thomas From The Third Congressional District of the State of North Carolina* (Washington, D.C.: Government Printing Office, 1901), testimony of Capt. John C. McMillan, 1017, hereinafter cited as *Fowler vs. Thomas*, testimony of Capt. John C. McMillan. Other testimony in the case will be similarly cited. In North Carolina, testimony in this contested election was heard in local stores and courthouses of the Third Congressional District. It appears from the testimony that the public attended the hearings in large numbers and local newspapers followed the case. The testimony was then sent on to the clerk of the U.S. House of Representatives and passed on to the respective Committee on Elections Number 2. A

longer version of this essay appeared in the *North Carolina Historical Review*. Used with permission.

2. *Fowler vs. Thomas*, testimony of Capt. John C. McMillan, 1017–1018.

3. There are some excellent books on Populism, in particular southern Populism, but few focus much attention on the demise of the Populist Party at the local level and the role of the rank and file during the late 1890s. However, there is much useful information and context in the seminal works on the Populist Party and the movement. See, for example, Norman Pollack, *The Populist Response to Industrial America: Midwestern Populist Thought* (Cambridge, MA: Harvard University Press, 1962); Lawrence Goodwyn, *Democratic Promise: The Populist Moment in America* (New York: Oxford University Press, 1976); Bruce Palmer, *"Man Over Money": The Southern Populist Critique of American Capitalism* (Chapel Hill: University of North Carolina Press, 1980). Two other classic works are still vital: C. Vann Woodward, *Tom Watson: Agrarian Rebel* (New York: Oxford University Press, 1938); John D. Hicks, *The Populist Revolt: A History of the Farmers' Alliance and the People's Party* (Minneapolis: University of Minnesota Press, 1931). Some excellent examples of local studies with rank-and-file voices in the South do exist. See, in particular, Barton C. Shaw, *The Wool-Hat Boys: Georgia's Populist Party* (Baton Rouge: Louisiana State University Press, 1984).

4. Skinner lost his bid for reelection in 1898. For more details on the complex nature of Populist Party politics in North Carolina, particularly divisions after 1896, see James M. Beeby, *Revolt of the Tar Heels: The North Carolina Populist Movement, 1890–1901* (Jackson: University Press of Mississippi, 2008). On local, grassroots Populism, Gregg Cantrell, "John B. Rayner: A Study in Black Populist Leadership," *Southern Studies* 24 (winter 1985): 432–443; Lawrence Goodwyn, "Populist Dreams and Negro Rights: East Texas as a Case Study," *American Historical Review* 76 (December 1971): 1435–1456; Samuel L. Webb, "A Jacksonian Democrat in Postbellum Alabama: The Ideology and Influence of Journalist Robert McKee, 1869–1896," *Journal of Southern History* 62 (May 1996): 239–274; James M. Beeby, "'Equal Rights to All and Special Privileges to None': Grass-Roots Populism in North Carolina," *North Carolina Historical Review* 78 (April 2001): 156–186; Alicia E. Rodriquez, "Disfranchisement in Dallas: The Democratic Party and the Suppression of Independent Political Challenges in Dallas, Texas, 1891–1894," *Southwestern Historical Quarterly* 108 (July 2004): 42–64.

5. Until the last ten years or so, little historical work focused on Populism in North Carolina. Indeed, no work successfully detailed the various wings within the party, the radicalization of the Alliance toward the People's Party, and how the Populists organized themselves and worked with the Republicans to topple the Democrats. However, that has changed recently. James L. Hunt, *Marion Butler and American Populism* (Chapel Hill: University of North Carolina Press, 2004), based on his lengthy dissertation, effectively analyzes the pivotal role of Populist U.S. senator and North Carolina leader Marion Butler and Hunt successfully resuscitated Butler's career and legacy. See also Philip R. Muller, "New South Populism: North Carolina, 1884–1900" (Ph.D. diss., University of North Carolina at Chapel Hill, 1971); Craig M. Thurtell, "The Fusion Insurgency in North Carolina: Origins to Ascendancy, 1876–1896" (Ph.D. diss., Columbia University, 1998); Simeon Delap, "The Populist Party in North Carolina," *Trinity Archives* 14 (1922): 40–74. A very good and rather specialized analysis of Populism in the Old North State is Joe Creech, *Righteous Indignation: Religion and the Populist Revolution* (Urbana:

The Demise of Grassroots Populism in North Carolina . . . 195

University of Illinois Press, 2006). For the most complete analysis of the People's Party in North Carolina, Beeby, *Revolt of the Tar Heels*. Scholars of Tar Heel Populism should consult the Marion Butler Papers (hereinafter cited as Butler Papers) and the Cyrus Thompson Papers, both in the Southern Historical Collection, Manuscripts Department, Wilson Library, University of North Carolina at Chapel Hill, as well as the local Populist newspapers such as the Clinton *Caucasian*, Charlotte *People's Paper*, Hickory *Mercury*, Pittsboro *Chatham Citizen*, Raleigh *Hayseeder*, Raleigh *Home Rule*, Wadesboro *Plow Boy*, and others.

6. For a good discussion of the 1898 white supremacy campaign: Glenda Gilmore, *Gender and Jim Crow: Women and the Politics of White Supremacy in North Carolina, 1896-1920* (Chapel Hill: University of North Carolina Press, 1996); Robert Wooley, "Race and Politics: The Evolution of the White Supremacy Campaign of 1898 in North Carolina" (Ph.D. diss., University of North Carolina at Chapel Hill, 1977); H. Leon Prather, "The Red Shirt Movements in North Carolina, 1898-1900," *Journal of Negro History* 62 (1977): 174-184. This is the best treatment of the Red Shirts. For an excellent discussion of the effects of the Wilmington "riot," see David S. Cecelski and Timothy Tyson, eds., *Democracy Betrayed: The Wilmington Race Riot of 1898 and Its Legacy* (Chapel Hill: University of North Carolina Press, 1998).

The historiography of disfranchisement is lengthy. For North Carolina, the latest work is by Michael Perman, *Struggle for Mastery: Disfranchisement in the South, 1888-1908* (Chapel Hill: University of North Carolina Press, 2001), 148-173. But the best book on disfranchisement still remains J. Morgan Kousser, *The Making of Southern Politics: Suffrage Restriction and the Establishment of the One-Party South, 1880-1910* (New Haven, CT: Yale University Press, 1974). See also, Hunt, *Marion Butler*; Beeby, *Revolt of the Tar Heels*, 189-214; Dwight Billings, *Planters and the Making of a "New South": Class Politics, and Development in North Carolina, 1865-1900* (Chapel Hill: University of North Carolina Press, 1979), 191; Helen Edmonds, *The Negro and Fusion Politics in North Carolina, 1894-1901* (Chapel Hill: University of North Carolina Press, 1951), 178; Alexander Mabry, "'White Supremacy' and the North Carolina Suffrage Amendment," *North Carolina Historical Review* 8 (1936): 1-24, especially 3-10. Although this essay does not question the central arguments of these excellent works, it does seek to incorporate a local-history approach with attention to the grassroots and the role of the Populist Party in the unfolding story.

7. There is no *direct* evidence that the Democrats stole the Third Congressional District in 1898, but the surviving evidence, particularly the Red Shirt violence in Duplin County, suggests that the Democrats did in fact steal the district. See Beeby, *Revolt of the Tar Heels*, 172-188.

8. For the revised returns for the 1894 election, see House Committee on Elections, *Cyrus Thompson vs. John G. Shaw*, 54th Cong., 1st sess., 1896, H. Rept. 1635, 27, 1-2; Beeby, "'Equal Rights to All, Special Privileges to None,'" 163 and 183. For the official result in 1896, 1898, and 1900, *Contested Election Case of John E. Fowler vs. Charles R. Thomas From The Third Congressional District of the State of North Carolina*, Exhibit H (1900 election), Exhibit I (1898 election), and Exhibit J (1896 election). Evidence for the contestant, 327-328.

9. Prather, "The Red Shirt Movement in North Carolina, 1898-1900," 175-177.

10. The best treatment of Marion Butler and his leadership is the excellent biography by James L. Hunt, *Marion Butler*; for this period, see 171-185. For more details on the

1900 elections throughout the state and its effect on the November election, see Prather, "The Red Shirt Movement in North Carolina, 1898–1900"; Perman, *Struggle for Mastery*, 148–173; Beeby, *Revolt of the Tar Heels*, 189–214; Billings, *Planters and the Making of a "New South"*; Edmonds, *The Negro and Fusion Politics in North Carolina*; Mabry, "'White Supremacy' and the North Carolina Suffrage Amendment"; Benjamin R. Justesen II, "George Henry White, Josephus Daniels, and the Showdown over Disfranchisement, 1900," *North Carolina Historical Review* 77 (January 2000): 1–33; Eric Anderson, *The Black Second: Race and Politics in North Carolina, 1872–1901* (Baton Rouge: Louisiana State University Press, 1981), 296–312.

11. Collins and Goodwyn, *Members of the General Assembly of North Carolina, 1895* (Raleigh: Edwards and Broughton Printers and Binders, 1895), 11.

12. *Fowler vs. Thomas*, testimony of A. J. Ward, 159. Prather, "The Red Shirt Movement in North Carolina," 180–183.

13. Prather, "The Red Shirt Movement in North Carolina," 180–183. Prather did not utilize the contested election testimony and thus his work relies mainly on newspaper accounts from the period. For other work on the Red Shirts in the 1900 election, Beeby, *Revolt of the Tar Heels*, 202–210; Hunt, *Marion Butler*, 178–180.

14. *Fowler vs. Thomas*, testimony of Moses Judge, 166.

15. *Fowler vs. Thomas*, testimony of Dave Kennedy, 124.

16. *Fowler vs. Thomas*, testimony of Ivey Blount, 99–100. See also Tim Middleton, 125. It is not certain whether he was related to A. R. Middleton.

17. A. R. Middleton played a key role in the 1894 state election and in the 1895 state assembly as a cooperationist leader (Middleton was the N.C. General Assembly doorkeeper; in 1895, he stopped a white Democrat from leaving the state assembly, inflaming the Democratic press). Beeby, *Revolt of the Tar Heels*, 113–114. *Fowler vs. Thomas*, testimony of A. R. Middleton, 118–120.

18. *Fowler vs. Thomas*, testimony of Lafayette Hussy, 137; Middleton, 138; and J. S. Hamilton, 146.

19. *Fowler vs. Thomas*, testimony of Whittington Spear, 428. There are dozens of examples from James City. See testimony of James Burden, 448–449; Philip Burden, 451; Sam Bizzell, 453; Haywood Green, 455–456; Hilliard Edmondson, 458–459; Edward Sanders, 468–469; Charlie Woodward, 469–470; Thomas Becton, 470; Aaron Little, 479.

20. *Fowler vs. Thomas*, testimony of Jobb Grimes, 429.

21. *Fowler vs. Thomas*, testimony of Mac Oden, 429.

22. For other examples, see *Fowler vs. Thomas*, testimony of James Wilson, 432; Isaac Aydlett, 432–433; Samuel Williams, 434; Homer Simmons, 436–437; William Bembry, 438–439; James Russell, 443; and Cary Wilson, 447–448. For Duplin County, see *Fowler vs. Thomas*, testimony of A. J. Ward, 158–159; and A. R. Middleton, 118–121. For Cumberland County, see *Fowler vs. Thomas*, testimony of William McLean, 682–683; Irvin Painter, 683; Jackson Campbell, 683; George Walker, 684; Robert Halliday, 684; George Fuller, 684; Jack Mills, 684; and Oliver Armstrong, 685; testimony of African American voters in Cross Creeks Number Three Precinct, 705–725; Orlando F. Goddard, 726–727.

23. For examples of intimidation in the courtroom, *Fowler vs. Thomas*, testimony of Edward Dixon Sr., 79–81; Richard Best, 81–82.

24. For Craven County, *Fowler vs. Thomas*, testimony of Sam Stallings, 425; Henry Latham, 426; Angus Moore, 427; Jacob Dennis, 430; Samuel Adams, 431; Alexander

Delemar, 431; John Q. Smith, 433; Lewis Williams, 435; John T. Vale, 436; Abram Harvey, 438; Riley Branch, 439; Benjamin Harris, 441; John Webber, 443; Henry Hardy, 450; Sutton Burden, 451; Primos Roberts, 454; Peter Haddock, 455; and scores of others.

25. John E. Fowler to Marion Butler, July 25, 1900, Butler Papers. *Fowler vs. Thomas*, Notice of Contest, 2–16, from John E. Fowler, *Contestant, and lawyer*, William W. Clark. Testimony of J. W. Mallard, 33; Sam B. Newton, 150–151; C. C. Vann, 154; J. C. Summerlin, 149; O. L. Ward, 190; Henry J. Faison, 194; R. W. Blackmore, 84–86; J. W. Mallard, 32–34; Z. J. Quinn, 123; C. C. Vann, 154; R. C. Seawall, 168. For more examples of the Red Shirts preventing Populist leaders from speaking: Hickory *Times- Mercury*, August 1, 1900; Charlotte *People's Paper*, July 13, 1900; Maury Ward to Marion Butler, July 26, 1900; A. B. Winner to Marion Butler, July 25, 1900; R. W. Blackmore to Marion Butler, July 28, 1900, all three in the Butler Papers. Some local leaders and organizers in the Third Congressional District wrote to Populist senator Marion Butler describing the inflammatory speeches Democrats used to intimidate voters: J. J. Jones to Marion Butler, July 26, 1900; Maury Ward to Marion Butler, July 26, 1900, both in Butler Papers. See also, Marion Butler, "Election in North Carolina," *The Independent* 12 (August 16, 1900); and Prather, "The Red Shirt Movement in North Carolina," 180–183.

26. *Fowler vs. Thomas*, testimony of J. W. Mallard, 34.

27. *Fowler vs. Thomas*, testimony of V. N. Seawall, 31–32.

28. *Fowler vs. Thomas*, testimony of Edward Wagoner, 213.

29. *Fowler vs. Thomas*, testimony of B. L. Blackmore, 73–75.

30. *Fowler vs. Thomas*, testimony of J. T. Wilkins, 160–162. For others noted, *Fowler vs. Thomas*, testimony of John E. Fowler, 64; W. H. Pope, 67; Peter Fisher, 224–226; William R. Dixon, 296–297; W. P. Faison, 90; see also Junius Bell, 36; O. L. Ward, 190–193; A. A. McCaskill, 691–692; Duncan C. Downing, 700–703; J. R. Wilson, 86–87; J. F. Williams, 111–112; R. D. Carr, 121–123; Y. F. Jones, 143–144; Simeon Garner, 148–149; Adam Williams, 149–150; Sam B. Newton, 150–152; and Henry Faison, 194–195.

31. *Fowler vs. Thomas*, testimony of C. C. Vann, 154–158.

32. For the rebuttal testimony, *Fowler vs. Thomas*, testimony of C. C. Vann, 1020–1021.

33. *Fowler vs. Thomas*, testimony of Frank Faison, 70.

34. *Fowler vs. Thomas*, testimony of A. J. Ward, 158–160.

35. *Fowler vs. Thomas*, testimony of Willie Powell, 70; Bunyan Ezzell, 71; Christopher Taylor, 71; B. L. Blackmore, 73–75; Jacob Bronson, 93–94; Jerry Gillespie, 96; Richard Williams, 100; F. L. Johnson, 162–163; Allen Kelly Jr., 167; Henry Cannon, 244–245; Isaiah Ebron, 344; Charles H. Miller, 344; Isaac Holloway, 345. Before the election of 1900, some local Populists in the eastern part of the state, not just in the Third Congressional District, complained about registration problems: R. C. Carr to Marion Butler, July 3, 1900, Butler Papers. On issues facing African Americans: James D. Thomas to Marion Butler, July 3, 1900; William J. Leary to Marion Butler, July 3, 1900; B. B. Lassiter to Marion Butler, July 3, 1900; J. S. Basnight to Marion Butler, July 3, 1900; William Powell to Marion Butler, July 6, 1900, D. M. Hall to Marion Butler, July 16, 1900; D. G. McLellan to Marion Butler, July 16, 1900; P. B. Lockerman to Marion Butler, July 16, 1900; J. W. Lee to Marion Butler, July 16, 1900; J. R. Hines to Marion Butler, July 16, 1900; W. D. Longhorn to Marion Butler, July 16, 1900; J. K. Gore to Marion Butler, July 18, 1900; J. W. Canadam to Marion Butler, July 18, 1900; W. D. Bartlett to Marion Butler, July 18, 1900; W. R. White to Marion Butler, July 14, 16, 1900, all in the Butler Papers; "The Law on Registration and Challenges,"

July 23, 1900; Circular, July 24, 1900, Butler Papers. P. H. Bright to Hal Ayer, July 12, 1900; G. L. Williams to Marion Butler, July 4, 1900; R. R. Harris to Marion Butler, July 2, 1900; D. M. Konegay to Marion Butler, July 16, 1900; A. E. Holton to Marion Butler, July 17, 1900, all in the Butler Papers; "Instructions to Judges of Election," 1900, clipping file, North Carolina Collection, Wilson Library, University of North Carolina, Chapel Hill.

36. *Fowler vs. Thomas*, testimony of W. N. Bass, 68–69.

37. *Fowler vs. Thomas*, testimony of John A. Gavin, 127–130.

38. *Fowler vs. Thomas*, testimony of John A. Fowler, 69; Henry Butler, 68–69; J. H. Sutton, 97; Jacob Dobson, 98; Joseph Low, 99; Enoch Hill, 99; Hark Middleton, 101; Nathan Huggins, 246–247; Starkey Northcott, 245–246; Cicero Cooper, 247; Luke Neal, 247; Robert Williams, 251–252; Allen Jackson, 252–253; Gibbs Spencer, 253; Anthony Harker, 254–255; Charles M. Harriss, 347; and many others.

39. *Fowler vs. Thomas*, testimony of R. D. Carr, 123.

40. *Fowler vs. Thomas*, testimony of O. L. Ward, 190–193; J. J. Blanchard, 78–79. This was corroborated by R. F. Polloch, 82–84. R. W. Blackmore, 84–86; W. S. Loftin, 91–92; R. D. Carr (Democratic Registrar), 123; R. C. Seawell, 168–169; Eli W. Mobley, 170–173; Robert Hancock, 545–549.

41. *Fowler vs. Thomas*, testimony of John E. Fowler, 64–65.

42. *Fowler vs. Thomas*, testimony of J. J. Matthis, 66.

43. *Fowler vs. Thomas*, testimony of Robert Hancock, 489–492; Jessie Basnight, 492–495.

44. *Fowler vs. Thomas*, testimony of John E. Fowler, 64–65; W. H. Hope, 67; J. T. Matthis, 67; W. G. McCullen, 67–68; William R. Dixon, 296–297; Lewis H. Outlaw, 423–424. For the testimony in Thurman Precinct: Robert Hancock, 489–492; Jessie Basnight, 492–495. For Cumberland County: A. L. McCaskill, 692–697; A. G. Thornton, 728–731; Frank Carr, 734–735; N. A. Williams, 735–736; Alex McNeill, 736–737; and N. E. McMillan, 737. For Sampson County: John B. Williams, 742; W. T. Britt, 742; R. A. Ingram, 742; and Octave Robinson, 746.

45. House Committee on Elections, *John E. Fowler vs. Charles R. Thomas*, 57th Cong., 1st sess., 1902, H. Rept. 1514, 1–4. The committee consisted of M. E. Olmstead (Chairman), J. M. Miller, G. Sutherland, Henry D. Green, J. M. Robinson, Samuel L. Powers, F. D. Currier, and John J. Feely.

46. For details on the post-1900 period: Hunt, *Marion Butler*, 186–212; David Roller, "The Republican Party of North Carolina, 1900–1916" (Ph.D. diss., Duke University, 1965), 65–92. Unlike some southern states, many North Carolina Populist leaders joined the Republican fold and pushed for a Progressive-era agenda in that party. Harry Skinner was the first to do so, but he was joined by John Fowler, Cyrus Thompson, and many others. Marion Butler finally declared for the GOP in 1904. It is impossible to tell exactly what happened to the rank-and-file of the Populists but it is clear that thousands joined the Republicans in such counties as Sampson (which became a solidly Republican County until World War Two).

Agrarian Producerism after Populism

SOCIALISM AND GARVEYISM IN THE RURAL SOUTH

—JAROD ROLL

Insofar as the southern Populist movement fed on a single idea it was this: "Wealth belongs to him who creates it . . . 'If any will not work, neither shall he eat.'"[1] The Omaha platform of 1892, the founding document of the Populist Party, legitimized the third-party revolt by casting it as a defense of this ideological complex, which was both political and religious. One dimension of this belief system was what historians have called "producerism," a moral logic whereby "free men rightfully received the 'fruits of their labor' and, conversely, that those who did not make a contribution to tangible production had no legitimate claims on its results."[2] For rural people, particularly southerners, the authority of agrarian producerism stemmed from a set of religious convictions and practices at the heart of evangelical Protestantism. Rural believers were well versed in the epistle of James and his admonition that it was "by works a man is justified, and not by faith only" (James 2:24), a theology of work that also justified the punishment of sin. Farmers were just as familiar with the Apostle Paul's admonition "that if any would not work, neither should he eat" (2 Thess. 3:10), the scriptural basis of the Omaha platform.[3] Yet, this was a worldview in crisis, nowhere so as in the South, where falling commodity prices, expensive credit, and rapid market integration made independent farming difficult, or worse. Southern farmers read in Populist political rhetoric a means to save themselves. The nation, according to the preamble to the 1892 platform, was on "the verge of moral, political, and material ruin" because "the fruits of the toil of millions are boldly stolen to build up colossal fortunes for a few." By stopping the "impoverishment of the producing class," the Populists hoped to achieve nothing less than "the salvation of the Republic and the uplifting of mankind."[4]

Southern Populists were thus driven by a religious ideal: the fervent belief in the ability of ordinary people to purify the nation's political and economic ills and create a more just civilization that would enable producers to uphold their God-given duties.[5] The faith of southern farmers in Populist political economy, with its interlocking religious, moral, and historical components, fell squarely within the nineteenth-century American religious tradition of postmillennialism that had its roots in the antebellum years. In short, postmillennialists believed that Christ would return only after the faithful had created their own millennium by redeeming this world from injustice and corruption through hard work, devotion, and sacrifice. In this Whiggish view (literally the belief in divinely ordained progress), good works by man led gradually to Christ's triumph and the creation of heaven on earth. As the historian Joe Creech concluded in his study of the People's Party in North Carolina, "Populists ... wove their political and economic reforms into a grand cosmic narrative pitting the forces of God and democracy against those of Satan and tyranny" that imbued "the movement with a sacred, even apocalyptic sense of urgency." While this intellectual framework was not unique to southern Populists, their evocation of it as a political cause was at least as consistent and coherent as it was in the most religious parts of the movement elsewhere. This was a set of ideas that attracted thousands of African Americans as well as whites across the South because it drew on deep regional traditions about the relationship between faith, work, and politics, and because economic developments in the South in the 1890s, unmatched anywhere else, threatened that relationship. Reliable reports state that as many as 400,000 black people counted themselves as Populists around the time of the founding of the People's Party in Omaha in 1892.[6]

And yet, where did the "apocalyptic sense of urgency" that inspired hundreds of thousands of rural southerners to support the Populist insurgency go after the demise of the People's Party in the late 1890s? According to most scholars, the Populist movement, one of the largest, most vibrant, and most consequential mass political movements in American history, died abruptly and un-mourned at the close of the nineteenth century, its ideas anachronistic and unfit for modern America.[7] The historian Robert C. McMath, for example, concluded that Populism as a "movement of producers" was "rooted in the political and cultural values of the nineteenth century" and thus did not "fit well with the political and bureaucratic structures that accompanied industrial capitalism."[8] Other historians have argued that Progressivism either absorbed or stymied the Populist movement after

1900: by co-opting its best reform policies into government bureaucracies or, as was the case in much of the Jim Crow South, by enforcing and rationalizing white one-party rule through disenfranchisement. All of this resulted, according to the historian Michael Kazin, in the cutting of the link between religion and producerist politics that lay at the heart of Populist ideology. A set of ideas once closely held by hundreds of thousands of rural southerners, white and black, was gone.[9]

But do such bedrock ideas end with the political parties that espouse them? Given the strength of agrarian producerism as a belief system among southerners throughout the nineteenth century, it would seem remarkable for it to collapse so quickly after the demise of the People's Party, which was, after all, simply the latest institutional vehicle in a long tradition of agrarian movements in the region that included the Farmers' Alliance, the Colored Farmers' Alliance, the Knights of Labor, and the Agricultural Wheel. Some historians have located surviving traces of agrarian producerism in the demagoguery of white supremacists who tried to lure Populists back into the fold of the Democratic Party after 1900, men such as Ben Tillman and Tom Watson. Certainly, their campaigns to defend the prerogatives of white men functioned according to the language of nineteenth-century ideals, if only as rhetoric. The best example of the use of producerism as a political slogan was perhaps Arkansan Jeff Davis, first as governor then as a U.S. senator. Davis's homespun witticisms and excoriations of national trusts earned him the fervent loyalty of many poor whites, but his devotion to the cause of working people seemed to end at the stump. What these conservative, "small-p" populists could not replicate was the sense of religious mission at the heart of earlier iterations of agrarian producerism. Their interpretation was at some remove from the way agrarian producerism had functioned in the Populist movement, and it obviously did not appeal to black people. Indeed, the turn toward racism by white Populists such as Watson led many black Populists to safeguard their visions for the future in separatist movements, a desire for racial independence that built upon the autonomy black Populists had exercised through the Colored Farmers' Alliance. Although now divided along racial lines, many black and white southerners continued to follow and interpret the spirit of the Omaha platform after 1900: they shared a belief in their duty and power to fulfill God's design through hard work that would in time secure their "salvation" and the "uplifting of mankind."[10]

This essay will trace the career of agrarian producerism as an explicitly religious political vision in two of the largest oppositional grassroots movements in the South in the early twentieth century: the Socialist Party and Marcus Garvey's Universal Negro Improvement Association (UNIA). This pairing may at first seem curious given the marked differences between the socialist and Garveyite movements. Although both groups claimed large and important membership across the rural South, socialists, most of whom were white, aimed to rescue American democracy through the realization of the Cooperative Commonwealth, an idea first popularized in 1884 by Laurence Gronlund, a northern socialist. Meanwhile, Garveyites pursued the self-determination of black people worldwide through the redemption of Africa and the African Diaspora from white tyranny, a goal that had animated black and white thinkers since the early nineteenth century.[11] Yet the rural southern members of both groups, although divergent in aims and strategies, drew ideological power from the common well of agrarian producerism, an inheritance bequeathed by the Populist movement, and in doing so revalued the political currencies of socialism and Garveyism to support and defend their southern Christian attachments to productive farming as a devotion to community, nation, and God. Indeed, these two movements were perhaps the most important inheritors of that Populist movement impulse. While Progressivism claimed a Populist source, it could not excite ordinary people to mobilize as the People's Party had because of its penchant for disenfranchisement and bureaucratization. Located in the precise areas where Populism had been strong, by contrast, southern Garveyites and socialists both organized mass political movements based on a valorization of productive labor as the lodestone of a future society defined by virtue, justice, and Christian morality, whether they called it the Cooperative Commonwealth or a redeemed Africa. Irrespective of perceived differences, these African American and white activists shared a particularly southern agrarianism that lent their lives and labors on the land tremendous meaning that was rooted in family and religious tradition. This tradition inspired a vision of southern change that relied on a postmillennial faith in the righteous labor of committed individuals as the means to triumph over evil in this world, which included rising tenancy and landlessness, debt, political disenfranchisement, and racial violence, and usher in God's millennial reign of peace and justice. Southern Garveyites and socialists were not just speaking in universal languages of reform. Rather, their agrarian producerist interpretations of those languages often clashed with their counterparts elsewhere, particularly the socialists and black nationalists who lived in American cities. In short, agrarian producerism did not dissolve with the People's Party; the ideas that inspired that movement continued to empower rural southerners to challenge ruling regional elites after 1900, and to bring a distinctly southern agrarian vision to these two diverse, global causes. Agrarian Garveyites and socialists shared with their Populist forebears a belief in man's potential to enact a divinely inspired design for the perfection of a future society. For all three, that restorationist task began with the duties of productive labor as proscribed in the Bible.[12]

In 1907, a worried Texas newspaper editor wrote to Tom Watson, still the standard-bearer of the then nearly defunct People's Party, to warn him that many younger Populists were "sliding into the Socialist party or what they think is such." Although worrisome, these defectors could be brought back into the People's Party fold, the editor believed, because the socialist movement that attracted them was "really an aggravated case of Populism."[13] Watson's disastrous stand for the presidency the following year belied the editor's confidence. The Watson campaign received just over 29,000 votes nationwide in 1908 in what would be the last gasp of the People's Party. His appeal was limited, since over 16,000 of those votes came from Watson's own native Georgia. Compared to the electoral strength of Populism in the 1890s, this final showing was pathetic.[14]

Although the correspondent from Texas misjudged the fortunes of the People's Party, he accurately identified the growing popularity of the Socialist Party among rural people who formerly would have identified themselves as Populists. In 1908, more than 40,000 rural voters in Louisiana, Arkansas, Oklahoma, Tennessee, Texas, Alabama, Mississippi, and Missouri voted for Eugene V. Debs, the presidential candidate of the Socialist Party. While Watson retreated to finish his career in the senate and the People's Party faded into oblivion, the socialists gained strength in these southern states. Four years later, Debs garnered over 90,000 votes from these areas. Electoral growth was in some ways the tip of the socialist iceberg, especially considering the Jim Crow restrictions on voting. Votes for Debs represented a thriving grassroots movement comprised of committed radical activists, local Socialist Party groups, and a growing regional press with local newspapers in Mississippi, Oklahoma, Louisiana, Arkansas, Missouri, and Texas. In many cases, these voters claimed a direct connection to the Farmers' Alliance or the People's Party. For example, thousands of socialists joined the movement from the Texas Farmers' Union and the Indiahoma Farmers' Union, formed in 1902 and 1905, respectively, by former Populists alienated by fusion with the Democratic Party in 1896. Among them was S. O. Daws, who had been central to the founding of the Farmers' Alliance in Texas in the 1880s and had been perhaps the most influential organizer in the Populist movement. With the leadership of Daws and other veterans of the Alliance, the Farmers' Unions served as an organizational and institutional conduit from Populism to the Socialist Party in Oklahoma and Texas. As the historian Jim Bissett has shown, the Indiahoma Farmers' Union shared an overlapping membership with the Socialist Party between 1905 and 1908; it limited membership to producers only, arguing that "none but tillers of the soil should be members of the union." "Now, let's wake up," wrote one soil tiller from Oklahoma, "and get the right man in front, that is, the farmer" who actually worked the land, "not the man that owns hundreds of acres of land and never works a foot of it himself." Although relatively short lived, the Farmers' Unions acted as a direct feeder of producerist thought to the emerging southern socialist movement.[15]

Where such institutional or individual links ceased to exist, the socialist press maintained ideological continuity between Populism and the socialist movement. In Mississippi, the state's first socialist paper, *The Grander Age*, published in Biloxi, had started life as a Populist sheet but rejected Bryan's fusion with the Democrats. Elsewhere, the *Appeal to Reason*, which would become the most influential socialist newspaper with over 700,000 subscribers nationwide, followed the political philosophy of its founder and managing editor Julius A. Wayland, a former People's Party supporter who also broke toward socialism following the debacle of 1896. His "one-hoss philosophy," honed first in the pages of the *Coming Nation* and then the *Appeal*, was rooted in producerist thought and expectations of postmillennial Christian deliverance. A native of Indiana and an acolyte of the utopian Christian socialist John Ruskin, Wayland experimented with the direct application of these ideas by founding a cooperative settlement called Ruskin near Tennessee City, Tennessee, in 1894. From Ruskin, he published the *Coming Nation* and advocated for the People's Party. Wayland did not last long in Ruskin or the Populist movement. By 1897, he had moved to southeast Kansas and fully into the socialist camp. In the pages of the *Appeal*, his new paper, Wayland argued that the problems of modern industrial society all stemmed from the abuse of those who worked by those who did not. Socialism, he declared, promised "social harmony—and perfect social harmony means the millennium." He despaired that while many devout believers prayed "for the Millennium, for 'on earth as it is in heaven,'" they did not know how to make it so because they had been cowed by "the arrogance of the slave power—the power of the property class to make money out of the labor of others." Many essentially voted "for their own enslavement," as he believed those who had supported William Jennings Bryan in 1896 had done.[16] Wayland was not the only rural socialist intellectual to espouse these ideas in the late 1890s. Fred Warren, a close friend of Wayland's and editor of the *Bates County Critic* in western Missouri, also articulated a vision of socialist revolution that promised millennial deliverance for producers. In 1899, he argued that socialism would mean "the gradual elimination, and finally the abolition of all useless and unproductive toil," would require that "every person of suitable age and physical and mental ability must work or starve," and guarantee that everyone would "receive the full value of his or her labor." Warren gave these aims legitimacy and appeal by citing the same scripture (2 Thess. 3:10) as the Omaha platform: "He that will not work shall not eat."[17]

These were not the thoughts of rustic cranks, at least not unpopular ones. The *Appeal* under the leadership of Wayland and Warren, who became its editor in 1904, rapidly emerged as the main mouthpiece of the southern socialist movement. Although the editorial pair received their ideas from eclectic sources, their evocation of producerism fit into a deep tradition of southern popular political thought that immediately appealed to hundreds of thousands of rural people across the region. In January 1908, the *Appeal* reported 22,615 subscribers in Oklahoma, 19,127 subscribers in Texas, and 9,879 subscribers in Arkansas. By June 1912, these states were home to 29,197, 38,157, and 13,344 socialist subscribers, respectively; the state of New York claimed just over 26,000. Overall that summer, the states of the Old Confederacy, plus Kentucky, Oklahoma, and West Virginia, claimed over 127,000 subscribers to the *Appeal*, almost 23 percent of the paper's national circulation. Even in Mississippi, a state not known to be friendly to radical politics, the *Appeal* claimed between 1,400 and 2,300 subscribers annually; more than 20,000 Magnolia State socialists subscribed to the paper in the run-up to the 1919 election, when the party made its last challenge for the governorship.[18] The *Appeal* was a national paper, but it spoke most clearly and compellingly to rural southerners.

Those drawn to the pages of the *Appeal to Reason*, whether cotton farmers, coal miners, or timber cutters, did not share the same economic position of many of their Populist forebears. Where most members of the Alliances and the People's Party tended to own property, particularly some land, and aimed to participate in reformed national markets, the southerners who became socialists after 1900 either struggled to hold onto their land or worked as tenants on someone else's farm or for wages in extractive industries. In Mississippi and southeast Missouri, for example, many socialists were the owners of small farms who were on the brink of slipping into tenancy while others cut timber for a living. In Oklahoma and Texas, by contrast, a large proportion of party supporters were already tenants. Some of them had owned land before losing it, while others were the first in their families to fail to acquire their own farm. "Sawmills laying off men. No sale for cotton. Farmers up against it," the Mississippi socialist R. G. Pratt lamented in 1914.[19] Several scholars have used the centrality of landlessness to socialist thought and action in these areas to argue that southern socialists thought more in proletarian or Marxist terms than as producers since they no longer owned land and the products of their labor. The persistence of producerist and postmillennial ideology in the socialist movement suggests, however, that this was more a demographic and chronological difference than one of ideas. As numerous scholars have demonstrated, the great problems that animated the Populists in the 1890s had by the 1900s become widespread, acute crises. Debt and landlessness did not abate with Bryan's defeat in 1896 but increased dramatically. The rise of tenancy meant that young people could no longer expect to climb the agricultural ladder through renting into landownership, as many of their parents had done. In this sense, Tom Watson's Texas informant offered powerful insight into the generational dynamics of the growth of socialist sentiment. He had said that "the old populists are all right, but it is the younger who need looking after."[20]

The spread of rural wage labor and permanent tenancy threatened to subject rural people to a condition of dependence. Fearful of creeping "wage slavery," many young farmers looked to socialism as a means to create, or restore, a safe future. In the new cotton counties of southeast Missouri, farmers fearful of rising rates of landlessness rallied to the electoral goals of the Socialist Party after 1906. They were led by Phil Hafner, a one-time Democratic editor with Populist sympathies, who started a rival socialist newspaper, the *Scott County Kicker*, in 1902 out of disgust with the Democratic Party. "The Scott County Kicker is the People's Paper," declared the masthead, and "it is not Muzzled!" Hafner challenged all independent farmers to read the *Kicker* and "wear no Man's Collar."[21] Worsening opportunities, however, did not mean that socialists like Hafner and his followers identified with the urban working classes. Rather, the tragedy of tenancy was that those caught in it continued to believe that they could and should one day establish their independence through landownership. They joined the Socialist Party because they were farmers who aspired to be landowners but would most likely never own land. They believed, as had their parents and grandparents, in the centrality of hard work and production to one's claims to citizenship and selfhood but were prevented by economic changes from fulfilling these duties. Their radicalism was born not of new Marxist ideas, but from stymied producerist certainties.

Southern socialists championed small producers in a world they believed beset by monopolists. At the heart of their appeal lay a reverence for the natural, even divine, rights of laborers. "Labor is honorable, exalted," Hafner wrote in 1906, it is "healthful and necessary to happiness." Relying on a common-sense reading of the labor theory of value, Hafner argued that "capital is that which labor creates. If you raise a crop of corn with your labor," he continued, "the result is your capital. It should all be yours—every ear of it." This was a right rooted in biblical command, not some fancy new theory. "Under just conditions no man should have any product (capital) unless he creates it," Hafner argued, because "the Bible directs that you eat your bread in the sweat of your face."[22] Oscar Ameringer, the famed socialist organizer and author from Oklahoma, made this argument the subject of his 1912 pamphlet, "Socialism for the Farmer Who Farms the Farm," which declared that "if there [is] such a thing as natural right, the right to the use of the land should be foremost" because "land is the storehouse of nature, from which mankind draws the material to sustain life" and "labor applied to land creates wealth." This was a right guaranteed by Leviticus and denied by capitalists. "The Old Testament is rather hard on the private ownership of the land and the New Testament holds still less consolation for the landlord," Ameringer pointed out.[23] As decreed in Leviticus 25:18–19, those who obeyed God's law "shall dwell in the land in safety. And the land shall yield her fruit, and ye shall eat her fruit." No amount of economic or political power could permanently deny this promise. The right of producers was a "natural right," the *Kicker* declared, which "cannot be forfeited, nor by special privileges justly acquired." In short, "no man can give another the right to rob him."[24]

Yet the producer's claim to this natural right was weaker than ever. Patrick S. Nagle, the editor of the Kingfisher, Oklahoma, *Tenant Farmer*, argued that merchants and creditors used unjust, illegitimate power to oppress tenants. Others agreed that this state of affairs was possible because of the complete corruption of politics and the economy. W. M. Stingley, a member of the Indiahoma Farmers' Union, declared in 1906 that "the capitalist masters own, not only the natural and mechanical machinery of production, but they own the full machinery of our government from justice of the peace up."[25] The web of rent, profit, and interest that this unholy alliance supported was plain robbery, according to Texas socialist Tom Hickey. Southern socialists frequently likened this injustice to enslavement. "The renter is a slave," argued one Oklahoma socialist, because "a large part of his life work is lost to him."[26] "No man is free so long as another man owns the means by which he must earn a living," Hafner argued. Before 1863, the "chattel slave power used the lash to drive men to work," he concluded, while "today the wage slave power has substituted hunger and want for the lash."[27] When socialists evoked "wage slavery," they tapped a widespread rural abhorrence, rooted in antebellum America, especially the South, of the dependent relationships created when one relied on another for work. To the agrarian mind, farm workers who labored for wages on a permanent basis became perpetual dependents, like slaves, and thus relinquished claims to their manhood and even citizenship. Still, the *Kicker* insisted that through the millennial power of socialism, "wage slavery is as surely doomed as was chattel slavery."[28] One Texas correspondent agreed. The only way to avoid "becoming a slave," he declared in the pages of *The Rebel*, Hickey's newspaper, was to join the socialist "army of emancipation."[29]

Socialism offered a modern means to restore the natural rights of producers. The Socialist Party, according to the editor of Oklahoma's *Strong City Herald*, was for the "hard-working, frugal, honest souls that have labored hard all these years, and are to-day without a legal right to stay upon the earth, simply because they have been robbed of the greater amount of the products of their labor."[30] This cause was consistent with the ideological roots of American political tradition. "It is the rising Socialist movement that has the mission to restore democracy," Hafner argued, "to make the best part of the Declaration of Independence something more than clanging brass, and to insure that a government of the people, by the people and for the people shall not perish from off the earth."[31] To achieve this mission, however, good citizens would need to take back their government. "What we need in office is men of our own class," the Missouri socialist organizer J. W. Adams claimed. "There are but two forces—one that produces and consumes, and another that consumes without producing," he continued. "It seems to me that it does not require much effort for the farmer to discover to what class he belongs."[32] The 1912 platform of the Socialist Party in Oklahoma made this commitment to producerism clear. The main aim of the party, it stated, was "to facilitate the passing of the land from the possession of the landlords into the hands of the actual tillers of the soil."[33] "We in Oklahoma want every farmer who owns land and farms his land to keep it," Ameringer declared at the Socialist Party's national convention in Chicago in 1910, because "the more he works and produces, the better for us, and the more he improves it the better for mankind."³⁴

Framed in these terms, southern socialism offered a vision of justice through the redemptive power of American ideals. "Socialists propose a complete overthrow of present conditions," Hafner declared. "Change is sure to come," he concluded, and "there is no heading it off."³⁵ That change would be realized in the Cooperative Commonwealth, a political and economic reordering that many socialists referred to as the "coming nation," an idea of transformation that had animated Wayland's Populist and Ruskinite newspaper of that name in the 1890s. The dream of future restoration drew upon the postmillennial Christian tradition, a vision articulated by agrarian socialists with the distinct cadences of southern evangelical belief. "God is the author and founder of the economic social cooperative commonwealth of the nation," a socialist in Oklahoma declared in 1902.³⁶ Divine authorship guaranteed that the commonwealth would come to pass through the faithful labors of committed activists. "Be Ye of good cheer," Hickey reassured Texas socialists, many of them mired in poverty and landlessness, "for the day is coming when, with spirit of the Lord in your hearts and with your footsteps lighted with the lamp of Socialism ... we will, with that old prophet Nehemiah, say to the rulers of the nation: 'Restore, I pray you, even to this day, their land, their vineyards, and their houses.' And they shall be restored."³⁷ A. C. Walker shared his prayer for divine deliverance with Hickey in early 1915: "May the great god of heaven help us to secure our liberty and freedom," he wrote. "He has promised to help those who help themselves."³⁸ Socialism facilitated the millennium because, an Oklahoma editor explained in 1912, "it teaches the fulfillment of the natural laws and prepares a man so that he can truthfully pray, 'Thy Kingdom come. Thy will be done, in earth as it is in heaven.'"³⁹ This enunciation of agrarian producerism matched almost word for word what Wayland had written in the pages of the *Appeal* eleven years before. H. B. Cochran, of Bonham, Texas, concurred with both when he said that socialism brought man "face to face with what generations have longed, hoped, prayed, yes, even died for: the Brotherhood of Man ... the fulfillment of the Nazarene's promise—the Millennium."⁴⁰ This religious view of political change flowed directly from the People's Party and its 1892 vow to restore the independence of producers and thereby ensure "the salvation of the Republic and the uplifting of mankind."⁴¹

When in 1910 Oscar Ameringer encouraged the national Socialist Party to focus organizing efforts on farmers because their liberation would be "better for mankind," he was tapping into a religious agrarian tradition that discomfited many of his urban socialist comrades.[42] The determination of southern socialists to hold onto agrarian producerist ideas was distinctive within the party. The Socialist Party's candidate for vice president in 1900, Job Harriman, a lawyer from California, had gone so far as to argue that "farmers do not belong to the working class, because the farmers own the farms."[43] Socialists like Harriman and those further to the party's left, people such as Big Bill Haywood and others in the International Workers of the World, tended to take a stricter Marxist interpretation of class to argue that only those who had no share in the means of production belonged in the movement. As far as farmers went, these socialists argued that the party had room only for the rural proletariat of tenants and wage workers, not small landowners. Their interpretation supported a broadly held view that in the future Cooperative Commonwealth all land would be owned collectively as would all the other means of production. In response, southern socialists argued strenuously, based on the tenets of agrarian producerism, for the party to amend its platform so that it would back the farmers' right, in the words of the Oklahomans, "to have the use and occupancy of the land sufficient for a home and the support of his family."[44] To publicly denounce all landownership as a capitalist crime, as most urban socialists did, would be to attack the most potent symbol of agrarian independence and doom the Socialist Party in the South. At the party's 1910 convention, A. M. Simons, a correspondent for the *Appeal to Reason*, submitted a proposed plank for the party platform that would pledge to allow small landowning farmers to own their farms and contribute to collective bargaining and marketing cooperatives, much like the cooperative plans put forward by the Farmers' Alliance in the 1880s. Simons cautioned against narrow Marxist definitions of class. "Any program that neglects the largest single division of the producing class," explained Simons, "can not rightly call itself a working class movement."[45] To protect agricultural production would be in the interest "both of the farmers as producers and of the rest of the population as purchasers."[46] Ameringer could not have agreed more. "In the case of the farmer who farms the farm," he told the convention, "the Socialist movement has no right to interfere with that relationship." "The thing we want to do is to give the land to the man who uses the land," he explained, "to give to the working people the product of their labor."[47]

Southern socialists held the producerist line because of principle not expedience. Opposition from urban socialists was fierce. At the 1910 convention, T. J. Lewis, a Welsh-born silver miner from Oregon, shouted back at Ameringer that the farmer was historically "the greatest enemy to organized labor." "Take your book and tear it up and throw your button in the ditch," Lewis taunted the Oklahoman, because the Socialist Party was revolutionary and would not "toady to the farmer." Lewis received wide applause.[48] After more hair-tearing debate, A. M. Simons rebutted Lewis's tirade with electoral fact. The party simply could not exclude farmers who represented "twelve millions of people of the producing classes, without whom we stand no more chance of a Socialist victory in this country than we do of changing the orbit of the comet."[49] The convention reporter recorded no applause in response to Simon's argument. His proposal failed. At the party convention in Indianapolis in 1912, Simons and Ameringer made the same arguments and faced the same resistance, but successfully re-worded a plank to vow support for "the toilers of the fields as well as those in the shops, factories and mines of the nation in their struggles for economic justice."[50] Even then, the strength of the movement in Oklahoma and Texas, two of the biggest socialist vote producers in the nation, could do no better than this vague gesture from the national party.

The southern socialist movement did not prevail. Voting fraud, intimidation, and the crushing patriotism of the World War I years (which banned periodicals such as the *Appeal to Reason* from the mail) all combined to thwart grassroots revolutionary politics after 1912. The failure of socialist electoral strategies did not, however, mark the end of producerism as a political idea for those who had joined the party of Debs. Many turned to violence as a means of resistance, as isolated groups such as the Reelfoot Lake rebels in Tennessee or the Night Riders of the Kentucky and Tennessee Black Patch had done following the demise of the People's Party. Across the terrain of southern socialism, from southeast Missouri to Oklahoma and Texas, tenant farmers lashed out at the landlords, plantation bosses, and corporate elite they perceived as the enemies of the rural producing classes. Crucially, like many frustrated white Populists had done in the 1890s, white socialists also struck at African Americans, who many within their ranks considered to be the tools of elite enemies as tenants and sharecroppers on white-owned plantations. Agrarian violence against planters and black farmers was often inspired by the same sense of religious mission that had guided socialist organization. "I have known night riders to pray before they saddled their horses and reached for their Winchesters," Patrick Nagle confirmed in 1915.[51] Many vigilantes justified their acts with the logic of producerism itself. "If economic conditions don't soon change," a Missouri socialist warned, the people "will stampede the storage houses and take back part of the product of their toil, robbed from them by rich speculators." And "Jesus will not find fault with them," he added.[52] After all, another writer confirmed, "the Carpenter walked into the temple in broad daylight and scourged out the money changers."[53]

That southern white agrarians directed their frustrations at perceived African American competitors reflected the general tendency of both the People's Party and the Socialist Party to exclude black workers from their conceptions of producerism. Despite some success with interracial political cooperation in the 1890s, neither group could overcome the power of white supremacy. For southern socialists like Tom Hickey and Phil Hafner, African American farmers represented a powerful reminder of their own loss of independence (indeed, of the dependence of enslavement) rather than an opportunity to build an all-encompassing agrarian movement. Any such opportunity was quickly lost. What little effort there was to bring blacks into the Socialist Party was overwhelmed by white hostility. Rural white conceptions of manhood and citizenship simply did not include African Americans, even though they shared many of the same concerns and ambitions. Black farmers had, for example, founded hundreds of independent, all-black towns throughout central Oklahoma and Texas beginning in the 1890s as a means to secure their own social and economic independence. These rural settlements operated according to the same producerist ethic that had animated white settlers. "Nothing makes a colored man feel prouder than to stand on his own property and call it home," declared Oklahoma's *Langston City Herald* in 1894.[54] Like their white socialist counterparts, black farmers found this aim increasingly difficult to achieve. But they were not content to wait for socialists to abandon white supremacy before seeking a common remedy. The inability to control the products of their labor caused black farmers to look for political solutions in other places. In the 1910s, thousands of African Americans who had migrated west joined separatist campaigns to establish a land of their own, whether in the far western United States, Canada, or Mexico. That they joined such improbable movements as that organized by black nationalist Chief Alfred Charles Sam said more about the tragic flaws of the socialist movement than it did about African American faith in producerism.[55]

By the mid-1920s, Marcus Garvey's UNIA had become the largest political movement among southern black farmers since Populism. Nearly half of the 1,176 UNIA divisions in the world were located in southern states; that is, the Old Confederacy plus Kentucky, southern Missouri, Oklahoma, and West Virginia. The majority of these, 354 divisions, took root in farming communities, with the largest concentration of Garveyite sentiment located in the Mississippi River Valley; in southwestern Georgia; in the coastal communities of Virginia and the Carolinas, and in the all-black settlements of Oklahoma and Texas. While most of these divisions were small, anywhere from seven to fifty paying members each, those who joined carried influence in their communities. Rural Garveyites were men (and some women), usually over thirty-five years of age, who were small landowners, successful renters, aspiring sharecroppers, teachers, and preachers who headed family, work, and religious groups. According to the historian Claudrena Harold, southern Garveyites were "striving blacks" who "measured economic success in terms of one's ability to purchase a home, open up a business, or acquire a small amount of land."[56]

Recent scholarly attention on the rural southern wing of Garveyism has revealed important connections to black agrarian activism before 1900. "Garveyism," according to the historian Steven Hahn, "exemplified the vitality and adaptability of popular 'organizing traditions' whose genealogies extend deep into the history of slavery and early emancipation."[57] Although the record of this organizational ancestry is fragmentary, it is possible to trace connections. In Phillips County, Arkansas, for example, African Americans sustained five UNIA divisions in the 1920s. These represented only the most recent in a long lineage of local political mobilizations that included the Colored Farmers' Alliance in the 1890s and the Knights of Labor in the 1880s. Omar Ali, one of the few historians to give extended treatment to black involvement in the Populist movement, argued that "black Populism" was itself "an independent movement of African-Americans for economic and political reform" that "grew out of the unique experiences of southern" blacks. Black Populism, in Ali's view, paralleled its often closely aligned white counterpart but on an autonomous trajectory that extended to "the Garvey movement."[58] It is difficult to identify individuals who belonged to both groups because neither organization left a great store of records. The kinds of local documents that would enable a search for rank-and-file members have either been lost (to fire in the case of the UNIA) or destroyed. Moreover, many leading black Populists, such as John B. Rayner of Texas and Walter Pattillo of North Carolina, died before the advent of Garveyism. Geographical continuity between the two, however, is easier to demonstrate, suggesting the same kind of intergenerational continuities that linked white Populists to the Socialist Party. Major sites of black Populist strength: east-central Texas, and eastern Arkansas, eastern North Carolina, and, for a brief moment, the Mississippi Delta became major sites of Garveyite strength thirty years later. For example, the concentration of intense Garveyite support in counties along the estuarial backwaters of eastern North Carolina, home to almost forty rural UNIA divisions in the 1920s, making it one of the largest state contingents, neatly mirrored the location of black support for the People's Party and Colored Farmers' Alliance in the 1890s. The same pattern held true in the black farming settlements along the Sabine, Neches, and Angelina rivers in east-central Texas. The all-black towns in Nacogdoches County that supported UNIA divisions where within twenty miles of districts that had been home to Colored Alliances in the 1890s. This pattern of geographical continuity is too specific and widespread for coincidence. The durability of the idea of agrarian producerism among southern blacks was not defined solely by geographical continuity, however, as mass migration during the period from the 1890s to the 1920s severed many of the direct links between place and ideas.[59]

Even so, the very act of migrating from one rural place to another in a search of economic independence testified to the centrality of agrarian ambition among black farmers. Between 1880 and 1920 hundreds of thousands of black farmers moved west in search of land and peace. Their progression westward occurred in stages. The brightest beacon initially was the wooded backcountry of Mississippi's Yazoo Delta where pioneers, most of whom were ex-slaves or their children, carved settlements out of isolated swamps in the 1880s. These settlements for a time became a locus of black Populist activism, particularly in Leflore County. Although a violent white backlash crushed the Colored Farmers' Alliance in Mississippi, it did not quell rural black efforts to secure landed autonomy. Thousands continued moving westward, first to the lowlands of eastern Arkansas and ultimately to all-black farming settlements in Oklahoma and Texas. The ideals of agrarian producerism continued to motivate the migrants to Kingfisher County, Oklahoma, who declared themselves in 1894 to be "farmers skilled and trained at the calling" and encouraged more settlers from "that class of energetic, enthusiastic, frugal, industrious, and hard working farming talent, to populate and settle this vast, vacant, invaluable and productive soil."[60] Few purer descriptions of agrarian producerism exist. Rural black migration between southern places would continue into the 1920s when as many as 15,000 African Americans moved to the newly developed lowlands of southeast Missouri. One of these migrants captured the motivation behind the general pattern in early 1923 when he explained that he was in search of a land were he could prove "that he was a good farmer and a good citizen," phrasing that could easily have come from a black Populist. African Americans in the Missouri county this farmer settled in would during the next two years form five UNIA divisions.[61]

African American farmers in these areas found in Garveyism a cause that legitimized and reenergized their quest. Founded in Jamaica in 1914, the UNIA attracted wide support after Garvey arrived in Harlem in 1916. From there he transformed the UNIA into a worldwide movement to build "a strong and powerful Negro nation" led by powerful black men.[62] Garvey argued that economic strength and autonomy was the best way for black people to realize a country of their own where they could develop free of white interference. This message captured a sense of urgency among African Americans after World War I. "Whatsoever my future is to be is my own creation," Garvey and his followers concluded, and "as of the individual so of the race."[63] Garveyites envisioned the redemption of Africa from colonial rule at the heart of that future. The mission for African redemption itself carried religious power as the founding of a new age, an epochal moment that would finally bring earthly peace and prosperity—a black millennium. The black farmers across the South who joined the UNIA after 1920 saw themselves as key actors in a collective movement that promised the autonomy of all black people worldwide. This sense of mission was especially potent among black farmers in the cotton southwest, in particular, Arkansas, Mississippi, Missouri, and Oklahoma. These areas represented a new agricultural frontier, where fecund lands were continually opened to settlement even into the 1920s. The black families that moved there and remained were committed to farming, especially if they stayed put through the Great Migration. Furthermore, the UNIA divisions they created were among the largest, most active of all those in the rural South. As the historian Mary Rolinson has noted, these Garveyites also "showed more outward signs of upward economic mobility" than those in eastern states.[64] As small property owners, whether of land, mules, or tools; as heads of households and kin groups; and as employers of younger kin and neighbors, they viewed themselves as, in the words of the *Negro World*, "the leaders in the social, the civil and the business life of" their communities. "They have the light and they should have the leading of the race into higher and better conditions."[65] From the perspective of urban Garveyites in Harlem and elsewhere, southern black farmers made unlikely candidates for race leadership, given the preoccupations of urban black nationalists with modern notions of social and physical hygiene, white-collar business models, and the building of global commercial and diplomatic institutions. Yet,

Garvey's rural followers interpreted his ideas and aims through their own lived experience and preexisting ideas. In their minds, the UNIA offered a promising new global vehicle for their agrarian producerist beliefs, a faith rooted in the rural southern past.[66]

Adhering to the logic of producerism, rural Garveyites stressed the duty of individuals to work toward their own redemption. The UNIA became a means to secure the products of their toil for the first time. Producerism worked differently for Garveyites than it did for white socialists. Unlike whites who looked to reclaim lost or failing autonomy, African Americans saw in the logic of hard work and just reward a means to achieve upward economic mobility, with its attendant benefits of autonomy, independence, and self-possession. "Self-reliance is the key to human progress," wrote a Garveyite from Plantersville, Alabama. "The Negro is learning to stand upon his own feet and fight his way to the top by his own efforts," he concluded.[67] Rural Garveyites almost always described their activities using a language of work or labor. "Blytheville is up and at work, looking forward to better days," reported M. L. Poole from northeastern Arkansas.[68] Many believed that Garvey's significance lay in his ability to show black people how to work for themselves. The problem of African Americans was that whites had too often stolen the products of their toil, whether through enslavement or the frauds of Jim Crow. "It is time to start working for ourselves," declared Louisa Love of Hermondale, Missouri, because "we have been working for the other race so long."[69] Mollie Bynum of Blytheville, Arkansas, urged inculcating rural black youth with Garvey's ideas "before they begin to work in jobs at starvation wages" for whites.[70] Precocious thirteen-year-old Robert Jones of Acmar, Alabama, agreed that it "is time for we Negroes down here in the South to get on the job to save our race."[71] This was an idea with roots in black Populism. At its founding in 1886, the Colored Farmers' Alliance of Texas had expressed a very similar aim "to aid its members to become more skillful and efficient workers" on their own behalf.[72]

These rural Garveyites believed that the redemption of Africa was their main task, the completion of which would enable their economic independence. Bynum concluded her call for the mobilization of black youth with a prayer "to God for the redemption of Africa."[73] Queenie Sudduth of Sunflower, Mississippi, said that she was "anxious for the redemption of Africa and a government for our race.... May God bless the work."[74] The day-to-day business of local UNIA divisions, and by extension the day-to-day efforts of the members themselves, took on central importance in this world-historical drama. A liberated Africa would bring the "better days" that M. L. Poole looked forward to. Speaking in New Madrid in 1923, W. M. Davis, a UNIA leader from Cairo, Illinois, emphasized "the importance of the work in which we are engaged, the greatest work of the century, the greatest and noblest task that any race could undertake."[75] That task was, as Missourian D. D. Daniels, who had been born a slave in Mississippi, said later, "the great work of Negro Uplift and African Redemption."[76] Despite the different context, Daniels articulated a goal not far removed from that in the 1892 Omaha platform for "the uplifting of mankind." Attaching the same epic importance to Garveyism, Davis lauded the formation of the new division at Lilbourn, Missouri, as another link in "the ever growing chain of the U.N.I.A. which is encircling the globe."[77] So convincing were such "testimonies," that the division "enrolled fourteen new members to the *Cause Afric*" and everyone declared "to go on with the fight until Africa is redeemed."[78] The promise of a better day in the future validated their current struggles to accomplish the task.

The Garveyite emphasis on racial redemption through work carried a strong postmillennial inflection. Work on behalf of the race was a religious duty that God would reward. "Faith without works," Arkansan Bennie Bember said, quoting the Apostle Paul, "is dead."[79] This was in line with Garvey's own thinking, as well as the producerist tradition. "God is not going to save you," Garvey preached. "He has given you a life to live, and if you do not exercise your own will in your own behalf you will be lost."[80] A better world for black people would only come through the faithful toil of black people. God had made it this way, and there could be no alternative. Reverend Johnson preached to the members of the Wyatt, Missouri, division "in strong terms of the Negro depending upon God to do for them that which they themselves can do."[81] He argued that if they wanted more, they would have to get it themselves. Fellow Missourian E. W. Pinkard concurred. "A man who thinks that he is fitted for something better and is willing to work and suffer to get it," he told readers of the *Negro World*, "will eventually reach a higher plane."[82] Such an interpretation of the outcome of Garveyism stoked a sense of empowerment, as well as responsibility. A three-day UNIA convention in Pine City, Arkansas, included two talks that hammered this point home: "Faithful to Duty" and "Get out of the Rut of Slothfulness and Shiftiness and Look to a Higher Thing."[83] Black tenant farmers in the Jim Crow South were telling themselves, not simply *being* told, that only they could save themselves, neither God nor Garvey would do it for them. "Praying alone for justice won't get justice," Bember concluded, "and praying alone for a government won't get you a government. It makes no difference how much faith you have in God if you make no effort to get it you will never get justice.... you must put forth some effort."[84] Looking beneath the Garveyite usage, this construction resonated with the challenge Eugene V. Debs had levied in speeches to white southern socialists a decade before, when he told audiences that "people must do things for themselves."[85]

What Garveyites actually did in the rural South contrasted sharply with the activities of their UNIA counterparts elsewhere, especially those in cities, reflecting how the southern religious meaning of agrarian producerism altered the outcomes of the Garveyite organizing it inspired. Rural southern Garveyites spent the majority of their time and resources on the cause of African redemption, not as a mass movement to resettle on African shores, but in order to reiterate and reinforce the ideological and political power of their efforts as black agrarians among hostile neighbors. Garveyites in cities, meanwhile, created a range of community service organizations, including cooperatives, schools, and medical units, in a bid to build autonomous institutions. Rural Garveyites did none of this. They remained resolutely focused on the religious mission of their work, as both farmers and black nationalists, as the Garveyites of the Pine City, Arkansas, division expressed when they opened their meeting with the hymn, "We are marching on": "We are marching on, with shield and banner bright / we will work for God and battle for the right / we will praise His Name, rejoicing in His might / and we'll work till Jesus calls / ... [us] to the promised land where living waters flow."[86]

For black southerners, these ideas had deep roots in the emigration and missionary movements they had launched in the late nineteenth century. In the final years of Reconstruction, African Americans, especially in the African Methodist Episcopal Church and the American Colonization Society, crafted an intense belief that they were chosen by God to carry civilization to Africans. In the process, they would create their own millennial haven on African shores and secure the destiny of the race. "We feel it no less a duty than a pleasure," the Liberia Exodus Arkansas Colony declared in the late 1870s, "to give the Gospel, Christianity and civilization to our Fatherland." As the historian Kenneth Barnes concluded, these African Americans imagined themselves as central actors in "a sort of black manifest destiny."[87] This postmillennial mission, anchored in Psalm 68:31, which prophecies that "Princes shall come out of Egypt; Ethiopia shall soon stretch out her hands unto God," would not be achieved in a flash but rather through generations of faithful service, whether in support of missionaries, by establishing Liberian farms, or by building businesses to help carry light to the Dark Continent. J. A. Shazier, of Perkinston, Mississippi, summed up the Garveyite interpretation of this legacy when he declared that "Africa is our motherland, and it is up to us to help redeem it. We are the ones to re-establish the land and have an independent government," he concluded. "Let us work to that end."[88]

Popular mobilizations around agrarian producerism, white and black, failed of course to stem the structural reorganization of the southern agricultural economy in the 1920s and 1930s. Tenancy itself diminished as landlords displaced renters and sharecroppers from the land in favor of casual wage workers and machines. As the real basis for producerist belief literally disappeared, so did the postmillennial expectations that accompanied it. Indeed, apocalyptic interpretations of crisis and change increasingly replaced gradualist visions of working toward Christ's triumph on earth. Some turned to violence. Others, both black and white, especially those in new Pentecostal-Holiness churches, looked for immediate deliverance through what they believed would be Christ's imminent return. This process did not spell the end of popular political movements in the rural South. Indeed, far from it. In the 1930s, the responsiveness of the New Deal state to popular political pressure, particularly when applied by labor unions, encouraged southern farmers to reframe their claims for economic security. Increasingly unable in the context of the Great Depression to use their productive labor to legitimize citizenship rights, southern agrarians, most of whom were now landless, began to deploy a more universal, what some might call more modern, claim that as citizens they deserved the right to support themselves through gainful work. In this vein, new interracial, working-class organizations like the Southern Tenant Farmers' Union abandoned demands for widespread landownership in order to lobby for higher wages, public housing, and government health programs. Although the political argument had changed, the influence of Populism could still be felt in the STFU, which brought together white socialists and former Garveyites in concerted action. That influence echoed in the ministrations of the white union organizer and preacher Claude Williams, a one-time socialist who hailed from the old Populist stronghold of western Tennessee and was very popular among black nationalist farmers. The crux of his appeal in the mid-1930s was rooted deep: "We have to build the Kingdom of God on earth," he preached, by reforming the social order according to Christ's principles, "an order of justice and brotherhood for everybody.

There is an abundance for all if we seek this order. We pray to our Father—not the white man's Father, not the black man's Father—but *Our* Father. We ask, Thy will be done on *earth* as it is in heaven." "It is not God's will that men and women and children should toil in the fields from sunup to sundown to grow cotton, and go naked." Jesus, Williams promised, "will stop debts and debtors, wipe them all out: there won't be any need for ... commissaries and robissaries if you receive what you produce."[89]

Notes

1. "The Omaha Platform, 1892," reprinted in George Brown Tindall, ed., *A Populist Reader: Selections from the Works of American Populist Leaders* (Gloucester, MA: Peter Smith, 1976), 90.

2. Nancy Cohen, *The Reconstruction of American Liberalism, 1865–1914* (Chapel Hill: University of North Carolina Press, 2002), 29; Shelton Stromquist, "The Crisis of 1894 and the Legacies of Producerism," in *The Pullman Strike and the Crisis of the 1890s: Essays on Labor and Politics*, ed. Richard Schneirov, Shelton Stromquist, and Nick Salvatore (Urbana: University of Illinois Press, 1999), 181. For the roots of agrarian producerism: Matthew Hild, *Greenbackers, Knights of Labor, and Populists: Farmer-Labor Insurgency in the Late-Nineteenth-Century South* (Athens: University of Georgia Press, 2007), 8–24, 217–218; Steven Hahn, *A Nation under Our Feet: Black Political Struggles in the Rural South from Slavery to the Great Migration* (Cambridge, MA: The Belknap Press of Harvard University Press, 2003), 135–146, 414–425; Michael Kazin, *The Populist Persuasion: An American History* (New York: Basic Books, 1995), 3–35; Steven Hahn, *The Roots of Southern Populism: Yeoman Farmers and the Transformation of the Georgia Upcountry, 1850–1890* (New York: Oxford University Press, 1983), 1–11, 252; Joe Creech, *Righteous Indignation: Religion and the Populist Revolution* (Urbana: University of Illinois Press, 2006), 86–89; Shelton Stromquist, *Re-inventing "The People": The Progressive Movement, the Class Problem, and the Origins of Modern Liberalism* (Urbana: University of Illinois Press, 2006), 5, 13–16; and Omar H. Ali, *In the Lion's Mouth: Black Populism in the New South, 1886–1900* (Jackson: University Press of Mississippi, 2010), 76. For more on producerism, see Daniel T. Rodgers, *The Work Ethic in Industrial America, 1865–1920* (Chicago: University of Chicago Press, 1978), 30–63; Stephen D. Kantrowitz, *Ben Tillman and the Reconstruction of White Supremacy* (Chapel Hill: University of North Carolina Press, 2000), 18, 106–122; and Leon Fink, *Workingmen's Democracy: The Knights of Labor and American Politics* (Urbana: University of Illinois Press, 1982), 3–4.

3. For more on the religious dimensions of southern producerist thought: Creech, *Righteous Indignation*, 3, 35–38; Ali, *In the Lion's Mouth*, 8; Wayne Flynt, "One in the Spirit, Many in the Flesh: Southern Evangelicals," in *Varieties of Southern Evangelicalism*, ed. David Edwin Harrell Jr. (Macon, GA: Mercer University Press, 1981), 27–30; Wayne Flynt, *Poor but Proud: Alabama's Poor Whites* (Tuscaloosa: University of Alabama Press, 1989), 232–236; and Jarod Roll, *Spirit of Rebellion: Labor and Religion in the New Cotton South* (Urbana: University of Illinois Press, 2010), 1–10; 27–51.

4. "The Omaha Platform, 1892," reprinted in Tindall, ed., *A Populist Reader*, 90.

5. Creech, *Righteous Indignation*, xxiii–xxiv; James M. Beeby, *Revolt of the Tar Heels: The North Carolina Populist Movement, 1890-1901* (Jackson: University Press of Mississippi, 2008), 1; Charles Postel, *The Populist Vision* (New York: Oxford University Press, 2007), 4.

6. Creech, *Righteous Indignation*, xviii–xix (quote). This revisionist trend is in marked contrast to Richard Hofstadter's account of Populism: Richard Hofstadter, *The Age of Reform: From Bryan to F.D.R.* (New York: Vintage, 1955), 62–63. For further treatments of postmillennial thought: Timothy P. Weber, *In the Shadow of the Second Coming: American Premillennialism, 1875-1925* (New York: Oxford University Press, 1979), 9; Randall L. Stephens, *The Fire Spreads: Holiness and Pentecostalism in the American South* (Cambridge, MA: Harvard University Press, 2008), 31; Daniel Walker Howe, *What Hath God Wrought: The Transformation of America 1815-1848* (New York: Oxford University Press), 285–286. Creech referred to this eschatological tradition as "patriotic millennialism." Creech, *Righteous Indignation*, 5–6. For the scale and scope of black involvement in the Populist movement, see Omar H. Ali, "Black Populism in the New South, 1886–1898" (Ph.D. diss., Columbia University, 2003), 217; and Ali, *In the Lion's Mouth*.

7. Cohen, *The Reconstruction of American Liberalism*, 5; Hild, *Greenbackers, Knights of Labor, and Populists*, 217; Creech, *Righteous Indignation*, 177–183; Lawrence Goodwyn, *Democratic Promise: The Populist Moment in America* (New York: Oxford University Press, 1976), 516–531; Hahn, *The Roots of Southern Populism*, 287–288. For an excellent summary of this point, Samuel L. Webb, "From Independents to Populists to Progressive Republicans: The Case of Chilton County, Alabama, 1880–1920," *Journal of Southern History* 59 (November 1993): 707–736.

8. Robert C. McMath Jr., *American Populism: A Social History, 1877-1898* (New York: Hill and Wang, 1993), 210.

9. Postel, *The Populist Vision*, 271, 286; Webb, "From Independents to Populists to Progressive Republicans," 707–736; Connie L. Lester, *Up From the Mudsills of Hell: The Farmers' Alliance, Populism, and Progressive Agriculture in Tennessee, 1870-1915* (Knoxville: University of Tennessee Press, 2006), 208–212; Creech, *Righteous Indignation*, xxvii–xxviii; Stromquist, *Re-Inventing "The People,"* 3–7; Beeby, *Revolt of the Tar Heels*, 213–217; Kazin, *The Populist Persuasion*, 3–4, 50; Ali, "Black Populism in the New South," 217–222.

10. "The Omaha Platform, 1892," reprinted in Tindall, ed., *A Populist Reader*, 90. For the producerist tinge in white supremacist demagoguery, see Kantrowitz, *Ben Tillman and the Reconstruction of White Supremacy*, 2–7; C. Vann Woodward, *Tom Watson: Agrarian Rebel* (New York: Oxford University Press, 1938; Galaxy Books ed., 1967), 370–395. On Jeff Davis, see C. Vann Woodward, *Origins of the New South, 1877-1915* (Baton Rouge: Louisiana State University Press, 1951), 376–377; James R. Green, *Grass-Roots Socialism: Radical Movements in the Southwest, 1895-1943* (Baton Rouge: Louisiana State University Press, 1978), 63, 78. On the separatist impulse in black Populism, see Ali, *In the Lion's Mouth*, 8–9.

11. See Laurence Gronlund, *The Co-Operative Commonwealth in its Outline, An Exposition of Modern Socialism* (Boston: Lee and Shepard, 1884); and Edwin S. Redkey, *Black Exodus: Black Nationalist and Back-to-Africa Movements, 1890-1910* (New Haven, CT: Yale University Press, 1969), 1–23.

12. Melissa Walker, *Southern Farmers and Their Stories: Memory and Meaning in Oral History* (Lexington: University Press of Kentucky, 2006), 78–79, 216; Roll, *Spirit of Rebellion*, 1–10. Ali, the foremost scholar of African American involvement in the Populist movement, concluded that the "ideological and political connections between the various black movements and organizations in the early twentieth century and their continuity with Black Populism are important areas of research that need further investigation to better understand the legacy of Black Populism." See Ali, "Black Populism in the New South," 221, n. 8.

13. Taylor McRae to Tom Watson, January 23, 1907, quoted in Woodward, *Tom Watson*, 404.

14. Woodward, *Tom Watson*, 399–400.

15. Indiahoma Farmers' Union, 1906 (first quote) and *Durant Independent Farmer*, 1905 (second quote), quoted in Jim Bissett, *Agrarian Socialism in America: Marx, Jefferson, and Jesus in the Oklahoma Countryside, 1904–1920* (Norman: University of Oklahoma Press, 1999), 27. For state vote totals, see http://www.statemaster.com/graph/pre_1908_pop_vot_for_eug_deb-1908-popular-votes-eugene-debs and http://www.presidentelect.org/e1912.html (both accessed November 11, 2009). For the location of local socialist newspapers, see James Weinstein, *The Decline of Socialism in America, 1912–1925* (New York: Vintage Books, 1969), 94–102; Stephen Cresswell, "Grassroots Radicalism in the Magnolia State: Mississippi's Socialist Movement at the Local Level, 1910–1919," *Labor History* 33 (1992): 82, 85; Green, *Grass-Roots Socialism*, 12–13, 180–185, 244–269; Daniel Letwin, *The Challenge of Interracial Unionism: Alabama Coal Miners, 1878–1921* (Chapel Hill: University of North Carolina Press, 1998), 128; Robin D. G. Kelley, *Hammer and Hoe: Alabama Communists during the Great Depression* (Chapel Hill: University of North Carolina Press, 1990), 17, 28; Bissett, *Agrarian Socialism in America*, 21–88, 125. I consider the South to include all or parts of the following states: Alabama, Arkansas, Florida, Georgia, Kentucky, Louisiana, Mississippi, Missouri, North Carolina, Oklahoma, South Carolina, Tennessee, Texas, Virginia, and West Virginia. See John Shelton Reed, "The South: What is it," in *The South for New Southerners*, ed. Paul D. Escott and David R. Goldfied (Chapel Hill: University of North Carolina Press, 1991), 18–41.

16. Julius A. Wayland, quoted in Elliott Shore, *Talkin' Socialism: J. A. Wayland and the Radical Press* (Lawrence: University Press of Kansas, 1988), 34 (first and second quotes), 40 (third and fourth quotes). On *The Grander Age*, Cresswell, "Grassroots Radicalism in the Magnolia State," 90.

17. *Bates County Critic*, 1899, quoted in Shore, *Talkin' Socialism*, 142–143.

18. Green, *Grass-Roots Socialism*, 17–19, 128–142; Shore, *Talkin' Socialism*, 51–77, 165–183, 206; Cresswell, "Grassroots Radicalism in the Magnolia State," 89. For circulation numbers, see "Circulation of the Appeal to Reason by States," *Appeal to Reason*, January 25, 1908; and "Circulation Report Week Ending June 22," *Appeal to Reason*, July 6, 1912.

19. R. G. Pratt, quoted in Cresswell, "Grassroots Radicalism in the Magnolia State," 97.

20. McRae to Watson, 1907, quoted in Woodward, *Tom Watson*, 404. For this interpretation of the Populists: Lester, *Up From the Mudsills of Hell*, 195–196, 205–206; Postel, *The Populist Vision*, 32–37. For the demographics of socialism in Mississippi and Missouri: Cresswell, "Grassroots Radicalism in the Magnolia State," 84–85; and Jarod H. Roll, "Gideon's Band: From Socialism to Vigilantism in Southeast Missouri," *Labor History* 43 (November 2002): 490–492. For these interpretations of socialism in Oklahoma and

Texas: Green, *Grass-Roots Socialism*, 10–27; Neil Foley, *The White Scourge: Mexicans, Blacks, and Poor Whites in Texas Cotton Culture* (Berkeley and Los Angeles: University of California Press, 1997), 64–69.

21. "The Scott County Kicker is the People's Paper," *Scott County Kicker*, June 2, 1906; Roll, "Gideon's Band," 489–490.

22. "In a Nut Shell," *Scott County Kicker*, December 1, 1906.

23. Oscar Ameringer, *Socialism for the Farmer Who Farms the Farm*, Rip Saw Series No. 15 (St. Louis, MO: National Rip Saw Publishing Co., 1912), 14–15; Green, *Grass-Roots Socialism*, 85.

24. "Private Ownership of the Earth is a Crime Against Mankind," *Scott County Kicker*, August 22, 1908.

25. W. M. Stingley, 1906, quoted in Bissett, *Agrarian Socialism in America*, 63.

26. *Social Economist*, June 6, 1901, quoted in Green, *Grass-Roots Socialism*, 27.

27. "Observations by the Kicker," *Scott County Kicker*, August 10, 1910.

28. "Farmer and Socialism," *Scott County Kicker*, May 16, 1908.

29. "Flashes from Our Correspondents," *The Rebel*, March 16, 1912, quoted in Foley, *The White Scourge*, 101 (quote); *Tenant Farmer*, September 1915, in Green, *Grass-Roots Socialism*, 140; Foley, *The White Scourge*, 94–101; Rodgers, *The Work Ethic in Industrial America*, 30–33; David R. Roediger, *The Wages of Whiteness: Race and the Making of the American Working Class* (London: Verso, 1991), 44–47.

30. *Strong City Herald*, October 12, 1916, quoted in Bissett, *Agrarian Socialism in America*, 107.

31. "Something to Think About," *Scott County Kicker*, July 9, 1910.

32. "A Farmer Writes," *Scott County Kicker*, October 26, 1907.

33. Platform of the Oklahoma Socialist Party, 1912, quoted in Bissett, *Agrarian Socialism in America*, 68.

34. Oscar Ameringer, floor debate, May 19, 1910, reprinted in Socialist Party USA, *Proceedings of the First National Congress* (Chicago: H. G. Adair, 1910), 223.

35. "Observations by the Kicker," *Scott County Kicker*, July 11, 1908 (first quote), and "Farmer and Socialism," *Scott County Kicker*, May 16, 1908 (second quote).

36. *Oklahoma Socialist*, August 21, 1902, quoted in Bissett, *Agrarian Socialism in America*, 100. See also Green, *Grass-Roots Socialism*, 163–164; and Shore, *Talkin' Socialism*, 55–63.

37. Tom Hickey, 1912, quoted in Green, *Grass-Roots Socialism*, 163.

38. A. C. Walker to Tom Hickey, February 7, 1915, quoted in Green, *Grass-Roots Socialism*, 308.

39. *New Century*, April 26, 1912, quoted in Bissett, *Agrarian Socialism in America*, 100.

40. H. B. Cochran, Bonham Texas, 1901, quoted in Green, *Grass-Roots Socialism*, 164.

41. "The Omaha Platform, 1892," reprinted in Tindall, ed., *A Populist Reader*, 90.

42. Ameringer, floor debate, May 19, 1910, reprinted in Socialist Party USA, *Proceedings of the First National Congress*, 223.

43. Harriman, 1900, quoted in Bissett, *Agrarian Socialism in America*, 65. For a discussion of the variants within the Socialist Party, Weinstein, *The Decline of Socialism in America*, 3–5.

44. "Farmer's Program of the Socialist Party of Oklahoma," reprinted in Socialist Party USA, *Proceedings of the First National Congress*, 215. For more on the resistance of

urban socialists, see Bissett, *Agrarian Socialism in America*, 65–69; and Green, *Grass-Roots Socialism*, 28–29.

45. A. M. Simons, "Suggestions for Farmers' Committee," reprinted in Socialist Party USA, *Proceedings of the First National Congress*, 215.

46. Lee, "Farmer's Program of the Socialist Party of Oklahoma," reprinted in Socialist Party USA, *Proceedings of the First National Congress*, 219.

47. Ameringer, floor debate, May 19, 1910, reprinted in Socialist Party USA, *Proceedings of the First National Congress*, 222.

48. T. J. Lewis, floor debate, May 19, 1910, reprinted in Socialist Party USA, *Proceedings of the First National Congress*, 224–225. U.S. Census Bureau, Manuscript Census, 1910 ("Thomas J. Lewis," Beaver Creek, Clackamas County, Oregon).

49. A. M. Simons, floor debate, May 19, 1910, reprinted in Socialist Party USA, *Proceedings of the First National Congress*, 231.

50. Platform of the Socialist Party, 1912, in Bissett, *Agrarian Socialism in America*, 69.

51. Patrick S. Nagle, May 1915, quoted in Green, *Grass-Roots Socialism*, 303.

52. Gibson *Justice*, September 11, 1914, 4.

53. Gibson *Justice*, June 5, 1914, 4 (quote). For more on the transition from socialism to vigilantism in the South, see Green, *Grass-Roots Socialism*, 316–395; Roll, "Gideon's Band," 500–503; Lester, *Up From the Mudsills of Hell*, 217–231; Foley, *The White Scourge*, 104–106.

54. *Langston City Herald*, 1894, in Bonnie Lynn-Sherow, *Red Earth: Race and Agriculture in Oklahoma Territory* (Lawrence: University Press of Kansas, 2004), 42.

55. For more on rural black nationalism in Oklahoma before 1920, Green, *Grass-Roots Socialism*, 265. For discussions of how African Americans complicated rural white notions of independence: Foley, *The White Scourge*, 104–106; Roll, "Gideon's Band," 483–503. For more on rural black settlements, see Lynn-Sherow, *Red Earth*, 4–10; and Thad Sitton and James H. Conrad, *Freedom Colonies: Independent Black Texans in the Time of Jim Crow* (Austin: University of Texas Press, 2005), 1–27.

56. Claudrena N. Harold, *The Rise and Fall of the Garvey Movement in the Urban South, 1918–1942* (New York: Routledge, 2007), 69 (quote). On the locations and membership of the UNIA in the rural South, "Locations of UNIA Divisions and Chapters," in Robert A. Hill and Barbara Bair, eds., *The Marcus Garvey and Universal Negro Improvement Association Papers*, vol. 7: *November 1927–August 1940* (Berkeley and Los Angeles: University of California Press, 1990), 986–996; Mary G. Rolinson, *Grassroots Garveyism: The Universal Negro Improvement Association in the Rural South, 1920–1927* (Chapel Hill: University of North Carolina Press, 2007), 109, 197–199; and Membership Record Card File, 1925–1927, Box 22B, UNIA Central Division Records, Schomburg Center, Harlem, New York Public Library (hereafter Central Division Records, NYPL). On the demographics of rural Garveyism: Hahn, *A Nation under Our Feet*, 472; Roll, *Spirit of Rebellion*, 52–75.

57. Hahn, *A Nation under Our Feet*, 473.

58. Ali, "Black Populism in the New South," 5–6 (first three quotes), 221 (final quote).

59. For more suggestions of the connections between rural Garveyism and black Populism: Ali, "Black Populism in the New South," 224–226; Hahn, *A Nation under Our Feet*, 415, 474; "Locations of UNIA Divisions and Chapters," in Hill and Bair eds., *The Marcus Garvey and Universal Negro Improvement Association Papers*, vol. 7, 986–996. For more on black Populists, see Beeby, *Revolt of the Tar Heels*, 80–82, 124–125; Jack

Abramowitz, "John B. Rayner: A Grass-Roots Leader," *Journal of Negro History* 36 (April 1951): 160–193; and Lester, *Up From the Mudsills of Hell*, 83–85. In east-central Texas, the all-black town of James City had a Colored Alliance in the 1890s, less than thirty miles from all-black towns such as Cushing that supported Garveyism. See Ali, "Black Populism in the New South," 100; "Locations of UNIA Divisions and Chapters," in Hill and Bair, eds., *The Marcus Garvey and Universal Negro Improvement Association Papers*, vol. 7, 995.

60. Daniel F. Littlefield Jr. and Lonnie E. Underhill, "Black Dreams and 'Free' Homes: The Oklahoma Territory, 1891–1894," *Phylon* 34 (1973): 354–355.

61. "Editorial," *Sikeston Standard*, January 19, 1923 (quote). On rural black migration westward, see James C. Cobb, *The Most Southern Place on Earth: The Mississippi Delta and the Roots of Regional Identity* (New York: Oxford University Press, 1994), 72; William Cohen, *At Freedom's Edge: Black Mobility and the Southern White Quest for Racial Control, 1861–1915* (Baton Rouge: Louisiana State University Press, 1991), 252–258; Loren Schweninger, *Black Property Owners in the South, 1790–1915* (Urbana: University of Illinois Press, 1997), 143–184; Hahn, *A Nation under Our Feet*, 135–146, 457–458; John C. Willis, *Forgotten Time: The Yazoo-Mississippi Delta after the Civil War* (Charlottesville: University Press of Virginia, 2000), 41–75; Kenneth C. Barnes, *Journey of Hope: The Back-to-Africa Movement in Arkansas in the Late 1800s* (Chapel Hill: University of North Carolina Press, 2004), 35–39; Roll, *Spirit of Rebellion*, 52–75.

62. Marcus Garvey speech, January 1924, reprinted in Cary D. Wintz, ed., *African American Political Thought, 1890–1930: Washington, Du Bois, Garvey and Randolph* (New York: M. E. Sharpe, 1996), 234.

63. "U.N.I.A., Nearing the Greatest World Conference of Race, Calls Upon Negroes Everywhere to Rise Up and Be Men," *The Negro World*, April 27, 1929.

64. Rolinson, *Grassroots Garveyism*, 109.

65. "Preach the Gospel of Conservation of Race Resources," *The Negro World*, August 13, 1927 (quote). For more on the eschatological roots and routes of Garveyism, and the strength of this belief in the rural South: Timothy W. Fulop, "'The Future Golden Day of the Race': Millennialism and Black Americans in the Nadir, 1877–1901," *Harvard Theological Review* 84 (January 1991): 78; Rolinson, *Grassroots Garveyism*, 1–8, 197–199; Jarod Roll, "Garveyism and the Eschatology of African Redemption in the Rural South, 1920–1936," *Religion and American Culture: A Journal of Interpretation* 20 (January 2010): 27–56.

66. For more on urban black nationalists and the UNIA, see Michele Mitchell, *Righteous Propagation: African Americans and the Politics of Racial Destiny after Reconstruction* (Chapel Hill: University of North Carolina Press, 2004), 144–145, 218–239; and Colin Grant, *Negro with a Hat: The Rise and Fall of Marcus Garvey* (London: Vintage Books, 2009), 217–297.

67. "Self Reliance is the Mainspring of Success," *The Negro World*, February 6, 1926.

68. "North Arkansas Alive in the Good Work," *The Negro World*, June 7, 1924.

69. "A Well Wisher Who Reads the Negro World," *The Negro World*, June 7, 1924.

70. "Mollie Bynum Prays for the Redemption of Africa," *The Negro World*, June 7, 1924.

71. "Thirteen-Year-Old Boy Who Thinks Far Ahead," *The Negro World*, December 20, 1924.

72. Colored Farmers' Alliance of Texas, quoted in, Ali, "Black Populism in the New South," 87.

73. "Mollie Bynum Prays for the Redemption of Africa," *The Negro World*, June 7, 1924.

74. "She is Working for the Negro World," *The Negro World*, May 24, 1924.

75. "Charleston, Mo.," *The Negro World*, December 15, 1923.

76. D. D. Daniel and R. H. Starks, New Madrid, to the Attorney General, November 1, 1925, Folder 9, Box 1160A, Record Group 42, Department of Justice Pardon Case Files, Record Group 204, National Archives and Records Administration, College Park, Maryland.

77. "Charleston, Mo.," *The Negro World*, December 15, 1923.

78. "New Madrid," *The Negro World*, October 27, 1923.

79. Bennie Bember, Tuckermann, Arkansas to the Editor, *The Negro World*, February 16, 1929.

80. Marcus Garvey quoted in Randall K. Burkett, *Garveyism as a Religious Movement: The Institutionalization of a Black Civil Religion* (Metuchen, NJ: Scarecrow Press, 1978), 49.

81. "Wyatt, Mo.," *The Negro World*, December 8, 1928.

82. E. W. Pinkard, Hermondale, Missouri to the Editor, *The Negro World*, September 5, 1925.

83. "Pine City Div., Arkansas Holds 3-Day Convention," *The Negro World*, October 6, 1923.

84. Bember to the Editor, *The Negro World*, February 16, 1929.

85. "Renters Union," Gibson *Justice*, November 13, 1914.

86. On the activities of urban Garveyites, see Harold, *The Rise and Fall of the Garvey Movement in the Urban South*, 30–59, 91–92. See also, Roll, *Spirit of Rebellion*, 66–71. "Pine City, Ark.," *The Negro World*, March 28, 1925; "We are marching on with shield and banner bright," Oremus online, http://www.oremus.org/hymnal/w/wo42.html (last accessed April 30, 2009).

87. Barnes, *Journey of Hope*, 2–19; 125–133 (first quote, 133; second quote, 131).

88. J. A. Shazier, Perkinston, Mississippi to the Editor, *The Negro World*, February 7, 1925.

89. Claude Williams, ca. 1936, quoted in Cedric Belfrage, *Let My People Go* (London: Victor Gollancz, 1940), 311 (first two quotes), 312 (third quote), and 313 (fourth quote) [italics in original]; Roll, *Spirit of Rebellion*, 103–80; Erik S. Gellman and Jarod Roll, *The Gospel of the Working Class: Labor's Southern Prophets in New Deal America* (Urbana: University of Illinois Press, 2011).

CONTRIBUTORS

OMAR H. ALI is associate professor of African American and Diaspora Studies at the University of North Carolina, Greensboro. The author of *In the Lion's Mouth: Black Populism in the New South, 1886–1900* (2010) and *In the Balance of Power: Independent Black Politics and Third-Party Movements in the United States* (2008), he has also served as guest editor for *Souls: A Critical Journal of Black Politics, Culture, and Society*.

JAMES M. BEEBY is associate professor of history and chair of the history department at Indiana University Southeast. He is also a Fellow of the Royal Historical Society of Great Britain. He is the author of *Revolt of the Tar Heels: The North Carolina Populist Movement, 1890–1901* (2008) and several published articles and book chapters on southern politics and the rise of Jim Crow. His next project is a study of race and class in the 1937 Ohio River flood and the politics of the New Deal and disaster relief.

MATTHEW HILD is a visiting assistant professor of history at the University of West Georgia and an affiliate instructor at the School of History, Technology, and Society at the Georgia Institute of Technology. His published works include *Greenbackers, Knights of Labor, and Populists: Farmer-Labor Insurgency in the Late-Nineteenth-Century South* (2007) and articles and essays in *Agricultural History*, the *Arkansas Historical Quarterly*, *Atlanta History*, the *Georgia Historical Quarterly*, and the *Gulf South Historical Review*. He is currently researching the life and career of Major John F. Hanson, a prominent industrialist and Republican Party leader in post-Reconstruction Georgia who played a pivotal role in the establishment of what is now the Georgia Institute of Technology.

MICHAEL PIERCE is associate professor of history at the University of Arkansas. He is author of *Striking with the Ballot: Ohio Labor and the Populist Party* (2010). His essay in this volume is a revised version of a paper he gave at the meeting of the St. George Tucker Society marking the seventy-fifth anniversary of C. Vann Woodward's *Tom Watson, Agrarian Rebel*. He thanks David L. Chappell, members of the St. George Tucker Society, and the Watson-Brown Foundation for the support and feedback he received at that meeting.

LEWIE REECE is assistant professor of history at Anderson University, South Carolina. A historian of nineteenth-century America, his work has focused on political culture, law, and race. He is currently completing his book *Pure Despotism: South Carolina's Route to Disfranchisement, 1815–1915*, a study which seeks to explain the role of race and class in the disfranchisement process. Dr. Reece is author of several articles and book chapters on Reconstruction and desegregation in South Carolina.

ALICIA E. RODRIQUEZ is associate professor of history at California State University, Bakersfield. She has published in the *Southwestern Historical Quarterly*, and is completing an article-length study, "Ku Klux Kern: The 1920s Ku Klux Klan in Kern County, California." She is currently finishing her book, *The Urban Roots of Populist Reform: The People's Party in Dallas, Texas, 1887–1900*.

JAROD ROLL teaches American history at the University of Sussex in Brighton, England, where he is also the founding director of the Marcus Cunliffe Centre for the Study of the American South. He is the author of *Spirit of Rebellion: Labor and Religion in the New Cotton South* (2010), which won the Herbert G. Gutman Prize from the Labor and Working-Class History Association. He also coauthored *The Gospel of the Working Class: Labor's Southern Prophets in New Deal America* (2011), a biography of two working-class southern preachers whose interpretation of evangelical Christianity provided a penetrating critique of America's political and economic problems during the Great Depression and World War II. He is currently writing about religion and black politics in the Jim Crow South.

DAVID SILKENAT is assistant professor of history and education at North Dakota State University. He is the author of *Moments of Despair: Suicide, Divorce, and Debt in Civil War Era North Carolina* (2011). He is currently working on a book on Civil War refugees.

JOEL SIPRESS is professor of history at the University of Wisconsin-Superior. His work on late nineteenth-century Louisiana has appeared in *Louisiana History* and the *Journal of the Gilded Age and Progressive Era*. His work on the scholarship of teaching and learning has appeared in the *Journal of American History*. He is engaged in an ongoing analysis and critique of the "coverage" model of the introductory college history course and has also embarked upon a study of Ojibwa resistance to Indian removal in the mid-nineteenth century.

INDEX

Adams, J. W., 208
Adams, Thomas B., 19
African Americans, 5; in 1892 Georgia election, 3–4; in 1892 Louisiana election, 21–25; and African Methodist Episcopal Church, 133, 134, 218; in Dallas, Texas, 59; in Grant Parish, Louisiana, 7–9, 11–15, 17, 30n15; in North Carolina and attitudes toward debt, 101–2, 107–9, 111–12, 117, 118; and Populism in the Deep South, 145; relationship with People's Party in Grant Parish, Louisiana, 22–25, 26; relationship with People's Party in North Carolina, 178–98; in Republican Party, 14; testimony of, 183–98; and United Negro Improvement Association, 202–20
Aldrich, William, 163
Ali, Omar H., 213, 222n12
Allen, William, 86
American Federation of Labor, 83, 89, 92
Ameringer, Oscar, 207, 209–10, 211
Appeal to Reason, 204, 205, 209, 210, 211
Archer, Samuel, 101
Arnett, Alex, 162
Atlanta Constitution, 37
Augusta Chronicle, 43
Aycock, Charles B., 183–86, 192, 193
Ayers, Edward, 79n38, 132

Bamber, Bennie, 217
Basnight, Jessie, 190–91
Beddingfield, Eugene, 119
Beeby, James M., 131, 141n8
Belk, William Henry, 110–11
Blanchard, Newton C., 10, 18, 30n18, 32n29

Brian, Benjamin F., 11, 12, 16, 20, 21, 23, 24, 25, 26, 31n22, 31n23
Brian, Hardy L., 19, 21, 23
Bright, P. H., 189
Brown, Benjamin, 45
Bryan, William Jennings, 94, 165–66, 167, 168–69, 193, 204
Burton, Orville Vernon, 133
Butler, Marion, 97, 101–2, 116, 120, 166, 167, 179, 180, 181, 182, 186, 193, 197n25, 198n46
Bynum, Mollie, 216

Calvin, Martin, 45
Carr, Elias, 115
Carter, J. W., 150
Cleburne Demands, 58
Cleveland, Grover, 86, 162
Cleveland Citizen, 89
Cochran, H. B., 209
Colfax Chronicle, 9, 13, 19, 21, 22, 23, 30n15
Colfax Massacre, 7, 13
Colored Farmers' Alliance, xv, 102, 114, 128–44, 149–51, 152–53, 201, 213; in Florida, 128, 129; in Georgia, 150; in Mississippi, 151, 153; in Texas, 216
Colored Farmers' Union, 16–18, 19, 20, 23
Coxey, Jacob, 85–86, 87, 91, 92, 96, 100n36; in Atlanta, 93; and People's Party, 88, 91–94
Cramer, H. M., 48, 50
Creech, Joe, 200
Crumwell, James, 51
Cunningham, John, 164

Dallas Demands, 58
Dallas Morning News 69, 72, 73, 75–76, 78n9

Dancy, John, 111
Daniels, D. D., 217
Davis, W. M., 217
Daws, S. O., 146, 203–4
Debs, Eugene, 87, 88, 94, 203, 218
Democratic Party, xi, 147, 153; in Alabama, 157–58; in Georgia, 37–55; in Grant Parish, Louisiana, 8–11, 13, 18, 20; in Mississippi, 152–53; in North Carolina, 177–98, 202; in Texas, 60, 65, 67, 70
Destler, Chester McArthur, 56
Dickson, Patrick, 132
Diffey, J. P., 62
Dixon, Edward, Sr., 186
Doyle, Henry S., 3, 4, 129, 134, 136–37, 160–61
Du Bois, W. E. B., 112
Dunning, N. A., 148

Eight-Hour Convention, 59, 60
Eight-Hour Labor League, 62–64, 65, 69, 70, 71, 76
Elections: of 1892, 3, 23–26, 42, 74–77, 88, 119, 157, 158, 161–64; of 1894, 88, 90, 120, 163; of 1896, 38, 94–97, 163, 165–68, 178; of 1900, 88–90, 120, 163

Farmers' Alliance and Industrial Union, xixn3, 15, 18, 63, 145–48, 152; in Alabama, 151, 156–58; and Cleburne Demands, 58; in Dallas, Texas, 57, 59; Dallas Demands, 58; in Georgia, 46–47, 146, 151, 153–54; in North Carolina, 102–3, 114–15, 118; in Texas, 63, 75–76, 203–4
Felton, Rebecca Latimer, 45, 54n29, 163
Felton, William H., 37, 45, 49, 163
Fink, Leon, 36, 38, 52n8
Fitzgerald, James, 71, 73
Foster, James F., 48
Fowler, John E., 178, 179, 180, 181, 182–87, 190–93, 193n1, 198n46
Franklin, John Hope, 106
Freeman, George, 135

Gaines, George W., 137
Gaither, Gerald, 131, 140
Gavin, John A., 189

George, Henry, 60
Gerteis, Joseph, 131
Gibbs, Barnett, 70, 76
Golden, P. H., 60, 63, 68–69, 72–73, 74, 76
Goldston, J. J., 116
Goodwyn, Lawrence, xi, 139
Gompers, Samuel, 83
Gordon, John B., 151
Gould, Jay, 10
Grandy, Moses, 106–7
Grange (Patrons of Husbandry), 113; and Colored Grange, 133
Graves, Anton, 137
Great Southwest Strike, 57
Greenback Party, xi, 14, 154
Greensboro Daily Democrat, 129
Grimes, Jobb, 185
Grimes, John Bryan, 135
Guice, Thomas J., 17, 19
Gunby, A. A., 166, 167
Guynes, William P., 14, 15, 16, 32n30

Hafner, Phil, 206, 207, 208, 209
Hahn, Steven, 131, 213
Harriman, Job, 210
Harrison, Benjamin, 161, 167
Hayes, John W., 48
Hickey, Tom, 208
Hicks, John D., xi, 83, 132
Hild, Matthew, 83
Hogg, James, 58
Hofstadter, Richard, xi
Huff, William A., 44–45
Humphrey, R. M., 149–50

Jones, Thomas G., 157–58
Journal of the Knights of Labor, 40
Judge, Moses, 184

Knights of Labor, Noble and Holy Order of the, 36, 51n5, 55, 83, 94; in Atlanta, 39, 41–42, 48; in Augusta, 39, 42–43, 48, 85; decline in Georgia, 46–50; in Georgia, 36–55; legacy in Georgia, 49–50; in Macon, 39, 43–44; in North Carolina, 113, 135; and Populists, 46–50;

in Savannah, 39–41, 52n9; in Texas, 57, 59
Kolb, Reuben, 145, 151, 156–58, 163

Lamb, W. R., 72, 73, 74
Laurent, L. D., 155
Lewis, T. J., 210–11
Livingston, Lon, 154
Lloyd, Henry Demarest, 88, 89, 91, 94
Lodge Election Bill, 66, 128–29, 134, 152
Louisiana Farmers' Union, 15, 25; in Grant Parish, 15–16, 17–18, 25
Louisiana Populist, 26
Love, Louisa, 216

Macon Daily Telegraph, 44
Macune, Charles W., 18, 146, 147, 152
Mallard, J. W., 187
Manning, Joseph, 156–57, 158, 163, 169
Matthis, J. J., 190
McBee, Alexander, 108
McBride, John, 86, 87, 88, 89, 92; and American Federation of Labor, 89; and People's Party, 88; and United Mine Workers of America, 86
McCord, Charles Z., 45
McKinley, William, 95, 167, 168
McLaurin, Melton, 47
McMath, Robert C., xi, 46, 56, 200
McMillan, John C., 177–78, 193n1
Meynardie, J. Simmions, 43
Middleton, Abe, 184–85, 196n17
Moore, John L., 128–29, 134, 141n8
Murdock, James, 117
Murray, George Washington, 129, 136, 140

Nagle, Patrick S., 207
Negro World, 215

Ocala Platform, 63–64, 82, 96, 151, 156
Oden, Mac, 185
Omaha Platform, x, 82, 83, 90, 96, 164, 199, 201

Palmer, Bruce, xv
Pattillo, Walter A., 129, 134, 140, 213

Peffer, William, 86, 91
People's Party (Populist Party/Populism): and African Americans, xv, 22–26 128–44, 162; in Alabama, 145, 157, 158, 162–64; in Arkansas, 166; and attitudes toward debt, 120; in Dallas, Texas, 56–57, 59, 65, 68, 70–77; in Georgia, 3–4, 37–45, 46–50, 145, 154, 159–61, 162, 167; in government with Republicans, 120–21, 138; in Illinois, 88, 89; and legacy of, 26–27, 49–50, 76–77, 121–22, 169–70, 203; in Louisiana, 3–35, 145, 154–55, 161, 164–65; in Michigan, 88; in Milwaukee, 88; in Minneapolis, 88, 89; in Mississippi, 161–62, 169; in 1900 campaign, 183–98; in North Carolina, 101–27, 177–98; in Ohio, 88, 94; and religion, 200, 202, 218; and Socialists, 205–7; in Texas, 71, 75
People's Party Paper, 85, 86, 87, 90, 92, 163–64
Pinkard, E. W., 217
Polk, Leonidas L., 110, 113, 115, 119–20, 147, 152–53, 155–56
Pollack, Norman, xi
Poole, M. L., 216, 217
Postel, Charles, xxin6, 4, 122, 131, 140
Powderly, Terence, 38, 44, 46, 47, 48, 58
Pratt, R. G., 206
Price, J. C., 111
Progressive Farmer, 114, 115, 117, 130, 147

Rayner, John B., 129, 213
Red Shirts, 138, 177, 178, 181–87, 191–93, 195n7
Reed, Silas C., Jr., 43
Republican Party, xi; and African Americans, 14, 21; in Georgia, 37–39; in Grant Parish, Louisiana, 7–12, 14, 17; in Louisiana, 26, 155–56; in North Carolina, 120, 138, 189–90; in Texas, 60
Robertson, J. P., 65
Rodriquez, Alicia, 83
Roxborough, Charles, 155
Russell, Phillip M., 40

Salisbury Carolina Watchman, 116
Sanges, James C., 47
Savannah Morning News, 39–41
Schofield, James E., 44–45
Schwartz, John, 40–41
Scott County Kicker, 206, 207, 208
Seawall, Virgil N., 187
Shazier, J. A., 219
Simmons, Furnifold, 183, 193
Simons, A. M., 210
Socialist Party, 202–12; and African Americans, 212; in Arkansas, 203; in Louisiana, 203; in Mississippi, 203, 204; in Missouri, 203, 205, 208, 211; in Oklahoma, 203, 205, 206, 207–8, 211; and relation to Populism, 199–226; in Texas, 203–9
Southern Tenant Farmers' Union, 219
Spear, Oscar, 185
Spencer, T. H. A., 64, 73, 74
Stingley, W. M., 207
Subtreasury, x, 18, 100n38, 114–15, 151–52
Sudduth, Queenie, 216

Tannehill, Robert L., 24, 25
Taubeneck, Herman, 90, 91, 94, 97
Taylor, A. D., 119
Texas State Federation of Labor, 60–61
Thomas, Charles H., 14, 17, 20
Thomas, Charles R., 179, 181, 183, 192
Thomas, John, 184
Thomasson, Basil Armstrong, 105–6
Thompson, Cyrus, 180, 193, 198n46
Thompson, Henry B., 24, 25
Toombs, Robert, 84, 96
Tourgee, Albion, 137
Traylor, L. A., 20, 33n45
Turner, J. H., 148

Universal Negro Improvement Association, 202, 212–20; in Arkansas, 215; and Marcus Garvey, 212–13, 215; and Garveyism, 202; and *Langston City Herald*, 212; in the Mississippi Delta, 213, 214, 215, 219; in Missouri, 214, 215–17; in North Carolina, 213, 214; in Oklahoma, 214, 215; and religion, 218–19; in the South, 202, 212–20; in Texas, 214, 215

Vance, Zebulon B., 119–20
Vann, C. C., 188

Wade, Melvin, 59, 65
Wagoner, Edward, 187
Walker, Corey, 133
Ward, A. J., 183, 189
Warren, Fred, 205
Warmoth, Henry, 165
Washington, Booker T., 112
Watson, Thomas E., 3, 49–50, 56, 82, 84, 90, 91, 100n36, 100n38, 100n43, 136, 145, 159, 161–63, 166, 168, 201, 203; and attitudes towards industrial workers, 82–100; and the 1896 campaign, 94–97; and fear of labor movement, 83, 85, 91–92, 93; and Pullman strike, 87
Wayland, Julius A., 204–5, 209
Weaver, James, 47–48, 90, 97, 156, 161
White, George H., 110
White Man's Party, 8–9
Wilkins, J. T., 188
Williams, Claude, 219–20
Wilson, Anthony, 137
Woodward, C. Vann, xi, xii, 3, 4, 27, 28n2, 34n58, 56, 90, 96, 129–30, 138–39
Woodward, James G., 41, 42
Worth, Jonathan, 107
Wyne, William, 160

www.ingramcontent.com/pod-product-compliance
Lightning Source LLC
Chambersburg PA
CBHW030618230426

43661CB00053B/2044